# Power Pivot and Power BI:
# The Excel User's Guide to DAX, Power Query, Power BI
# & Power Pivot in Excel 2010-2016

by
## Rob Collie
## &
## Avichal Singh

T0206619

Holy Macro! Books
PO Box 541731
Merritt Island, FL 32954

# Power Pivot and Power BI

Author: Rob Collie & Avichal Singh

Layout: Jill Bee

Technical Editor:  Scott Senkeresty

Cover Design: Shannon Travise & Jocelyn Collie

Indexing: Nellie J. Liwam

Published by: Holy Macro! Books, PO Box 541731 Merritt Island FL 32954 USA

Distributed by: Independent Publishers Group, Chicago, IL

2nd Printing: November 2016

Printed in black & white: September 2021

ISBN: 978-1-61547-075-4 Print

LCCN: 2015940638

# Table of Contents

# Dedications

Rob:

To everyone who has ever gotten excited about a PivotTable. We all share a kindred and wonderful sickness.

Avi:

To my Mom and Dad. For teaching me that it is good to be important, but more important to be good.

# Supporting Workbooks and Data Sets

The supporting workbooks and datasets can be downloaded from:

http://ppvt.pro/bookfiles

Note that these are being provided on an *informal* basis. You may find the supporting files helpful but we've made every effort to provide full coverage of topics within the book. You'll never find us using these files as an escape hatch and saying something like "take a look at the supporting files if this isn't clear".

*Figure 1 Thanks to SQLBI team for providing a useful resource to the community*

# Errata and Book Support

We have made every effort to ensure the accuracy of this book. If you do find an error, please report it using the "Errata" button on http://ppvt.pro/daxbook page.

# A Note on Hyperlinks

You will notice that all of the hyperlinks in this book look like this:

http://ppvt.pro/<foo>

Where <foo> is something that is short and easy to type. Example:

http://ppvt.pro/1stBlog

 These links are **CaSe SeNsItIvE!** If the link in the book ends in "**1stBlog**" like above, typing "**1stblog**" or "**1st-BLOG**" will not take you to the intended page!

**This is a "short link" and is intended to make life much easier for readers of the print edition.** That link above will take you to the first blog post Rob ever published, which went live in October of 2009.

Its "real" URL is this:

http://www.PowerPivotpro.com/2009/10/hello-everybody/

Which would *you* rather type?

So just a few notes:

1. **These short links will *always* start with http://ppvt.pro/** – which is short for "PowerPivotPro," the name of our blog.
2. **Not all of these links will lead to our blog** – some will take you to Microsoft sites for instance.
3. **The book does not rely on you following the links** – the topics covered in this book are intended to be complete in and of themselves. The links provided are strictly optional "more info" type of content.

## "State of the Union" November 2015 – What's Changed?

As we wrapped up final edits on this book, Avi and Bill said, "OK Rob, you know those first two chapters? The ones that set the stage and give perspective to this whole thing? It's time for you to revise those and bring them up to date."

They had a point – it *had* been more than three years since I wrote those chapters. And a *lot* has changed since then in our landscape, reshaped as it is by Microsoft's vigorous seismic activity.

**But when I re-read those two chapters, I found very little that I wanted to alter.** I'm leaving those largely untouched, which is a rare move for me.

Why did I choose to forgo such a writing opportunity, since I enjoy it so much?

**Here's why: those chapters talk about things that fundamentally do *not* change** – the importance of people, the importance of Excel, the massive opportunities afforded to "data people," and Microsoft's continued investment in all of the above.

I suspect that ten years from now, if we're revising this book for the Nth edition, those chapters will again largely remain unchanged – except that we will be talking about a data revolution that's already run its course, rather than one that's in progress ☺

Instead I'm going to use this Foreword to reflect a bit on some things that truly *have* changed. Let's start with the 800 pound gorilla, my former employer (and Avi's)...

The Microsoft Corporation.

## What Has Changed at Microsoft? Virtually Everything.

Let's see here, just a few things:

**Ballmer out, Nadella in** – the change at the top of Microsoft is not to be underestimated. Satya brings a very different and more open perspective to the game, and that absolutely makes a difference to us. For example, today's Microsoft does not stubbornly ignore iOS and Android, whereas the old regime acted like "if we ignore them long enough, they will go away." (A few years back when MS announced their earliest plans for mobile-friendly BI, and it revolved solely around the soon-to-be-released Windows 8 while ignoring other platforms, I chortled for two months consecutive before eventually having to see a doctor to make it stop.) It's worth reflecting how far we have come since then. Microsoft Power BI is available in the *Apple App Store*, for crying out loud, and it's not at *all* weird to see it there? Times have changed.

**Power Query** – when the first edition of this book went to press, I don't think we'd even *heard* of Power Query. Microsoft already had a world-changing data engine – the DAX/Power Pivot engine – and that was more than enough, in my eyes, to kickstart a total revolution in how the world operates. So to have them surprise us, out of the blue, with a relatively user-friendly desktop engine for shaping and cleaning data... a "sibling" that does virtually everything that Power Pivot could not do on its own... um, yeah. Power Query is a big deal, folks, and even though they are retiring that name, the "M Engine" is here to stay, and our professional lives are forever altered. Dramatically for the better.

**Unity** – CEO isn't the only place where MS has changed people. There have also been several changes in leadership on the relevant engineering teams at Microsoft. Some new arrivals on the SQL side of the house and some old friends "coming home" on the Excel side of the house have already made a monster impact over the past two years. Above all, I'm struck by how *unified* Microsoft seems to be in the BI space these days. Not *perfectly* unified, but dramatically more so than I have *ever* seen before. Everyone seems to be pulling in the same direction – both within the SQL team's many factions (who, in my time there, were in open war with one another), and across the SQL/Office boundary. The latter is particularly important, because the Excel team is now 100% "in" on Power Pivot. They understand its value and strategic importance to their own product, whereas before, the Excel team regarded Power Pivot with suspicion – as something that had been *done to* their product.

**PowerBI.com and Power BI Desktop** – consider this: at the beginning of 2015, *neither of these things actually existed.* In eleven short months, I've been through the full cycle of opinions: the "this is vaporware" phase, the "oh no they're de-emphasizing Excel" phase, the "what the heck is this Desktop thing, they really don't get it do they" phase.... And now, the "wow this is all pretty cool, Excel Services is in PowerBI.com, Desktop opens Power Pivot models, I guess they actually DO have a good roadmap that includes Excel, and it's all actually *working*" phase. Seriously, I've gone from feeling ambushed to feeling like we've been given a tremendous gift. And oh yeah – a free cloud version for publishing that anyone can use, and that's easy to sign up for? With an open source visuals platform? This is *Microsoft* doing all this? Are you KIDDING ME. And it all happened this year.

**Pace** – you can put this together from the previous bullet, but MS is now moving at a frightening pace. Frightening? Did I say frightening? Well, it's only frightening if you write books. There's now an ever-present danger of us writing an entire chapter on how you deal with a particular problem, and then three weeks later, them adding a feature that makes that problem go away, rendering the entire chapter obsolete, and thereby making the authors look silly. Actually, this is virtually *guaranteed* to happen. But outside of the authoring world, yeah, this is a very good thing. Not having to wait two years for key omissions and/or bugs to be addressed has precious little downside.

# What's Changed in *My* Corner of the World? Also Everything.

I always tell first-time public speakers and bloggers to talk about their own personal experiences. You are, in fact, the world's #1 expert on what has happened in your own life.

That's what I'm going to do here, because hey, I can't be wrong! Yes, it is a "skewed" view in some ways, to take small-scale observations from one person and put them next to the changes happening at a goliath like Microsoft, but I *do* have what they call a ringside seat for this particular show. There's relevance here, especially when it comes to hard numbers and economics.

Let's stick to that list format:

**4x Community Growth** - Judging by PowerPivotPro.com blog stats, our community – those who are aware of and using Power Pivot and Power BI – is now approximately four times the size as it was when the first edition went to print. That's right, there are a lot more "new" people at this point than grizzled veterans. As it should be! This will continue to hold true for quite some time. Welcome everyone ☺

**Team Growth** – at time of writing there are now seventeen human beings with PowerPivotPro.com email addresses. Guess how many humans had such addresses three years ago? Zero – not even *I* had one! Not *all* of the seventeen are doing Power Pivot / Power BI work, but *most* of them are. And the handful who play auxiliary roles are in some ways even more telling: *we now have an organization which is large enough to require auxiliary roles.* I find that incredibly satisfying, and not just on the personal front – our organization wouldn't be growing unless the *demand* for our services was growing. We're not traditional BI consultants, and we're not spreadsheet consultants. We're a new breed and the market is saying "yes, this is a good mutation, your virus may continue to grow." In fact I'm aware of several brand-new firms that have joined us in this "new style," and the world of data is so large that there's zero sense of competition, only a shared sense of joy in changing the rules in a positive way.

**Avi** – among those seventeen is our esteemed co-author, Avi Singh, who has been working himself half to death on this 2nd Edition. This is great news, because there was *zero* chance I'd have been able to do this alone. (I've never been busier, as a professional, than I am today). So First Edition would probably have remained Only Edition without Avi on board. If anything, Avi believes in this stuff *more* than I do – anyone who says "I'm coming to work with you even if you can't pay me" is a bit crazy, but the right kind of crazy. We are lucky to have him, and yes, we *do* pay him ☺

**Microsoft Relationship** – our relationship with the "mother ship" is in a much better place today than three years ago. It's not like there was friction before, and I *do* still have a lot of friends there, but there was *also* a longstanding mutual sense that there wasn't much ROI in cooperating. For the most part, I ignored Microsoft and they returned the favor by ignoring me. But my views and their views on the world have converged quite a bit over the past three years, and I would attribute that to "everyone getting smarter" rather than one of us adopting the other's longstanding stance. Today, our messaging helps Microsoft reach customers, and Microsoft likewise connects us with people who need help. This may sound like a subtle point, but it could not feel any more different. Surprising as it sounds, this ex-Microsoft employee (and High Priest of their data platform) feels like he's back in the family for the first time in six years. And again, this reflects on Microsoft's positive direction as well as the market.

**Confidence** – this one is my favorite. Three years ago, I was "sure" that The New Way was going to replace The Old Way. So "sure," in fact, that I'd happily argue vigorously with anyone who disagreed or questioned it. Today though I'm not just "sure" – I am *sure*. For example, a few weeks back I watched a debate unfold in the comments thread of a Power PivotPro.com blog post, in which one "combatant" was questioning whether this stuff was catching on or not. Three years ago I would have waded into the fray, guns blazing. But this time I sat it out – my pulse didn't rise, I didn't take the bait. I just moved on to the next task. Someone else was taking up the good fight anyway (thanks Greg). The point here is that before, my certainty was *predictive* in nature, and that naturally carries some insecurity. Today's certainty comes from having seen it happen – we are no longer talking about what *will be*, we are talking about what undeniably *is*. I'm a lot more at peace, a happier person, and very much at ease with the way things are unfolding. I hope you share that same confidence already, or that you soon will.

**Happy** – OK, I lied. *This* one is my favorite. If you ask us what's the #1 service we provide these days, the most important thing we do for people, my answer will not be related to money, or efficiency, or time. Yes, we do help people quite a bit when measured in those terms. But the thing that strikes us all as most important, is *making people happy.* It's fair to call Power Pivot a "hard skill," and it's one that delivers ROI on a grand scale (ex: one of our one-week projects ended up saving the client $25 Million a year). But the "soft" stuff is what really energizes us. This stuff makes people *happier*, and you cannot put a price on that. We live charmed lives – working in data and solving valuable problems is the sort of thing that we "expect" to be boring and dehumanizing, but when it actually works, it's exactly the opposite.

Welcome to Happy Data Land.

-Rob Collie, November 2015

# Introduction - Our Two Goals for this Book

**Fundamentally of course, this book is intended to train you on Power Pivot and Power BI.** It captures the techniques we've learned from many years of teaching Power Pivot and its "cousin technologies" (in person and on PowerPivotPro. com), as well as applying it extensively in our everyday work.

Unsurprisingly, then, the contents herein are very much instructional – a "how to" book if ever there was one.

**But we also want you to understand how to maximize the impact on your career.** This isn't *just* a better way to do PivotTables. It isn't *just* a way to reduce manual effort. It's not *just* a better formula engine.

Even though Rob worked on the first version of Power Pivot while at Microsoft, he had no idea how impactful it would be until about two years after he left to form his own company. He had to experience it in the real world to see its full potential, and even then it took some time to overwhelm his skeptical nature (his Twitter profile now describes him as "skeptic turned High Priest.")

**This is the rare technology that can (and will) fundamentally change the lives of millions of people** – it has more in common with the invention of the PC than with the invention of, say, the VCR.

The PC might be a particularly relevant example actually. At a prestigious Seattle high school in the early 1970's, Bill Gates and Paul Allen discovered a mutual love for programming, but there was no widespread demand for programmers at that point. Only when the first PC (the Altair) was introduced was there an opportunity to properly monetize their skills. Short version: they founded Microsoft and became billionaires.

But zoom out and you'll see much more. *Thousands* of people became millionaires at Microsoft alone (sadly, we both missed that boat by a few years). Further, without the Altair, there would have been no IBM PC, no Apple, no Mac, no Steve Jobs. No iPod, no iPhone, no Appstore. No Electronic Arts, no Myst. No World of Warcraft. **The number of people who became wealthy as a result of the PC absolutely dwarfs the number of people who had anything to do with inventing the PC itself!**

**We think Power Pivot and Power BI offer the same potential wealth-generation effect to Excel users as the PC offered budding programmers like Gates and Allen:** your innate skills remain the same but their value becomes many times greater. Before diving into the instructional stuff in Chapters 2 and beyond, Chapter 1 will summarize your exciting new role in the changing world.

And like many things in when you hang around with Rob, the story starts with a movie reference ☺

# 1 - A Revolution Built On YOU

## Does This Sound Familiar?

*(Updated Fall 2015, but we decided to leave this part in Rob's first-person "voice" – because the authenticity is better-preserved).*

In the movie *Fight Club*, Edward Norton's character refers to the people he meets on airplanes as "single serving friends" – people he befriends for three hours and never sees again. I have a unique perspective on this phenomenon, thanks to a real-world example that is relevant to this book.

A woman takes her seat for a cross-country business flight and is pleased to see that her seatmate appears to be a reasonably normal fellow. They strike up a friendly conversation, and when he asks her what she does for a living, she gives the usual reply: "I'm a marketing analyst."

That answer satisfies 99% of her single-serving friends, at which the conversation typically turns to something else. However, this guy is the exception, and asks the dreaded follow-up question: "Oh, neat! What does that *mean*?"

She sighs, ever so slightly, because the honest answer to that question always bores people to death. Worse than that actually: it often makes the single-serving friend recoil a bit, and express a sentiment bordering on pity.

But she's a factual sort of person, so she gives a factual answer: "well, basically I work with Excel all day, making Pivot-Tables." She fully expects this to be a setback in the conversation, a point on which we share no common ground.

Does this woman's story sound familiar? Do you occasionally find yourself in the same position?

Well imagine her surprise when this particular single-serving friend actually becomes **excited** after hearing her answer! He lights up – it's the highlight of his day to meet her.

Because, you see, on this flight, she sat down next to me. And I have some exciting news for people like her, which probably includes you ☺

## Excel Pros: The World Is Changing in Your Favor

If you are reading this, I can say confidently that the world is in the early stages of an incredible discovery: it is about to realize how immensely valuable YOU are. In large part, this book is aimed at helping you reap the full rewards available to you during this revolution.

That probably sounds pretty appealing, but why am I so comfortable making bold pronouncements about someone I have never met? Well, this is where the single-serving friend thing comes in: I have met **many** people like you over the years, and to me, you are very much 'my people.'

In fact, for many years while I worked at Microsoft, it was my **job** to meet people like you. I was an engineer on the Excel team, and I led a lot of the efforts to design new functionality for relatively advanced users.

Meeting those people, and watching them work, was crucial, so I traveled to find them. When I was looking for people to meet, the only criteria I applied was this: you had to use Excel for ten or more hours per week.

I found people like that (like you!) all over the world, in places ranging from massive banks in Europe to the back rooms of automobile dealerships in Portland, Oregon. There are also many of you working at Microsoft itself, working in various finance, accounting, and marketing roles, and I spent a lot of time with them as well (more on this later).

Over those years, I formed a 'profile' of these 'ten hour' spreadsheet people I met. Again, see if this sounds familiar.

**Attributes of an Excel Pro:**

- They grab data from one or more sources.
- They prep the data, often using VLOOKUP.
- They then create pivots over the prepared data.
- Sometimes they subsequently index into the resulting pivots, using formulas, to produce polished reports. Other times, the pivots themselves serve as the reports.
- They then share the reports with their colleagues, typically via email or by saving to a network drive.
- They spend at least half of their time re-creating the same reports, updated with the latest data, on a recurring basis.

At first, it seemed to be a coincidence that there was so much similarity in the people I was meeting. But over time it became clear that this was no accident. It started to seem more like a law of physics – an inevitable state of affairs. Much like the heat and pressure in the earth's crust seize the occasional pocket of carbon and transform it into a diamond, the demands of the modern world 'recruit' a certain kind of person and forge them into an Excel Pro.

Aside: Most Excel Pros do not think of themselves as Pros: I find that most are quite modest about their skills. However, take it from someone who has studied Excel usage in depth: if you fit the bulleted criteria above, you are an Excel Pro. Wear the badge proudly.

I can even put an estimate on how many of you are out there. At Microsoft we used to estimate that there were 300 million users of Excel worldwide. This number was disputed, and might be too low, especially today. It's a good baseline, nothing more. But that was **all** users of Excel – from the most casual to the most expert. Our instrumentation data further showed us that only 5-10% of all Excel users *created* PivotTables.

'Create' is an important word here – many more *consume* pivots made by others, but only 5-10% are able to *create* them from scratch. Creating pivots, then, turns out to be an overwhelmingly accurate indicator of whether someone is an Excel Pro. We might as well call them Pivot Pros.

You may feel quite alone at your particular workplace, because statistically speaking you *are* quite rare – less than 0.5% of the world's population has your skillset! But in absolute numbers you are **far** from alone in the world – in fact, you are one of approximately thirty million people. If Excel Pros had conferences or conventions, it would be quite a sight.

I, too, fit the definition of an Excel Pro. It is no accident that I found myself drawn to the Excel team after a few years at Microsoft, and it is no accident that I ultimately left to start an Excel / Power Pivot-focused business (and blog). While I have been using the word 'you' to describe Excel Pros, I am just as comfortable with the word '**we.**'

As I said up front, I am convinced that our importance is about to explode into the general consciousness. After all, we are already crucial.

# Our Importance Today

As proof of how vital we are, here's another story from Microsoft, one that borders on legend. The actual event transpired more than ten years ago and the details are hazy, but ultimately it's about you; about us.

Someone from the SQL Server database team was meeting with Microsoft CEO Steve Ballmer. They were trying to get his support for a 'business intelligence' (BI) initiative within Microsoft – to make the company itself a testbed for some new BI products in development at that time. If Steve supported the project, the BI team would have a much easier time gaining traction within the accounting and finance divisions at Microsoft.

In those days, Microsoft had a bit of a 'prove it to me' culture. It was a common approach to 'play dumb' and say something like, "okay, tell me why this is valuable." Which is precisely the sort of thing Steve said to the BI folks that day.

To which they gave an example, by asking a question like this: "If we asked you how much sales of Microsoft Office grew in South America last year versus how much they grew the year before, but only during the holiday season, you probably wouldn't know."

Steve wasn't impressed. He said, "sure I would," triggering an uncomfortable silence. The BI team **knew** he lacked the tools to answer that question – they'd done their homework. Yet here was one of the richest and most powerful men in the world telling them they were wrong.

One of the senior BI folks eventually just asked straight out, "Okay, **show** us how you'd do that."

Steve snapped to his feet in the center of his office and started shouting. Three people hurried in, and he started waving his arms frantically and bellowing orders, conveying the challenge at hand and the information he needed. This all happened with an aura of familiarity – this was a common occurrence, a typical workflow for Steve and his team.

Those three people then vanished to produce the requested results. In Excel, of course.

## Excel at the Core

Let that sink in: the CEO of the richest company in the world (and one of the most technologically advanced!) relied **heavily** on Excel Pros to be his eyes and ears for all things financial. Yes, I am sure that now, many years later, Satya Nadella has a broad array of sophisticated BI tools at his disposal. However, I am equally sure that his reliance on Excel Pros has not diminished by any significant amount.

Is there anything special about Microsoft in this regard? Absolutely not! This is true everywhere. No exceptions. Even at companies where they claimed to have 'moved beyond spreadsheets,' I was always told, off the record, that Excel still powered more than 90% of decisions. (Indeed, an executive at a large Microsoft competitor told me recently that his division, which produces a BI product marketed as a 'better' way to report numbers than Excel, uses Excel for **all** internal reporting!)

Today, if a decision – no matter how critical it is, or how large the organization is – is informed by data, it is overwhelmingly likely that the data is coming out of Excel. The data may be communicated in printed form, or PDF, or even via slide deck. But it was *produced* in Excel, and therefore by an Excel Pro.

The message is clear: today we are an indispensable component of the information age, and if we disappeared, the modern world would grind to a halt overnight. Yet our role in the world's development is just getting started.

# Three Ingredients of Revolution

There are three distinct reasons why Excel Pros are poised to have a very good decade.

## Ingredient One: Explosion of Data

The ever-expanding capacity of hardware, combined with the ever-expanding importance of the internet, has led to a truly astounding explosion in the amount of data collected, stored, and transmitted.

Estimates vary widely, but in a single day, the internet may transmit more than a thousand *exabytes* of data. That's 180 CD-ROMs' worth of data for each person on the planet, in just 24 hours!

However, it's not just the volume of data that is expanding; the number of *sources* is also expanding. Nearly every click you make on the internet is recorded (scary but true). Social media is now 'mined' for how frequently a certain product is mentioned, and whether it was mentioned positively or negatively. The thermostat in your home may be 'calling home' to the power company once a minute. GPS units in delivery vehicles are similarly checking in with 'home base.'

This explosion of volume and variety is often lumped together under the term 'Big Data.' A few savvy folks are front-running this wave of hype by labeling themselves as 'Big Data Professionals'. By the time you are done with this book, you might rightfully be tempted to do the same.

There's a very simple reason why 'Big Data' equals 'Big Opportunity' for Excel Pros: human beings can only understand a single page (at most) of information at a time. Think about it: even a few hundred rows of data is too big for a human being to look at and make a decision. We need to summarize that data – to 'crunch' it into a smaller number of rows (i.e. a report) – before we can digest it.

So 'big' just means 'too big for me to see all at once.' The world is producing Big Data, but humans still need Small Data. Whether it's a few hundred rows or a few billion, people need an Excel Pro to shrink it for human consumption. The need for you is only growing.

 For more on Big Data, see http://ppvt.pro/SaavyBigData.

## Ingredient Two: Economic Pressure

Much of the world has been in an economic downturn since 2008, and in general this is a bad thing. If played properly, however, it can be a benefit to the Excel Pro.

Consider, for a moment, the BI industry. BI essentially plays the same role as Excel: it delivers digestible information to decision makers. It's more formal, more centralized, and more expensive – an IT function rather than an Excel Pro function – but fills the same core need for actionable information.

A surprising fact: paradoxically, BI spending increases during recessions, when spending on virtually everything else is falling. This was true during the dot-com bust of 2000 and is true again today.

Why does this happen? Simply put: when the pressure is on, the value of smart decisions is increased, as is the cost of bad ones. I like to explain it this way: when money is falling from the sky, being 'smart' isn't all that valuable. At those times, the most valuable person is the one who can put the biggest bucket out the window. However when the easy money stops flowing, and everyone's margins get pressured, 'smart' becomes valuable once again.

Unlike BI spending, spending on spreadsheets is *not* measured – people buy Microsoft Office every few years no matter what, so we wouldn't notice a change in 'Excel spending' during recessions. I suspect, however, that if we could somehow monitor the number of hours spent in Excel worldwide, we would see a spike during recessions, for the same reason we see spikes in BI spending.

So the amount and variety of data that needs to be 'crunched' is exploding, and at the same time, the business value of *insight* is increasing. This is a potent mixture.

All it needs is a spark to ignite it. And boy, do we have a bright spark.

## Ingredient Three: Dramatically Better Tools

The world's need for insights is reaching a peak. Simultaneously, the amount of data is exploding, providing massive new insight opportunities (raw material for producing insights). Where is the world going to turn?

It is going to take an *army* of highly skilled data professionals to navigate these waters. Not everyone is cut out for this job either – only people who *like* data are going to be good at it. They must also be trained already – there's no time to learn, because the insights are needed now!

I think you see where I am going. **That army exists today, and it is all of YOU.** You already enjoy data, you are well-versed in the nuances of your particular business, and you are already trained on the most flexible data analysis tool in the world.

However, until now there have been a few things holding you back:

1. **You are very busy.** Many of you are swamped today, and for good reason. Even a modestly complex Excel report can require hundreds of individual actions on the part of the author, and most of those actions need to be repeated when you receive new data or a slightly different request from your consumers. Our labor in Excel is truly "1% inspiration and 99% perspiration," to use Edison's famous words.

2. **Integrating data from multiple sources is tedious.** Excel may be quite flexible, but that does not mean it makes every task effortless. Making multiple sources 'play nicely' together in Excel can absorb huge chunks of your time.

3. **Truly 'Big' Data does not fit in Excel.** Even the expansion of sheet capacity to one million rows (in Excel 2007 and newer) does not address all of today's needs. In my work at Pivotstream I sometimes need to crunch data sets exceeding 100 million rows, and even data sets of 100,000 rows can become prohibitively slow in Excel, particularly when you are integrating them with other data sets.

4. **Excel has an image problem.** It simply does not receive an appropriate amount of respect. To the uninitiated, it looks a lot like Word and PowerPoint – an Office application that produces documents. Even though those same people could not *begin* to produce an effective report in Excel, and they rely critically on the insights it provides, they still only assign Excel Pros the same respect as someone who can write a nice letter in Word. That may be depressing, but it is sadly true.

**The answer is here**

The Power BI family of tools addresses all of those problems. I actually think it's fair to say that it completely wipes them away.

**You** are the army that the world needs. You just needed an upgrade to your toolset. Power Pivot and its close cousin Power BI provide that upgrade and then some. I would say that we probably needed a 50% upgrade to Excel, but what we got is more like a 500% upgrade; and that is not a number I throw around lightly.

 Imagine the year is 1910, and you are one of the world's first biplane pilots. One day at the airfield, someone magically appears and gives you a brand-new 2020 jet plane. You climb inside and discover that the cockpit has been designed to mimic the cockpit of your 1910 biplane! You receive a *dramatic* upgrade to your aircraft without having to re-learn how to fly from scratch. That is the kind of 'gift' that Power Pivot provides to Excel Pros.

I bet you are eager to see that new jet airplane. Let's take a tour.

# 2 - Power Pivot and the Power BI Family: Making Sense of the Various Versions

## It's a Family of Products Built on Shared Engines

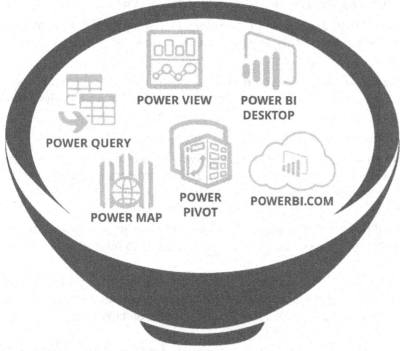

*Figure 2 "Power Soup" – There are at Least Six MS Data Products Running Around with the "Power" Prefix. But don't worry! We are here to clear all that up.*

### "Should I use Power Query or Power Pivot or Power View or Power BI?"

Ah, a fair question, but one with a surprisingly simple answer: you ALWAYS use Power Pivot! There is, indeed, an entire family of closely-related Microsoft products in this data analysis and reporting space, but they all revolve around Power Pivot. Let's start simple and then add pieces back to the puzzle.

### Power Pivot is the Center of the Power BI Universe

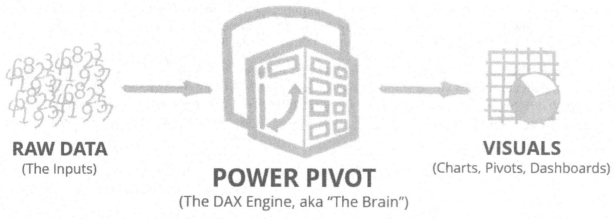

*Figure 3 Power Pivot is the centerpiece, no matter which "family members" you're using!*

Power Pivot is the central engine that powers all of your souped-up workbooks and BI solutions. It is the brain, the heart, and the spinal cord all in one. We like to say that Power Pivot is the piece that turns data into information – feed it "large" quantities of data (where sometimes even 100 rows is "large") and it will help you crunch it down into meaningful metrics.

As Microsoft continues to evolve its strategy and messaging, we've started to refer to Power Pivot as "the DAX engine." That's because it (Power Pivot) is starting to appear in more products, and in some of those products (such as Power

BI Desktop), the "Power Pivot" moniker has been retired. Rest assured, however that the DAX Engine / Power Pivot is THE crown jewel (AND brain / heart / spinal cord – yes, we love metaphors around here) of everything in Microsoft's BI suite. As they used to say on the pasta sauce commercials, "It's in there!" (Even though the ingredients list of Power BI Desktop omits it).

Using Power Pivot / the DAX engine, you build a data model, create relationships, write calculated column and measure formulas, etc. We will primarily focus on this portion in our book, because the Power Pivot data model is what subsequently drives all of the reporting/visualization/analysis tools.

## Power Query is a Close Second in Importance

But an engine needs fuel, and in this case, the fuel is data: whether big or small, 100 rows or 100 million rows, coming from the web or a database, a text file or a spreadsheet. You will want to pull all of your business data into Power Pivot (not all in one day ☺ of course. Start small, iterate fast: Power BI is agile BI).

So this brings us to our second-favorite component of the Power BI family…

Power Query!

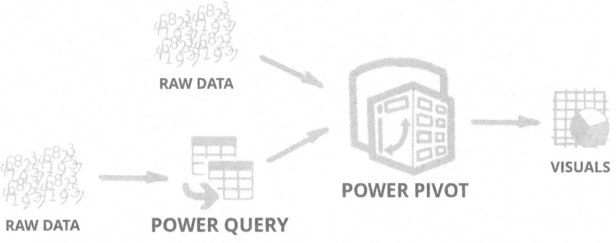

*Figure 4 Two ways to get data into Power Pivot: direct import, or via Power Query*

Power Pivot can grab data directly from a wide variety of sources (covered in the chapter on Loading Data). But sometimes it needs a little help. Sometimes, before you can bring the data into Power Pivot, you need to do some shaping, some cleanup, and maybe some data transformation. There is a tool built specifically for that – Power Query. And boy, does it shine at that task. Power Query is a great way to bring data into Power Pivot.

> ℹ️ For a long time our biggest reservation with Power Query was the lack of ability to easily automate the refresh of Excel workbooks that employ Power Query. We are thrilled to offer the **Power Update** tool (co-created by PowerPivotPro) which can help you do that and a lot more. Get it at http://ppvt.pro/pwrupdate

So Power Query is an optional piece of the puzzle: you aren't **forced** to use it, but it's there if you need it. In our experience, whether you need it depends primarily on this: do you have good database support? If most (or all) of your data is coming from databases, AND the people who run those databases are responsive to your requests, you are a member of a very fortunate minority! In such an environment, you can get your data cleaned and re-shaped before it ever reaches your desktop, and so Power Query has less utility.

But most environments are "noisier" than that, and Power Query really shines in those places – as a complement to Power Pivot. More specifically, we can view it as a "pre-processor" that cleans and shapes "noisy" data, before it's imported, so that Power Pivot can do its best work.

*Figure 5 Power Query in Excel 2013: For Shaping and Cleaning Data Before Power Pivot Ever "Sees" It.*

As of mid-2015, Microsoft is completely retiring the "Power Query" name: In Excel 2016, it no longer has its own ribbon tab for instance, and is instead called "Get & Transform" on the Data ribbon tab. That's entirely sensible in our opinion, and the important thing is that the engine remains the same.

Similarly, Power BI Desktop (described below) includes Power Query but no longer calls it that. Instead, you get to it via buttons like "Get Data" and "Queries." Again, entirely sensible, and again, the engine remains the same.

So, much like we now often refer to the Power Pivot engine as the "DAX Engine," you will also see us refer to Power Query's engine as the "M Engine."

See the chapter specifically on Power Query for more info.

# Visuals: The Crucial "Last Mile"

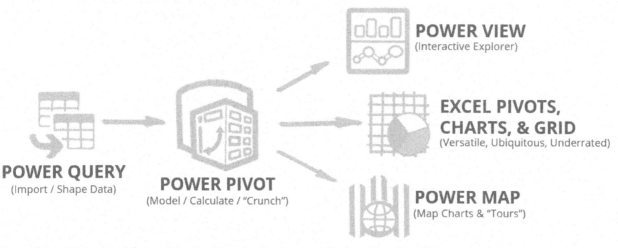

*Figure 6 Power View and Power Map are Visualization Layers... But so is Excel Itself!*

Power Pivot itself offers no visualization options – it can calculate meaningful metrics, but cannot display them effectively to end consumers and decision makers. Think of Power Pivot as a Calculation Layer that provides robustly-calculated metrics to a variety of Visualization Layers.

- **Excel**: The most popular visualization layer of all is Excel itself. Most people build Excel pivot tables and charts connected to their Power Pivot data model (not to mention another favorite of ours, cube formulas!) Excel visuals are a great option, and within the Excel-based flavors of Power BI, it's still the option we recommend most frequently. You also have several other visualization layers to choose from, however, so we'll mention those here as well.

- **Power Map**: Introduced in Excel 2013, we're not entirely sure that Microsoft plans to feature Power Map all that heavily in its future plans. In Excel 2016, it has been renamed to just "3d Maps." You absolute CAN use it to visualize Power Pivot data, but it's become enough of a "niche" product that we don't use it in our business.

- **Power View**: Power View is another 'client' that can render Power Pivot data onto interactive dashboards. There's a version of Power view included in Excel 2013 (Pro Plus version only), another one in Excel 2016 (although it's hidden from the Excel ribbon), and even a bit of an outlier: a version that exists solely within SharePoint 2010 and higher. It's fair to say, however, that Power View does NOT figure heavily in Microsoft's future plans, and we don't recommend going "all in" on Power View as your organization's visualization layer of choice. Increasingly, it's becoming clear that the two primary visualization "horses" in Microsoft's stable are going to be Excel itself, and Power BI Dashboards, which we will cover next.

- **Power BI Dashboards:** Until recently, Excel has been the only "environment" in which the Power BI tools were available. If you wanted to do some Power Pivot / DAX modeling, you launched Excel and went from there. But in 2015, Microsoft released a second environment, called Power BI Desktop. Power BI Desktop includes the two engines (Power Pivot and Power Query), as well as a brand-new visualization layer called Dashboards. Dashboards looks a bit like Power View, but whereas Power View was somewhat of a frustrating half-step, Power BI Dashboards are very robust/complete. They offer MANY visualization types that are not available in native Excel, the list of visualizations grows seemingly with every release, AND they have opened the platform up so that third-party programmers can add their own custom visualization types. Power BI Desktop and its companion cloud service are therefore worthy of their own chapter, which you will find later in this book.

- **Others**: As if this isn't excitement enough, we also have SQL Server Reporting Services, Datazen and many other Microsoft and non-Microsoft tools – it seems everyone is "lining up" to connect their visualization software to the Power Pivot engine, and for good reason.

> ⓘ To enable some of these other visualization options you will need a true "Server" version of Power Pivot. We'll cover that in our chapter on "YouTube for Workbooks."

Once your Power Pivot data model is built, reporting becomes "**cheap**" – a matter of mouse clicks in a field list (the field list provided by the visualization layer, such as Excel's PivotTable field list). New reports, and variants on existing reports, are borderline-effortless to assemble since all the business logic has been built at that point. With all the heavy lifting taken care of by your Power Pivot data model, you can easily use not just one but many reporting tools.

Power Pivot then becomes your single source of truth, the single engine that powers all your reporting across various reporting platforms and serving various groups of audiences.

> ⓘ You will rarely, if ever, catch a glimpse of Power Pivot (or Power Query for that matter) in any of Microsoft's public Power BI Demos. In their materials, the limelight is squarely on the sexy visualizations. And we're okay with that. Microsoft's competitors have long used that approach to sell their wares, and Microsoft is just borrowing a page from that book. But anyone getting down to implementing Power BI quickly learns that behind the scenes, Power Pivot is the engine driving Power BI.

> ⓘ Microsoft made an announcement in Oct, 2015 rolling out their "Reporting Roadmap". It promises:
> - Symmetry across On-Premise and Cloud. Currently the cloud options on PowerBI.com have raced ahead of any On-Premise reporting options.
> - Making various reporting options - SSRS, Power BI Desktop, Datazen etc. - work together in harmony.
> - A rejuvenated SQL Server Reporting Services (make it look like a tool from this century, as James Phillips put it)
> For more, see http://ppvt.pro/rptroadmap

# Power BI Desktop: Two Tools for the (Learning) Price of One!

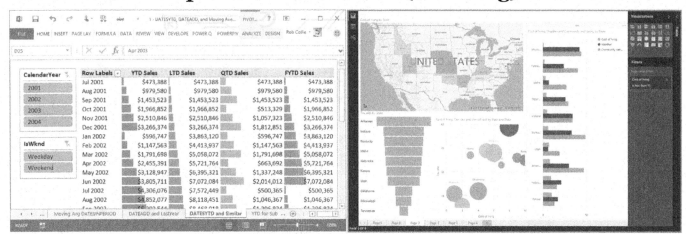

*Figure 7 Excel Power Pivot (left) versus Power BI Desktop: Visually Distinct, but the same "Under the Hood."*

## Same Engines, Just Different Visuals

We will cover Power BI Desktop in greater depth in a subsequent chapter, but we think it's important to lodge this in your brain up-front: when you are learning Power Pivot in Excel, you are also learning Power BI Desktop. The "tough" things to learn, which are also the valuable things to learn, are the same in both Power Pivot (Excel) and Power BI (Desktop). In fact, that's important enough that it warrants its own callout...

The "tough" things to learn, which are also the valuable things to learn, are the same in both Power Pivot (Excel) and Power BI (Desktop).

So when you learn one, you are actually learning two amazing tools for the price of one.

So here's the upside of all this "Power Soup" confusion: as the dust settles in Microsoft's evolving strategy, we have been given TWO amazing tools: Power Pivot in Excel, and Power BI Desktop, and we don't have to "invest double" in order to "win double."

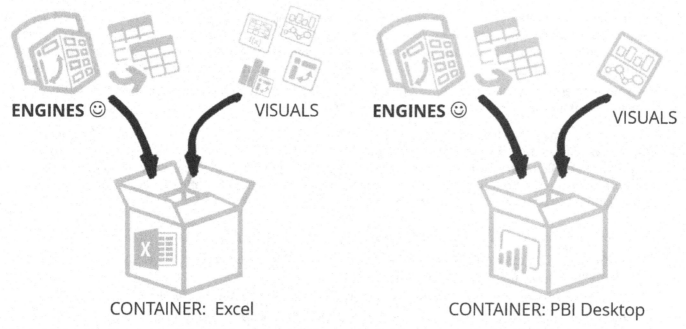

*Figure 8 Think of it this way: Excel and PBI Desktop are the "containers." The engines are the same in both places, only the visualization layers differ.*

## What do we mean by the "tough" or "valuable" stuff?

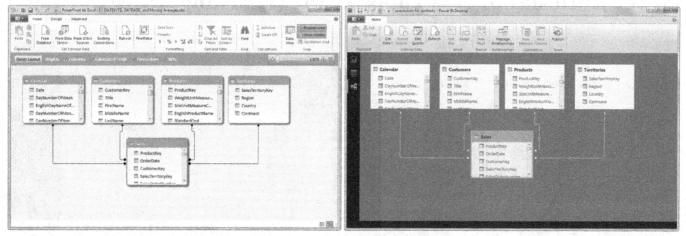

*Figure 9 Power Pivot's Diagram View sure looks a LOT like Power BI's Relationship View, because the DAX Engine is the heart of both.*

"Hrm," you say. "The view with the boxes and the lines is the same, but I'm still not convinced. I mean, there can still be a lot of OTHER differences hiding in there, right?"

Well sure! You haven't even seen the formulas yet! Let's see if you can spot the difference between a "Year to Date Sales" formula in Power Pivot versus Power BI...

Power Pivot version:

```
YTD Sales=
CALCULATE ( [Total Sales], DATESYTD( Calendar[Date] ) )
```

And the Power BI Desktop version:

```
YTD Sales=
CALCULATE ( [Total Sales], DATESYTD( Calendar[Date] ) )
```

**Trick question, they are EXACTLY the same!** Because, hey, it's the DAX engine in both places.

 In Power BI Desktop, the DAX Engine doesn't get its own separate special name like "Power Pivot." Its capabilities are just exposed in the Relationship view, and in the formulas you write. This makes sense to us – less name clutter. DAX Jedi (or Jedi-in-training) like you, dear reader, should not be concerned by this cosmetic "lack of name."

So, to recap, the engines are the same in both Power Pivot and Power BI. Here's one final summary diagram:

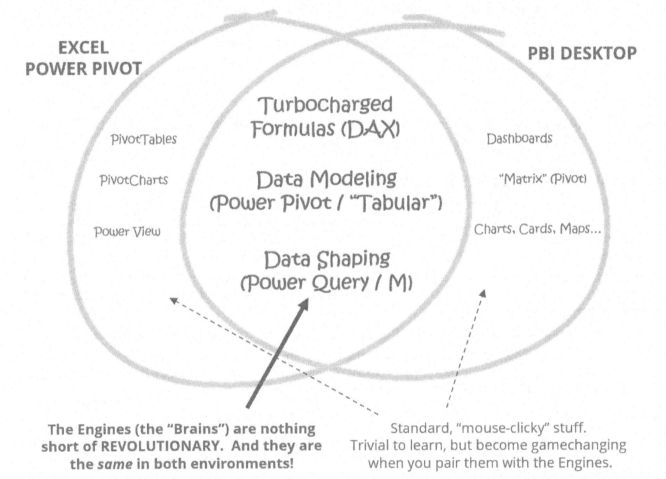

**EXCEL POWER PIVOT**

PivotTables

PivotCharts

Power View

Turbocharged Formulas (DAX)

Data Modeling (Power Pivot / "Tabular")

Data Shaping (Power Query / M)

**PBI DESKTOP**

Dashboards

"Matrix" (Pivot)

Charts, Cards, Maps...

**The Engines (the "Brains") are nothing short of REVOLUTIONARY. And they are the *same* in both environments!**

Standard, "mouse-clicky" stuff. Trivial to learn, but become gamechanging when you pair them with the Engines.

*Figure 10 Excel Power Pivot and PBI Desktop overlap in the stuff that warrant your time reading books like this one. Visuals, by contrast, are easy-to-learn, mouse-clicky stuff. You don't really need to "read the manual" to figure out how to build a chart in either environment.*

 In the official Microsoft messaging, "Power Pivot" now refers strictly to the DAX engine in Excel, with its Power Pivot ribbon tab and Power Pivot window, and "Power BI" now refers strictly to Power BI Desktop (and its accompanying PowerBI.com cloud publishing mechanism).

Over time we will be slowly adopting this official naming as well, but the community will understandably take some time to adjust.

We will come back to Power BI Desktop in its own dedicated chapter. But in the meantime, just remember that everything you're learning in subsequent chapters is useful in BOTH Power Pivot and Power BI.

# Power Pivot (in Excel) Versions

Focusing specifically on Power Pivot (the Excel-based version of these tools) there have now been four different major releases:

- **Power Pivot 2008 R2 (v1)** – We simply call this "Power Pivot v1." The "2008 R2" relates back to a version of SQL Server itself and has little meaning to us. This runs exclusively in Excel 2010, and since it's been superseded, there is very little reason to use this version. (If you are running a version of Power Pivot that starts with a 10, like 10.x.xxxx, that version is WAY out of date and should upgrade – we will NOT cover v1 in this book at all).

- **Power Pivot 2012 (v2)** – unsurprisingly we call this "Power Pivot v2." Again the 2012 relates to SQL Server, and again, we don't care that much. But we DO care that THIS is THE version to be running if you are running Excel 2010. **Whenever we refer to Power Pivot 2010 in this book, we are referring to THIS version.** (Make sure you are running 11.0.5058 or newer).

- **Power Pivot 2013** – released with Excel 2013.

- **Power Pivot 2016** – released with Excel 2016.

**You will get the same value out of this book regardless of the Excel version you are using.** Under the covers, fundamentals are the same and little has changed. We will talk about some of the cosmetic changes in the User Interface (UI) changes in this chapter. (The 2016 release **has** introduced some new DAX functions, which are covered in a separate chapter, but those should be thought of as "extras" rather than overhauls.)Here is a primer on how you can use Power Pivot based on your version of Excel.

## Power Pivot for Excel 2010

If you have Excel 2010, we exclusively recommend the v2 version, which offers many improvements over v1, which is now dead to us and will get no "air time" in this book. You can download the v2 version at: http://ppvt.pro/ppaddin2010SP2

## Power Pivot for Excel 2013 - Only Available in "Pro Plus" Excel

Microsoft really surprised us at the last minute, just as 2013 was officially released. It was quietly announced that Power Pivot would only be included in the "Pro Plus" version of Office 2013. This is NOT the same thing as "Professional" – Pro Plus was only available through volume licensing or subscription and was not available in any store. And unlike with 2010, there is no version of Power Pivot that you can just download for Excel 2013.

This put Power Pivot out of reach for many individuals. After much noise, on our part and others, Microsoft softened their stance and now individuals can get Power Pivot by either buying Excel 2013 Standalone or an Office 365 Pro Plus subscription. For more on this, see http://ppvt.pro/2013ProPlus

This was an improvement, but still a source of great frustration (just read the comments on the link shared above).

Office 2016 offers further improvement to this story, by including Power Pivot (and Power Query) in Standalone Excel (just like 2013), and all versions "Pro" and higher (whereas 2013 required Pro Plus). Still though, it is not included in all versions, so be careful to get Pro or Excel Standalone when making your purchase.

# Differences in User Interface: 2010, 2013, 2016

The User Interface (UI) of Power Pivot differs - in cosmetic ways ONLY - between Excel 2010, 2013, and 2016. Mostly it's just the names of buttons that have changed, but there are a few others, too. **Whenever there's a notable difference in UI between the versions, we will "pause" here in this book and show what it looks like in each version, at the moment where we first "introduce" that functionality.**

 Aside from Rob: When I worked at Microsoft, I used to LOVE renaming features. I'd see a button that I thought had been poorly-named in a previous version and say "let's improve it!" I even tried to rename PivotTables! Now that I'm on the receiving end of that behavior, I see the hubris in my younger self. Poetic justice, that I now suffer the consequences of my former peers' desire to constantly improve things. (I STILL think pivots should be renamed SummaryTables, though. Kidding. Mostly.)

The "default" version for screenshots in this book will be 2010, because that version usually yields the most helpful screenshots (see "awkward" below). Many of the screenshots and figures will therefore have the 2010 appearance. However, we want to again stress:

1. **All concepts covered in this book are 100% applicable to 2010, 2013, AND 2016,** because it's the DAX engine in all three cases, and that has changed hardly at all.

2. **The differences between the three versions are purely cosmetic in nature.** All of the core functionality – such as formulas and functions - behaves the same. The main difference is in the user interface (UI), e.g. which button you click to edit a formula or insert a pivot table.

3. **Whenever there's a UI difference that is significant, we will cover that in the book.** And we will do that in the context of introducing each new button or other UI element.

If you ever want to see all the notable 2010/2013/2016 UI differences in one place, this page - http://ppvt.pro/UIchanges - collects them all into an online "appendix" of sorts. See example below.

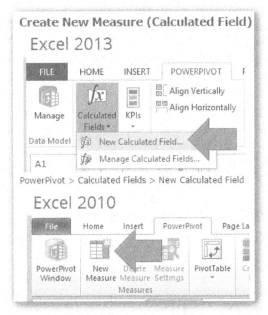

Figure 11 http://ppvt.pro/UIchanges *maps all the UI changes from Power Pivot across Excel 2010, 2013, and 2016.*

## When We Said "Cosmetic" We Meant "Awkward"

There is no way to sugar coat it, the user interface took a step **backward** from 2010 to 2013. It became harder to perform some routine data modeling steps - such as to find and edit formulas, or to insert a pivot or slicer. It's more awkward (more mouse clicks, harder to find) to perform these actions in 2013 than it is in 2010.

2016 has restored most, but not all, of the convenient UI functionality. Our consolation again, is that everything under the hood, beyond the minor UI changes, works just the same and just as well.

OK, we got that off our chests. Let us continue ☺

## 32-bit or 64-bit?

Each of the three versions of Power Pivot is available in two "flavors" – 32-bit and 64-bit. Which one should you use?

On the Microsoft download websites, 32-bit is labeled "x86" and 64-bit is labeled "AMD64." You know, just to make things interesting.

**If you have a choice, we *highly* recommend 64-bit.** 64-bit lets you work with larger volumes of data but is also more stable during intensive use, even with smaller data volumes. We run 64-bit on all of our computers.

For example, I (Rob) have a 300 million row data set that works fine on my laptop with 4 GB of RAM, but with 32-bit Power Pivot, *no* amount of RAM would make that possible. (In fact, it would not work even if I cut it down to 20 million rows).

So if you have a choice, go with 64-bit – it offers more capacity and more stability. That said, you may not have that luxury. You have to match your choice to your copy of Excel.

 You *cannot* run 64-bit Power Pivot with 32-bit Excel, or vice versa!

So the first question you need to answer is whether you are running 32-bit or 64-bit Excel.

In Excel 2010, you can find that answer here, on the Help page

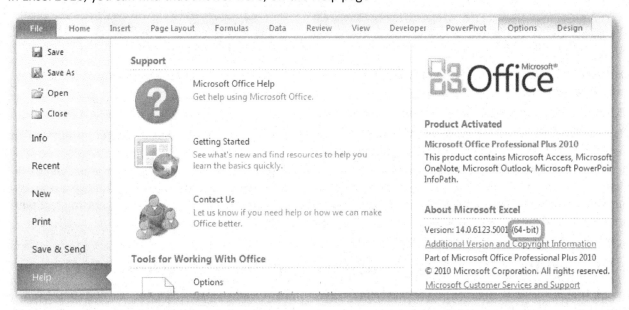

Figure 12 *Finding whether your version of Excel is 32-bit or 64-bit*

**If you are running 32-bit Excel, you are not alone: most people are running 32-bit.** We actually can think of no reason to run 64-bit Office except Power Pivot itself, so the 64-bit trend is really just getting started. (Who needs 64-bit Outlook, Word, and PowerPoint? No one does).

Certain Office addins only run in 32-bit, so double check that before you decide to uninstall 32-bit Office and switch to 64-bit.

The 64-bit problem is often solved by having a second computer purely for Power Pivot "authoring" purposes, and maintaining your original computer on 32-bit for compatibility with other Office addins. In cases where that's not practical, we've also frequently seen IT set up shared computers with 64-bit, and then Power Pivot authors can remotely use those computers via Remote Desktop. Lastly, this is one of the big reasons to consider Power BI Desktop, since you can run it in 64-bit without disrupting your Office install, which can remain 32-bit.

# Office 2010 or Newer is Required

No, sadly you cannot run Power Pivot with Excel 2007 or earlier versions.

There were very good technical reasons for this, and it was not an attempt by Microsoft to force people into Office 2010. Remember, the Power Pivot addin is free, and it would have been better for Microsoft, too, if Power Pivot worked with 2007.

If you are curious as to the reasons behind the "2010 or newer" requirement, see this post:

http://ppvt.pro/PP2007

# 3 - Learning Power Pivot "The Excel Way"

## Power Pivot is Like Getting Fifteen Years of Excel Improvements All at Once

**Power Pivot was first released in 2009, but development began *fifteen years* prior to that, in 1994.** Back then, it was called Microsoft SQL Server Analysis Services (SSAS). Actually, SSAS is very much alive and well as a product today – it remains the #1-selling analytical database engine in the world. SSAS was/is an industrial strength calculation engine for business, but targeted at highly specialized IT professionals.

In late 2006, Microsoft architect Amir Netz launched a secret incubation project (codename: Gemini) with an ambitious goal: make the full power of SSAS available and understandable to Excel Pros. A few months later he recruited me (Rob) to join the effort (he and I had collaborated before when I was on the Excel team). Gemini was eventually released under the name Power Pivot in 2009.

Continuing with the "biplane and jet" metaphor, think of SSAS as the jet plane, and Power Pivot as the effort to install an Excel-style cockpit and instrument panel so that Excel Pros can make the transition.

The key takeaway for you is this: **Power Pivot is a much, *much* deeper product than you would expect from something that appeared so recently on the scene.**

This actually has two very important implications:

1. **It is very hard to exhaust Power Pivot's capabilities.** Its long heritage means that a staggering number of needs have been addressed, and this is very good news.
2. **It is very helpful to learn it in the right sequence.** When touring the cockpit of your new jet, much will be familiar to you – the SUM() function is there, so is ROUND(), and even our old friend RAND(). But there are new functions as well, with names like FILTER() and EARLIER() and CALCULATE(). Naturally you want to start with the simplest and most useful functions, but it is hard to know which ones those *are*.

That second point is very important, and worth emphasizing.

## Learn Power Pivot As You Learned Excel: Start Simple & Grow

**When you were first introduced to Excel (or spreadsheets in general), you likely started simple:** learning simple arithmetic formulas and the "A1" style reference syntax. You didn't dive right into things like pivots until later. (In fact pivots didn't even exist in the first few versions of Excel).

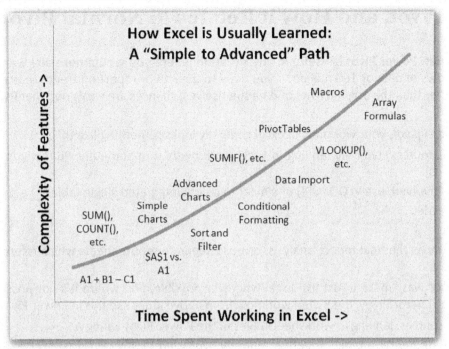

*Figure 13 An Approximate Representation of the Typical Excel Learning Curve*

You started with the simple stuff, got good at it, and only *then* branched out to new features. Incrementally, you added to your bag of tricks, over and over.

**Power Pivot is no different.** There are simple features (easy to learn and broadly useful) and advanced features (harder to learn and useful in more specific cases).

**We have carefully sequenced the topics in this book** to follow the same "simple to advanced" curve we developed and refined while training Excel pros over the past few years. The result is an approach that has proven to be very successful.

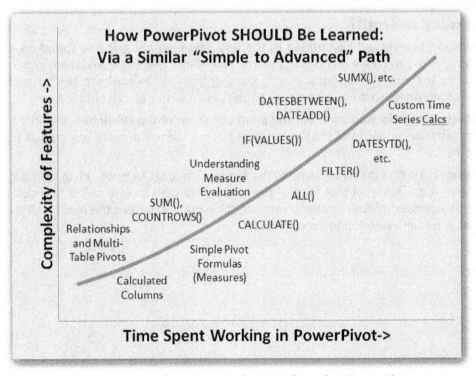

*Figure 14 The learning curve we advocate to Excel Pros as they adopt Power Pivot*

**We highly recommend that you proceed through the book "in order."** You will see that the chapters in this book are organized in roughly the order pictured above.

# When to Use Power Pivot, and How it Relates to Normal Pivot Usage

**We hear this question a lot. Simply put, Power Pivot is useful in any situation where you would normally want to use a pivot.** Whether you have 100 rows of data or 100 million, if you need to analyze or report on trends, patterns, and/or aggregates from that data, rather than the original rows of data themselves, chances are very good that Power Pivot has something to offer.

When you use a traditional (non Power-) pivot, your workflow in Excel generally looks something like this:

1. **Grab data** from one or more sources, typically landing in Excel worksheets (but sometimes directly in the "pivotcache" in advanced cases).
2. **If multiple tables of data are involved,** use VLOOKUP() or similar to create integrated single tables
3. **Add calculated columns** as needed
4. **Build pivots** against that data
5. **Either use those pivots directly** as the final report/analysis, or build separate report sheets which reference into the pivots using formulas

Our guiding philosophy on Power Pivot was "make it just like Excel wherever possible, and where it's not possible, make it 'rhyme' very closely with Excel." Accordingly, the 5-step workflow from above looks like this in Power Pivot:

1. **Grab data** from one or more sources, landing in worksheet-tables in the Power Pivot window.
2. **Use relationships to quickly link multiple tables together,** entirely *bypassing VLOOKUP()* or similar tedious formulas.
3. **Optionally supplement that data with calculated columns and measures,** using Excel functions you have always known, *plus some powerful new ones*.
4. **Build pivots** against that data
5. **Either use those pivots directly** as the final report/analysis, or *convert pivots into formulas* with a single click for flexible layout, or you can still build separate report sheets which reference into the pivots using formulas.

 On net you should think of Power Pivot as "Excel++" – the only new things you have to learn should bring you tremendous benefit.

## What This Book Will Cover in Depth

**Simple Guideline: the more "common knowledge" something is, the less pages we are going to spend on it.** We figure, for instance, that the button you use to create pivots is not worth a lot of ink. That topic, and many others, has been covered in depth by Bill Jelen's first Power Pivot book, http://ppvt.pro/MRXLPP. **By contrast, the formula language of Power Pivot needs a lot of attention,** so it receives many chapters and consumes most of the book.

**But even in topics that are relatively straightforward, we will still point out some of the subtleties,** the little things that you might not expect. So for instance, in our brief chapter on Data Import, we will provide some quick tips on things we have discovered over time.

**And what is this "DAX" thing anyway?** "DAX" is the name given to the formula language in Power Pivot, and it stands for Data Analysis eXpressions. We're not actually all that fond of the name – we wish it were called "Formula+" or something that sounds more like an extension to Excel rather than something brand new. But the name isn't the important thing – the fact is that DAX *is* just an extension to Excel formulas.

OK, let's load some data.

# 4 - Loading Data Into Power Pivot

## No Wizards Were Harmed in the Creation of this Chapter

We don't intend to instruct you on how to use the import wizards in this chapter. They are mostly self-explanatory and there is plenty of existing literature on them. Instead we want to share with you the things we have learned about data import over time.

**Think of this chapter as primarily "all the things we learned the hard way about data import."**

That said, all chapters need to start somewhere, so let's cover a few fundamentals...

## Everything Must "Land" in the Power Pivot Window

As we hinted in previous chapters, all of your relevant data MUST be loaded into the Power Pivot window rather than into normal Excel worksheets. But this is no more difficult than importing data into Excel has ever been. It's probably easier in fact.

### Launching the Power Pivot Window

The Power Pivot window is accessible via this button on the Power Pivot ribbon tab in Excel:

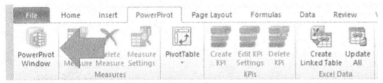

*Figure 15 Excel 2010: Launch the Power Pivot window*

*Figure 16 Excel 2013: Launch the Power pivot window*

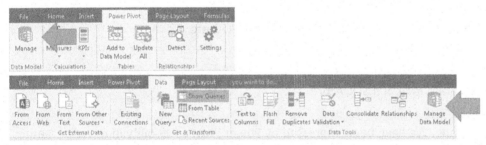

*Figure 17 Excel 2016: Offers not one but two ways to launch Power Pivot window*

 If the Power Pivot ribbon tab does not appear for you, the Power Pivot addin is either not installed or not enabled. Watch the videos on http://ppvt.pro/UIchanges which help you install and enable Power Pivot.

### One Sheet Tab = One Table

Every table of data you load into Power Pivot gets its own sheet tab. So if you import three different tables of data, you will end up with something like this:

*Figure 18 Three tables loaded into Power Pivot. Each gets its own sheet tab.*

### You Cannot Edit Cells in the Power Pivot Window

That's right, the Power Pivot sheets are read-only. You can't just select a cell and start typing.

You can delete or rename entire sheet tabs and columns, and you can add calculated columns, but you cannot modify cells of data, ever.

Does that sound bad? Actually, it's a good thing. It makes the data more trustworthy, but even more importantly, it forces you to do things in a way that saves you a *lot* of time later.

## Everything in the Power Pivot Window Gets Saved into the Same XLSX File

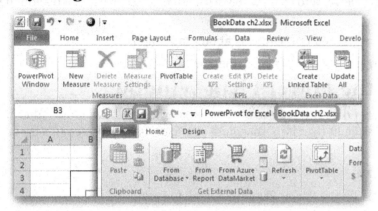

*Figure 19 Both windows' contents are saved into the same file, regardless of which window you save from*

 Each instance of the Power Pivot window is tightly "bound" to the XLSX (or XLSM/XLSB) you had open when you clicked the Power Pivot Window button in Excel. You can have three XLSX workbooks open at one time, for instance, and three different Power Pivot windows open, but the contents of each Power Pivot window are only available to (and saved into) its original XLSX.

# Many Different Sources

Power Pivot can "eat" data from a very wide variety of sources, including the following:

- From normal Excel sheets in the current workbook
- From the clipboard – any copy/pasted data that is in the shape of a table, even tables from Word for instance
- From text files – CSV, tab delimited, etc.
- From databases - like Access and SQL Server, but also Oracle, DB2, MySQL, etc.
- From SharePoint lists
- From MS SQL Server Reporting Services (SSRS) reports
- From cloud sources like Azure DataMarket and SQL Azure
- From so-called "data feeds"

So there is literally something for everyone. We have been impressed by Power Pivot's flexibility in terms of "eating" data from different sources, and have always found a way to load the data we need. And now you have Power Query, which further extends the data sources you can connect to and send the data into Power Pivot.

For each of the Power Pivot methods above, we will offer a brief description and our advice.

# Linked Tables (Data Source Type)

If you have a table of data in Excel like this:

| CalendarYear | MonthNumberOfYear | SalesTerritoryRegion | EnglishProductSubcateg |
|---|---|---|---|
| 2001 | 7 | Australia | Mountain Bikes |
| 2001 | 7 | Australia | Road Bikes |
| 2001 | 7 | Canada | Mountain Bikes |
| 2001 | 7 | Canada | Road Bikes |
| 2001 | 7 | France | Mountain Bikes |
| 2001 | 7 | France | Road Bikes |

*Figure 20 Just a normal table of data in a normal Excel sheet*

You can "link" this to a Power Pivot table. This will duplicate the selected Excel table into the Power Pivot window, and also keep them in sync. Here's how to "link" tables for each of the Excel versions.

**Excel 2010**: Use "Create Linked Table" button to quickly grab the table into Power Pivot:

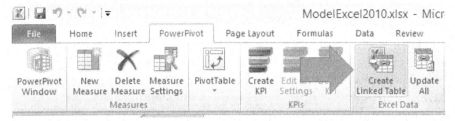

*Figure 21 Excel 2010: From Excel "Power Pivot" tab > click Create Linked Table*

**Excel 2013**: Here the button is called "Add to Data Model"

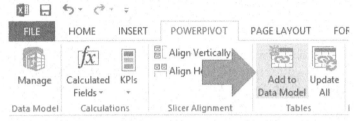

*Figure 22 Excel 2013: From Excel "Power Pivot" tab > click Add to Data Model*

**Excel 2016**: For 2016, the button is still called "Add to Data Model"

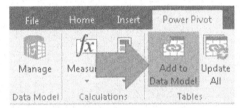

*Figure 23 Excel 2016: From Excel "Power Pivot" tab > click Add to Data Model*

 In Excel 2013/2016, you're better off if you format your data as an Excel table and then give the table a proper name. Do this before you add these to your Power Pivot Data Model. Else your Pivot Table Field List may continue to show the unfortunate default name of Table1, Table2…; even when you rename them on the Power Pivot side.

## Advantages

- This is the quickest way to get a table from Excel into Power Pivot
- If you edit the data in Excel – change cells, add rows, etc. – Power Pivot will pick those changes up. So this is a sneaky way to work around the "cannot edit in Power Pivot window" limitation.
- If you add columns, those will *also* be picked up. We call this out specifically because Copy/Paste (below) does *not* do this, and we frequently find ourselves wishing we had used Link rather than Copy/Paste for that reason.

## Limitations

- **You cannot link a table in Workbook A to the Power Pivot window from Workbook B.** This only creates a linked table in the Power Pivot window "tied" to the XLSX where the table currently resides.
- **This is *not* a good way to load *large* amounts of data** into Power Pivot. A couple thousand rows is fine. But ten thousand rows or more may cause you trouble and grind your computer to a halt.
- **By default, Power Pivot will update its copy of this table *every* time** you leave the Power Pivot window and come back to it. That happens whether you changed anything in Excel or not, and leads to a delay while Power Pivot re-loads the same data.
- **Linked Tables cannot be scheduled for auto-refresh** on a Power Pivot server. They can only be updated on the desktop.

- **You cannot subsequently change over to a different source type** – this really isn't a limitation specifically of linked tables. This is true of every source type in this list: whatever type of data source is used to create a table, that table cannot later be changed over to use another type of data source. So if you create a Power Pivot table via Linked Table, you cannot change it in the future to be sourced from a text file, database, or any other source. You will need to delete the table and re-create it from the new source.

 It is often very tempting to start building a Power Pivot workbook from an "informal" source like Linked Tables or Copy/Paste, with a plan to switch over and connect the workbook to a more robust source (like a database) later. Resist this temptation whenever possible! If you plan to use a database later, load data from your informal source (like Excel) into that database and then import it from there. The extra step now will save you *loads* of time later.

## Tips and Other Notes

- **To work around the "large data" problem,** we often save a worksheet as CSV (comma separated values) and then import that CSV file into Power Pivot. We have imported CSV files with more than 10 million rows in the past. See "Importing from Text Files" later in this chapter for more.

- **Rename your Excel Table first**, before you bring them into Power Pivot when using Excel 2013/2016. This is an annoying behavior in Excel 2013 and 2016, that even if you rename a Linked Table in Power Pivot, the old (Excel) table name continues to show in the PivotTable Field List. To avoid this, simply rename your Excel Table before bringing it in to Power Pivot.

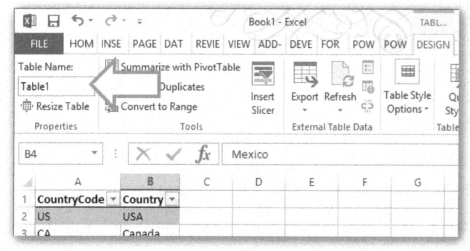

*Figure 24 For Excel 2013/2016 rename table before adding to Power Pivot*

- **To avoid the delay** every time you return to the Power Pivot window, we highly recommend changing this setting in the Power Pivot window to "Manual". Afterwards you can click Update All or Update Selected buttons to refresh the linked tables manually.

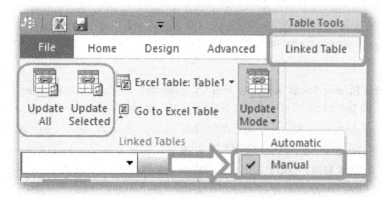

*Figure 25 Change the Update Mode to Manual*

# Pasting Data Into Power Pivot (Data Source Type)

If you copy a table-shaped batch of data onto the Windows clipboard, this button in the Power Pivot window will light up:

*Figure 26 This button could have been named "Paste as New Table"*

## Advantages

- **You can paste from any table-shaped source** and are not limited to using just Excel (unlike Linked Tables)
- **You can paste from other workbooks** and are not limited to the same workbook as your Power Pivot window

**Pasted tables support both "Paste/Replace" and "Paste/Append"** as shown by the buttons here:

*Figure 27 These paste methods can come in handy*

## Limitations

- **Suffers from the same "large data set"** drawback as Linked Tables.
- **You can never paste in an additional column.** Once a table has been pasted, its columns are fixed. You can add a calculated column but can never change your mind and add that column you thought you omitted the first time you pasted. This becomes more of a drawback than you might expect.
- **Not all apparently table-shaped sources are truly table-shaped.** Tables on web pages are notorious for this. Sometimes you are lucky and sometimes you are not.
- **Cannot be switched to another data source type** (true of all data source types).

# Importing From Text Files (Data Source Type)

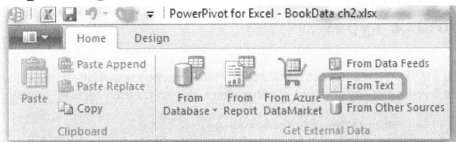

*Figure 28 The text import button in the Power Pivot window*

## Advantages

- **Can handle nearly limitless data volumes**
- **You can add new columns later** (if you are a little careful about it, see below)
- **Text files can be located anywhere** on your hard drive or even on network drives and Power Pivot can connect to them directly. If on a website, you can use Power Query to connect to them and send the output to Power Pivot. So some backend process might update a text file every night in a fixed location (and filename), for example, and all you have to do is refresh the Power Pivot workbook the next day to pick up the new data.
- **Can be switched to point at a different text file,** but still cannot be switched to an entirely different source type (like database).

## Limitations

- **No reliable column names** – unlike in a database, text files are not robust with regard to column names. If the order of columns in a CSV file gets changed, that will likely confuse Power Pivot on the next refresh.
- **Cannot be switched to another data source type** (true of all data source types).

# Databases (Data Source Type)

## Advantages

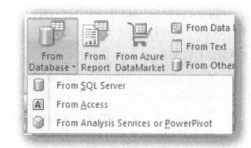

- **Can handle nearly limitless data volumes**
- **You can add new columns later**
- **Can be switched to point at a different server, database, table, view, or query.** Lots of "re-pointability" here, but you still can't switch to another data source type.
- **Databases are a great place to add calculated columns.** There are some significant advantages to building calculated columns in the database, and then importing them, rather than writing the calculated columns in Power Pivot itself. This is particularly true when your tables are quite large. We will talk about this later in the Performance chapter.

*Figure 29 The Database import button in the Power Pivot window*

- **Power Pivot really shines when paired with a good database.** There is just an *incredible* amount of flexibility available when your data is coming from a database. More on this in the following two links.

 If you are curious, you can read the following posts about why Power Pivot is even better when "fed" from a database: http://ppvt.pro/DBpart1, and http://ppvt.pro/DBpart2

## Limitations

- **Not always an option.** Hey, not everyone has a SQL Server at their disposal, and/or not everyone knows how to work with databases.
- **Cannot switch between database types.** A table sourced from Access cannot later be switched over and pointed to SQL Server. So in reality, these are separate data source types, but they are similar enough that we did not want to add a completely separate section for each.
- **Cannot be switched to another data source type** (true of all data source types).

# Less Common Data Source Types

## SharePoint Lists

These are great when you have a data source that is maintained and edited by human beings, especially if more than one person shares that editing duty. But if your company does not use SharePoint, this isn't terribly relevant to you.

 Only SharePoint 2010 and above can be used as a Power Pivot data source.

The Great Power Pivot FAQ is an example of a public SharePoint list, where myself and others from the community can record the answers to frequently-asked questions, which are then shared with the world. It is located here: http://ppvt.pro/TheFAQ

## Reporting Services (SSRS) Reports

This is another example of "if your company already uses it, it's a great data source," but otherwise, not relevant.

 Only SSRS 2008 R2 and above can be used as a Power Pivot data source.

## Cloud Sources Like Azure DataMarket and SQL Azure

**Folks, we are a huge, huge, HUGE fan of Azure DataMarket, and they improve it every day.** Would you like to cross-reference your sales data with historical weather data for every single store location over the past three years? That data is now easily within reach. International exchange rate data? Yep, that too. Or maybe historical gas prices? Stock prices? Yes and yes. There are *thousands* of such sources available on DataMarket.

We don't remotely have space here to gush about DataMarket, so we will point you to a few posts that explain what it is, how it works, and why we think it is a huge part of our future as Excel Pros. In the second post we explain how you can get 10,000 days of free weather data: http://ppvt.pro/DataMktTruth, http://ppvt.pro/DataMktWeather and http://ppvt.pro/UltDate

**SQL Azure** is another one of those "if you are using it, it's relevant, otherwise, let's move on" sources. But like DataMarket, we think most of us will be encountering SQL Azure in our lives as Excel Pros over the next few years.

## "Data Feeds"

Data Feeds are essentially a way in which a programmer can easily write an "adapter" that makes a particular data source available such that Power Pivot can pull data from it.

In fact, SharePoint and SSRS are exposed to Power Pivot via the Data Feed protocol – that is how those source types were enabled "under the hood."

So we are mentioning this here in case your company has some sort of custom internal server application and you want to expose its data to Power Pivot. The quickest way to do that may be to expose that application's data as a data feed, as long as you have a programmer available to do the work.

For more on the data feed protocol, which is also known as OData, see: http://www.odata.org/

# Other Important Features and Tips

## Renaming up Front – VERY Important!

**The names of tables and columns are going to be used everywhere in your formulas.** And Power Pivot does NOT "auto-fix" formulas when you rename a table or column! So if you decide to rename things later, you may have a lot of manual formula fixup to do.

And besides, bad table and column names in formulas just make things harder to read. So it's worth investing a few minutes up front to fix things up.

 We *strongly* recommend that you get into the habit of "import data, then immediately rename before doing anything else." It has become a reflex for us. Don't be the person whose formulas reference things like "Column1" and "Table1" OK?

 Excel 2016/Power BI Desktop: Renames are automatically handled within your data model. That means, if you rename a table, column or a measure all dependent calculations are updated to reflect the new name. WooHoo! Well, not so fast. If you created reports connected to your model, they may still be affected. Thus it's still a best practice to rename upfront.

## Don't Import More Columns than You Need

We will explain why in a subsequent chapter, but for now just follow this simple rule:

 If you don't expect to use a column in your reports or formulas, don't import it. You can always come back and add it later if needed, unless you are using Copy/Paste.

## Table Properties Button

This is a very important button, but it is hiding on the second ribbon tab in the Power Pivot window:

*Figure 30 For all data source types other than Linked Tables and Copy/Paste, you will need this button*

**This button is what allows you to modify the query behind an existing table.** So it's gonna be pretty important to you at some point. We know someone who used Power Pivot for two months before realizing that there was a second ribbon tab!

When you click it, it returns you to one of the dialogs you saw in the original import sequence:

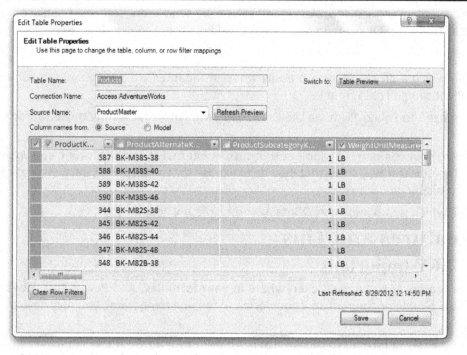

*Figure 31 Here you can select columns that you originally omitted, or even switch to using a different table, query, or view in a database. Table Properties button. Don't leave home without it.*

## Existing Connections Button

Also useful is the Existing Connections button. Clicking this brings up a list of all connections previously established in the current workbook:

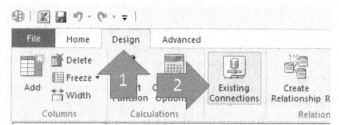

*Figure 32 Excel 2010: Existing Connections is under the "De-sign" ribbon tab*

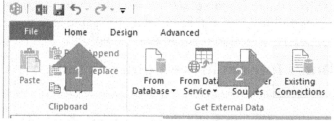

*Figure 33 Excel 2013 & Excel 2016: Existing Connections is under the "Home" ribbon tab*

This dialog is important for two reasons:

1. **The Edit button lets you modify existing connec-tions.** In the screenshot above, you see a path to an Access database. If we want to point to a dif-ferent Access database, we would click Edit here. Same thing if we want to point to a different text file, or if we want to point to a different SQL Serv-er database, etc.

2. **The Open button lets you quickly import a new table from that existing connection.** We *highly* recommend doing this rather than starting over from the "From Database" button on the first ribbon tab. You get to skip the first few screens of the wizard this way, AND you don't litter your workbook with a million connections pointing to the same exact source.

*Figure 34 List of connections established in the current work-book*

# 5 - Intro to Calculated Columns

## Two Kinds of Power Pivot Formulas

When we talk about DAX (the Power Pivot formula language, which you should think of as "Excel Formulas+"), **there are two different places where you can write formulas: Calculated Columns and Measures.**

Calculated Columns are the less "revolutionary" of the two, so let's start there. In this chapter we will introduce the basics of calculated columns, and then return to the topic later for some more advanced coverage.

## Adding Your First Calculated Column

You cannot add calculated columns until you have loaded some data. So let's start with a few tables of data loaded into the Power Pivot window:

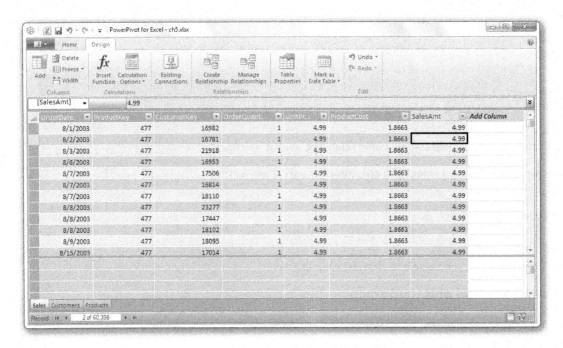

Figure 35 Three tables loaded into Power Pivot, with the Sales table active

## Starting a Formula

You see that blank column on the right with the header "Add Column?" Select any cell in that blank column and press the "=" key to start writing a formula:

Figure 36 Select any cell in the "Add Column", press the "=" key, and the formula bar goes active

## Referencing a Column via the Mouse

Using the mouse, click any cell in the SalesAmt column:

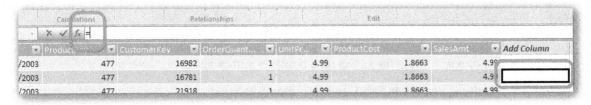

Figure 37 Clicking on a column while in formula edit mode adds a column reference into your formula

# Referencing a Column by Typing and Autocomplete

We are going to subtract the ProductCost column from the SalesAmt column, so we type a "-" sign.

Now, to reference the ProductCost column, we type "[" (an open square bracket). See what happens:

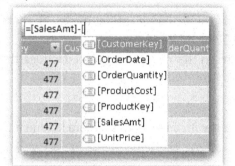

*Figure 38 Typing "[" in formula edit mode triggers column name autocomplete*

We can now type a "P" to further limit the list of columns:

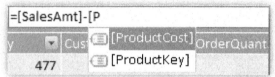

*Figure 39 Typing the first character of your desired column name filters the autocomplete list*

Now we can use the up/down arrow keys to select the column name that we want:

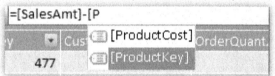

*Figure 40 Pressing the down arrow on the keyboard selects the next column down*

And then pressing the up arrow also does what you'd expect:

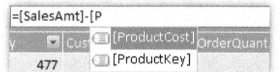

*Figure 41 The up arrow selects the next column up*

Once the desired column is highlighted, the <TAB> key finishes entering the name of that column in our formula:

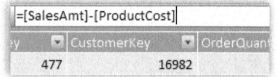

*Figure 42 <TAB> key enters the selected column name in the formula and dismisses autocomplete*

Now press <ENTER> to finish the formula, just like in Excel, and the column calculates:

| =[SalesAmt]-[ProductCost] | | | | | |
|---|---|---|---|---|---|
| erKey | OrderQuant... | UnitPr... | ProductCost | SalesAmt | CalculatedColumn1 |
| 16982 | 1 | 4.99 | 1.8663 | 4.99 | 3.1237 |
| 16781 | 1 | 4.99 | 1.8663 | 4.99 | 3.1237 |
| 21918 | 1 | 4.99 | 1.8663 | 4.99 | 3.1237 |
| 16953 | 1 | 4.99 | 1.8663 | 4.99 | 3.1237 |
| 17506 | 1 | 4.99 | 1.8663 | 4.99 | 3.1237 |

*Figure 43 Pressing <ENTER> commits the formula. Note the entire column fills down, and the column gets a generic name.*

**Notice the slightly darker color of the calculated column?** This is a really nice feature that is new in v2, and helps you recognize columns that are calculated rather than imported.

# Just like Excel Tables!

If that whole experience feels familiar, it is. The Tables feature in "normal" Excel has behaved just like that since Excel 2007. Here is an example:

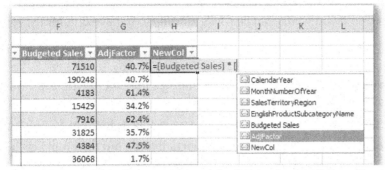

*Figure 44 Power Pivot Autocomplete and column reference follows the precedent set by Excel Tables*

OK, the Excel feature looks a bit snazzier – it can appear "in cell" and not just in the formula bar for instance – but otherwise it's the same sort of thing.

## Rename the New Column

Notice how the new column was given a placeholder name? It's a good idea to immediately rename that to something more sensible, just like we do immediately after importing data. Right click the column header of the new column, choose Rename:

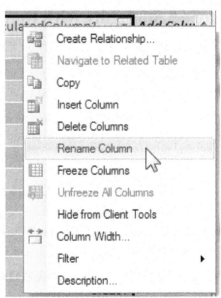

*Figure 45 Right click header to rename*

## Reference the New Column in Another Calculation

Calculated columns are referenced precisely the same way as imported columns. Let's add another calculated column with the following formula:

        =[Margin] / [SalesAmt]

And here is the result:

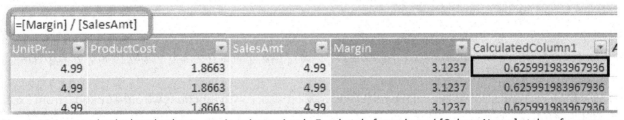

*Figure 46 A second calculated column, again using a simple Excel-style formula and [ColumnName]-style references*

Notice how we referenced the [Margin] column using its new (post-rename) name, as opposed to its original name of [CalculatedColumn1]? In Power Pivot, the column names are not just labels. They also serve the role of named ranges. There isn't one name used for display and another for reference; they are one and the same. This is a good thing, because you don't have to spend any additional time maintaining separate named ranges.

# Properties of Calculated Columns

## No Exceptions!

**Every row in a calculated column shares the same formula.** Unlike Excel Tables, you cannot create exceptions to a calculated column. One formula for the whole column. So if you want a single row's formula to behave differently, you have to use an IF().

## No "A1" Style Reference

**Power Pivot *always* uses named references like [SalesAmt].** There is no A1-style reference in Power Pivot, ever. This is good news, as formulas are much more readable as a result.

**Columns are referenced via [ColumnName].** And yes, that means column names can have spaces in them.

**Columns can *also* be referenced via 'TableName'[ColumnName].** This becomes important later, but for simple calculated columns within a single table, it is fine to omit the table name.

**Tables are referenced via 'TableName'.** Single quotes are used around table names. But the single quotes can be omitted if there are no spaces in the table name (meaning that TableName[ColumnName] is also legal, without single quotes, in the event of a "spaceless" table name).

## Stored Statically with the File

For each row, the value of the Calculated column is computed and upon file save, is saved back to the XLSX file with our Power Pivot data model. This has performance implications which we will cover in the chapter dedicated to performance.

Also, note the use of the term "static". Calculated column computation is only triggered by three events

- Definition or Redefinition: When you define (or edit) the formula for the calculated column and hit enter, the column values are recalculated
- Data Refresh: When the Power Pivot table holding the calculated column is refreshed the column values are recalculated.
- "Upstream" changes: re-definition or refresh of any column that is referenced by this column's formula will also trigger re-calc.

Thus calculated columns are "static" as opposed to Measures (introduced in the next chapter) which are "dynamic". We'll see an example of this when we revisit calculated columns in the chapter on Advanced Calculated Columns.

# *Slightly* More Advanced Calculations

Let's try a few more things before moving on to measures.

## Function Names Also Autocomplete

Let's write a third calc column, and this time start the formula off with "=SU"...

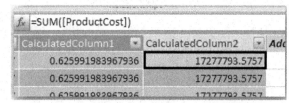

*Figure 47 The names of functions also autocomplete. Note the presence of two familiar functions – SUM() and SUBSTITUTE() – as well as two new ones – SUMMARIZE() and SUMX()*

We'll get to SUMMARIZE() and SUMX() later in the book. For now, let's stick with functions we already know from Excel, and write a simple SUM:

| $f_x$ =SUM([ProductCost]) | |
| --- | --- |
| CalculatedColumn1 | CalculatedColumn2 |
| 0.625991983967936 | 17277793.5757 |
| 0.625991983967936 | 17277793.5757 |
| 0.625991983967936 | 17277793.5757 |

*Figure 48 SUM formula summed the entire column*

## Aggregation Functions Implicitly Reference the Entire Column

Notice how SUM applied to the entire [ProductCost] column rather than just the current row? Get used to that – **aggregation functions like SUM(), AVERAGE(), COUNT(), etc. will *always* "expand" and apply to the entire column.**

## Quite a Few "Traditional" Excel Functions are Available

Many familiar faces have made the jump from normal Excel into Power Pivot. Let's try a couple more.

        = MONTH ( [OrderDate] )

and

        = YEAR ( [OrderDate] )

To receive the following results:

| | |
|---|---|
| 8 | 2003 |
| 8 | 2003 |
| 8 | 2003 |
| 8 | 2003 |
| 8 | 2003 |

*Figure 49 MONTH() and YEAR() functions also work just like they do in Excel*

If you'd like to take a quick tour through the function list in Power Pivot, you can do so by clicking the little "fx" button, just like in Excel:

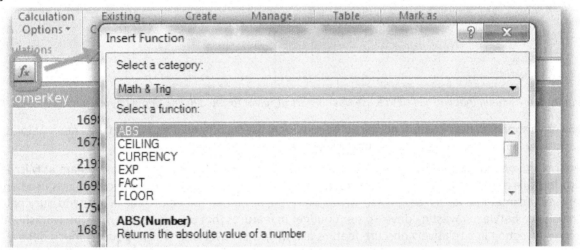

*Figure 50 Power Pivot also has a function picker dialog. Note the presence of many familiar functions.*

## Excel functions Are Identical in Power Pivot

**If you see a familiar function, one that you know from normal Excel, you already know how to use it.** It will have the same parameters and behavior as the original function from Excel.

OK, before anyone calls us a liar, we'll qualify the above and say that it's true 99.9% of the time. The keen eye of Bill Jelen has found one or two places where things diverge in small ways, but Power Pivot has done a frankly amazing job of duplicating Excel's behavior, in no small part due to the Excel team helping them out. In most cases, Power Pivot uses exactly the same programming "under the hood" as Excel.

# Enough Calculated Columns for Now

There is nothing inherently novel or game changing about calculated columns really. If that were the only calculation type offered by Power Pivot, it would definitely not be analogous to a "Biplane to jetplane" upgrade for Excel Pros.

We will come back to calculated columns a few more times during the course of the book, but first we want to introduce measures, the real game changer.

# 6 - Introduction to DAX Measures

## "The Best Thing to Happen to Excel in 20 Years"

That's a quote from MrExcel himself, Bill Jelen. He was talking about Power Pivot in general, but specifically measures. So what are measures?

**On the surface, you can think of Measures as "formulas that you add to a pivot."** But they offer you unprecedented power and flexibility, and their benefits extend *well* beyond the first impression. Several years after we started using Power Pivot professionally, we're still discovering new use cases all the time.

## Aside: A Tale of Two Formula Engines

Some of you may already be saying, "hey, pivots have always had formulas."

Why yes, yes they have. Here's a glimpse of the formula dialog that has been in Excel for a long time:

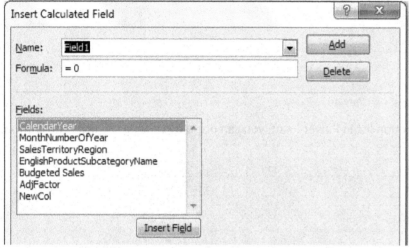

*Figure 51 Power Pivot measures mean that you will NEVER use this "historical" pivot formula dialog again (if you ever used it at all)*

**This old feature has never been all that helpful, nor has it been widely used.** (Oh and if you think it has been helpful, great! Power Pivot measures do all of this and much, much more).

It has not been very helpful or widely used because it never received much investment from the Excel team at Microsoft. The Excel pivot formula engine is completely separate from the primary formula engine (the one that is used on worksheets). Whenever it came time for us to plan a new version of Excel, we had to decide where to spend our engineering budget. The choice between investing development budget in features that everyone sees, like the worksheet formula engine, versus investing in a relatively obscure feature like this, was never one which required much debate. The pivot formula engine languished, and never really improved.

**Remember the history of Power Pivot though? How we said it sprang from the longstanding SSAS product?** Well, SSAS is essentially one big pivot formula engine. So now, all at once, we have a pivot formula engine that is the result of nearly 20 years of continuous development effort by an entire engineering team. Buckle up ☺

## Adding Your First Measure

There are two ways you can add a measure:

1.  **In the Excel window** (attached to a pivot)
2.  **In the Power Pivot window** (in the measure grid). Note that this is called Calculation Area in the UI but we call it the measure grid since it only contains measures.

**We highly recommend starting out with the first option – in the Excel window,** attached to a pivot, because that gives you the right context for validating whether your formula is correct.

 **Both ways of adding measures are equivalent**: Even though they may feel different, they both have the same end-result – of adding the measure in the Power Pivot Data Model. Let us emphasize that. Even when you add a Measure from the Excel window, the measure is still created in the Power Pivot Data Model. You can check that by going over to the Power Pivot window.

## Create a Pivot

With that in mind, let us create a pivot connected to our Power Pivot data model. This is slightly different across the Excel versions. **We'll show you the easiest method** to create a pivot for each Excel version.

**Excel 2010**: From Excel, click the Power Pivot ribbon tab, then click Pivot Table.

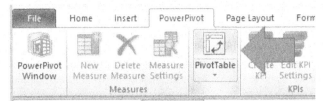

*Figure 52 Excel 2010: Creating a pivot from Excel's Power Pivot ribbon tab*

**Excel 2013/2016**: From Excel > Launch Power Pivot window > In Power Pivot window > Click Pivot Table button

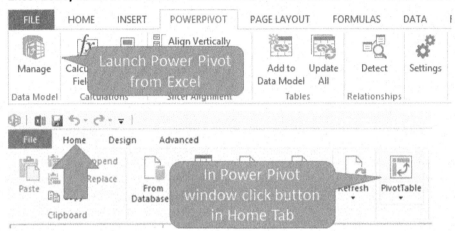

*Figure 53 Excel 2013 and 2016: Creating a pivot is best done from the Power Pivot window*

With Excel 2016, you can easily do it from the Excel side as well:

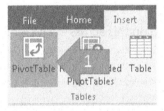

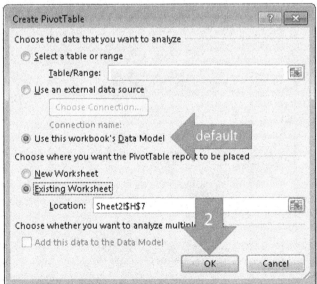

*Figure 54 Excel 2016: From Excel "Insert" ribbon tab, click Pivot Table and then OK. Note that it defaults to use the workbook Data Model (a.k.a. Power Pivot Data Model)*

This yields a blank pivot on a new worksheet:

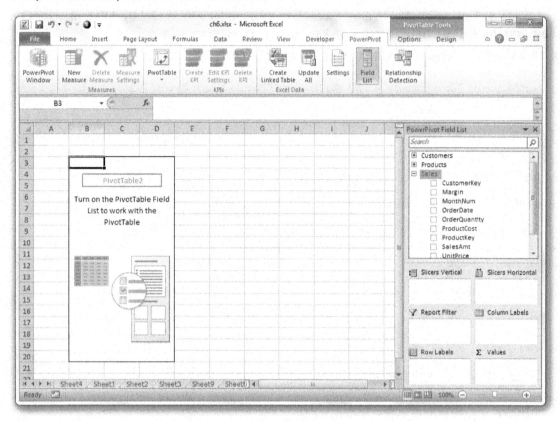

*Figure 55 Blank pivot. Every table from the Power Pivot window is available in the field list.*

Notice how the pivot field list contains all three tables from the Power Pivot window? **For now, we are going to ignore the other tables and just focus on Sales.** Exploring the advantages of multiple tables is covered later on.

## Add a Measure!

Let us create our first measure. Since the interface is slightly different, We'll show you how to do this across each Excel version.

**Excel 2010**: Make sure you have selected a cell inside the Pivot Table we just created. Then you can either

> Click the Excel "Power Pivot" ribbon tab > click New Measure

OR

> Right click a table in the PivotTable Field List > click Add New Measure.

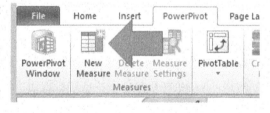

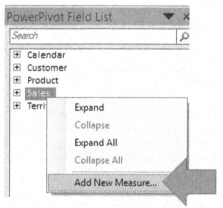

*Figure 56 Excel 2010: Creating a New Measure Button*

**Excel 2013**: Click the Excel "Power Pivot" ribbon tab > Click "Calculated Fields" > Click "New Calculated Field"

 In Excel 2013, "Measures" were renamed as "Calculated Fields". We were never fond of this new name and ranted about it incessantly. We are glad to report that in Excel 2016 and in Power BI Desktop, we are back to the original name of "Measures". If you are using Excel 2013, know that "Calculated Field" and "Measures" mean the same thing.

*Figure 57 Excel 2013: Creating a New Measure (Calculated Field)*

**Excel 2016**: You can either

> Click the Excel "Power Pivot" tab > Measures > New Measure...

OR

> Right click a table in the PivotTable Field List > click Add Measure

This brings up the Measure Settings dialog, which we will often refer to as the measure editor, or often as just "the editor."

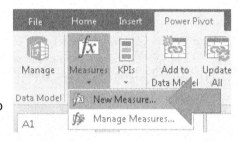

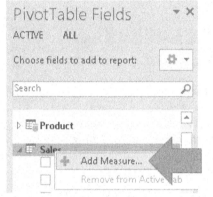

*Figure 58 Excel 2016: Creating a New Measure*

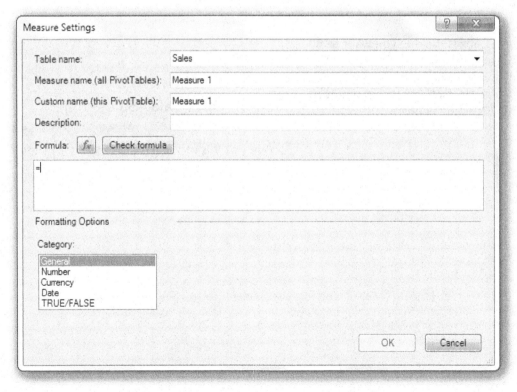

*Figure 59 Measure Settings, also known as the Measure Editor, or The Editor* ☺

There's a lot going on in this dialog, but for now let's ignore most of it and just write a simple formula:

```
= SUM ( Sales[SalesAmt] )
```

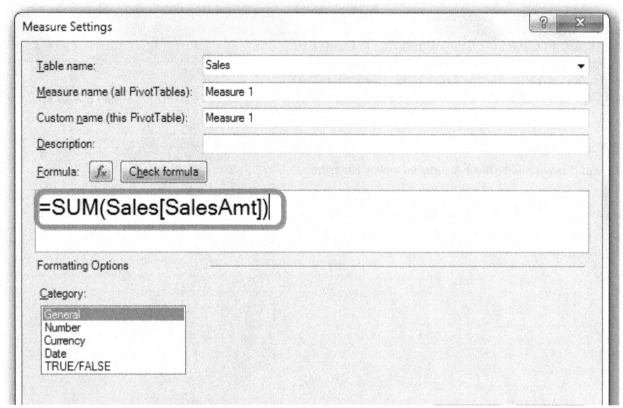

Figure 60 Entering a simple measure formula

## Name the Measure

Before clicking OK, we will give the measure a name. This is just as important as giving sensible names to tables and columns.

 The "Measure name" box is the one you want to fill in. Ignore the "Custom name" box for now – that will automatically match what you enter in the "Measure name" box. (In fact, Microsoft removed the box from Excel 2013 and higher!)

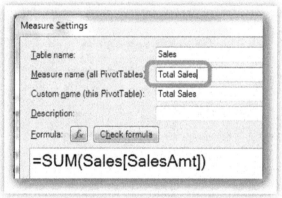

Figure 61 It is very important to give the measure a sensible name

## Results

Click OK, and we get:

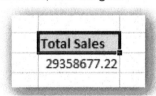

| Total Sales |
|---|
| 29358677.22 |

Figure 62 The resulting pivot

Figure 63 New checkbox added to the field list for the measure, and measure added to Values dropzone

## Works As You Would Expect

Let's do some "normal pivot" stuff. We are going to drag MonthNum to Rows and Year to Columns, yielding:

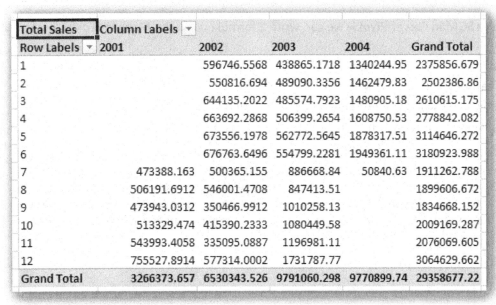

| Total Sales | Column Labels | | | | |
|---|---|---|---|---|---|
| Row Labels | 2001 | 2002 | 2003 | 2004 | Grand Total |
| 1 | | 596746.5568 | 438865.1718 | 1340244.95 | 2375856.679 |
| 2 | | 550816.694 | 489090.3356 | 1462479.83 | 2502386.86 |
| 3 | | 644135.2022 | 485574.7923 | 1480905.18 | 2610615.175 |
| 4 | | 663692.2868 | 506399.2654 | 1608750.53 | 2778842.082 |
| 5 | | 673556.1978 | 562772.5645 | 1878317.51 | 3114646.272 |
| 6 | | 676763.6496 | 554799.2281 | 1949361.11 | 3180923.988 |
| 7 | 473388.163 | 500365.155 | 886668.84 | 50840.63 | 1911262.788 |
| 8 | 506191.6912 | 546001.4708 | 847413.51 | | 1899606.672 |
| 9 | 473943.0312 | 350466.9912 | 1010258.13 | | 1834668.152 |
| 10 | 513329.474 | 415390.2333 | 1080449.58 | | 2009169.287 |
| 11 | 543993.4058 | 335095.0887 | 1196981.11 | | 2076069.605 |
| 12 | 755527.8914 | 577314.0002 | 1731787.77 | | 3064629.662 |
| Grand Total | 3266373.657 | 6530343.526 | 9791060.298 | 9770899.74 | 29358677.22 |

Figure 64 MonthNum field on Rows, Year on Columns, Total Sales Measure just "does the right thing"

OK, our first measure is working well. Let's take stock of where we stand before moving on.

# "Implicit" Versus "Explicit" Measures

We have done nothing special so far, we are just laying the groundwork. We mean, a simple SUM of the SalesAmt column is something we always could have done in normal pivots.

In fact, we can uncheck the [Total Sales] measure and then just click the [SalesAmt] checkbox, and get precisely the same results as before:

Figure 65 Unchecked the [Total Sales] measure, checked the [SalesAmt] checkbox

| Total Sales | Column Labels | | | | |
|---|---|---|---|---|---|
| Row Labels | 2001 | 2002 | 2003 | 2004 | Grand Total |
| 1 | | 596746.5568 | 438865.1718 | 1340244.95 | 2375856.679 |
| 2 | | 550816.694 | 489090.3356 | 1462479.83 | 2502386.86 |
| 3 | | 644135.2022 | 485574.7923 | 1480905.18 | 2610615.175 |
| 4 | | 663692.2868 | 506399.2654 | 1608750.53 | 2778842.082 |
| 5 | | 673556.1978 | 562772.5645 | 1878317.51 | 3114646.272 |
| 6 | | 676763.6496 | 554799.2281 | 1949361.11 | 3180923.988 |
| 7 | 473388.163 | 500365.155 | 886668.84 | 50840.63 | 1911262.788 |
| 8 | 506191.6912 | 546001.4708 | 847413.51 | | 1899606.672 |
| 9 | 473943.0312 | 350466.9912 | 1010258.13 | | 1834668.152 |
| 10 | 513329.474 | 415390.2333 | 1080449.58 | | 2009169.287 |
| 11 | 543993.4058 | 335095.0887 | 1196981.11 | | 2076069.605 |
| 12 | 755527.8914 | 577314.0002 | 1731787.77 | | 3064629.662 |
| Grand Total | 3266373.657 | 6530343.526 | 9791060.298 | 9770899.74 | 29358677.22 |

Figure 66 Yields the same exact pivot results

 Just like in normal pivots, if you check the checkbox for a numerical column, that will default to creating a SUM in the Values area of the field list. And checking a non-numeric field will place that field on Rows by default.

**So we have two ways to "write" a SUM in Power Pivot** – we can write a formula using the Measure Editor, or we can just check the checkbox for a numeric column.

We have our own terms for this:

1. **Explicit Measure** – a measure you create by writing a formula in the Editor
2. **Implicit Measure** – what you get when you just check a numeric column's checkbox

Turns out, we have a very strong opinion about which of these is better.

 **We never, ever, EVER create implicit measures!** Even if it's a simple SUM that we want, we *always* fire up the measure editor, write the formula, and give the measure a sensible name. We think it is important that checking a numeric checkbox does what it does, because that matches people's expectations from normal Excel. But that does not mean you should do it! Trust us on this one, you want to do things explicitly. There are too many benefits to the explicit approach. You will not see us create another implicit measure in this book. They are dead to us ☺

# Referencing Measures in Other Measures

We'll show you one reason why we prefer explicit measures right now.

## Another Simple Measure First

First, let us create another simple SUM measure, for Margin:

```
= SUM ( Sales[Margin] )
```

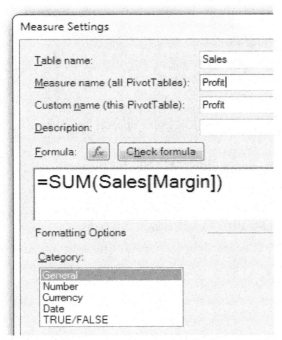

Figure 67 Creating a new measure, that we named Profit

Figure 68 Profit measure added to field list

| Row Labels | 2001 Total Sales | Profit | 2002 Total Sales | Profit | 2003 Total Sales | Profit | 2004 Total Sales | Profit | Total Total Sales | Total Profit |
|---|---|---|---|---|---|---|---|---|---|---|
| 1 | | | 596746.557 | 240320.91 | 438865.172 | 183728.206 | 1340245 | 554959.023 | 2375856.679 | 979008.139 |
| 2 | | | 550816.694 | 219507.52 | 489090.336 | 205186.474 | 1462479.8 | 604917.116 | 2502386.86 | 1029611.11 |
| 3 | | | 644135.202 | 259370.475 | 485574.792 | 203897.055 | 1480905.2 | 612934.286 | 2610615.175 | 1076201.82 |
| 4 | | | 663692.287 | 267392.109 | 506399.265 | 212618.101 | 1608750.5 | 662243.34 | 2778842.082 | 1142253.55 |
| 5 | | | 673556.198 | 271926.439 | 562772.565 | 238672.303 | 1878317.5 | 779974.147 | 3114646.272 | 1290572.89 |
| 6 | | | 676763.65 | 273032.243 | 554799.228 | 235050.708 | 1949361.1 | 806300.87 | 3180923.988 | 1314383.82 |
| 7 | 473388.163 | 190967.542 | 500365.155 | 202013.054 | 886668.84 | 362115.145 | 50840.63 | 28365.7176 | 1911262.788 | 783461.459 |
| 8 | 506191.6912 | 203872.516 | 546001.471 | 221445.745 | 847413.51 | 353404.118 | | | 1899606.672 | 778722.379 |
| 9 | 473943.0312 | 188489.502 | 350466.991 | 142096.9 | 1010258.13 | 420575.209 | | | 1834668.152 | 751161.611 |
| 10 | 513329.474 | 206121.74 | 415390.233 | 172136.184 | 1080449.58 | 449117.105 | | | 2009169.287 | 827375.029 |
| 11 | 543993.4058 | 218924.75 | 335095.089 | 136436.673 | 1196981.11 | 496559.426 | | | 2076069.605 | 851920.849 |
| 12 | 755527.8914 | 303229.82 | 577314 | 241171.901 | 1731787.77 | 711809.271 | | | 3064629.662 | 1256210.99 |
| Grand Total | 3266373.657 | 1311605.87 | 6530343.53 | 2646850.15 | 9791060.3 | 4072733.12 | 9770899.7 | 4049694.5 | 29358677.22 | 12080883.6 |

Figure 69 Profit measure added to pivot, along with Total Sales measure

# Creating a Ratio Measure

OK, time for some fun. Here's a new measure:

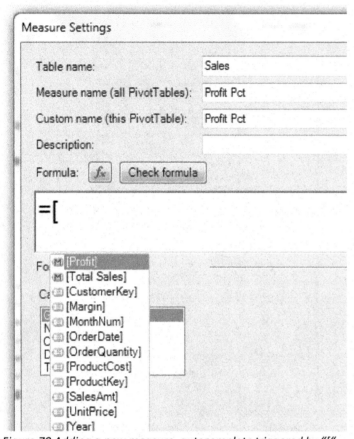

Figure 70 Adding a new measure, autocomplete triggered by "["

Do you see the first item in the autocomplete list? Zooming in:

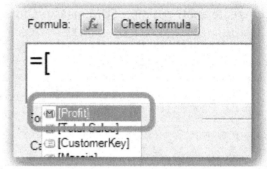

Figure 71 The [Profit] measure appears in autocomplete!

There's even a little "M" icon, for measure, next to [Profit] in the autocomplete.

[Total Sales] is also in there, so let's try:

```
= [Profit] / [Total Sales]
```

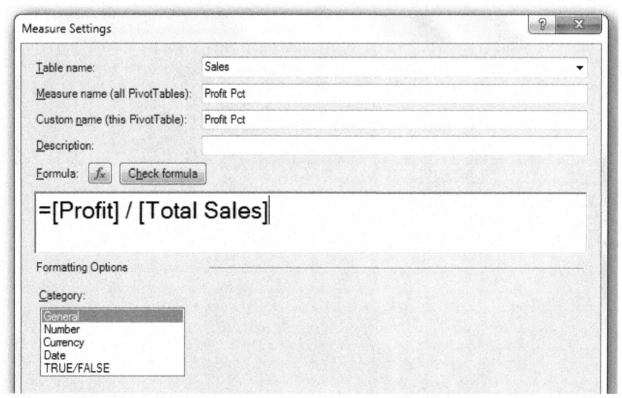

Figure 72 Measures can reference other measures, useful for creating things like ratios and percentages (and a million other things)

# Original Measures Do NOT Have to Remain on the Pivot

We'll click OK now and create this new [Profit Pct] measure, but then we'll uncheck the other two measures so we just see [Profit Pct] in the pivot:

| Profit Pct | Column Labels | | | | |
|---|---|---|---|---|---|
| Row Labels | 2001 | 2002 | 2003 | 2004 | Grand Total |
| 1 | | 0.402718553 | 0.418643851 | 0.414072833 | 0.412065318 |
| 2 | | 0.398512831 | 0.41952674 | 0.413624246 | 0.411451613 |
| 3 | | 0.402664648 | 0.41990865 | 0.413891648 | 0.412240696 |
| 4 | | 0.402885666 | 0.419862579 | 0.411650736 | 0.411053783 |
| 5 | | 0.403717522 | 0.424100815 | 0.415251491 | 0.414356167 |
| 6 | | 0.403438103 | 0.423668052 | 0.413623143 | 0.413208183 |
| 7 | 0.403405824 | 0.403731259 | 0.408399539 | 0.55793403 | 0.40991823 |
| 8 | 0.402757532 | 0.405577196 | 0.417038569 | | 0.409938747 |
| 9 | 0.397704976 | 0.405450167 | 0.416304701 | | 0.409426419 |
| 10 | 0.401538877 | 0.414396319 | 0.415676135 | | 0.41179956 |
| 11 | 0.40244008 | 0.407158079 | 0.41484316 | | 0.410352739 |
| 12 | 0.40134828 | 0.417748228 | 0.411025694 | | 0.409906295 |
| Grand Total | 0.401548019 | 0.405315607 | 0.415964461 | 0.414464851 | 0.411492778 |

*Figure 73 [Profit Pct] measure displayed by itself – its two "ancestor" measures are not required on the pivot*

# Changes to "Ancestor" Measures Flow Through to Dependent Measures

Let's simplify the pivot a bit, and put the [Profit] measure back on:

| Row Labels | Profit Pct | Profit |
|---|---|---|
| 1 | 0.412065318 | 979008.1385 |
| 2 | 0.411451613 | 1029611.111 |
| 3 | 0.412240696 | 1076201.816 |
| 4 | 0.411053783 | 1142253.551 |
| 5 | 0.414356167 | 1290572.89 |
| 6 | 0.413208183 | 1314383.821 |
| 7 | 0.40991823 | 783461.4593 |
| 8 | 0.409938747 | 778722.3793 |
| 9 | 0.409426419 | 751161.6111 |
| 10 | 0.41179956 | 827375.029 |
| 11 | 0.410352739 | 851920.8486 |
| 12 | 0.409906295 | 1256210.991 |
| Grand Total | 0.411492778 | 12080883.65 |

*Figure 74 Removed [Year] from Columns, added [Profit] measure back*

Let's focus just on that first row for a moment:

| Row Labels | Profit Pct | Profit |
|---|---|---|
| 1 | 0.412065318 | 979008.1385 |

*Figure 75 About 41% for [Profit Pct], and 979k for [Profit]*

What happens if we modify the formula for the [Profit] measure? Let's find out.

Right click the [Profit] measure in the field list and choose Edit formula:

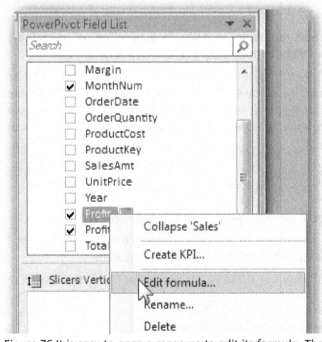

*Figure 76 It is easy to open a measure to edit its formula. They took this right-click edit away in 2013 and gave it back in 2016. In 2013, you have to use the Manage Calculated Fields button on the ribbon.*

Now let's do something silly. Let's arbitrarily boost our profits by 10%, by multiplying the original SUM formula by 1.1:

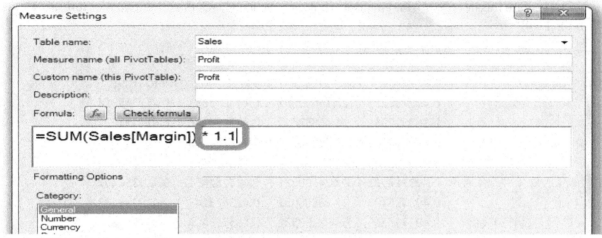

*Figure 77 You would never do this in real life, unless you are, say, Enron*

Click OK and let's look at the first row in the pivot again:

| Row Labels ▼ | Profit Pct | Profit |
|---|---|---|
| 1 | 0.45327185 | 1076908.952 |

*Figure 78 [Profit] is now 10% higher, as expected. But that ALSO impacted [Profit Pct], since [Profit Pct] is based in part on [Profit].*

## Cases Where This Makes Real Sense

The model we're working with here is pretty simple at the moment, and lacks things like Tax, Shipping, and Discount. It's not hard to imagine defining [Profit] or [Total Sales] in ways that include/exclude those other miscellaneous amounts, and sometime later (perhaps much later) realizing that you need to change that.

In fact, it might just be a change in the business that triggers you to change your definition of [Total Sales] – it is not necessary that you made a mistake!

**You may ultimately find yourself with literally dozens of measures (if not hundreds) that all depend back to more fundamental measures.** Those dependencies can even run many "layers" thick – [X] depends on [Y] which depends on [Z] etc.

**When you realize that you have hundreds of impacted calculations, but you only need to change a single formula to fix EVERYTHING**, it is a glorious moment indeed.

**It's worth driving this point home, so we will restate it:** Imagine having an entire suite of sophisticated Excel reports that all assume a certain calculation method for Profit and Sales. And then something fundamental changes, rendering that approach invalid. You could be performing spreadsheet surgery for days, perhaps weeks. If you use Power Pivot properly, that same situation might only take a few seconds to address.

 The first time you experience this "I fix one thing and everything is updated" moment, you will know that your life has changed. How often do you find statements like that in a book about *formulas*? We're guessing never, but it's the truth ☺

## Reuse Measures, Don't "Redefine"

In order to reap the benefit outlined above, it's important to use the names of measures in formulas rather than the formula that defined the original measure.

For instance, these two formulas for [Profit Pct] would return the same results:

```
= SUM ( Sales[Margin] ) / SUM ( Sales[SalesAmt] )
```

would yield the same results as:

```
= [Profit] / [Total Sales]
```

But only the second approach gives you the "fix once, benefit everywhere" payoff. So act accordingly.

Instinctively, I (Rob) expected that tying everything tightly together like this, building "trees" of measures that depend on other measures, sometimes in layers, would lead to inflexibility and problems later on. In practice, that has never been the case. It has been all benefit in my experience.

Related: if you discover places where you need, for example, a Sales measure that is calculated differently, the right approach is just to define a second Sales measure with an appropriate name, such as [Sales – No Tax] or [Sales Incl Commissions], etc. That works splendidly. Seriously, I am smiling as I type this.

# Other Fundamental Benefits of Measures

There are a few more benefits that no chapter titled "Intro to Measures" would be complete without. Let's cover those quickly before continuing.

## Use in Any Pivot

Up until now we have just been working with a single pivot. But if we create a brand-new pivot, guess what? All of the measures we created on that first pivot are still available in our new pivot!

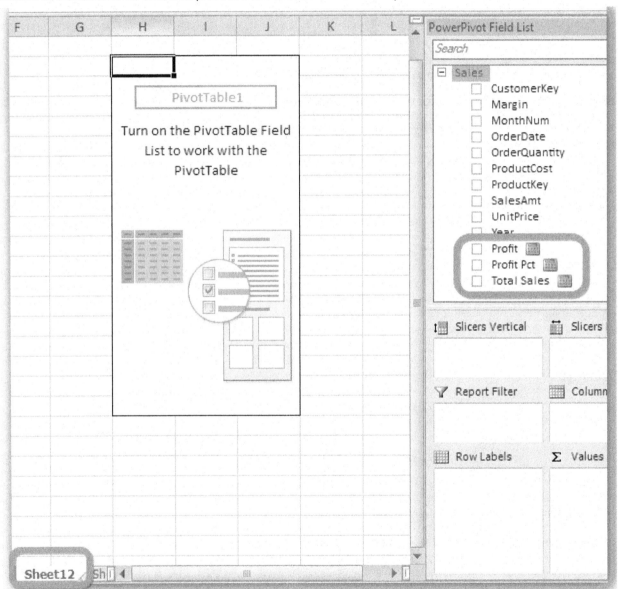

*Figure 79 New pivot, new worksheet, but the measures are still available for re-use!*

# Centrally-Defined Number Formatting

So far, we've been looking at ugly-formatted measures. Let's add all three measures to this new pivot to illustrate:

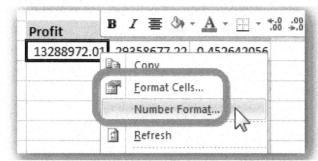

| Profit | Total Sales | Profit Pct |
|--------|-------------|------------|
| 13288972.01 | 29358677.22 | 0.452642056 |

*Figure 80 Unformatted measures in our pivot*

We can always use Format Cells, or even better, Number Format, to change this:

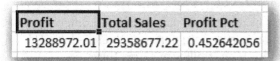

*Figure 81 These two ways to format numbers in a pivot are SO antiquated! Be gone!*

Instead, let's bring up the measure editor for one of these measures:

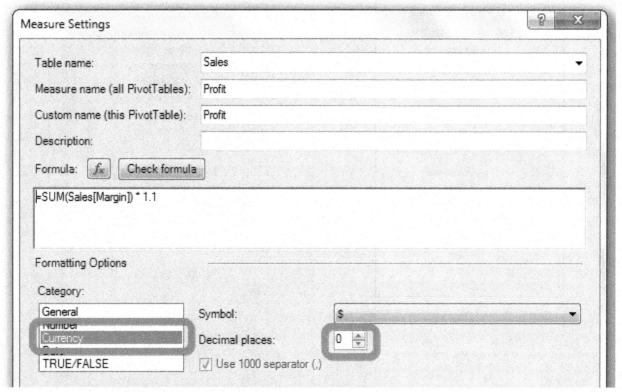

*Figure 82 Setting [Profit] to be formatted as Currency, with 0 decimal places*

The results are the same as if we had used Format Cells or Number Format:

| Profit | Total Sales | Profit Pct |
|--------|-------------|------------|
| $13,288,972 | 29358677.22 | 0.452642056 |

*Figure 83 [Profit] measure is now formatted nicely in the pivot, just as if we had used Format Cells or Number Format.*

But that format now applies everywhere! Let's return to our previous pivot and Refresh it:

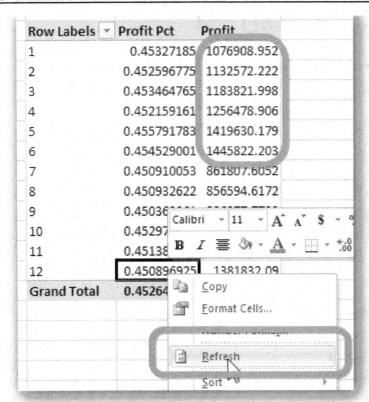

Figure 84 We return to the first pivot, where [Profit] is still formatted "ugly," and choose Refresh

The pivot picks up the new formatting!

Figure 85 Currency formatting on [Profit] now shows up on original pivot, too

A refresh is not strictly required and is actually a bad idea in 2013 and higher because that triggers a refresh of the data model. Any manipulation of the other pivot will cause the formatting to be "picked up." Reorder fields, click a slicer, click a "+" to drill down, etc. – all of these will cause the formatting to be picked up.

Now let's set a percentage format on the [Profit Pct] measure:

The results are as expected:

| Row Labels | Profit Pct | Profit |
|---|---|---|
| 1 | 45.3 % | $1,076,909 |
| 2 | 45.3 % | $1,132,572 |
| 3 | 45.3 % | $1,183,822 |
| 4 | 45.2 % | $1,256,479 |
| 5 | 45.6 % | $1,419,630 |
| 6 | 45.5 % | $1,445,822 |
| 7 | 45.1 % | $861,808 |
| 8 | 45.1 % | $856,595 |
| 9 | 45.0 % | $826,278 |
| 10 | 45.3 % | $910,113 |
| 11 | 45.1 % | $937,113 |
| 12 | 45.1 % | $1,381,832 |
| Grand Total | 45.3 % | $13,288,972 |

Figure 87 Percentage format? Check.

Figure 86 Formatting as Number, Percentage, 1 Decimal Place

# Whetting Your Appetite: COUNTROWS() and DISTINCTCOUNT()

This chapter is running a bit long, but hey, there's a lot of value to convey. And we still want to end with some "sizzle."

Let's use a couple of new functions to define two measures:

```
[Transactions] =
COUNTROWS ( Sales )
```

and

```
[Days Selling] =
DISTINCTCOUNT ( Sales[OrderDate] )
```

 When you see us use the syntax [Foo] = <formula>, that means we are creating a new measure named [Foo], with that formula. That way we don't have to show screenshots of the Measure Editor every time we add a measure.

Let's see what that looks like:

| Row Labels | Total Sales | Days Selling | Transactions |
|---|---|---|---|
| 1 | $2,375,857 | 93 | 5,017 |
| 2 | $2,502,387 | 85 | 5,059 |
| 3 | $2,610,615 | 93 | 5,178 |
| 4 | $2,778,842 | 90 | 5,589 |
| 5 | $3,114,646 | 93 | 6,064 |
| 6 | $3,180,924 | 90 | 6,080 |
| 7 | $1,911,263 | 124 | 4,019 |
| 8 | $1,899,607 | 92 | 4,256 |
| 9 | $1,834,668 | 89 | 4,229 |
| 10 | $2,009,169 | 92 | 4,536 |
| 11 | $2,076,070 | 90 | 4,536 |
| 12 | $3,064,630 | 93 | 5,835 |
| Grand Total | $29,358,677 | 1124 | 60,398 |

*Figure 88 [Transactions] and [Days Selling] – introduction to COUNTROWS() and DISTINCTCOUNT()*

## COUNTROWS(Sales)

This function does exactly what it sounds like – it returns the number of rows in the table you specify. So for instance, in the figure above, there are 5,017 rows in the Sales table that have a MonthNum of 1.

 We named this measure [Transactions] only because we know that each row in our Sales table is a transaction. But if a single transaction were spread across multiple rows, we couldn't do that. We'd have to use DISTINCTCOUNT() against a Transaction ID column, which we don't have in this example.

## DISTINCTCOUNT(Sales[OrderDate])

Again, this function does what it sounds like it does. It returns the number of distinct (unique) values of the column you specify.

So while there are 5,017 rows for MonthNum 1, and all of them obviously have a value for the [OrderDate] column, there are only 93 different unique values for [OrderDate] in those 5k rows.

## Deriving More Useful Measures From These Two

Now we define two more measures that depend on the two measures above.

```
[Sales per Transaction] =
[Total Sales] / [Transactions]
```

and

```
[Sales per Day] =
[Total Sales] / [Days Selling]
```

Results:

| Row Labels ▼ | Total Sales | Days Selling | Transactions | Sales per Transaction | Sales per Day |
|---|---|---|---|---|---|
| 1 | $2,375,857 | 93 | 5,017 | $473.56 | $25,547 |
| 2 | $2,502,387 | 85 | 5,059 | $494.64 | $29,440 |
| 3 | $2,610,615 | 93 | 5,178 | $504.17 | $28,071 |
| 4 | $2,778,842 | 90 | 5,589 | $497.20 | $30,876 |
| 5 | $3,114,646 | 93 | 6,064 | $513.63 | $33,491 |
| 6 | $3,180,924 | 90 | 6,080 | $523.18 | $35,344 |
| 7 | $1,911,263 | 124 | 4,019 | $475.56 | $15,413 |
| 8 | $1,899,607 | 92 | 4,256 | $446.34 | $20,648 |
| 9 | $1,834,668 | 89 | 4,229 | $433.83 | $20,614 |
| 10 | $2,009,169 | 92 | 4,536 | $442.94 | $21,839 |
| 11 | $2,076,070 | 90 | 4,536 | $457.69 | $23,067 |
| 12 | $3,064,630 | 93 | 5,835 | $525.22 | $32,953 |
| Grand Total | $29,358,677 | 1124 | 60,398 | $486.00 | $26,120 |

*Figure 89 Two meaningful business measures – can't do these in normal pivots!*

## Rearrange Pivot, Measures Automatically Adjust!

We remove MonthNum from Rows, drag ProductKey on instead, then drag Year to slicers and select 2002:

| Year | | | |
|---|---|---|---|
| 2001 | 2002 | 2003 | 2004 |

| ProductKey ▼ | Total Sales | Days Selling | Transactions | Sales per Transaction | Sales per Day |
|---|---|---|---|---|---|
| 312 | $658,402 | 123 | 184 | $3,578.27 | $5,353 |
| 313 | $608,306 | 111 | 170 | $3,578.27 | $5,480 |
| 310 | $608,306 | 107 | 170 | $3,578.27 | $5,685 |
| 314 | $568,945 | 99 | 159 | $3,578.27 | $5,747 |
| 311 | $504,536 | 106 | 141 | $3,578.27 | $4,760 |
| 371 | $235,609 | 76 | 108 | $2,181.56 | $3,100 |
| 377 | $235,609 | 80 | 108 | $2,181.56 | $2,945 |
| 369 | $219,902 | 70 | 90 | $2,443.35 | $3,141 |
| 370 | $202,798 | 66 | 83 | $2,443.35 | $3,073 |
| 375 | $185,433 | 64 | 85 | $2,181.56 | $2,897 |
| 368 | $175,921 | 58 | 72 | $2,443.35 | $3,033 |

*Figure 90 Completely scrambled the pivot, but our measure formulas still work!*

Slicers are a native Excel functionality but work beautifully with PivotTables connected to Power Pivot. Adding Slicers to Power Pivot PivotTables has changed across Excel versions. Given how useful Slicers can be, we'll take a brief side-trip to show you how that works in each Excel version.

Also note that one Slicer can be "connected" to multiple pivot tables. That makes them great to build a dashboard where all Pivot Tables/Charts are controlled by a single set of slicers.

# Slicers in Different Versions of Excel

**2010 Slicers:** Power Pivot Field List has a dedicated area for slicers, where you can just drag and drop the fields. The slicers also auto-arrange.

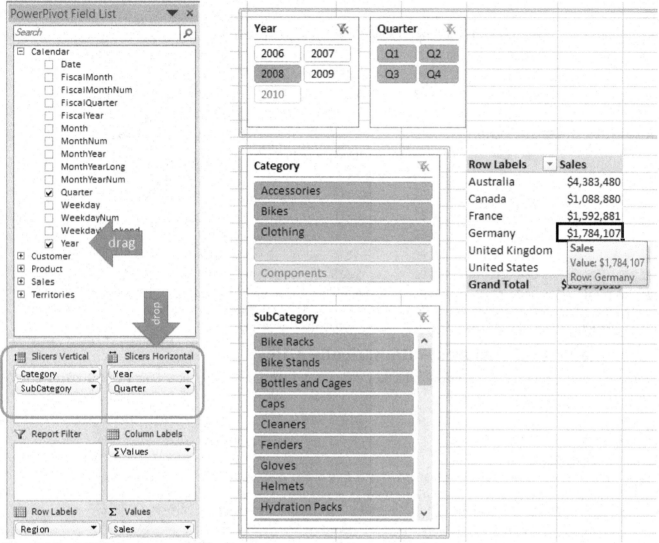

Figure 91 Excel 2010: So easy to add slic-   Figure 92 Excel 2010: Slicers auto-arrange in Vertical and Horizontal areas
ers to your Pivot

**Excel 2013 & Excel 2016 Slicers**: Slicers are slightly less friendly to use. Here's how you can add them to your Pivot.

Option 1 (Insert Single Slicer): Right Click in Field List > Add as Slicer

Option 2 (Insert Multiple Slicers):

PivotTable Tools > Analyze > Insert Slicer

Select Fields > Click OK

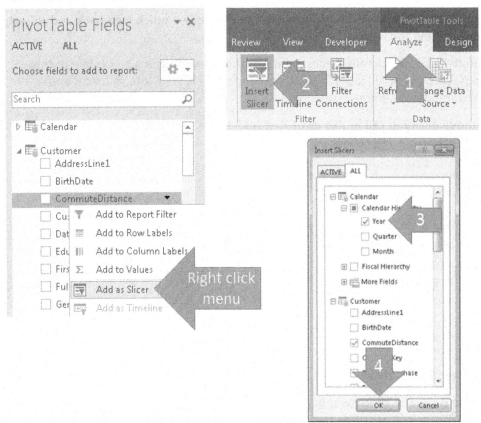

*Figure 93 Excel 2013 & Excel 2016: Adding a Slicer to your Pivot*

# Measures Are "Portable Formulas"

**Stop and think about that "rearrange the pivot and the formulas still work" point for a moment.** Let's say your work-group originally requested a report that displayed Sales per Day and Sales per Transaction, grouped by Month.

How would you build that report in normal Excel? You couldn't just write formulas in a pivot. You'd have to do some pretty serious formula alchemy to get it working.

And those formulas, in normal Excel, would be very much "hardwired" to the "I want to see it by month" requirement.

Then some executive sees the report, loves it, and says "Wow, if only I could see this grouped by Product instead!"

**Switching the normal Excel report over to be grouped by Product rather than Month (and sliceable by Year) would *not* be a modification. That would be starting from scratch, in many ways, and rebuilding the entire report.**

With Power Pivot, you just drag fields around in the field list.

> This is why we often describe measures as "portable formulas" – they can be used in many different contexts without needing to be rewritten. "Write once, use anywhere" is another way to say it. And even just the ability to re-use the same formula on another worksheet, in another pivot, by just clicking a checkbox, is a stunning example of portability. As your measure formulas become more sophisticated and powerful, this benefit becomes more and more impactful.
>
> I (Rob) even wrote a guest post for the official Excel blog on this topic, if you are interested:
> http://ppvt.pro/portableformulas

But before we go any further, we need to talk about how measures actually *work*.

# 7 - The "Golden Rules" of DAX Measures

## How Does the DAX Engine Arrive at Those Numbers?

In the previous chapter we showed you a bunch of examples of measures, displayed in various-shaped pivots. And of course, the numbers displayed in all of those cases are accurate.

**Since we're writing some pretty interesting formulas in pivots now, we need to take a quick step back and reflect, just a little bit, about how pivots work behind the scenes.**

 On an instinctive level, we're pretty sure you already understand everything we're going to explain in this chapter, but your understanding is informal and "loose." What we need to do is take your informal understanding and make it crisper. We need to put it into words.

For instance, if we asked you what the highlighted cell in this pivot "means," we're pretty sure you will immediately have an answer.

| Row Labels ▼ | Profit | Total Sales | Profit Pct |
|---|---|---|---|
| ⊟ 2001 | $287,087 | $652,367 | 44.0 % |
| 312 | $236,794 | $547,475 | 43.3 % |
| 328 | $2,831 | $6,292 | 45.0 % |
| 344 | $47,462 | $98,600 | 48.1 % |
| ⊟ 2002 | $337,581 | $768,886 | 43.9 % |
| 312 | $284,772 | $658,402 | 43.3 % |
| 328 | $5,347 | $11,885 | 45.0 % |
| 344 | $47,462 | $98,600 | 48.1 % |
| **Grand Total** | **$624,668** | **$1,421,253** | **44.0 %** |

*Figure 94 Question: Can you explain what the $98,600 "means?"*

**Let's make this multiple choice. Choose Answer A or Answer B:**

- **Answer A:** "$98,600 worth of product 344 was sold in the year 2001."
- **Answer B:** "When you filter the Sales table to just the rows where Year=2001 and ProductKey=344, then sum up the SalesAmt column over those remaining rows, you get $98,600."

**We bet you chose A.** Am I right? Yeah, I'm right. Don't lie to me. Unless you have actually merged with Excel over the years to form a cyborg calculator, you still think more like a person than a machine. And people think like Answer A.

**But Answer B is *exactly* how the DAX engine arrived at the $98,600 number.** So learning to think that way, just a little bit, is a goal of this chapter.

 It's important for you to get comfortable thinking about measures the way the DAX engine thinks about them - like Answer B. Thinking like a human (Answer A) is still important, too, and even when writing measures it's going to be okay most of the time. That's because most of the time, your measure formula just works the first time you write it. But when your measure formula doesn't do what you expect, you usually have to think "the DAX way" (Answer B) in order to fix it.

Teaching you to "think like DAX" is essentially the point of this chapter. Don't worry if you haven't grasped this yet, we're going to break it down a few ways for you.

## Stepping Through That Example

Let's step through that same "98,600" example from above, this time in the Power Pivot window so that we have a picture at each step.

Here's the Sales table:

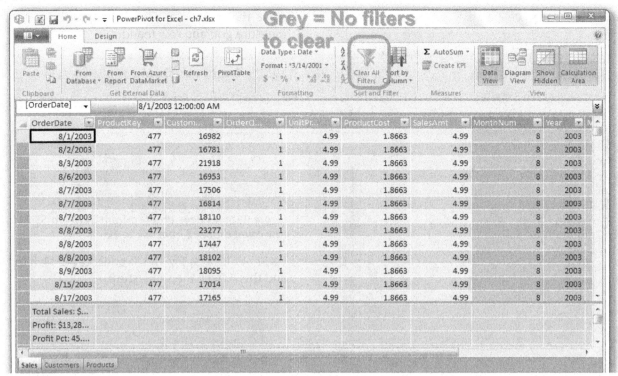

*Figure 95 Sales table with all filters cleared*

There are three elements of this window we'd like to call out.

1. **The "Clear All Filters" Button on the Ribbon.** Highlighted in the picture above. When this is greyed out like this, you know there are no filters applied on the current table.

2. **The row count readout.** Pictured here, it shows there are 60,398 rows in the Sales table when all filters are cleared.

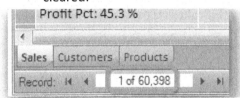

*Figure 96 Row Count Readout: 60,398 rows are currently being displayed in the Sale table.*

3. **The measure grid (the three cells at the bottom of the table).** Let's widen the first column so we can see what those were.

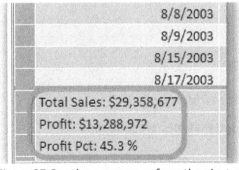

*Figure 97 Our three measures from the pivot also appear here, in the Measure Grid.*

**This area at the bottom of the table is the Measure Grid (Calculation Area).** This feature was introduced in Power Pivot v2 release, and lets you add measures from within the Power Pivot window. Most users would be comfortable with adding measures from Excel, but you can use either approach or go back and forth. The end-result is the same, a shiny new measure in your Power Pivot model. The bonus for Measure Grid is that it's superb for demonstrating "the DAX way," so we're gonna use it here to great effect.

All right, let's filter Year to be 2001:

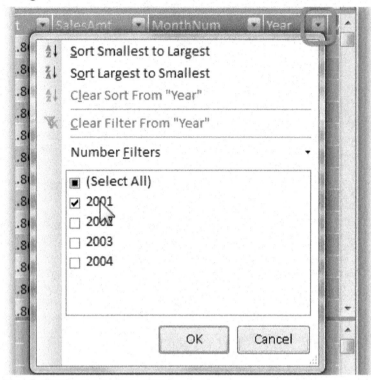

Figure 98 Filtering to Year=2001

After the filter is applied, let's check out the measure grid and row readout:

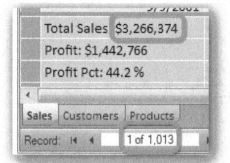

Figure 99 Sales have dropped from $27M to $3.2M, row count dropped from 60k to 1k

OK, now let's apply the ProductKey=344 filter and then check the same stuff:

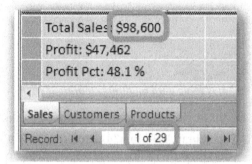

Figure 100 With both filters applied, we get the $98,600 number (the sum of SalesAmt from 29 rows)

Hey hey! It matches the pivot! Notice that [Profit] is displaying as $47,462 and [Profit Pct] as 48.1%? Those were the numbers in the pivot as well:

| Row Labels | Profit | Total Sales | Profit Pct |
|---|---|---|---|
| ⊟ 2001 | $287,087 | $652,367 | 44.0 % |
| 312 | $236,794 | $547,475 | 43.3 % |
| 328 | $2,831 | $6,292 | 45.0 % |
| 344 | $47,462 | $98,600 | 48.1 % |
| ⊟ 2002 | $337,581 | $768,886 | 43.9 % |
| 312 | $284,772 | $658,402 | 43.3 % |
| 328 | $5,347 | $11,885 | 45.0 % |
| 344 | $47,462 | $98,600 | 48.1 % |
| Grand Total | $624,668 | $1,421,253 | 44.0 % |

Figure 101 [Profit] and [Profit Pct] in the pivot also match up to what we see in the filtered Measure Grid.

Hey, where are our other measures? If we make the measure grid taller, we see that they are here too:

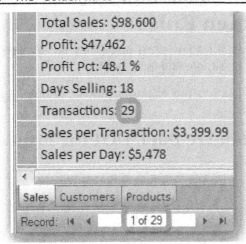

*Figure 102 All of our measures are here. Note that [Transactions] = 29, which is also what the row readout tells us.*

Do you think the [Days Selling] = 18 number is correct? Of course it is, but double checking it is a good excuse to show you another trick we use a lot. We dropdown the OrderDate filter:

*Figure 103 Scroll through this list and count how many dates show up. (Hint: there are 18).*

> ⓘ Dropping down the filters in the Power Pivot window is a very helpful trick. It will only show you the values that are "legal" in the context of the filters applied to all other columns at the moment, just like in normal Excel Autofilter. This trick is especially useful for seeing whether there are any Blank values in this column once the other column filters are respected. (Even when there are too many values in the column, and you see the "Not all items shown" warning, the Blanks checkbox will show up if there are blanks, and if it's missing, you know there are none).

Enough examples. We promised you some Golden Rules, and Golden Rules We shall deliver.

# Translating the Examples Into Three Golden Rules

We've been teaching these, that we call the Golden Rules of DAX measures, for a few years now. They serve as the foundation – once you understand these, most everything that follows will be simple and incremental.

 When you are reading these rules, we encourage you to reference back to the examples above to help clarify what the rules mean.

## Rule A: DAX Measures Are Evaluated Against the Source Data, NOT the Pivot

**It is very tempting to think that the Grand Total cell at the bottom of a pivot is the sum of the cells above it, but that is NOT the way it is calculated.** As far as DAX is concerned, the fact that the Grand Total matches the sum of the numbers above it borders on *coincidence*.

So when you are thinking about how to construct a measure formula, or are debugging one that isn't quite working, **visualize the underlying table in the Power Pivot window, because the DAX engine is doing its work in that context.**

For an example of this, we need look no further than the age-old problem of "the average of averages is meaningless."

| Row Labels | Profit | Total Sales | Profit Pct |
|---|---|---|---|
| ⊟ 2001 | $287,087 | $652,367 | 44.0 % |
| 312 | $236,794 | $547,475 | 43.3 % |
| 328 | $2,831 | $6,292 | 45.0 % |
| 344 | $47,462 | $98,600 | 48.1 % |
| ⊟ 2002 | $337,581 | $768,886 | 43.9 % |
| 312 | $284,772 | $658,402 | 43.3 % |
| 328 | $5,347 | $11,885 | 45.0 % |
| 344 | $47,462 | $98,600 | 48.1 % |
| **Grand Total** | **$624,668** | **$1,421,253** | **44.0 %** |

**Does NOT Match**

Average: 45.5 %    Count: 6    Sum: 272.8 %

*Figure 104 The six selected cells' Average is 45.5% but the pivot Grand Total is 44.0% - only a calculation against the individual rows in the Sales table will yield the right result.*

## Rule B: Each Measure Cell is Calculated Independently

When thinking about how your measure is calculated, it is best to think "one cell at a time."

So, pick a cell and visualize how it was calculated, as if it were an island.

 The value in one measure cell NEVER impacts the value in another measure cell. The measures are calculated independently, and calculated against the source table(s). See Rule A ☺

| Month | Profit |
|---|---|
| 1 | $1,076,909 |
| 2 | $1,132,572 |
| 3 | $1,183,822 |
| 4 | $1,256,479 |
| 5 | $1,419,630 |
| 6 | $1,445,822 |
| 7 | $861,808 |
| 8 | $856,595 |
| 9 | $826,278 |
| 10 | $910,113 |
| 11 | $937,113 |
| 12 | $1,381,832 |
| **Grand Total** | **$13,288,972** |

*Figure 105 The DAX engine may not calculate in precisely this 1-4 order, but you should think that it does*

# Rule C: DAX Measures are Evaluated in 6 Logical Steps

## Step 1: Detect Pivot Coordinates

**Before the DAX engine even *looks* at your formula, it detects the "coordinates" of the current measure cell (the Values-area cell from the pivot that is currently being calculated.)**

To illustrate this, let's use a slightly "richer" pivot:

The selected measure cell has three "coordinates", coming in from the Row, Column and the Slicer –

Sales[MonthNum]=8
Sales[Year]=2001, and
Sales[ProductKey]=313

Notice how we specify pivot coordinates in Table[Column] format; that may seem redundant now, but would come in handy once we start dealing with multiple tables, so get used to doing it this way.

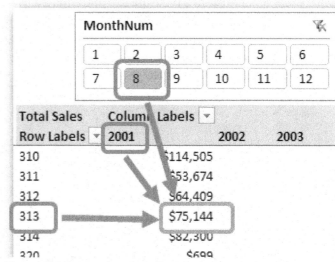

*Figure 106 Detect pivot coordinates*

 A measure cell's set of filter coordinates is often referred to as its **Filter Context**

## Step 2: CALCULATE Alters Filter Context

Covered later in the book. We'll skip the explanation for this for now and save it for later, where we can explain it in full. (The only reason we're mentioning it here is because later in the book, we want the number of the steps to remain consistent).

## Step 3: Apply Those Filter Coordinates to the Underlying Table(s)

Those coordinates (the filters in the filter context) are then applied to their respective underlying tables. In this case, all three coordinates/filters came from the Sales table, so that's the only table that will get filtered. (You never see this filtering of course- because it happens behind the scenes). In our case the Sales table is filtered based on MonthNum, Year, ProductKey values in our filter context.

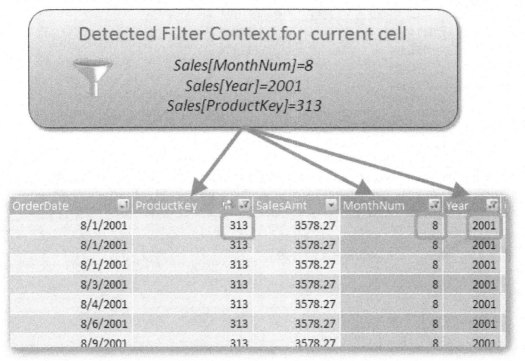

*Figure 107 Applying Filter Coordinates in Step 3: All Three Filters Get Applied to the Sales Table*

## Step 4: Filters Follow the Relationship(s)

Covered in Chapter 10. We'll skip this for now, too.

## Step 5: Evaluate the Arithmetic

Once the filter context of a measure cell (determined by its coordinates in the pivot) has been used to filter the underlying table(s), ONLY THEN is the arithmetic in your formula evaluated.

In our case, the arithmetic is simple: SUM(Sales[SalesAmt]), but complex arithmetic would run in similar manner on the filtered set of rows. **In other words, your SUM() or COUNTROWS() function doesn't run until the filter context has been applied to the source table(s).**

| OrderDate | ProductKey | SalesAmt | MonthNum | Year |
|---|---|---|---|---|
| 8/1/2001 | 313 | 3578.27 | 8 | 2001 |
| 8/1/2001 | 313 | 3578.27 | 8 | 2001 |
| 8/1/2001 | 313 | 3578.27 | 8 | 2001 |
| 8/3/2001 | 313 | 3578.27 | 8 | 2001 |
| 8/4/2001 | 313 | 3578.27 | 8 | 2001 |
| 8/6/2001 | 313 | 3578.27 | 8 | 2001 |
| 8/9/2001 | 313 | 3578.27 | 8 | 2001 |

*Figure 108 Evaluate the arithmetic against all the rows that "survived" the filtering process*

Note that Sales[SalesAmt] column itself was not filtered in Step 3, but the filters on the [ProductKey], [MonthNum], and [Year] reduced the number of rows in the entire Sales table, and as a result, the [SalesAmt] column now contains only a subset of its overall values. (We're running the risk of over-explaining something obvious here, but it's kinda beautiful, in an important way, so please indulge us).

## Step 6: Return Result

The result of the arithmetic is returned to the current measure cell in the pivot, then the process starts over at step 1 for the next measure cell.

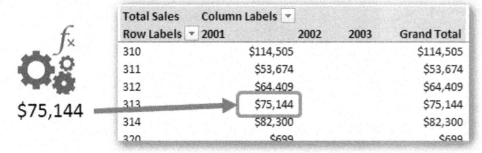

| Total Sales | Column Labels | | | |
|---|---|---|---|---|
| Row Labels | 2001 | 2002 | 2003 | Grand Total |
| 310 | $114,505 | | | $114,505 |
| 311 | $53,674 | | | $53,674 |
| 312 | $64,409 | | | $64,409 |
| 313 | $75,144 | | | $75,144 |
| 314 | $82,300 | | | $82,300 |
| 320 | $699 | | | $699 |

*Figure 109 Result is returned back to the Pivot*

**The evaluation steps can be thought of as occurring in two phases:** First the filters are applied, *then* the arithmetic. You can also think of these as two machines in an assembly line: the Filter Machine and then the Math Machine.

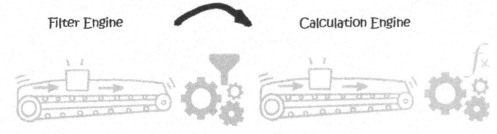

Filter Engine             Calculation Engine

*Figure 110 Some people find it helpful to visualize the calculation process as an assembly line: first things go into the Filter Machine, then the Math Machine.*

# How the DAX Engine Calculates Measures

Here is a recap of all six logical steps, which outline how the DAX engine works:

**1** **Detect Pivot Coordinates** of Current Measure Cell

**2** **CALCULATE Alters Filter Context**: ...

**3** **Apply the coordinates** in the filter context to each of the respective tables. This results in a set of "active" rows in each of those tables.

**4** **Filters Follow the Relationship(s)**: ...

**5** **Evaluate the Arithmetic**: Once all filters are applied, evaluate the arithmetic – SUM(), COUNTROWS(), etc. in the formula against the remaining active rows.

**6** **Return Result**: The result of the arithmetic is returned to the current measure cell in the pivot, then the process starts over at step 1 for the next measure cell.

*Figure 111 Measure evaluation proceeds as per steps outlined. Details on some steps to be filled-in in later chapters* **A Few More Tips**

## No "Naked Columns" in Measure Formulas

When you reference a column in a measure formula, it always has to be "wrapped" in some sort of function. A "naked" reference to a column will yield an error in a measure. Let's take a look at an example:

```
[My New Measure] =
Sales[Margin]
```

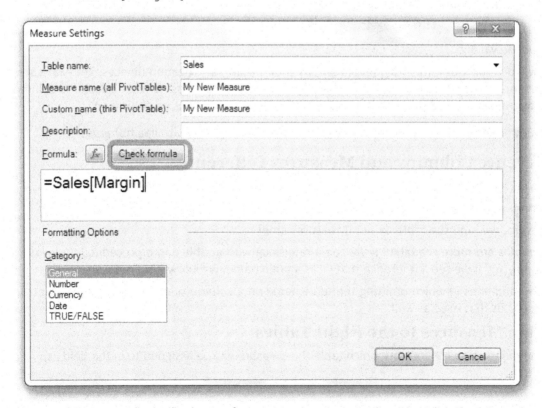

*Figure 112 We enter a "naked" column reference into the measure editor, then click Check Formula...*

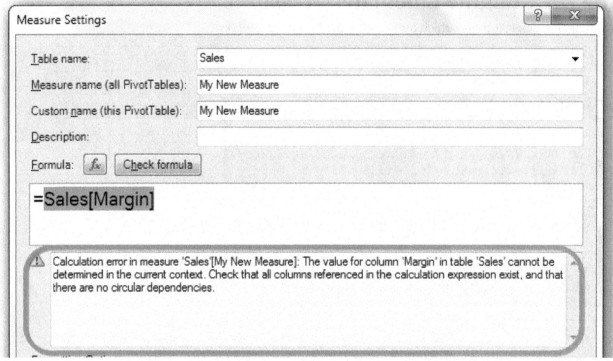

*Figure 113 ...leading to a relatively cryptic error message.*

Let's look at that error message:

*"Calculation error in measure 'Sales'[My New Measure]: The value for column 'Margin' in table 'Sales' cannot be determined in the current context. Check that all columns referenced in the calculation expression exist, and that there are no circular dependencies."*

Not a great error message. It really should be more helpful. But when you see this error, in your head you should translate this to be "I have a naked column reference somewhere."

> **ⓘ** "Cannot be determined in the current context" should become a trigger phrase for you to think "I have a naked column reference somewhere in my measure formula."

But all of the following would be valid:

Any aggregation function will do. Think of it this way: pivots are, by their nature, aggregation devices. They take sets of rows and turn them into more compact numerical results. Referencing "naked columns" is what calculated column formulas do. **Measure are aggregations, and they don't accept naked column references on their own.**

> **ⓘ** Remember, naked column references are OK in calculated columns. This rule only applies to *measures*.

## Best Practice: Reference Columns and Measures Differently

Whenever we are writing a measure formula,

- **To reference a column, we *include* the table name:** TableName[ColumnName]
- **To reference a measure, we *omit* the table name:** [MeasureName]

**We do this so that our formulas are more readable.** If we see a reference with a table name preceding it, we know immediately that it's a column, and if we see a reference that lacks a table name, we know it's a measure.

Additionally, there are many situations in which omitting the table name on a column reference will return an error. Following this best practice avoids that issue as well.

## Best Practice: Assign Measures to the Right Tables

The "Table name" box in the measure editor controls which table the measure will be assigned to in the field list.

Measure Settings

| | |
|---|---|
| Table name: | Sales ▼ |
| | Customers |
| Measure name (all PivotTables): | Sales |
| | Products |
| Custom name (this PivotTable): | Measure 1 |
| Description: | |

Formula:  [*fx*]  [ Check formula ]

=

Formatting Options

Category:

General
Number

*Figure 114 If you set this dropdown to the Sales table...*

*Figure 115 ...the measure will be "parented" to the Sales table in the field list.*

**Simple Rule:** We assign our measures to the tables that contain the numeric columns used in the formula.

ⓘ This is merely good hygiene so that your model is easier to understand later (by you or by someone else). If a measure is returning numbers from a column in the Sales table, I (Rob) assign that measure to the Sales table. Assigning it to the Customers table would confuse me later on – it would make me think this somehow evaluated number of customers rather than amount of sales. (I used to think that which table you assigned a measure to actually impacted the *results* of measures, but that isn't the case. You would get the same results.)

# 8 - CALCULATE() – Your New Favorite Function

## A Supercharged SUMIF()

Have you ever used the Excel function SUMIF(), or perhaps its newer cousin, SUMIFS()?

We describe CALCULATE() as "the SUMIF/SUMIFS you always wish you'd had." You are going to love this function, because it works wonders.

In case you are one of the pivot pros who managed to skip SUMIF() and SUMIFS() in normal Excel, they are both very useful functions: they sum up a column you specify, but filter out rows that don't fit the filter criteria you specify in the formula. So for instance, you can use SUMIF to sum up a column of Sales figures, but only for rows in the table where the Year column contains 2012.

Does that sound familiar? It sounds a lot like the Golden Rules from the prior chapter – "filter, then arithmetic." An interesting similarity, and CALCULATE() continues in that same tradition.

Anyway, CALCULATE() is superior to SUMIF() and SUMIFS() in three fundamental ways:

1.  **It has cleaner syntax.** This is the smallest of the three advantages, but it *feels* good. And a *happier* formula writer is a *better* formula writer.

2.  **It is an "anything" IF, and not limited to SUM/COUNT/AVERAGE.** There is no MAXIF() function in Excel for instance. That always bugged us. Nor is there a MINIF(), and there is definitely no STDEVIF(). CALCULATE() is literally unlimited – it allows you to take *any* aggregation function (or even a complex multi-function expression!) and quickly produce an IF version of it.

3.  **It can be used in pivots** (as part of a measure), which normal SUMIF() cannot.

## CALCULATE() Syntax

> **CALCULATE(<measure expression>, <filter1>, <filter2>, ...)**
> Ex: CALCULATE(SUM(Sales[Margin]), Sales[Year]=2001)
> Ex: CALCULATE([Sales per Day], Sales[Year]=2002, Sales[ProductKey]=313)

## CALCULATE() in Action – a Few Quick Examples

Let's start with a simple pivot. Year on rows, [Total Sales] measure on values:

OK, let's add a new measure, one that is always filtered to Year=2002:

```
[2002 Sales] =
CALCULATE ( [Total Sales], Sales[Year] = 2002 )
```

Three things to note in this formula:

1.  **We used the name of a measure for the <measure expression> argument** of CALCULATE. Any expression that is legal for a measure is okay there – that includes the name of a pre-defined measure, or any formula expression that could be used to define a measure.

2.  **In the <filter> argument, 2002 is *not* in quotes.** That's because the Year column is numeric. If it were a text column, we would have needed to use ="2002" instead.

3.  **We only used one <filter> argument this time,** but we could use as many as we want in a single CALCULATE formula.

And the results:

| Year | Total Sales |
|------|-------------|
| 2001 | $3,266,374 |
| 2002 | $6,530,344 |
| 2003 | $9,791,060 |
| 2004 | $9,770,900 |
| Grand Total | $29,358,677 |

*Figure 116 Simple pivot – the basis for our first foray into CALCULATE()*

| Year | Total Sales | 2002 Sales |
|------|-------------|------------|
| 2001 | $3,266,374 | $6,530,344 |
| 2002 | $6,530,344 | $6,530,344 |
| 2003 | $9,791,060 | $6,530,344 |
| 2004 | $9,770,900 | $6,530,344 |
| Grand Total | $29,358,677 | $6,530,344 |

*Figure 117 Our new measure matches the original measure's 2002 value in every situation!*

**Do those results surprise you?** We bet they are *close* to what you expected, but maybe not exactly. You might have expected years 2001 and 2003 to display zeroes for our new measure, and you might be scratching your head a bit about the grand total cell, but otherwise, having the new measure always return the 2002 value from the original measure is probably pretty instinctive.

**It's not very often that we write a CALCULATE measure that filters against a column that is also on the pivot (Sales[-Year] in this case).** That seldom makes any real-world sense. We just started out like this so you can see that the $6,530,344 number matches up.

So to make this a bit more realistic, let's take Year off of the pivot and put MonthNum on there instead: This probably makes even more sense than the prior pivot. The grand total is still that $6.5M number, but every other cell returns a distinct number – the sales from 2002 matching the MonthNum from the pivot.

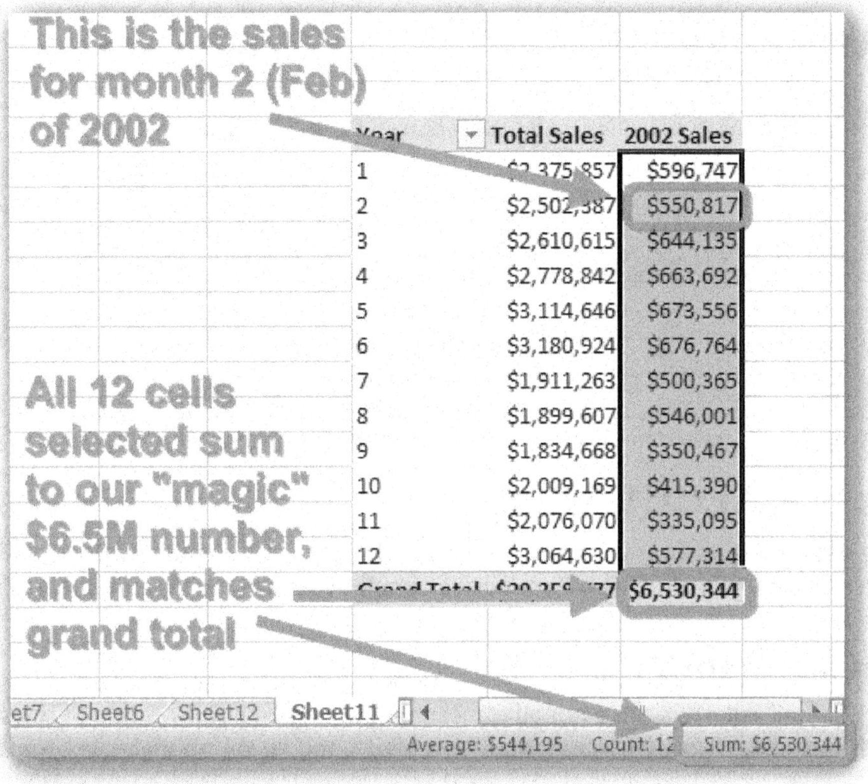

Figure 118 Previous results examined: each month of 2002 is returned separately, and the grand total matches all of 2002. Exactly what we want and expect!

# How CALCULATE() Works

Now that we've looked at a couple of examples, let's examine how CALCULATE() truly works, because that will clear up the handful of somewhat unexpected results in that first example.

**There are three key points to know about CALCULATE()**, specifically about the <filter> arguments:

1. **The <filter> arguments operate during the "filter" phase of measure calculation.** They modify the filter context provided by the pivot – this happens before the filters are applied to the source tables, and therefore also before the arithmetic phase.

2. **If a <filter> argument acts on a column that IS already on the pivot, it will *override* the pivot context for that column.** So in our first example above, the pivot is "saying" that Sales[Year]=2001, but we have Sales[-Year]=2002 in our CALCULATE(), so the pivot's "opinion" of 2001 is completely overridden by CALCULATE(), and becomes 2002. That is why even the 2001 and 2003 cells (and the grand total cell) in the first example returned the 2002 sales number.

3. **If a <filter> argument acts on a column that is NOT already on the pivot, that <filter> will purely *add* to the filter context.** In our second example, where we had Sales[MonthNum] on the pivot but not Sales[Year], the Sales[Year]=2002 filter was applied on top of the Month context coming in from the pivot, and so we received the intersection – 2002 sales for month 1, 2002 sales for month 2, etc.

So it is time to fill in Step #2 in our DAX Evaluation Steps diagram to explain where CALCULATE inserts itself, allowing us to alter the filter context:

**1** **Detect Pivot Coordinates** of Current Measure Cell

**2** **CALCULATE Alters Filter Context:** If applicable, apply <filters> from CALCULATE(), adding/removing /modifying coordinates and producing a new filter context.

**3** **Apply the Coordinates** in the filter context to each of the respective tables. This results in a set of "active" rows in each of those tables.

**4** **Filters Follow the Relationship(s):** ...

**5** **Evaluate the Arithmetic:** Once all filters are applied, evaluate the arithmetic – SUM(), COUNTROWS(), etc. in the formula against the remaining active rows.

**6** **Return Result:** The result of the arithmetic is returned to the current measure cell in the pivot, then the process starts over at step 1 for the next measure cell.

*Figure 119 The DAX Evaluation Steps from last chapter: revised to explain CALCULATE()'s impact on filter context*

# Two Useful Examples of CALCULATE()

The [2002 Sales] measure that we have been using as an example so far is a good way to show you how CALCULATE() works, but it might not seem terribly useful. So let us show you two quick examples that are much more broadly applicable.

## Example 1: Transactions of a Certain Type

Here is one that we see all the time in the retail sales business: not all transactions are normal sales. Some businesses record many different transaction types including "Normal Transaction," "Refund," and "Promotional Sales Transaction."

Our database has a column for that, so we went ahead and imported it into our Sales table (using Table Properties). Here, we see that it has three values:

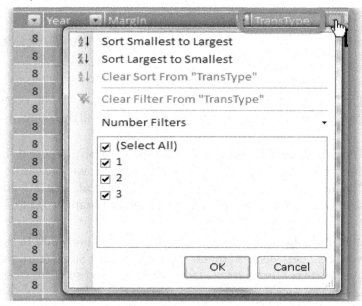

*Figure 120 Our newly-imported TransType column*

We now want to write four new measures, defined here in English:

- **"Normal" Sales** – Just transactions of type 1
- **"Promotional" Sales** – Just transaction of type 3
- **"Refunds"** – transactions of type 2, expressed as a negative number
- **"Net Sales"** – Regular plus Promotional sales, less Refunds

Now, here are the formulas for each:

```
[Normal Sales] =
CALCULATE ( [Total Sales], Sales[TransType] = 1 )


[Promotional Sales] =
CALCULATE ( [Total Sales], Sales[TransType] = 3 )


[Refunds] =
CALCULATE ( [Total Sales], Sales[TransType] = 2 )
     * -1


[Net Sales] =
[Normal Sales] + [Promotional Sales] + [Refunds]
```

> Note that our treatment of [Refunds] assumes that refunds are recorded as positive values in our Sales table. If they were recorded as negative values, we would remove the multiplication by -1 from the [Refunds] measure.

Results:

| Row Labels | Normal Sales | Promo Sales | Refunds | Net Sales |
|---|---|---|---|---|
| 2001 | $2,235,112 | $505,235 | ($526,027) | $2,214,320 |
| 2002 | $4,677,472 | $915,346 | ($937,525) | $4,655,293 |
| 2003 | $6,965,623 | $1,441,621 | ($1,383,817) | $7,023,427 |
| 2004 | $6,906,155 | $1,480,472 | ($1,384,273) | $7,002,355 |
| Grand Total | $20,784,362 | $4,342,674 | ($4,231,642) | $20,895,394 |

*Figure 121 All four measures added to pivot, with Year on rows*

Neat huh?

And then continuing down Practical Road, let's see what percentage of our sales are due to us running promotional campaigns:

```
[Pct Sales on Promo] =
[Promotional Sales]
     / ( [Normal Sales] + [Promotional Sales] )
```

Results:

| Row Labels | Normal Sales | Promo Sales | Refunds | Net Sales | Pct Sales on Promo |
|---|---|---|---|---|---|
| 2001 | $2,235,112 | $505,235 | ($526,027) | $2,214,320 | 18.4 % |
| 2002 | $4,677,472 | $915,346 | ($937,525) | $4,655,293 | 16.4 % |
| 2003 | $6,965,623 | $1,441,621 | ($1,383,817) | $7,023,427 | 17.1 % |
| 2004 | $6,906,155 | $1,480,472 | ($1,384,273) | $7,002,355 | 17.7 % |
| Grand Total | $20,784,362 | $4,342,674 | ($4,231,642) | $20,895,394 | 17.3 % |

*Figure 122 Highlighted measure tells us what percentage of our sales dollars come from promotional campaigns*

## Example 2: Growth Since Inception

We're going to define a new "base" measure that tracks how many customers were active in a given timeframe:

```
[Active Customers] =
DISTINCTCOUNT ( Sales[CustomerKey] )
```

 "Base measure" is how we refer to measures that do not refer to other measures, and are pure arithmetic like the one above.

And now a measure that always tells us how many customers were active in 2001 (our first year in business):

```
[2001 Customers] =
CALCULATE ( [Active Customers], Sales[Year] = 2001 )
```

Results:

| Year | Active Customers | 2001 Customers |
|------|-----------------|----------------|
| 2001 | 1013 | 1013 |
| 2002 | 2677 | 1013 |
| 2003 | 9309 | 1013 |
| 2004 | 11377 | 1013 |
| Grand Total | 18484 | 1013 |

*Figure 123 Active customers by year, and active customers for 2001 specifically*

And then a measure that tells us percentage growth in customer base since 2001:

```
[Customer Growth Since 2001] =
DIVIDE ( [Active Customers] - [2001 Customers], [2001 Customers] )
```

Results:

| Year | Active Customers | 2001 Customers | Customer Growth Since 2001 |
|------|-----------------|----------------|----------------------------|
| 2001 | 1013 | 1013 | 0.0 % |
| 2002 | 2677 | 1013 | 164.3 % |
| 2003 | 9309 | 1013 | 819.0 % |
| 2004 | 11377 | 1013 | 1023.1 % |
| Grand Total | 18484 | 1013 | 1724.7 % |

*Figure 124 Percentage growth in customer base since 2001*

# Alternatives to the "=" Operator in <Filters>

In a <filter> argument to CALCULATE(), you are not limited to the "=" operator. You can also use:

- < (Less than)
- > (Greater than)
- <= (Less than or equal to)
- >= (Greater than or equal to)
- <> (Not equal to)

# Evaluation of Multiple <filters> in a Single CALCULATE()

**All of the <filter> arguments in a single CALCULATE() behave as if they are wrapped in an AND() function.** In other words, a row must match every <filter> argument in order to be included in the calculation.

If you need an "OR()" style of operation, you can use the "||" operator. For instance:

```
=CALCULATE ( [Total Sales],
    Sales[TransType] = 1 || Sales[TransType] = 3 )
```

 When you use the || operator within one of the Calculate filter arguments, it can only be used between comparisons on a single column – TransType in this case. You cannot use || between comparisons that operate on different columns, such as TransType and Year.

# The "ALL" (aka "Unfiltered") Filter Context

That [Active Customers] measure provides an opportunity to explain how the Grand Total cell works in the pivot.

Let's look at the pivot again:

*Figure 125 Sum of all years is MUCH higher than the Grand Total cell*

A perfect example of why it's important to think about the measures evaluating against the source table(s) rather than in the pivot itself. Also, we've talked a lot about filter context to this point, but so far, we have not discussed the filter context of the grand total cell.

**It's pretty simple actually: the grand total cell represents the *absence* of a filter. In the context of that cell, it's as if the Year field is not even *on* the pivot.**

To drive this home, let's remove Year from the pivot:

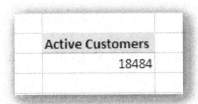

*Figure 126 Remove Year from the pivot, and the result matches the Grand Total cell from when Year IS on the pivot. This is not an accident!*

It makes sense: some of our customers from 2001 stuck around and bought things in 2002 (and later), and some 2002 customers similarly persisted into 2003. If we summed the individual totals for each year, we'd count those "carryover" customers more than once (and end up with 24,376). But when we clear the Year filter, the DISTINCTCOUNT(Sales[CustomerKey]) arithmetic runs against an unfiltered table, and only counts each customer once! We end up with 18,484, which is the correct answer.

Don't skip the paragraph above. The world won't end if you *do* skip it, but it's worth more attention than the average un-bolded text ☺

# Not all Totals Are Completely (or Even Partially) Grand

To clarify, let's drag Year to Columns, and add MonthNum to rows:

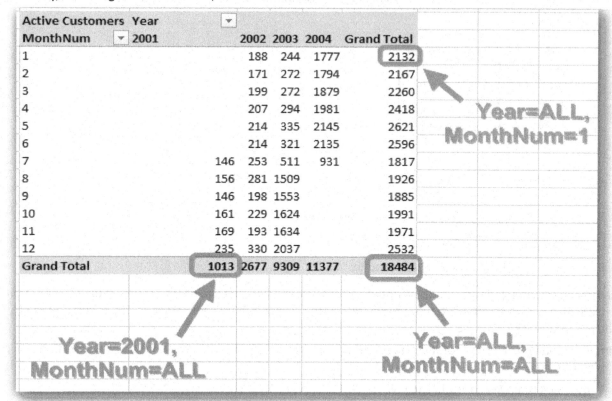

*Figure 127 Filter context for three different kinds of grand totals – total across Years, total across MonthNums, and total across both.*

**Every total in a pivot is really just the *absence* of one or more filters – a place where one or more of the pivot fields does not apply, as if the field were completely absent from the pivot.**

As you add more fields to rows and columns, you get many different variations of totals. For instance, nothing really changes when you nest one field under another. Let's nest MonthNum under Year on Rows as an example:

| Year-Month | Active Customers |
|---|---|
| ⊟ 2001 | 1013 |
| 7 | 146 |
| 8 | 156 |
| 9 | 146 |
| 10 | 161 |
| 11 | 169 |
| 12 | 235 |
| ⊟ 2002 | 2677 |
| 1 | 188 |
| 2 | 171 |
| 3 | 199 |

*Figure 128 Nesting does not really change anything. Note the subtotal for 2002 (2677) was a grand total cell when Year was on Columns (in the previous pivot).*

**ⓘ** **The physical location of a measure cell in the pivot is *not* important. Only its "coordinates" are important.** A filter context of Year=2002, Month=ALL is exactly the same to the DAX engine, no matter where the Year and MonthNum fields were located – rows, columns, report filters, or slicers.

# 9 - ALL() – The "Remove a Filter" Function

Given where the last chapter left off, this sure seems like a great time to introduce the ALL() function.

In fact, given last chapter's section on the "ALL" filter context, and the title of this chapter, you can probably already guess most everything you need to know about the ALL() function. So we won't bore you with long-winded explanations of the basics. We will keep it crisp and practical.

## The Crisp Basics

**The ALL() function is used within a CALCULATE(), as one of the <filter> arguments,** to remove a filter from the filter context.

Let's jump straight to an example. Consider the following pivot: [Net Sales] displayed by MonthNum, with Year on a slicer:

| Month | Net Sales |
|-------|-----------|
| 1 | $325,923 |
| 2 | $384,359 |
| 3 | $332,465 |
| 4 | $364,024 |
| 5 | $458,236 |
| 6 | $346,219 |
| 7 | $675,507 |
| 8 | $570,071 |
| 9 | $783,861 |
| 10 | $756,351 |
| 11 | $807,463 |
| 12 | $1,218,949 |
| Grand Total | $7,023,427 |

Year slicer: 2001, 2002, 2003 (selected), 2004

*Figure 129 We will use this pivot to demonstrate the usage of ALL().*

OK, time for a new measure:

```
[All Month Net Sales] =
CALCULATE ( [Net Sales], ALL ( Sales[MonthNum] ) )
```

And the results:

| Month | Net Sales | All Month Net Sales |
|-------|-----------|---------------------|
| 1 | $325,923 | $7,023,427 |
| 2 | $384,359 | $7,023,427 |
| 3 | $332,465 | $7,023,427 |
| 4 | $364,024 | $7,023,427 |
| 5 | $458,236 | $7,023,427 |
| 6 | $346,219 | $7,023,427 |
| 7 | $675,507 | $7,023,427 |
| 8 | $570,071 | $7,023,427 |
| 9 | $783,861 | $7,023,427 |
| 10 | $756,351 | $7,023,427 |
| 11 | $807,463 | $7,023,427 |
| 12 | $1,218,949 | $7,023,427 |
| Grand Total | $7,023,427 | $7,023,427 |

Year slicer: 2001, 2002, 2003 (selected), 2004

*Figure 130 Because ALL() removed the filter from MonthNum, every measure cell in the right column has precisely the same filter context (coordinates) as the grand total in the left column*

 We suppose you can also think of ALL() as a means by which to "reference" one of the total cells in a pivot, as long as you also understand that fundamentally, what you are doing is clearing/removing a filter from the filter context.

# The Practical Basics – Two Examples

Time for a couple of examples of where ALL() is useful.

## Example 1 – Percentage of Parent

Let's do a simple ratio of the two measures already on the pivot:

```
[Pct of All Month Net Sales] =
[Net Sales] / [All Month Net Sales]
```

Results:

| Year | | Month | Net Sales | All Month Net Sales | Pct of All Month Net Sales |
|------|------|-------|-----------|---------------------|----------------------------|
| 2001 | 2002 | 1 | $325,923 | $7,023,42? | 4.6 % |
| 2003 | 2004 | 2 | $384,359 | $7,023,42? | 5.5 % |
|      |      | 3 | $332,465 | $7,023,42? | 4.7 % |
|      |      | 4 | $364,024 | $7,023,42? | 5.2 % |
|      |      | 5 | $458,236 | $7,023,42? | 6.5 % |
|      |      | 6 | $346,219 | $7,023,42? | 4.9 % |
|      |      | 7 | $675,507 | $7,023,42? | 9.6 % |
|      |      | 8 | $570,071 | $7,023,42? | 8.1 % |
|      |      | 9 | $783,861 | $7,023,42? | 11.2 % |
|      |      | 10 | $756,351 | $7,023,42? | 10.8 % |
|      |      | 11 | $807,463 | $7,023,42? | 11.5 % |
|      |      | 12 | $1,218,949 | $7,023,42? | 17.4 % |
|      |      | Grand Total | $7,023,427 | $7,023,427 | 100.0 % |

*Figure 131 New measure returns each month's contribution to the "all month" total*

We can remove the original ALL measure from the pivot and the new "pct of total" measure still works:

| Year | | Month | Net Sales | Pct of All Month Net Sales |
|------|------|-------|-----------|----------------------------|
| 2001 | 2002 | 1 | $325,923 | 4.6 % |
| 2003 | 2004 | 2 | $384,359 | 5.5 % |
|      |      | 3 | $332,465 | 4.7 % |
|      |      | 4 | $364,024 | 5.2 % |
|      |      | 5 | $458,236 | 6.5 % |
|      |      | 6 | $346,219 | 4.9 % |
|      |      | 7 | $675,507 | 9.6 % |
|      |      | 8 | $570,071 | 8.1 % |
|      |      | 9 | $783,861 | 11.2 % |
|      |      | 10 | $756,351 | 10.8 % |
|      |      | 11 | $807,463 | 11.5 % |
|      |      | 12 | $1,218,949 | 17.4 % |
|      |      | Grand Total | $7,023,427 | 100.0 % |

*Figure 132 Pct of total measure still works without the ALL() measure on the pivot*

ℹ️ Yes, you can do this in Excel pivots without the use of ALL(). You can use the Show Values As feature and achieve the same visual result. But that conversion (from raw value to % of total) happens after the DAX engine has done its work, meaning that the DAX engine only has the raw value. In other words, if you ever want to use a "Pct of total" value in a DAX calculation, Show Values As is useless – you absolutely need to use ALL() as illustrated above.

# Example 2 – Negating a Slicer

This one is useful, but also a lot of fun. Let's start with the following pivot (we just added ProductKey as a slicer, and made a few selections).

*Figure 133 Pivot with product slicer*

Now add a measure that ignores any filters on ProductKey:

```
[Net Sales - All Products] =
CALCULATE ( [Net Sales], ALL ( Sales[ProductKey] ) )
```

And a measure that is the ratio of that to the original [Net Sales]:

```
[Selected Products Pct] =
[Net Sales] / [Net Sales - All Products]
```

Results:

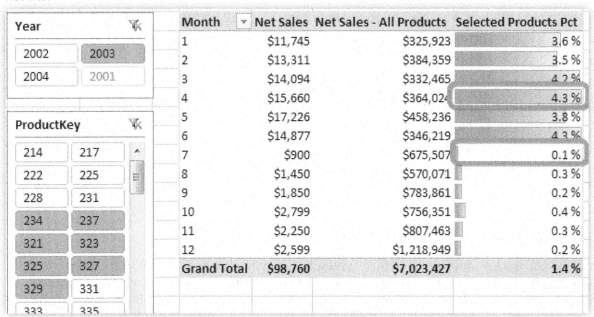

*Figure 134 The seven selected products account for 4.3% of all Net Sales in April 2003, but only 0.1% of all sales in July 2003.*

> ℹ️ We're a big believer in conditional formatting. We apply conditional formatting to our pivots almost instinctively at this point.

Now we change the selection of products on the slicer:

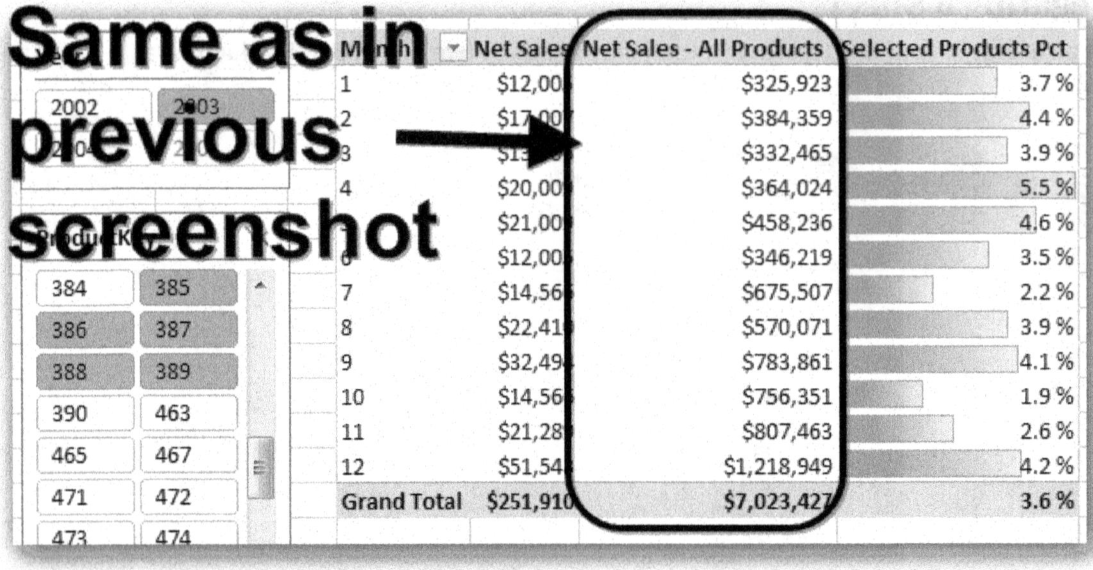

Figure 135 These five products account for a lot larger share of Net Sales than the previous seven. Note that the highlighted middle column (the ALL measure) is unchanged from the previous screenshot.

> ℹ️ You cannot achieve these results using Show Values As. ALL() is the only way.

# Variations

ALL() can be used with arguments other than a single column. Both of these variations are also valid:

- ALL(<Col1>, <Col2>, …) – You can list more than one column. *EX: ALL(Sales[ProductKey], Sales[Year])*
- ALL(<TableName>) – shortcut for applying ALL() to every column in the named table. *EX: ALL(Sales)*

# ALLEXCEPT()

- Let's say you have 12 columns in a table, and you want to apply ALL() to 11 of the 12, but leave 1 of them alone.
- You can then use ALLEXCEPT(<Table>, <col1 to leave alone>, <col2 to leave alone>…)
- Example:

```
ALLEXCEPT ( Sales, Sales[ProductKey] )
```

Is the same as listing out *every* column in the Sales table *except* ProductKey:

```
ALL (
    Sales[OrderQuantity],  Sales[UnitPrice],
    Sales[ProductCost],  Sales[CustomerKey],
    Sales[OrderDate], Sales[MonthNum],…
    <every other column except ProductKey>
)
```

So ALLEXCEPT() is a lot more convenient in cases like this.

> ℹ️ The other difference, besides convenience, is that if you subsequently add a new column to the Sales table, ALLEXCEPT() will "pick it up" and apply ALL() behavior to it, without requiring you to change your measure formula. The ALL(<list every column>) approach obviously will not apply to the new column until you edit the formula.

# ALLSELECTED()

This is a new one in Power Pivot v2, and it's something we have needed a few times in v1. We don't expect to use it super frequently, but when you need it, we have found there is no workaround – when you need this function, you *really* need it.

First, let us show you a trick that has nothing to do with DAX.

Did you know that a field on rows or columns or report filter can also be dragged to Slicers and be two places at once?

*Figure 136 MonthNum field on both Rows and Slicer – makes for quick filtering of the Row area without having to use the Row Filters dropdown*

ℹ️ Remember the people who consume the work of Excel Pros? The people who don't enjoy working with data as much as we do? They do not like using the Row Filters dropdown, at all. Nor do they like using Report Filters. Most of them do enjoy working with slicers though, so this "duplicate a field on Rows and on a Slicer" trick is something we do on their behalf. Actually, it's better for us, too.

Now let's just find the [All Month Net Sales] measure that we defined using ALL() and put that on the pivot:

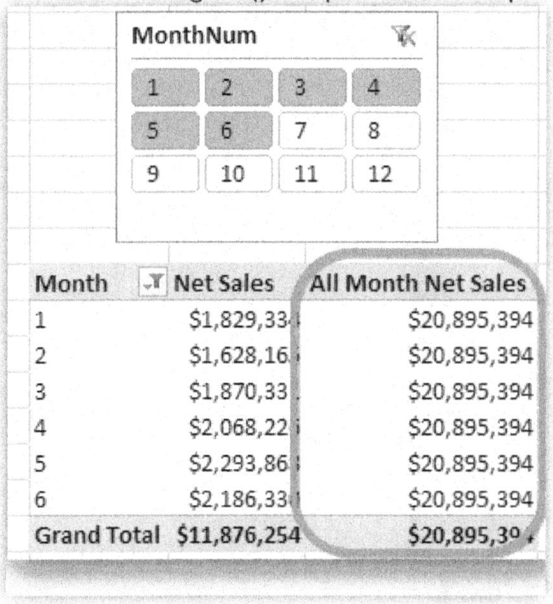

Now let's clear the filter on the slicer and see what we get:

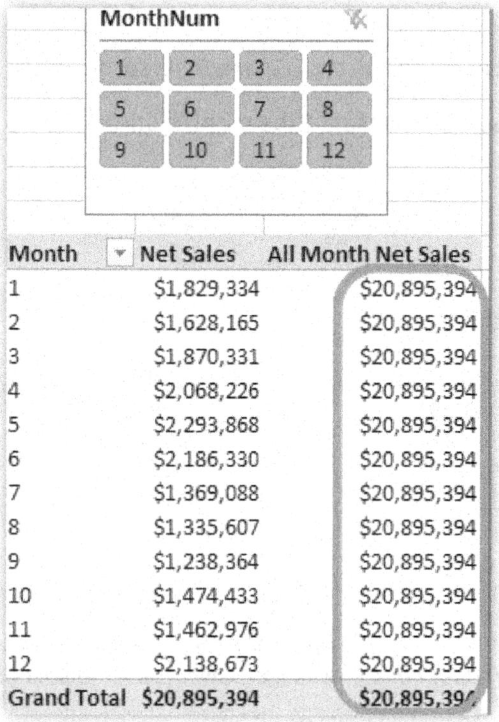

*Figure 137 The selected measure is defined with ALL(Sales[MonthNum])*

*Figure 138 The selected measure is defined with ALL(Sales[MonthNum])*

**But our goal here is to create a "percent of everything I *SEE*" measure. If we select six months on the slicer, we want a measure that returns *just the total of those six months.***

So let's define a new measure, and this time use ALLSELECTED() instead:

```
[Net Sales for All Selected Months] =
CALCULATE ( [Net Sales], ALLSELECTED ( Sales[MonthNum] ) )
```

And then a ratio measure:

```
[Pct of All Selected Months Net Sales] =
[Net Sales] / [Net Sales for All Selected Months]
```

Results:

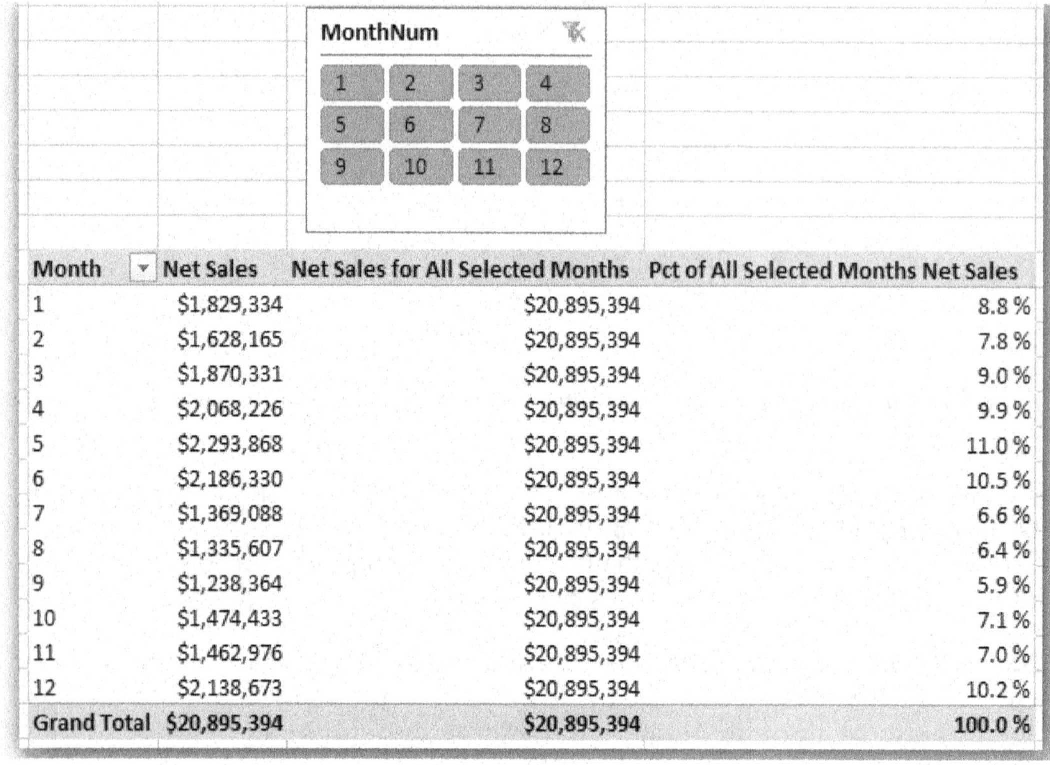

| Month | Net Sales | Net Sales for All Selected Months | Pct of All Selected Months Net Sales |
|---|---|---|---|
| 1 | $1,829,334 | $20,895,394 | 8.8 % |
| 2 | $1,628,165 | $20,895,394 | 7.8 % |
| 3 | $1,870,331 | $20,895,394 | 9.0 % |
| 4 | $2,068,226 | $20,895,394 | 9.9 % |
| 5 | $2,293,868 | $20,895,394 | 11.0 % |
| 6 | $2,186,330 | $20,895,394 | 10.5 % |
| 7 | $1,369,088 | $20,895,394 | 6.6 % |
| 8 | $1,335,607 | $20,895,394 | 6.4 % |
| 9 | $1,238,364 | $20,895,394 | 5.9 % |
| 10 | $1,474,433 | $20,895,394 | 7.1 % |
| 11 | $1,462,976 | $20,895,394 | 7.0 % |
| 12 | $2,138,673 | $20,895,394 | 10.2 % |
| Grand Total | $20,895,394 | $20,895,394 | 100.0 % |

*Figure 139 Looks the same as the ALL() measure, so far...*

But now let's select a subset of the months on the slicer:

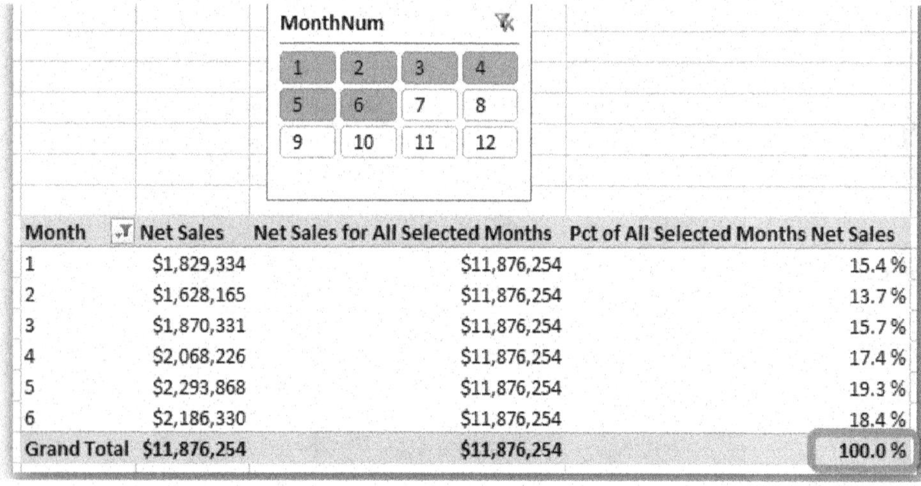

| Month | Net Sales | Net Sales for All Selected Months | Pct of All Selected Months Net Sales |
|---|---|---|---|
| 1 | $1,829,334 | $11,876,254 | 15.4 % |
| 2 | $1,628,165 | $11,876,254 | 13.7 % |
| 3 | $1,870,331 | $11,876,254 | 15.7 % |
| 4 | $2,068,226 | $11,876,254 | 17.4 % |
| 5 | $2,293,868 | $11,876,254 | 19.3 % |
| 6 | $2,186,330 | $11,876,254 | 18.4 % |
| Grand Total | $11,876,254 | $11,876,254 | 100.0 % |

*Figure 140 NOW we see a difference. Middle column is no longer over $20M. Also note the highlighted grand total is 100% - if we were using ALL(), that number would be lower (closer to 50% since 6 months are selected).*

That's enough about ALL() and its variants for now.

# 10 - Thinking in Multiple Tables

## A Simple and Welcome Change

In the opening chapters, we mentioned that Power Pivot offers a lot of benefits when you are working with multiple tables of data. But so far, we have shown none of those - we have only worked with the Sales table. Why have we waited?

Working with multiple tables is not complicated – it actually requires you to *unlearn old habits* more than it requires you to learn new ones. This is not going to be a difficult adjustment for you, just a little different.

The reason we waited until now to cover "multi table" is this: **All of the concepts covered so far work the same way with multiple tables as they do with one table.** We didn't want to risk confusing you by teaching the CALCULATE() function at the same time as multi-table.

**So this chapter really just extends what we have already covered, and shows how the same rules apply *across* tables as they do *within* tables.**

## Unlearning the "Thou Shalt Flatten" Commandment

**Normal Excel literally *requires* that all of your data resides in a single table** before you can build a pivot or chart against it. Since your data often arrives in multi-table format, Excel Pros have also become part-time Professional Data Flatteners.

- **That usually means flattening via VLOOKUP().** Sometimes it means *lots* of VLOOKUP().
- **Sometimes it involves database queries.** Some Excel Pros who know their way around a database also write queries that flatten the data into one table before it's ever imported.

**You do *not* need to do either of these anymore. In fact, you *should* not.**

 In Power Pivot there are many *advantages* to leaving tables separate. It may be tempting to pull columns from Table B into Table A, especially using the RELATED() function. You should resist this temptation. We sometimes use RELATED() to partially combine tables but only when debugging or inspecting our data. We delete that column when we are done with our investigation.

Got it? Just leave those tables alone. And if you already have flattened versions of your tables in your database, we actually recommend not using those versions – import the tables "raw" (separately). If flattened versions are the only ones available, consider unflattening them in the Database or by using Power Query, before you bring them into Power Pivot.

## Relationships Are Your Friends

Let's create our first relationship between two Power Pivot tables. Take a look at our Products table:

| ProductK... | EnglishProductNa... | StandardC... | FinishedGoodsF... | Color | Weight | SafetyStockLe... | ReorderPo... | ListPr... |
|---|---|---|---|---|---|---|---|---|
| 422 | LL Road Rear Wheel | 49.9789 | TRUE | Black | 1050 | 500 | 375 | 112.565 |
| 423 | ML Road Rear Wheel | 122.2709 | TRUE | Black | 1000 | 500 | 375 | 275.385 |
| 413 | LL Road Front Wheel | 37.9909 | TRUE | Black | 900 | 500 | 375 | 85.565 |
| 424 | HL Road Rear Wheel | 158.5346 | TRUE | Black | 890 | 500 | 375 | 357.06 |
| 414 | ML Road Front Wheel | 110.2829 | TRUE | Black | 850 | 500 | 375 | 248.385 |
| 415 | HL Road Front Wheel | 146.5466 | TRUE | Black | 650 | 500 | 375 | 330.06 |
| 557 | ML Crankset | 113.8816 | TRUE | Black | 635 | 500 | 375 | 256.49 |
| 556 | LL Crankset | 77.9176 | TRUE | Black | 600 | 500 | 375 | 175.49 |

*Figure 141 We have not yet used the Products table, but it contains a lot of useful columns!*

To create a relationship, click on the 'Create Relationship' button on the Design tab.

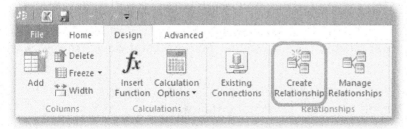

*Figure 142 Creating our first relationship*

We're going to create a relationship between Products and Sales, using the ProductKey column:

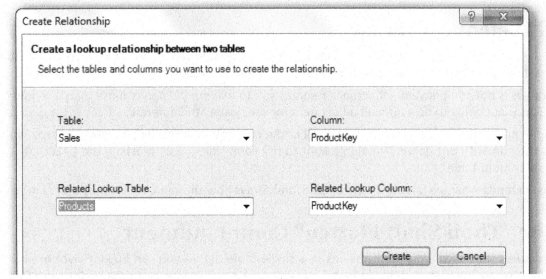

Figure 143 Relating Sales to Products

# "Lookup" Tables

**Note how we selected Products to be the Lookup table? That's important.** So important, in fact, that Power Pivot will not let us get it wrong. Let's try reversing the two and see what happens:

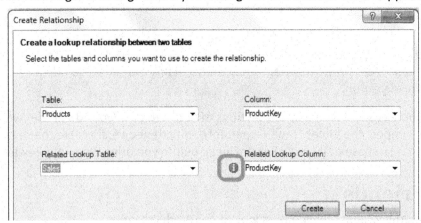

Figure 144 We reversed Sales and Products, selecting Sales as our Lookup table, and we get a warning

Hover over the warning icon and we get an explanation:

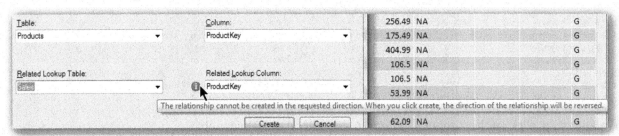

Figure 145 Power Pivot detects that we got the order wrong, and when we click OK, Products will be correctly used as the Lookup table!

The use of the word "Lookup" was deliberate. Back at Microsoft, we chose that word so that it would "rhyme" with Excel Pros' familiarity with VLOOKUP.

> Think of Lookup tables as the tables from which you would have "fetched" values when writing a VLOOKUP. Lookup tables tend to be the places where friendly labels are stored for instance.

**From here on, we will refer to the two tables' roles in a relationship as the "lookup table" and the "data table."**

## The Diagram View

**This feature was introduced in Power Pivot v2, and it becomes very helpful as your models grow more sophisticated.** But in smaller models, Diagram View is a fabulous gift to the authors of Power Pivot books, because we don't have to spend long hours making graphical representations of tables and relationships ☺

*Figure 146 Click the Diagram View button on the ribbon or in the bottom-right corner of the Power Pivot window.*

Clicking that button gives us:

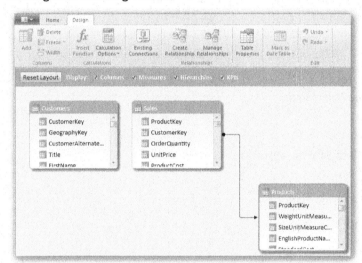

*Figure 147 Diagram View! All three tables displayed, with two of them linked by the relationship we just created.*

ⓘ Notice the direction of the arrow. Up through 2013, the arrow always points to the Lookup table. You can also create, edit and delete relationships in the diagram view. We will see an example later in this chapter.

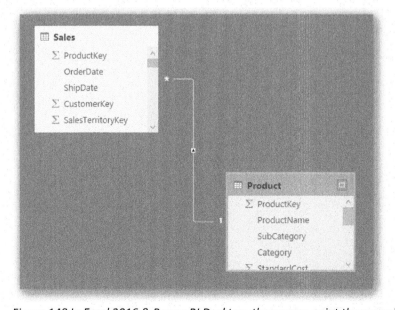

*Figure 148 In Excel 2016 & Power BI Desktop, the arrows point the opposite direction which is an improvement. Trust us.*

# Using Related Tables in a Pivot

Now let's revisit a pivot that uses ProductKey on Rows, and enhance it with some of the columns from this Products table.

| ProductKey ▾ | Normal Sales | Promo Sales | Refunds | Net Sales | Pct Sales on Promo |
|---|---|---|---|---|---|
| 214 | $54,934 | $11,932 | ($11,162) | $55,704 | 17.8 % |
| 217 | $52,170 | $10,742 | ($10,042) | $52,870 | 17.1 % |
| 222 | $52,205 | $11,547 | ($10,602) | $53,150 | 18.1 % |
| 225 | $13,854 | $3,012 | ($2,823) | $14,042 | 17.9 % |
| 228 | $14,897 | $2,899 | ($3,649) | $14,147 | 16.3 % |
| 231 | $16,247 | $2,200 | ($3,649) | $14,797 | 11.9 % |
| 234 | $16,047 | $2,500 | ($4,049) | $14,497 | 13.5 % |
| 237 | $14,197 | $3,399 | ($3,049) | $14,547 | 19.3 % |
| 310 | $862,363 | $150,287 | ($189,648) | $823,002 | 14.8 % |
| 311 | $669,136 | $164,600 | ($171,757) | $661,980 | 19.7 % |
| 312 | $837,315 | $182,492 | ($186,070) | $833,737 | 17.9 % |
| 313 | $722,811 | $196,805 | ($161,022) | $758,593 | 21.4 % |
| 314 | $755,015 | $157,444 | ($143,131) | $769,328 | 17.3 % |
| 320 | $9,088 | $2,097 | ($2,097) | $9,088 | 18.8 % |

*Figure 149 ProductKey pivot – but of course, ProductKey is meaningless to us.*

OK, let's remove ProductKey:

| Normal Sales | Promo Sales | Refunds | Net Sales | Pct Sales on Promo |
|---|---|---|---|---|
| $20,784,362 | $4,342,674 | ($4,231,642) | $20,895,394 | 17.3 % |

*Figure 150 Be gone, ProductKey! And never show your face on a pivot again.*

Now I'll add ProductName from the Products table instead:

*Figure 151 Checked the ProductName field in the field list, adding it to Rows*

| ProductName | Normal Sales | Promo Sales | Refunds | Net Sales | Pct Sales on Promo |
|---|---|---|---|---|---|
| Road-650 Black, 58 | $34,312 | $16,191 | ($7,494) | $43,009 | 32.1 % |
| Touring-1000 Blue, 54 | $226,487 | $104,899 | ($50,065) | $281,320 | 31.7 % |
| Touring-3000 Yellow, 54 | $23,013 | $8,166 | ($4,454) | $26,725 | 26.2 % |
| Mountain-100 Black, 38 | $108,000 | $37,125 | ($20,250) | $124,875 | 25.6 % |
| Mountain-400-W Silver, 46 | $68,485 | $23,085 | ($14,620) | $76,949 | 25.2 % |
| Touring-2000 Blue, 60 | $64,387 | $20,652 | ($13,363) | $71,676 | 24.3 % |
| Touring-1000 Yellow, 54 | $252,711 | $73,906 | ($50,065) | $276,552 | 22.6 % |
| Touring-3000 Yellow, 62 | $25,982 | $7,424 | ($3,712) | $29,694 | 22.2 % |
| Hitch Rack - 4-Bike | $26,880 | $7,560 | ($4,920) | $29,520 | 22.0 % |
| Mountain-500 Silver, 44 | $14,125 | $3,955 | ($3,955) | $14,125 | 21.9 % |
| Road-650 Red, 44 | $36,073 | $9,927 | ($8,529) | $37,472 | 21.6 % |
| Road-150 Red, 52 | $722,811 | $196,805 | ($161,022) | $758,593 | 21.4 % |
| Road-650 Black, 62 | $33,976 | $9,228 | ($5,844) | $37,360 | 21.4 % |
| Road-750 Black, 52 | $140,937 | $37,799 | ($29,699) | $149,037 | 21.1 % |
| Touring-3000 Blue, 58 | $28,209 | $7,424 | ($6,681) | $28,952 | 20.8 % |
| Road-550-W Yellow, 48 | $196,046 | $49,982 | ($37,777) | $208,251 | 20.3 % |
| Classic Vest, L | $8,255 | $2,096 | ($2,032) | $8,319 | 20.2 % |
| Touring-1000 Blue, 60 | $236,023 | $59,602 | ($54,834) | $240,791 | 20.2 % |

*Figure 152 ProductName replaced ProductKey: much more readable*

But we're not limited to using any one field from Products – all of them can be used now that we have a relationship established. Let's try a few different ones:

| Category | Normal Sales | Promo Sales | Refunds | Net Sales | Pct Sales on Promo |
|---|---|---|---|---|---|
| Accessories | $495,995 | $107,804 | ($96,961) | $506,838 | 17.9 % |
| Bikes | $20,047,702 | $4,188,222 | ($4,082,220) | $20,153,704 | 17.3 % |
| Clothing | $240,664 | $46,649 | ($52,460) | $234,852 | 16.2 % |
| **Grand Total** | **$20,784,362** | **$4,342,674** | **($4,231,642)** | **$20,895,394** | **17.3 %** |

*Figure 153 Category (from Products table) on Rows*

| Category-SubCat | Normal Sales | Promo Sales | Refunds | Net Sales | Pct Sales on Promo |
|---|---|---|---|---|---|
| **Accessories** | **$495,995** | **$107,804** | **($96,961)** | **$506,838** | **17.9 %** |
| Bike Racks | $26,880 | $7,560 | ($4,920) | $29,520 | 22.0 % |
| Bike Stands | $28,779 | $5,565 | ($5,247) | $29,097 | 16.2 % |
| Bottles and Cages | $40,697 | $8,151 | ($7,951) | $40,897 | 16.7 % |
| Cleaners | $5,032 | $1,185 | ($1,002) | $5,215 | 19.1 % |
| Fenders | $33,454 | $6,616 | ($6,550) | $33,520 | 16.5 % |
| Helmets | $159,309 | $34,220 | ($31,806) | $161,724 | 17.7 % |
| Hydration Packs | $27,825 | $6,654 | ($5,829) | $28,650 | 19.3 % |
| Tires and Tubes | $174,019 | $37,853 | ($33,657) | $178,216 | 17.9 % |
| **Bikes** | **$20,047,702** | **$4,188,222** | **($4,082,220)** | **$20,153,704** | **17.3 %** |
| Mountain Bikes | $7,199,563 | $1,360,830 | ($1,392,367) | $7,168,026 | 15.9 % |
| Road Bikes | $10,217,336 | $2,190,321 | ($2,112,927) | $10,294,730 | 17.7 % |
| Touring Bikes | $2,630,803 | $637,071 | ($576,927) | $2,690,947 | 19.5 % |
| **Clothing** | **$240,664** | **$46,649** | **($52,460)** | **$234,852** | **16.2 %** |
| Caps | $13,854 | $3,012 | ($2,823) | $14,042 | 17.9 % |
| Gloves | $24,514 | $5,486 | ($5,020) | $24,980 | 18.3 % |
| Jerseys | $122,990 | $22,606 | ($27,355) | $118,241 | 15.5 % |
| Shorts | $50,883 | $9,519 | ($10,918) | $49,483 | 15.8 % |
| Socks | $3,785 | $629 | ($692) | $3,722 | 14.3 % |
| Vests | $24,638 | $5,398 | ($5,652) | $24,384 | 18.0 % |
| **Grand Total** | **$20,784,362** | **$4,342,674** | **($4,231,642)** | **$20,895,394** | **17.3 %** |

*Figure 154 SubCategory (also from Products table) nested under Category*

| Color | Normal Sales | Promo Sales | Refunds | Net Sales | Pct Sales on Promo |
|---|---|---|---|---|---|
| Black | $6,272,549 | $1,267,427 | ($1,298,436) | $6,241,540 | 16.8 % |
| Blue | $1,531,913 | $400,061 | ($347,121) | $1,584,854 | 20.7 % |
| Multi | $75,241 | $14,009 | ($17,220) | $72,031 | 15.7 % |
| NA | $308,861 | $66,930 | ($59,326) | $316,465 | 17.8 % |
| Red | $5,417,765 | $1,153,707 | ($1,152,859) | $5,418,613 | 17.6 % |
| Silver | $3,721,517 | $713,957 | ($677,916) | $3,757,557 | 16.1 % |
| White | $3,785 | $629 | ($692) | $3,722 | 14.3 % |
| Yellow | $3,452,730 | $725,954 | ($678,071) | $3,500,614 | 17.4 % |
| Grand Total | $20,784,362 | $4,342,674 | ($4,231,642) | $20,895,394 | 17.3 % |

*Figure 155 Even Color can be used! (Another column from Products table)*

## Why That Works: Filter Context "Travels" Across Relationships

Let's examine a single measure cell and walk through the filter context "flow":

| Color | Normal Sales |
|---|---|
| Black | $6,272,549 |
| Blue | $1,531,913 |
| Multi | $75,241 |
| NA | $308,861 |
| Red | $5,417,765 |
| Silver | $3,721,517 |
| White | $3,785 |
| Yellow | $3,452,730 |
| Grand Total | $20,784,362 |

*Figure 156 Let's examine how filter context flows for the highlighted measure cell*

First, the Color="Red" filter is applied to the Products table:

| Produ... | StandardC... | FinishedGoodsF... | Color |
|---|---|---|---|
| 325 | 486.7066 | TRUE | Red |
| 324 | 413.1463 | TRUE | Red |
| 323 | 486.7066 | TRUE | Red |
| 322 | 413.1463 | TRUE | Red |
| 321 | 486.7066 | TRUE | Red |
| 320 | 413.1463 | TRUE | Red |
| 331 | 486.7066 | TRUE | Red |
| 330 | 413.1463 | TRUE | Red |
| 329 | 486.7066 | TRUE | Red |
| 328 | 413.1463 | TRUE | Red |
| 327 | 486.7066 | TRUE | Red |
| 326 | 413.1463 | TRUE | Red |
| 316 | 884.7083 | TRUE | Red |
| 315 | 884.7083 | TRUE | Red |
| 319 | 884.7083 | TRUE | Red |
| 318 | 884.7083 | TRUE | Red |
| 317 | 884.7083 | TRUE | Red |
| 372 | 1554.9479 | TRUE | Red |
| 371 | 1320.6838 | TRUE | Red |

*Figure 157 Products table filtered to Color="Red" as result of filter context*

The **ProductKey** column is not filtered directly, but it obviously *has* been reduced to a subset of its overall values, thanks to the Color="Red" filter on the table.

## Active Values for the Products[ProductKey] column:
### *{325; 324; 323; 322; 321; 320; 331; 330; 329; 328;*
### *... 245; 244; 243; 242; 241; 214; 213; 212}*

*Figure 158 Only those ProductKeys that correspond to Red products are left "active" at this point (63 ProductKey values out of a total of 397).*

That filtered set of 63 ProductKeys then flows across the relationship and filters the Sales table to that same set of ProductKeys:

| OrderQ... | ProductKey | UnitPr... | ProductCost | Custom... | OrderDate |
|---|---|---|---|---|---|
| 1 | 324 | 699.0982 | 413.1463 | 26620 | 7/3( |
| 1 | 324 | 699.0982 | 413.1463 | 20165 | 10/! |
| 1 | 324 | 699.0982 | 413.1463 | 19415 | 12/1! |
| 1 | 324 | 699.0982 | 413.1463 | 20558 | 1/7 |
| 1 | 324 | 699.0982 | 413.1463 | 18010 | 2/( |
| 1 | 324 | 699.0982 | 413.1463 | 25718 | 2/1( |
| 1 | 324 | 699.0982 | 413.1463 | 14737 | 2/2 |
| 1 | 324 | 699.0982 | 413.1463 | 18039 | 3/7 |
| 1 | 324 | 699.0982 | 413.1463 | 14746 | 3/9 |
| 1 | 324 | 699.0982 | 413.1463 | 25920 | 4/2( |
| 1 | 324 | 699.0982 | 413.1463 | 14755 | 4/2! |
| 1 | 324 | 699.0982 | 413.1463 | 19472 | 4/2! |
| 1 | 324 | 699.0982 | 413.1463 | 14756 | 4/2E |
| 1 | 324 | 699.0982 | 413.1463 | 25928 | 5/( |
| 1 | 324 | 699.0982 | 413.1463 | 14896 | 5/1! |
| 1 | 324 | 699.0982 | 413.1463 | 25947 | 6/1( |
| 1 | 325 | 782.99 | 486.7066 | 20577 | 7/2 |
| 1 | 325 | 782.99 | 486.7066 | 19924 | 7/1: |
| 1 | 325 | 782.99 | 486.7066 | 15155 | 7/1E |
| 1 | 325 | 782.99 | 486.7066 | 26021 | 7/2( |

| 2002 Sales: $... | Pct of All Month N... | Normal Sal... | Refunds: ($19,... | Pct Sales on... | Total Sales: $13 |

Sales | Customers | Products

*Figure 159 Sales table gets filtered (via relationship) to that same set of ProductKey values: {325; 324;...}*

**And then the arithmetic runs against the filtered Sales table. So it's the same Golden Rules as before. Those rules just extend across relationships.**

 During the filter phase of measure evaluation, filters applied to a Lookup table (Products in this case) flow through to the Data table(s) related to that Lookup table.

This does NOT, however, apply in reverse: filters applied to Data tables don't flow back "up" to Lookup tables.

# Visualizing Filters Flowing "Downhill" – One of Our Mental Tricks

In our heads, we always see Lookup tables floating above the Data tables. That way the filters flowing "downhill" into the Data tables.

We'll drag tables around in the Diagram View in order to represent that:

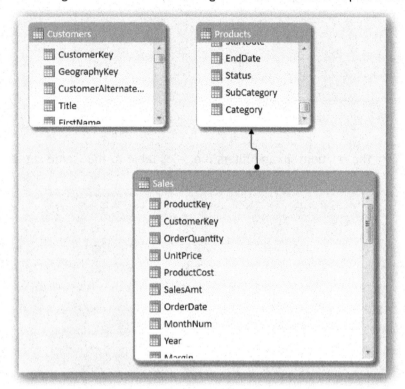

*Figure 160 Products table dragged to be "above" Sales table*

We also resized the tables so that the Data table (Sales) is bigger than the Lookup table (Products) – another mental trick.

We'll now create a relationship from Customers to Sales . This time we'll do so, within the Diagram View by dragging and dropping the key column that connects the two tables.

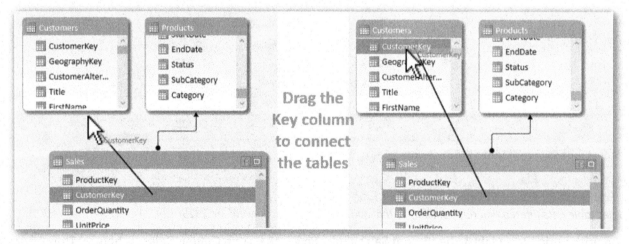

*Figure 161 Creating Relationships in the Diagram View*

 The direction in which you drag and drop the key column – from the Data to the Lookup table or from the Lookup table to the Data table – generally does not matter. Same as it didn't matter when we used the Create Relationship dialog, Power Pivot detects the "correct" direction of the relationship and sets it up in the correct direction.

Here's the updated diagram:

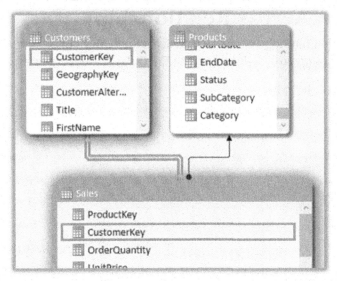

Figure 162 Two Lookup tables, both "above" the Data table that they filter

Note 1: Relationship lines/arrows in Diagram View can also be imagined as "**Filter Transmission Wires**". They "transmit" the filters applied on the uphill Lookup Tables to the downhill Data tables.

Note 2: It was a shame, in our opinion, that the relationship arrows flowed toward the Lookup tables in 2010 and 2013. Arrows point from Data to Lookup in the database world, but in Power Pivot we'd prefer that they point in the direction of filter flow. It's the little things that bug us.

This has been corrected in Power BI Desktop and Excel 2016, where the arrows point the right way now ☺

# Filters from All Related Lookup Tables Are Applied

Let's put columns from both Customers and Products on the same pivot:

| Total Sales | Marital Status ▾ | | |
|---|---|---|---|
| SubCategory ⤓ | M | S | Grand Total |
| Road Bikes | $7,419,057 | $7,101,527 | $14,520,584 |
| Mountain Bikes | $5,208,539 | $4,744,220 | $9,952,760 |
| Touring Bikes | $1,974,918 | $1,869,883 | $3,844,801 |
| Tires and Tubes | $140,253 | $105,276 | $245,529 |
| Helmets | $123,830 | $101,506 | $225,336 |
| Jerseys | $93,590 | $79,361 | $172,951 |
| Shorts | $43,604 | $27,716 | $71,320 |
| Bottles and Cages | $32,122 | $24,676 | $56,798 |
| Fenders | $27,079 | $19,540 | $46,620 |
| Hydration Packs | $22,821 | $17,487 | $40,308 |
| Bike Stands | $21,783 | $17,808 | $39,591 |
| Bike Racks | $22,920 | $16,440 | $39,360 |
| Vests | $19,558 | $16,129 | $35,687 |
| Gloves | $19,470 | $15,551 | $35,021 |
| Caps | $10,662 | $9,026 | $19,688 |
| Cleaners | $4,158 | $3,061 | $7,219 |
| Socks | $3,012 | $2,095 | $5,106 |
| **Grand Total** | **$15,187,376** | **$14,171,301** | **$29,358,677** |

Figure 163 Products[SubCategory] and [Customers[MaritalStatus] on the same pivot: they each impact measures, as expected

**This isn't worth belaboring really – we just wanted to point out that you can use more than one Lookup table on a single pivot with no issue.**

# CALCULATE() <Filters> *Also* Flow Across Relationships

Until now, all of our <filter> arguments in CALCULATE have been filtering columns in the Sales table. But <filter> arguments are completely legal against Lookup tables (in fact, encouraged!), so let's define a CALCULATE measure using a column in a Lookup table:

```
[Sales to Parents] =
CALCULATE ( [Total Sales],
    Customers[NumberChildrenAtHome] > 0 )
```

And compare that to its base measure, [Total Sales]:

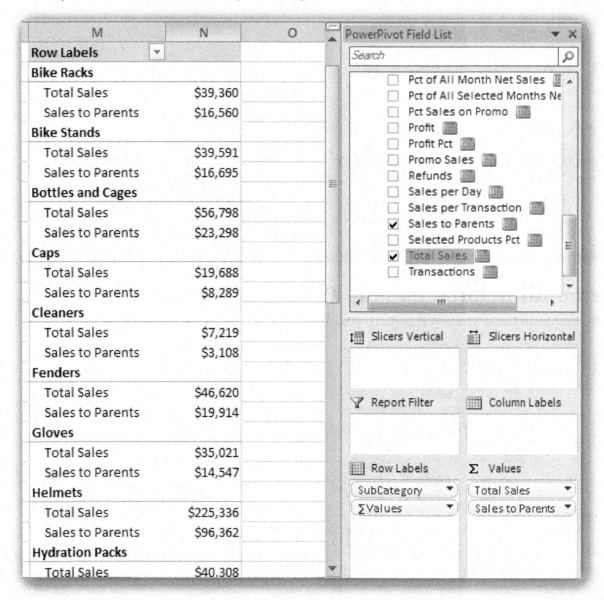

*Figure 164 Proof that CALCULATE <filters> also flow across relationships: [Sales to Parents] returns smaller numbers than its base measure [Total Sales]*

 We think that's probably sufficient to explain the concept, but to be super precise, we should also say that <filters> in CALCULATE() are applied *before* filters flow across relationships.

Taking that precision one step further, here's the final version of the DAX Evaluation Steps Diagram, with the crucial step#4 filled in:

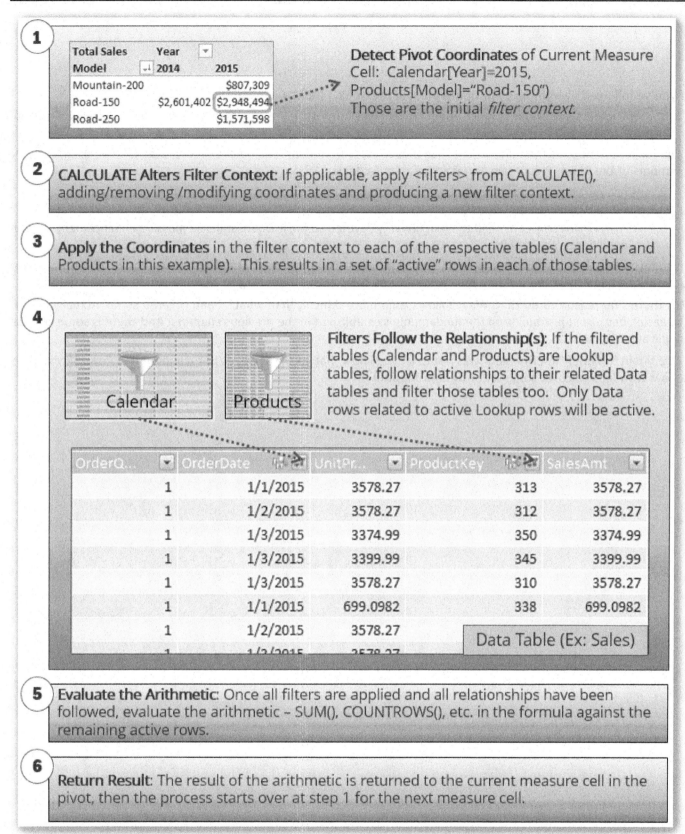

*Figure 165 DAX Evaluation Steps diagram updated to include step #4 showing that relationship traversal happens after CALCU-LATE() <filters> are applied*

You can download a digital copy of this and other useful PowerPivot/DAX tips in our 8-page reference card at
http://ppvt.pro/powerbirefcard

# 11 - "Intermission" – Taking Stock of Your New Powers

**If you've followed everything up until this point in the book, I (Rob) want you to know three things:**

1. You understand about as much about Power Pivot formulas (DAX) as I did after several months of experimenting on my own.

(And "experimenting" is the right word – I had moved away from Redmond before DAX was ready to be used, even by members of the Power Pivot team. So I learned as an "outsider.")

2. What you've read so far covers about the same amount of material as a full day of intensive training in one of my onsite, personalized courses.

3. If Power Pivot *only* contained the functionality covered so far, it would still be a *massive* enhancement to your capabilities as an Excel Pro.

**In other words, if you wanted, you could stop right now, close the book and file it away. You'd still improve the quantity and quality of the insights you can deliver by 4-5x, without needing to know anything covered hereafter.**

**But there's no reason to do that.** What follows is no more difficult than what's been covered so far. Actually I think it's easier, because it just builds on the fundamentals established in the previous chapters. **And there is some *serious* magic awaiting you** ☺

My point in this brief "intermission" was just to let you know that you're already VERY competent at Power Pivot. Take a bow. Now let's go cover some seriously amazing stuff ☺

# 12 - Disconnected Tables

**A disconnected table is one that you add to your Power Pivot model but *intentionally* do not relate it to any other tables.** At first that may seem a little strange – if there is no relationship between it and any other tables, filter context can never flow into it or out of it, so a disconnected table would never contribute anything meaningful to a pivot involving other tables.

But once you learn a simple new trick, it will make sense. It helps to have an example.

## A Parameterized Report

Let's work backwards this time: we will show you the result, and then explain how we did it.

Take a look at this pivot:

*Figure 166 Just a simple little pivot with two slicers, right?*

Nothing exciting on the surface. But let's change that "USD per EUR" from $1.10 to $1.80 and see what happens:

*Figure 167 Net Sales in Euros dropped sharply while the original Net Sales (in Dollars) remained unchanged*

Are you seeing what we're seeing? **This is a pivot where the user/consumer can dynamically input parameters (via slicers) and have those parameters reflected in calculations!**

This is absolutely real, and it's simple to build.

# Adding the Parameter Table

**We're going to ignore one of our own recommendations here and create a table via copy/paste.** We feel okay about doing so, because this is a table that isn't going to change frequently (if at all), and we're not going to write a bunch of formulas on this table (so if we needed to recreate it later, it would not be difficult to do).

**We create a single column table in Excel.** This is going to be the basis for our "USD per EUR" (dollars per euro) slicer:

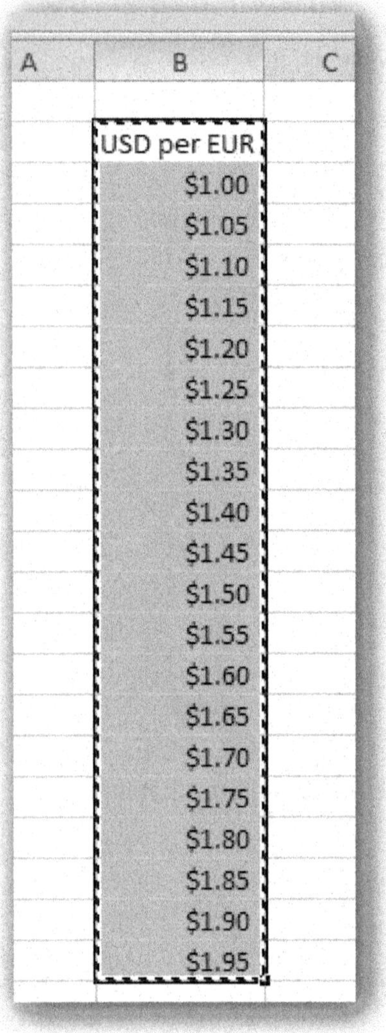

And then paste as new table in Power Pivot, yielding:

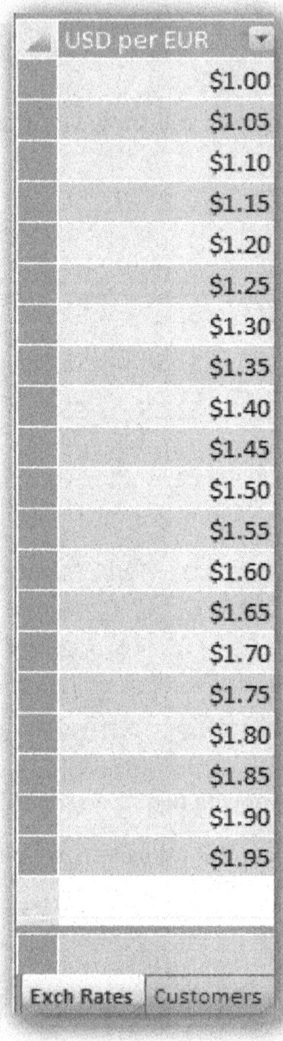

*Figure 168 Copying a simple table of data from Excel and Pasted as Exch Rates table in Power Pivot*

Now we can create a new pivot, and put that column on a slicer:

*Figure 169 New pivot, Category on Rows and the newly-pasted table/column on a slicer*

 Because we most often use Disconnected Tables as parameters, and those parameters are usually exposed as slicers, you may also think of them as "Slicer Tables" or "Parameter Tables."

## Adding a "Parameter Harvesting" Measure

Now we're going to do something interesting: we're going to add a measure on the Exch Rates table. This will be the first (but not last!) time that we create a measure on a non-data table.

The measure is:

```
[EURUSD] =
MAX ( 'Exch Rates'[USD per EUR] )
```

And the result:

| USD per EUR | | | | | | |
|---|---|---|---|---|---|---|
| $1.00 | $1.05 | $1.10 | $1.15 | $1.20 | $1.25 | $1.30 |
| $1.35 | $1.40 | $1.45 | $1.50 | $1.55 | $1.60 | $1.65 |
| $1.70 | $1.75 | $1.80 | $1.85 | $1.90 | $1.95 | |

| Row Labels | EURUSD |
|---|---|
| Accessories | $1.95 |
| Bikes | $1.95 |
| Clothing | $1.95 |
| Components | $1.95 |
| Grand Total | $1.95 |

*Figure 170 Measure that returns $1.95 all the time? Why would we want such a thing?*

The "punchline" here is that when we make a selection on the slicer, something neat happens:

*Figure 171 The measure returns whatever is selected on the slicer!*

**Cool! But this is just regular old filter context doing its thing.** Before the arithmetic (MAX) runs, the Exch Rates table gets filtered by the pivot, and the pivot is saying "[USD per EUR]=$1.45."

Because only a single row is selected when the user picks a single slicer value, we could also have used MIN() or AVERAGE() or even SUM() as the aggregation function in our [ExchangeRateEURUSD] measure – they all return the same result when a single value is selected. Your choice of function in cases like this is partly a matter of personal preference and partly a question of how you want to handle cases where the user picks more than one value. You can even decide to return an error – which we will cover in a later chapter.

# The Field List is Grumpy About This

At this point, the field list is giving us a warning:

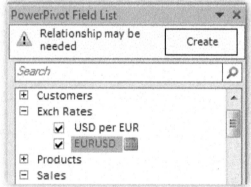

*Figure 172 Yes, there is no relationship between our Products table (where the Category field comes from) and our Exch Rates table (where this new measure comes from)*

**This warning, alas, merely goes with the territory of using Disconnected tables. And we don't like sacrificing real estate in our field list to a warning that tells us nothing. So we tend to turn this warning off using the Power Pivot ribbon in Excel:**

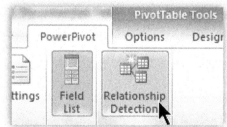

*Figure 173 Toggle this button to disable that warning (2010 only - in 2013 and beyond, you can dismiss the warning but not disable it)*

# Using the Parameter Measure for Something...Useful

OK, the [ExchangeRateEURUSD] measure is neat and all, but having a measure that tells the user what they've selected is of course pretty useless ☺

But now we can use that measure in other measures:

```
[Net Sales - EUR Equivalent] =
[Net Sales] / [EURUSD]
```

*Figure 174 New measure tells us what our sales would look like in Euros at the selected exchange rate!*

> We even used the formatting options in the measure editor to format the new measure in Euros. Oddly satisfying.

And we don't need the parameter measure displayed in order for it to work, so now we remove it to clean up the pivot:

*Figure 175 Remove the parameter measure to produce a cleaner report*

Add the Year column from the Sales table as a second slicer:

*Figure 176 Year slicer works like it always has*

# Parameter Table Can Be Used on Rows and Columns Too!

For grins, clear the slicer selection so that all exchange rates are selected, then drag that column to Rows instead:

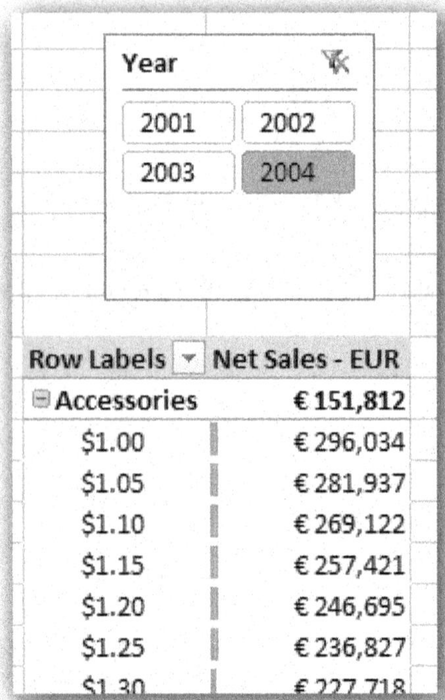

*Figure 177 Disconnected "slicer" field works on Rows too!*

**Are you surprised this works on Rows too?** It felt weird to us the first time we did this, but it shouldn't have. Each measure cell corresponds to a single value of the Exch Rate column. *This is no different from using a normal column (one that IS connected to the Sales table via relationship, or is IN the Sales table) on Slicers versus Rows.*

OK the result above is a little hard to see, let's rearrange a bit:

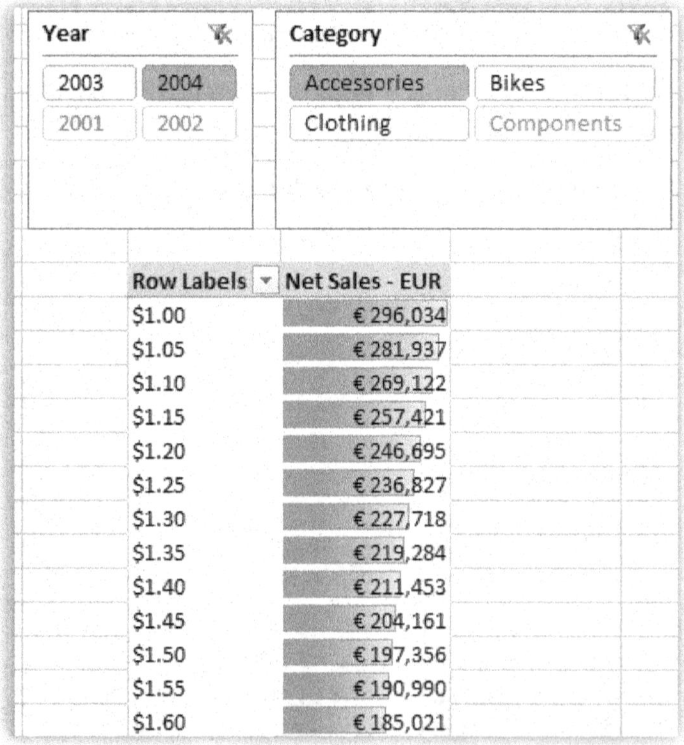

*Figure 178 Easier to see now with Category on slicer – EUR Equivalent Sales go down as Exchange Rate goes up*

 That may seem counterintuitive but it is accurate: if your country's currency is worth a lot relative to other countries' currencies, you make less money selling your products overseas than when your currency is worth less. So in some sense it's "better" for a country's currency to be worth less (and worse in other ways), but that's not exactly a DAX topic now is it? We just didn't want you thinking that we messed this one up ☺

# Why is it Important That They Be Disconnected?

**What would happen if our Exch Rates table *were* related to, say, the Sales table?**

**Short answer: nothing good.** What column would we use to form the relationship? There isn't a column in the Sales table that matches the values in the Exch Rates table. We could *invent* one we suppose, but then we'd have to arbitrarily assign transaction rows to individual exchange rate values, which would be nonsense.

And then when the user selected an exchange rate on the slicer, not only would that impact the [ExchangeRateEURUSD] measure (as desired) but it would *also* filter out rows from the Sales table (not desired). We'd undercount our sales figures, and in completely random fashion.

In real life, something like exchange rate is completely separate from Sales, so it shouldn't surprise us really that we can't create a meaningful relationship between them.

## A Very Powerful Concept

There are *many* variations on disconnected tables. In fact this concept borders on infinitely flexible. We will return to this topic and cover a few more variations as the book progresses. Let's look at one right now in fact.

# Disconnected Table Variation: Thresholds

In the previous example, we used a disconnected table to inject a numerical parameter into certain calculations, and give the report consumer/user control over that parameter.

Now let's try another example: giving the user control over "cutoffs," or thresholds, in terms of, say, which products should be included and which shouldn't.

Again, let's work backwards by showing you the desired result first:

*Figure 179 This pivot shows us, for instance, that there are 20 different products under the Clothing category that list for $50 or higher, and they accounted for $193k in sales.*

Nifty huh? The "how to" starts out just like the last example:

## Create a Disconnected Table to Populate the Slicer:

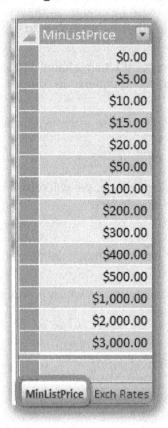

Figure 180 Another disconnected table

## Write a Measure to "Harvest" the User's Selection:

```
[MinListThreshold] =
  MAX ( MinListPrice[MinListPrice] )
```

Figure 181 "Harvester" measure [MinListThreshold] created on the disconnected table

## Diverging From the Prior Example: We Need to Filter, Not Perform Math

Hmm, now what? Last time, at this point we just divided an existing measure by our parameter measure to create something new. This time though, math isn't going to do it.

**Since we need to filter out Products unless they fit our criteria, we need to use our friend, CALCULATE().**

And hey, CALCULATE() supports the ">=" operator, so let's go ahead and do:

```
[Products Sales Above Selected List Price] =
CALCULATE ( [Total Sales],
    Products[ListPrice] >= [MinListThreshold] )
```

Enter it into the measure editor:

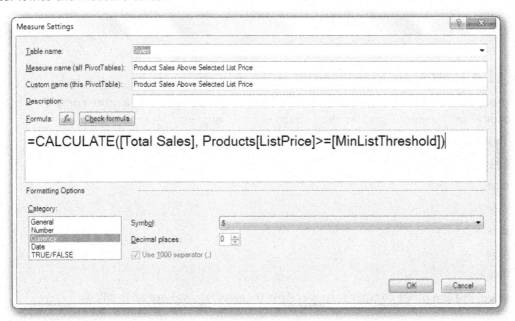

*Figure 182 [Products Sales Above Selected List Price] entered into measure editor*

And click Check Formula:

*Figure 183 Error: A function 'CALCULATE' has been used in a True/False expression that is used as a table filter expression. This is not allowed.*

That's a terribly-worded error message. In our opinion, here is what that error message *should* say:

'An expression was provided on the right side of a <filter> argument to CALCULATE. Only static values like 6 or "Red" are allowed in that location.'

**CALCULATE() requires that you provide a static value on the right side of a <filter> expression.**

## CALCULATE() Has a Limitation? Not really.

Hard to believe isn't it? CALCULATE *never* fails us!

**Well it's not failing us now either. It's actually protecting us, and there *is* a version of this formula that works:**

```
[Products Sales Above Selected List Price] =
CALCULATE (
    [TotalSales],
    FILTER ( Products,
        Products[ListPrice] >= [MinListThreshold] )
)
```

What is the FILTER() function, and what is it doing occupying one of our <filter> arguments to CALCULATE?

FILTER() is the next function on your Power Pivot journey. And while it's pretty straightforward, we don't want to "hide" it in this chapter. It deserves its own. So we will come back to this threshold example, but we will do it in the context of the FILTER() chapter.

# 13 - Introducing the FILTER() Function, and Disconnected Tables Continued

## When to Use FILTER()

**Simple rule:** use FILTER() when, in a <filter> argument to CALCULATE(), you need to perform a more complex test than "<column> equals <fixed value>" or "<column> greater than <fixed value>," etc.

**Examples of <filter> tests that *require* you to use FILTER():**

- <column> = <measure>
- <column> = <formula>
- <column> = <column>
- <measure> = <measure>
- <measure> = <formula>
- <measure> = <fixed value>

We used "=" in all of the above, but the other comparison operators (<, >, <=, >=, <>) are all implied.

> You can also use FILTER() as the <table> argument to functions like COUNTROWS() and SUMX() in order to have those functions operate on a subset of the table rather than all rows in the current filter context. This chapter will focus on its primary usage however, which is as a <filter> argument to CALCULATE().

## FILTER() Syntax

> FILTER(<table>, <single "rich" filter>)

## Why is FILTER() Necessary?

We mean, why can't we just slap any old complex test expression into the <filter> argument of CALCULATE()? Why the extra hassle?

We have made our peace with having to use FILTER(). We quite like it. Here's why.

### It's All About Performance (Speed of Formula Evaluation)

**Short answer:**

1. **Formulas written using just CALCULATE() are *always* going to be fast**, because CALCULATE() has built-in "safeties" that prevent you from writing a slow formula. "Raw" CALCULATE() refuses richer <filter> tests because those *can* be slow if used carelessly.
2. **FILTER() *removes* those safeties** and therefore gives you a mental trigger to be more careful – you can still write fast formulas using FILTER(), but if you are careless you can write something that is slow.

> We'd like to introduce three terms that we often use when we talk about formula speed:
>
> **Performance:** the practice of keeping your reports fast for your users. For instance, if someone clicks a slicer and it takes 30 seconds for the pivot to update, we would refer to that as "poor performance." If it responds instantly, we might call that "excellent performance," or we might say that the pivot "performs well."
>
> **Response time:** the amount of time it takes a report to respond to a user action and display the updated results. In the example above, we described a "response time" of 30 seconds as poor. Generally we try to keep response times to 3 seconds or less.
>
> **Expensive:** an operation is said to be "expensive" if it consumes a lot of time and therefore impacts performance/response time. For instance, above we could have described <column> = <static value> tests as "inexpensive" for the DAX engine, and richer comparisons like <column> = <measure> as "potentially expensive."
>
> **We will say more about these concepts in a subsequent chapter dedicated to Performance. For now this is enough.**

Anyway, the important thing to understand is that FILTER() removes the safeties and lets you perform an incredible variety of filter tests, but you have to be careful when you use it.

## How to Use FILTER() Carefully

You are going to love this, because the vast majority of "being careful" comes down to two simple rules:

1. **When you use FILTER(), use it against Lookup tables, *never* against Data tables.**
2. **Never use FILTER() when a "raw" CALCULATE() will get the job done.**

Pretty simple. For those of you who want to know more about the "why" behind that first rule, we are saving that for the chapter on Performance.

**The Secret of FILTER's Power**: We have already hinted at this. The secret is that it's an **iterator**, which just means it goes row by row through a table (first argument) to evaluate the filter condition (the second argument). FILTER is not alone in this, there is a **whole family of iterator function, or X functions** as they are often known. You would meet them in a subsequent chapter on X functions.

# Applying FILTER() in the "Thresholds" Example

## Revisiting the Successful Formula

Let's return to our "thresholds" example from the previous chapter, where we wanted to only include products whose Products[ListPrice] column was >= our [MinListThreshold] measure:

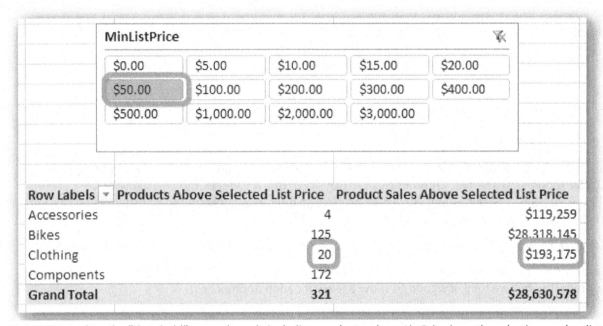

*Figure 184 Back to the "threshold" example: only including products whose ListPrice is >= the selection on the slicer.*

The formula we ended up using for the measure on the right was:

```
[Product Sales Above Selected List Price] =
CALCULATE (
    [Total Sales],
    FILTER ( Products,
        Products[ListPrice] >= [MinListThreshold] )
)
```

Are we following the rules for using FILTER() carefully? Let's check.

1. **Products is a Lookup table**, not a Data table (like Sales). **YES on rule #1.**
2. **We are comparing Products[ListPrice] to a measure**, which cannot be done in raw CALCULATE(). **YES on rule #2.**

OK, so now the [Products Above Selected List Price] measure – that gives us a count of products that pass the [MinListThreshold] test, and it's executed the same way as the measure above.

First though, we need a base measure that just counts products:

```
[Product Count] =
COUNTROWS ( Products )
```

Note how we assigned that measure to the Products table, since it counts rows in that table:

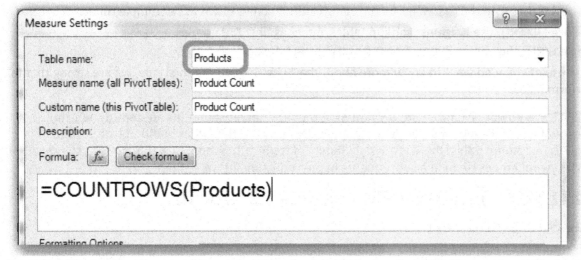

Figure 185 [Product Count] measure is assigned to the Products table since its arithmetic operates on the Product table (best practice)

Now we can create [Products Above Selected List Price] using that new base measure:

```
[Products Above Selected List Price] =
CALCULATE (
      [Product Count],
      FILTER ( Products,
            Products[ListPrice] >= [MinListThreshold] )
)
```

> We could have skipped the separate step of defining the [Product Count] measure, and just specified COUNTROWS(Products) as the first argument to CALCULATE(). But [Product Count] is likely to be a useful measure elsewhere too, and remember, it's a best practice to build measures on top of other measures, so that future changes to your model can be made in a single place.

## Verifying That the Measures Work

Well the measures are returning some numbers, but are they the right numbers? Let's investigate a little bit (we won't do this for every measure but we think it's good to show a few validation approaches).

**MinListPrice**

| $0.00 | $5.00 | $10.00 | $15.00 | $20.00 |
|-------|-------|--------|--------|--------|
| $50.00 | $100.00 | $200.00 | $300.00 | $400.00 |
| $500.00 | $1,000.00 | $2,000.00 | $3,000.00 | |

| Row Labels | Products Above Selected List Price | Product Sales Above Selected List Price |
|------------|-----------------------------------|----------------------------------------|
| Accessories | 4 | $119,259 |
| Bikes | 125 | $28,318,145 |
| Clothing | 20 | $193,175 |
| Components | 172 | |
| **Grand Total** | **321** | **$28,630,578** |

Figure 186 How do we know the measures are correct?

The first thing to do is just change slicer selection and make sure that it has an impact. Let's try $20 as our minimum list price:

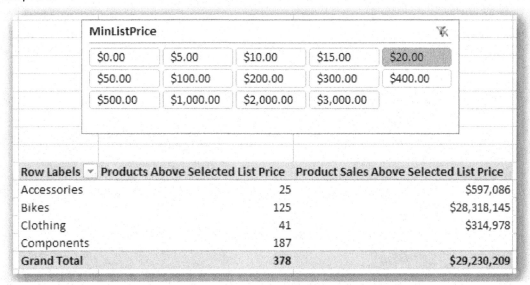

| Row Labels | Products Above Selected List Price | Product Sales Above Selected List Price |
|---|---|---|
| Accessories | 25 | $597,086 |
| Bikes | 125 | $28,318,145 |
| Clothing | 41 | $314,978 |
| Components | 187 | |
| Grand Total | 378 | $29,230,209 |

*Figure 187 We would expect both measures to return larger numbers with $20 as the selected threshold, and they both do*

A good sign. But let's make sure that the measures are truly counting the right products. Let's put Products[Product-Key] on Rows, and set the slicer to $3,000 since that should only show us a small number of products:

**MinListPrice**

| $0.00 | $5.00 | $10.00 | $15.00 | $20.00 |
| $50.00 | $100.00 | $200.00 | $300.00 | $400.00 |
| $500.00 | $1,000.00 | $2,000.00 | $3,000.00 | |

| Row Labels | Products Above Selected List Price | Product Sales Above Selected List Price |
|---|---|---|
| 310 | 1 | $1,202,299 |
| 311 | 1 | $1,005,494 |
| 312 | 1 | $1,205,877 |
| 313 | 1 | $1,080,638 |
| 314 | 1 | $1,055,590 |
| 344 | 1 | $197,199 |
| 345 | 1 | $142,800 |
| 346 | 1 | $166,600 |
| 347 | 1 | $122,400 |
| 348 | 1 | $165,375 |
| 349 | 1 | $151,875 |
| 350 | 1 | $202,499 |
| 351 | 1 | $192,374 |
| Grand Total | 13 | $6,891,018 |

*Figure 188 Only 13 products show up – another good sign*

But we really need to see the ListPrice. Let's put that on Rows too:

| Row Labels | Products Above Selected List Price | Product Sales Above Selected List Price |
|---|---|---|
| ⊟ 3374.99 | 4 | $712,123 |
| 348 | 1 | $165,375 |
| 349 | 1 | $151,875 |
| 350 | 1 | $202,499 |
| 351 | 1 | $192,374 |
| ⊟ 3399.99 | 4 | $628,998 |
| 344 | 1 | $197,199 |
| 345 | 1 | $142,800 |
| 346 | 1 | $166,600 |
| 347 | 1 | $122,400 |
| ⊟ 3578.27 | 5 | $5,549,897 |
| 310 | 1 | $1,202,299 |
| 311 | 1 | $1,005,494 |
| 312 | 1 | $1,205,877 |
| 313 | 1 | $1,080,638 |
| 314 | 1 | $1,055,590 |
| Grand Total | 13 | $6,891,018 |

*Figure 189 OK, all of the products showing up are indeed priced over $3k*

Lastly, over in the Power Pivot window, let's filter the Products table to ListPrice>=3000:

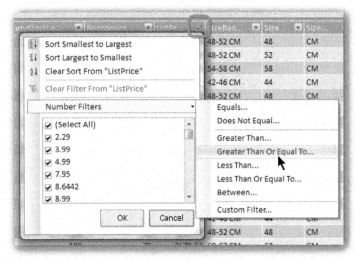

*Figure 190 This should result in 13 rows, matching the grand total from the pivot…*

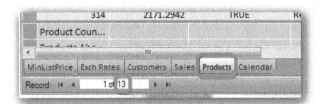

*Figure 191 …and it does*

**OK, this last step probably would be the first thing we would check.** But we wanted to show that both the Power Pivot window and the pivot itself are important tools for validating/debugging. We use both.

Since both measures use the same FILTER() logic, once we validate this one, we can be pretty confident that the other is working too. So there you have it: a simple threshold example driven by slicer, and it works.

## This Could Not Be Done with Relationships

Just to reinforce: the disconnected table approach was absolutely necessary for this threshold example. A given product, like a $75 shirt, belongs to many different price ranges – it is included in the $0, $5, $10$, $15, $20, and $50 price ranges. (In other words, the price ranges overlap with each other).

To see what we mean, imagine creating a column, in the Products table, to form the basis of the relationship. What would that column look like? If you committed to going down this road, you'd ultimately end up with multiple rows for each product (one for each price range that product "belongs to"). That would therefore require a "many to many" relationship with the slicer table (and with the Sales table), which Power Pivot does not support.

## Tip: Measures Based on a Shared Pattern – Create via Copy/Paste

**Notice how the two FILTER() measures above are identical except for their base measure?** One uses [Total Sales] as the first argument to CALCULATE() and the other uses [Product Count], but otherwise the formulas are the same.

You will do this all the time. And there's a quick way to do it:

1. You write the first measure. In this case, the [Total Sales] version.

2. Then you right click that measure in the field list (or in the Values dropzone) and choose edit:

*Figure 192 Edit your first measure*

3. Copy the existing formula:

*Figure 193 Copy the existing formula, which is conveniently selected already when you edit an existing measure*

4. Cancel out of the editor, create a new measure, and then paste the formula:

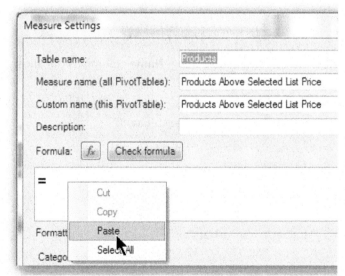

*Figure 194 Paste the original measure's formula*

5. Lastly, just replace the base measure reference ([Total Sales]) with the different desired measure ([Product Count]):

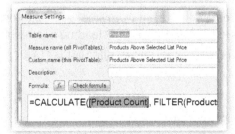

*Figure 195 The whole process takes just a few seconds*

You would discover this "trick" on your own pretty quickly (if you haven't already), but we do it so often that we wanted to make absolutely sure you are aware of it.

# More Variations on Disconnected Tables

## Upper and Lower Bound Thresholds

Let's take that Product[ListPrice] threshold example and extend it. Here's a new table:

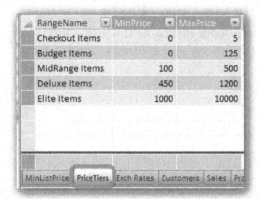

*Figure 196 A new disconnected table, but this time with min and max price columns*

 Note again that the price tiers overlap, meaning a given product can belong to more than one, thus making a relationship impossible.

Now we're going to define two "harvester" measures on that table:

```
[PriceTierMin] =
MIN ( PriceTiers[MinPrice] )
```

and

```
[PriceTierMax] =
MAX ( PriceTiers[MaxPrice] )
```

Now we're going to use RangeName column as our slicer:

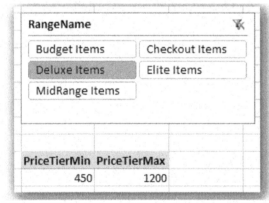

*Figure 197 You can use a label column from a disconnected table on your pivot. Both "harvester" measures again capture the user's selection, but this time based on columns that the user does not see.*

## Fixing the Sort Order on the Slicer: The "Sort By Column" Feature

In our first threshold example, we used a numerical field on the slicer, which naturally sorted from smallest to largest. In this label example however, "Budget" alphabetically precedes "Counter," and out sort order is misleading as a result.

In Power Pivot v1, we had to "fix" this by prepending strings for correct sorting, yielding slicers with values like "1 – Counter" and "2 – Budget" on them. Yuck.

In Power Pivot v2 however, we have a much better fix: the Sort By Column feature.

**First we need a single numerical (or text) column that sorts the table in the proper order.**

Doesn't matter how you go about creating this column – as long as you create one (or already have one), it works.

In this case we will use a new calculated column:

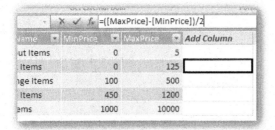

*Figure 198 Creating a column that will sort properly (in this case, our column will be the midpoint of each price tier)*

Now we select the RangeName column and click the Sort by Column button on the ribbon:

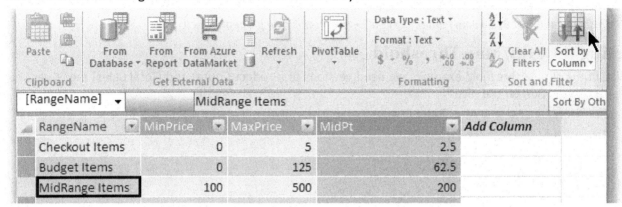

*Figure 199 Select label column, click Sort by Column*

In the dialog, set it to sort by the new MidPt column:

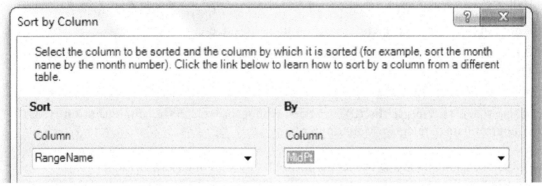

*Figure 200 Set the "sort by" column to the MidPt column*

Flip back over to Excel:

*Figure 201 Changing the Sort By Column triggers the "refresh" prompt*

Click the refresh button and the slicer sort order is fixed:

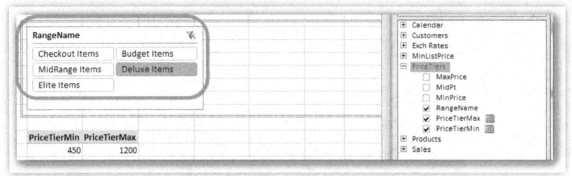

*Figure 202 Refresh, and the Sort By Column feature "kicks in" – the slicer is now properly sorted*

## Completing the Min/Max Threshold

Now, just like in the simple threshold example, we need versions of [Product Count] and [Total Sales] measures that respect the user's selection on the slicer:

```
[ProductCount MinMaxTier] =
CALCULATE (
    [Product Count],
    FILTER (
        Products,
        Products[ListPrice] >= [PriceTierMin]
            && Products[ListPrice] <= [PriceTierMax]
    )
)
```

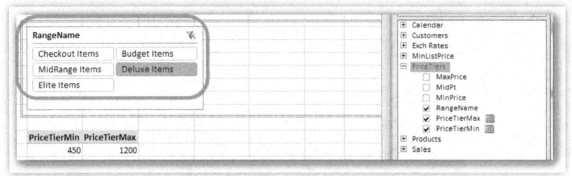

Since FILTER() only supports a single <rich filter> expression, we use the && operator – a row of Products table needs to meet both of those comparison tests in order to be included.

But since CALCULATE() itself *does* support multiple <filter> arguments, we could have done this without the && operator by using two FILTER() functions:

CALCULATE(<measure>, FILTER(…), FILTER(…) )

That would yield the same results. We use the && approach whenever we can though, because it is less expensive (in terms of performance) to do so. More on this later.

And then the [Total Sales] version, again employing the "copy/paste/change base measure" trick:

```
[Total Sales MinMaxTier] =
CALCULATE (
    [Total Sales],
    FILTER (
        Products,
        Products[ListPrice] >= [PriceTierMin]
            && Products[ListPrice] <= [PriceTierMax]
    )
)
```

Now we'll put both measures on the pivot, and remove the harvester measures:

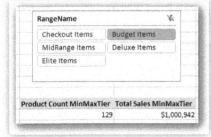

*Figure 203 It's alive!* ☺

## A Way to Visualize Disconnected Tables

**Disconnected tables, by definition, have no relation-ships to other tables in the model.** If we look at diagram view, we see that the PriceTiers table, for instance, is an island like we expect:

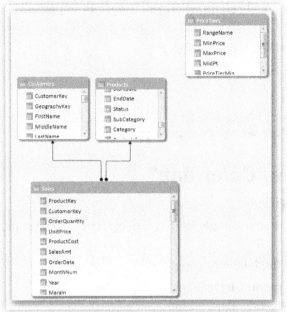

*Figure 204 PriceTiers Disconnected Table has no Relationship Arrows (as expected)*

**But when we use the "MinMaxTier" measures that we wrote above, the PriceTiers table *does* act a lot *like* a Lookup table**, since the PriceTiers filter context (such as user selections on the slicer) very much impacts the measure calculations and results.

So we often like to say that disconnected tables have a "dotted line" relationship with the tables that contain the corresponding FILTER() measures. In your head, you might think of it like this:

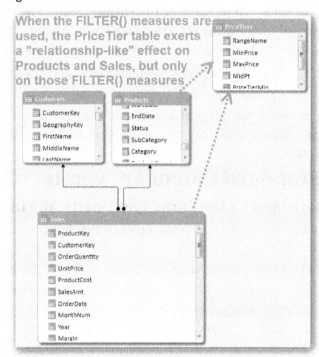

*Figure 205 In your head, you can imagine "dotted line" relationships*

 Disconnected tables only impact the measures that are specifically written to "pay attention" to them – so the PriceTiers table impacts [ProductCount MinMaxTier] and [Total Sales MinMaxTier], but no other measures in the Products and Sales tables.

# Putting This Chapter in Perspective

A couple things we want to emphasize before moving on:

- **We are not done with FILTER().** There's more to learn about FILTER() than what we have covered here, but we want to come back to those points later. It is not essential to learn the rest yet, and we are sticking to our philosophy of introducing things to you in the most learnable/useful order.

- **You will *not* use disconnected tables most of the time.** 90% of the pivots we create do *not* use disconnected tables. The other 10% of the time, they are very, *very* useful. We introduced disconnected tables in these last two chapters in large part because they are a great introduction to the FILTER() function (and *also* because they are a useful technique).

# 14 - Introduction to Time Intelligence

## At Last, It is Time!

(Get it? *Time?* There is no extra charge for humor of this quality).

**We've been eagerly awaiting this chapter. Power Pivot measures really shine when you use them to perform intelligent calculations against the calendar.**

It is a simple matter to perform calculations that answer questions like the following:

- How is our business performing relative to the same time last year?
- What were our Year to Date (YTD) sales as of June 1st?
- What was our best quarter over the past two years?

That is merely scratching the surface though. Good stuff. But before we dig in, a quick note about different types of calendars.

## "Standard Calendar" versus "Custom Calendar"

### Standard Calendars: The Focus of This Chapter

Right up front, we want to let you know that this chapter will be written strictly from the perspective of the standard calendar.

What do we mean by "standard calendar?" It's the calendar with the following properties:

- February has 28 days (29 in leap years) in it, and all other months have 30 or 31 days in them
- Quarters consist of three consecutive months – months whose lengths are described above
- Years have 365 days in them (366 in leap years)
- A given month this year might have more/less Saturdays (or any other day) in it than the same month last year

In other words, a standard calendar is the calendar that you have hanging on your wall.

**Power Pivot's time intelligence functions operate under the assumption that you use a standard calendar.** So they represent a natural place to start the topic of time intelligence.

### Custom Calendars: Perhaps Even More Important than Standard (Covered Later)

But many businesses do *not* measure themselves via the standard calendar. The standard calendar poses many problems that are often unacceptable:

- **Comparing this month to last month is often not "fair"** when last month had 31 days and this one has 30, for instance. Did we really perform 3% worse this month or is that just due to the different number of days?
- **Even two months of the same length are often not fair** comparisons since they contain different numbers of weekend days versus weekdays.
- **Sometimes the unit of time measured doesn't even** *resemble* **the wall calendar** – "Semesters" in the academic world and "Seasons" in the sports world for example
- **Going further, sometimes (such as in science), we want to literally compare** *time* **periods** instead of calendar periods – such as "the first five minutes after an event" compared to the following fifteen minutes etc.

In our experience, at least half of all organizations measure themselves by custom calendars. Retail businesses in particular are very sensitive to those first two problems.

**So have no fear, we will address custom calendars too. We are only going to** *start* **with the standard calendar. Stay tuned, in later chapters, for the custom calendar treatment.**

## Calendar: A Very Special Lookup Table

**Everything in time intelligence requires that you have a separate Calendar table.** (It does not have to be named "Calendar," but we usually use that name, or "Dates.")

### Where to Get a Calendar Table

There are many ways to create a calendar table. Here are a few options:

- **Import one from a database**. This is our favorite, for several reasons. But not everyone would have access to a database. See http://ppvt.pro/sqldate for one approach.

- **Create one in Excel.** Pretty much available to everyone. However may pose a problem when you need a dynamic action (e.g. trim calendar based on today's date). Download a sample Excel Calendar Generator at http://ppvt.pro/xlCalendar.

- **Generate using Power Query.** Best of both worlds, nearly available to everyone and offers easy dynamic capabilities. See http://ppvt.pro/udate2 and http://ppvt.pro/pqcalendar as examples.

- **Import one from Azure DataMarket (or elsewhere on the internet).** There's at least one calendar table available for free download on the internet, produced by the amazing Boyan Penev. See http://ppvt.pro/UltDate for more.

## Properties of a Calendar Table

A calendar table must:

- **Contain at least one column of "date" data type.**
- **Contain exactly one row per day.**
- **Contain completely consecutive dates, no gaps** – even if your business is never open on weekends, those days must be in the calendar
- **Be related to all of your Data tables (Sales, etc.)**
- **Contain columns for all of your desired grouping and labels** – things like MonthName, DayOfWeekName, IsWknd, IsHoliday, etc. (strictly, you *can* have a Calendar table with just the one date column, but the Calendar table is the place to put all of these other columns if you *do* have them).
- *Ideally* **only "spans" the relevant date ranges for your purposes.** If your business opened in 2001, it doesn't make sense for your Calendar table to start in 2000. And if today is June 20, 2012, it doesn't make sense for June 21, 2012 to be in the Calendar yet. This is one of the trickier requirements – it's the primary reason why we like to source our Calendar from a database. It really is optional, but you will find it very useful over time. Don't worry about it much for now.

## Our Calendar table: Imported and Related

| Date | DayNumberOfWeek | EnglishDayNameOfWeek | DayNumberOfMonth | Day |
|------|-----------------|----------------------|------------------|-----|
| 7/3/2003 | 5 | Thursday | 3 | |
| 7/4/2003 | 6 | Friday | 4 | |
| 7/5/2003 | 7 | Saturday | 5 | |
| 7/6/2003 | 1 | Sunday | 6 | |
| 7/7/2003 | 2 | Monday | 7 | |
| 7/8/2003 | 3 | Tuesday | 8 | |
| 7/9/2003 | 4 | Wednesday | 9 | |
| 7/10/2003 | 5 | Thursday | 10 | |
| 7/11/2003 | 6 | Friday | 11 | |
| 7/12/2003 | 7 | Saturday | 12 | |
| 7/13/2003 | 1 | Sunday | 13 | |
| 7/14/2003 | 2 | Monday | 14 | |
| 7/15/2003 | 3 | Tuesday | 15 | |
| 7/16/2003 | 4 | Wednesday | 16 | |
| 7/17/2003 | 5 | Thursday | 17 | |
| 7/18/2003 | 6 | Friday | 18 | |
| 7/19/2003 | 7 | Saturday | 19 | |
| 7/20/2003 | 1 | Sunday | 20 | |
| 7/21/2003 | 2 | Monday | 21 | |
| 7/22/2003 | 3 | Tuesday | 22 | |
| 7/23/2003 | 4 | Wednesday | 23 | |

stomers | Sales | Products | Calendar | Exch Rates | MinListPrice | PriceTiers

*Figure 206 Calendar table – now we can get started!*

Now we relate it to our Sales table, using the Date columns:

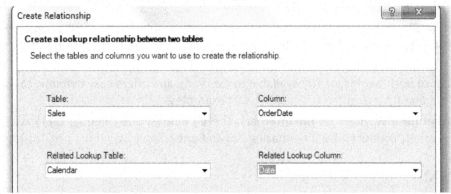

Figure 207 Relating Calendar to Sales

 In Power Pivot v1, the column used to relate Calendar to other tables *had* to be of data type Date. In v2, you can now relate using a column of a different data type, such as an integer, so you do *not* need a column of Type Date in your *Sales* table anymore, but you *do* still need a column of type Date in your *Calendar* table.

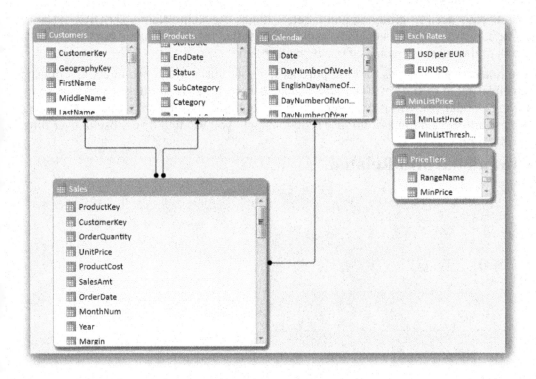

Figure 208 Updated diagram view: Calendar becomes the third lookup table

## Operates like a Normal Lookup Table

| DayNameOfWeek | Total Sales |
|---|---|
| Friday | $4,235,386 |
| Monday | $4,154,920 |
| Saturday | $4,342,674 |
| Sunday | $4,231,642 |
| Thursday | $4,113,749 |
| Tuesday | $4,153,093 |
| Wednesday | $4,127,215 |
| Grand Total | $29,358,677 |

Figure 209 [Total Sales] with Calendar[DayNameOfWeek] on Rows

And the Sort By Column feature works here too of course:

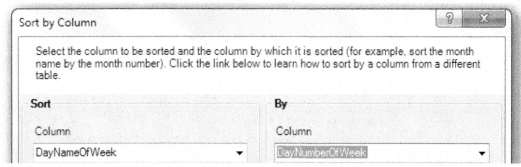

*Figure 210 Sort by Column Rides Again!*

| DayNameOfWeek ▾ | Total Sales |
|---|---|
| Sunday | $4,231,642 |
| Monday | $4,154,920 |
| Tuesday | $4,153,093 |
| Wednesday | $4,127,215 |
| Thursday | $4,113,749 |
| Friday | $4,235,386 |
| Saturday | $4,342,674 |
| **Grand Total** | **$29,358,677** |

*Figure 211 Days sorting in proper order (if you want Monday to be first, just create a calculated column in Calendar that starts with 1 for Monday and ends on 7 for Sunday, and use that as your sort by column instead)*

And we can repeat the same process for MonthName – every column can have its own separate sort by column:

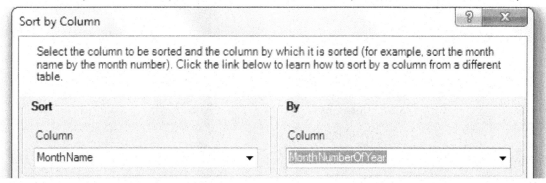

*Figure 212 Setting sort order for MonthName*

| MonthName ▾ | Total Sales |
|---|---|
| January | $2,375,857 |
| February | $2,502,387 |
| March | $2,610,615 |
| April | $2,778,842 |
| May | $3,114,646 |
| June | $3,180,924 |
| July | $1,911,263 |
| August | $1,899,607 |
| September | $1,834,668 |
| October | $2,009,169 |
| November | $2,076,070 |
| December | $3,064,630 |
| **Grand Total** | **$29,358,677** |

*Figure 213 Properly sorted month names!*

# First Special Feature: Enable Date Filtering via Mark as Date Table

With your Calendar table active, go to the Design tab of the ribbon and select Mark as Date Table:

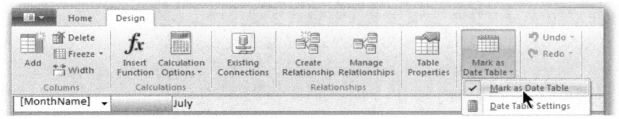

*Figure 214 Make this a habit for your Calendar/Date table*

Then, in the pivot, you get the special date filtering options:

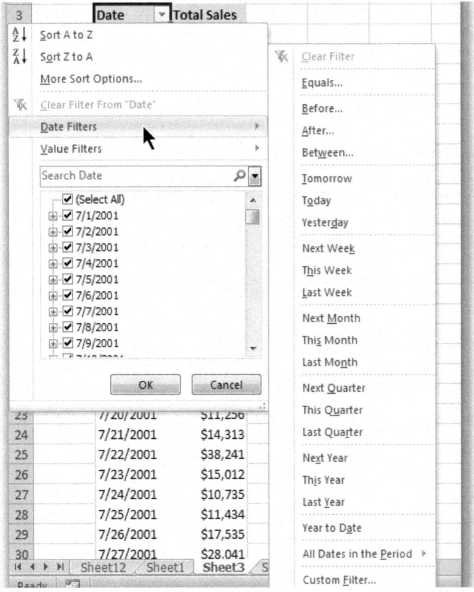

*Figure 215 Power Pivot "tells" Excel that this is a Date table, so Excel enables these filter options for you (most of which are useless with our sample data since the dates are ancient, but more useful in the real world)*

 If you are going to use a column of non-Date data type to relate your Calendar table to your Data tables, you MUST "mark it as date" in the Power Pivot window, or many other of the smart calculation features covered after this will not function properly.

# Second Special Feature: Time Intelligence Functions!

Power Pivot includes many new functions relating to time:

Figure 216 A subset of the DAX functions relating to time – a few are carryovers from normal Excel, but most are new.

## Diving in with DATESYTD()

There are so many functions that it was hard for us to choose which one to cover first. We picked DATESYTD() not because it's somehow special relative to the others, but just because it makes for a good example.

Let's start with a simple pivot:

| CalendarYear |
|---|

| Month ▼ | Total Sales |
|---|---|
| January | $1,340,245 |
| February | $1,462,480 |
| March | $1,480,905 |
| April | $1,608,751 |
| May | $1,878,318 |
| June | $1,949,361 |
| July | $50,841 |
| **Grand Total** | **$9,770,900** |

*(CalendarYear slicer: 2001, 2002, 2003, 2004 – 2004 selected)*

Figure 217 Our "testbed" for DATESYTD()

Now let's add a new measure, one that tracks Year to Date (YTD) sales:

```
[Total Sales YTD] =
CALCULATE ( [Total Sales], DATESYTD ( Calendar[Date] ) )
```

And...

| Month ▼ | Total Sales | Total Sales YTD |
|---|---|---|
| January | $1,340,245 | $1,340,245 |
| February | $1,462,480 | $2,802,725 |
| March | $1,480,905 | $4,283,630 |
| April | $1,608,751 | $5,892,380 |
| May | $1,878,318 | $7,770,698 |
| June | $1,949,361 | $9,720,059 |
| July | $50,841 | $9,770,900 |
| August | | $9,770,900 |
| **Grand Total** | **$9,770,900** | **$9,770,900** |

*(CalendarYear slicer: 2001, 2002, 2003, 2004 – 2004 selected)*

Figure 218 New measure shows us a running total of YTD sales for each month!

And like all good Power Pivot measures, this formula is "portable" into basically any report shape you desire, just by rearranging the pivot – no formula surgery required! Remove [Total Sales] and drag Year to Columns...

| Total Sales YTD | Year | | | | |
|---|---|---|---|---|---|
| Month | 2001 | 2002 | 2003 | 2004 | Grand Total |
| January | | $596,747 | $438,865 | $1,340,245 | $1,340,245 |
| February | | $1,147,563 | $927,956 | $2,802,725 | $2,802,725 |
| March | | $1,791,698 | $1,413,530 | $4,283,630 | $4,283,630 |
| April | | $2,455,391 | $1,919,930 | $5,892,380 | $5,892,380 |
| May | | $3,128,947 | $2,482,702 | $7,770,698 | $7,770,698 |
| June | | $3,805,711 | $3,037,501 | $9,720,059 | $9,720,059 |
| July | $473,388 | $4,306,076 | $3,924,170 | $9,770,900 | $9,770,900 |
| August | $979,580 | $4,852,077 | $4,771,584 | $9,770,900 | $9,770,900 |
| September | $1,453,523 | $5,202,544 | $5,781,842 | | $5,781,842 |
| October | $1,966,852 | $5,617,934 | $6,862,291 | | $6,862,291 |
| November | $2,510,846 | $5,953,030 | $8,059,273 | | $8,059,273 |
| December | $3,266,374 | $6,530,344 | $9,791,060 | | $9,791,060 |

*Figure 219 Our new [Total Sales YTD] measure, like all good DAX measures, automatically adjusts to any new pivot shape – just rearrange using the field list, and the measure does the hard work!*

## Anatomy of DATESYTD()

## Function Definition

 DATESYTD(<date column in calendar table>, <optional year end date>)

That first argument, <date column in calendar table>, is common to nearly all of the time intelligence functions. In Power Pivot itself, the function help just refers to it as Dates:

*Figure 220 What we call "<date column in calendar table>, Power Pivot calls "Dates" – whenever you see that, remember our version of it, because that's what "Dates" means in the time intelligence function definitions.*

**DATESYTD() is used as a <filter> argument to CALCULATE(), much like ALL() and FILTER().**

## How Does it Work?

Like almost everything else "magical" in Power Pivot, DATESYTD() operates by manipulating filter context.

Let's return to a simple pivot layout, and highlight a particular measure cell:

| CalendarYear | | | | | Month | Total Sales YTD |
|---|---|---|---|---|---|---|
| 2001 | 2002 | | | | January | $1,340,245 |
| | | | | | February | $2,802,725 |
| 2003 | 2004 | | | | March | $4,283,630 |
| | | | | | April | $5,892,380 |
| | | | | | May | $7,770,698 |
| | | | | | June | $9,720,059 |
| | | | | | July | $9,770,900 |
| | | | | | August | $9,770,900 |
| | | | | | Grand Total | $9,770,900 |

*Figure 221 For the highlighted measure cell...*

**DATESYTD() essentially identifies the latest date in the current filter context, and then "expands" the filter context backward from that date to the first date of the year (more specifically, to the first date in the year of that previously-identified latest date, which is 2004 in this case).**

OK, then DATESYTD() modifies that filter context. Here's how.

Again, visualizing the Calendar table in calendar form:

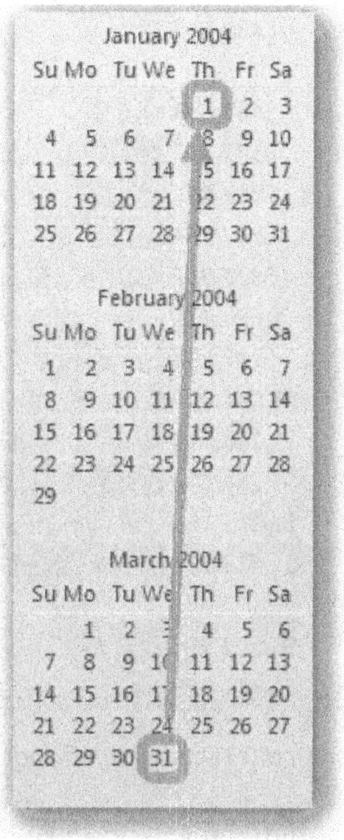

Resulting in a new filter context:

*Figure 222 If we imagine the Calendar table as a calendar rather than a table, where each row in Calendar is a single date, these are the active dates (rows) in the filter context for the measure cell highlighted in the prior figure.*

*Figure 223 DATESYTD() starts at the last date in the existing filter context, and then "expands" the filter context back to the first date of the year (the first date in the year of the current filter context)*

*Figure 224 New filter context highlighted (again visualizing the Calendar table as a calendar)*

## Changing the Year-End Date

That last argument to DATESYTD(), which is an optional argument that we left blank in the first example, allows you to customize your calendar just a little bit. That allows you to treat June 30 as the last day of the year, for instance, which is common in Fiscal Calendars.

Here's a measure that does just that:

```
[Total Sales Fiscal YTD] =
CALCULATE (
    [Total Sales],
    DATESYTD ( Calendar[Date], "6/30/2004" )
)
```

Now let's compare that to the original YTD measure, side by side. We've added Calendar[WeekNumOfYear] to Rows, nested under Month:

| CalendarYear | | Month | Total Sales YTD | Total Sales Fiscal YTD |
|---|---|---|---|---|
| 2001 | 2002 | ⊟ January | | |
| 2003 | 2004 | 1 | $64,297 | $2,788,930 |
| | | 2 | $160,190 | $2,884,823 |
| | | 3 | $266,720 | $2,991,353 |
| | | 4 | $361,655 | $3,086,288 |
| | | 5 | $438,865 | $3,163,498 |
| | | ⊟ February | | |
| | | 5 | $457,003 | $3,181,636 |
| | | 6 | $591,370 | $3,316,003 |
| | | 7 | $711,294 | $3,435,927 |
| | | 8 | $847,144 | $3,571,777 |
| | | 9 | $927,956 | $3,652,588 |
| | | ⊟ March | | |
| | | 9 | $937,992 | $3,662,625 |
| | | 10 | $1,061,270 | $3,785,903 |
| | | 11 | $1,168,840 | $3,893,473 |
| | | 12 | $1,284,089 | $4,008,722 |
| | | 13 | $1,371,790 | $4,096,423 |
| | | 14 | $1,413,530 | $4,138,163 |
| | | ⊟ April | | |
| | | 14 | $1,502,836 | $4,227,469 |
| | | 15 | $1,621,929 | $4,346,562 |

*Figure 225 Original YTD measure starts from 0 in January, but Fiscal YTD version already is approaching $3M.*

Note how we have sliced the pivot to 2003 even though we specified 6/30/2004 in the measure. The year itself does not matter in that last argument – the DATESYTD() function only looks at month and day and ignores the year (in that particular argument.)

Now let's scroll down and see what happens at the end of June:

| ⊟ June | | | |
|---|---|---|---|
| 23 | | $2,603,264 | $5,327,897 |
| 24 | | $2,750,811 | $5,475,444 |
| 25 | | $2,882,988 | $5,607,621 |
| 26 | | $3,004,735 | $5,729,367 |
| 27 | | $3,037,501 | $5,762,134 |
| ⊟ July | | | |
| 27 | | $3,194,171 | $156,670 |
| 28 | | $3,387,544 | $350,043 |
| 29 | | $3,563,304 | $525,802 |
| 30 | | $3,782,105 | $744,604 |
| 31 | | $3,924,170 | $886,669 |
| ⊟ August | | | |
| 31 | | $3,964,160 | $926,658 |
| 32 | | $4,182,052 | $1,144,551 |
| 33 | | $4,336,885 | $1,299,384 |
| 34 | | $4,529,375 | $1,491,874 |

*Figure 226 Fiscal YTD measure resets at the end of June, just as desired*

So the built-in time intelligence functions *are* capable of adapting to different year end dates. This still falls under what we call the Standard Calendar however, because the months are all still the same as the months on the wall calendar – June still has 30 days, July has 31, etc. Only when we start redefining our notions of Month/Quarter/Year to be a different from the wall calendar do we start to "break" functions like DATESYTD(). You will see what we mean when we get to that chapter.

## DATESMTD() and DATESQTD() – "Cousins" of DATESYTD()

These functions are the "month to date" and "quarter to date" versions of DATESYTD(), so we won't walk you through them – their usage is just like what we've illustrated for DATESYTD(). The only difference is that neither of them offer that optional second argument for YearEnd Date.

## TOTALYTD() – Another Cousin of DATESYTD()

TOTALYTD() is actually a replacement for CALCULATE(), one that "bakes in" a DATESYTD().

For example, our original YTD measure:

```
[Total Sales YTD] =
CALCULATE ( [Total Sales], DATESYTD ( Calendar[Date] ) )
```

Can be rewritten as:

```
[Total Sales YTD] =
TOTALYTD ( [Total Sales], Calendar[Date] )
```

We suppose that's a bit more readable – shorter for sure. But we don't see this as particularly necessary, we'd be fine without this function. Whether you choose to use it is really just a matter of personal preference.

# The Remaining (Many) Time Intelligence Functions – Grouped Into "Families"

As we said previously, there are *many* time intelligence functions. But it's pretty easy to group them into "families" (to continue the "cousin" metaphor). If we cover an example from each family, that will give you a foundation – the ability to quickly adopt whatever function you need – without us boring you to death covering every single function.

We've already covered the DATESYTD() family. Let's press forward, and take a tour of each remaining family.

# FIRSTDATE() and LASTDATE()

This is a simple family, and it only contains these two.

### Quite simply, these are the date versions of MIN() and MAX()

Briefly, let's define two measures:

```
[FIRSTDATE Example] =
FIRSTDATE ( Calendar[Date] )
```

And:

```
[LASTDATE Example] =
LASTDATE ( Calendar[Date] )
```

And look at them on our Month/Weeknum pivot:

| CalendarYear | | Month - WeekNumOfYear | FIRSTDATE Example | LASTDATE Example |
|---|---|---|---|---|
| 2001 | 2002 | ⊟ January | 1/1/2003 | 1/31/2003 |
| 2003 | 2004 | 1 | 1/1/2003 | 1/4/2003 |
| | | 2 | 1/5/2003 | 1/11/2003 |
| | | 3 | 1/12/2003 | 1/18/2003 |
| | | 4 | 1/19/2003 | 1/25/2003 |
| | | 5 | 1/26/2003 | 1/31/2003 |
| | | ⊟ February | 2/1/2003 | 2/28/2003 |
| | | 5 | 2/1/2003 | 2/1/2003 |
| | | 6 | 2/2/2003 | 2/8/2003 |
| | | 7 | 2/9/2003 | 2/15/2003 |
| | | 8 | 2/16/2003 | 2/22/2003 |
| | | 9 | 2/23/2003 | 2/28/2003 |
| | | ⊟ March | 3/1/2003 | 3/31/2003 |
| | | 9 | 3/1/2003 | 3/1/2003 |

*Figure 227 FIRSTDATE() and LASTDATE() in action*

In the field list we placed both of these measures on the Calendar table since their "arithmetic" operates on the Calendar itself – they return dates rather than sales data or product counts, etc.

# ENDOFMONTH(), STARTOFYEAR(), etc.

These return single dates, and have special handling for different "size" periods of time.

Again, let's illustrate by example:

| ENDOFMONTH Measure | Column Labels | | | | |
|---|---|---|---|---|---|
| Row Labels | 2001 | 2002 | 2003 | 2004 | Grand Total |
| January | | 1/31/2002 | 1/31/2003 | 1/31/2004 | 1/31/2004 |
| February | | 2/28/2002 | 2/28/2003 | 2/29/2004 | 2/29/2004 |
| March | | 3/31/2002 | 3/31/2003 | 3/31/2004 | 3/31/2004 |
| April | | 4/30/2002 | 4/30/2003 | 4/30/2004 | 4/30/2004 |
| May | | 5/31/2002 | 5/31/2003 | 5/31/2004 | 5/31/2004 |
| June | | 6/30/2002 | 6/30/2003 | 6/30/2004 | 6/30/2004 |
| July | 7/31/2001 | 7/31/2002 | 7/31/2003 | 7/31/2004 | 7/31/2004 |
| August | 8/31/2001 | 8/31/2002 | 8/31/2003 | 8/31/2004 | 8/31/2004 |
| September | 9/30/2001 | 9/30/2002 | 9/30/2003 | | 9/30/2003 |
| October | 10/31/2001 | 10/31/2002 | 10/31/2003 | | 10/31/2003 |
| November | 11/30/2001 | 11/30/2002 | 11/30/2003 | | 11/30/2003 |
| December | 12/31/2001 | 12/31/2002 | 12/31/2003 | | 12/31/2003 |
| Grand Total | 12/31/2001 | 12/31/2002 | 12/31/2003 | 8/31/2004 | 8/31/2004 |

Figure 228 Does about what you expect right?

Now let's swap out Month for Quarter on Rows:

| ENDOFMONTH Measure | Column Labels | | | | |
|---|---|---|---|---|---|
| Quarter | 2001 | 2002 | 2003 | 2004 | Grand Total |
| 1 | | 3/31/2002 | 3/31/2003 | 3/31/2004 | 3/31/2004 |
| 2 | | 6/30/2002 | 6/30/2003 | 6/30/2004 | 6/30/2004 |
| 3 | 9/30/2001 | 9/30/2002 | 9/30/2003 | 8/31/2004 | 8/31/2004 |
| 4 | 12/31/2001 | 12/31/2002 | 12/31/2003 | | 12/31/2003 |
| Grand Total | 12/31/2001 | 12/31/2002 | 12/31/2003 | 8/31/2004 | 8/31/2004 |

Figure 229 9/30/2001 is the last date in the last month of Q3 2001

Make sense? If you feed more than a single month to ENDOFMONTH(), it will find the last date in the last month.

**But when you feed it a filter context of "size" *less* than a month**, we get something different:

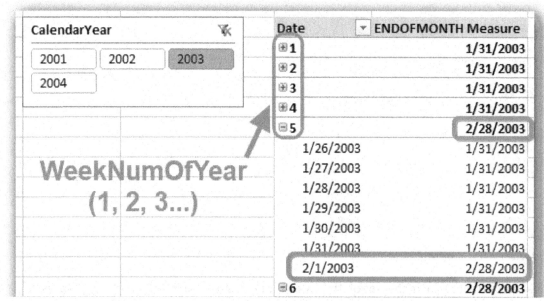

Figure 230 ENDOFMONTH() returns the last day of the month even if that day is NOT part of the current filter context.

The rest of this family behaves in much the same way.

# CLOSINGBALANCEMONTH(), CLOSINGBALANCEYEAR(), ETC.

These functions are CALCULATE() replacements that have "hardwired" date logic equivalent to ENDOFMONTH(), STARTOFYEAR(), etc.

 CLOSINGBALANCEMONTH(<measure expression>,<Date Column>,<optional filter>)

Example measure:

```
[Total Sales CLOSINGBALANCEMONTH] =
CLOSINGBALANCEMONTH ( [Total Sales], Calendar[Date] )
```

| CalendarYear | | Row Labels ⍋ | Total Sales | Total Sales CLOSINGBALANCEMONTH |
|---|---|---|---|---|
| 2001 | 2002 | ⊟ January | $97,267 | $17,469 |
| 2003 | 2004 | 1/24/2003 | $13,759 | $17,469 |
| | | 1/25/2003 | $6,298 | $17,469 |
| | | 1/26/2003 | $20,301 | $17,469 |
| | | 1/27/2003 | $5,275 | $17,469 |
| | | 1/28/2003 | $11,451 | $17,469 |
| | | 1/29/2003 | $13,474 | $17,469 |
| | | 1/30/2003 | $9,240 | $17,469 |
| | | 1/31/2003 | $17,469 | $17,469 |
| | | ⊟ February | $489,090 | $12,772 |
| | | 2/1/2003 | $18,138 | $12,772 |
| | | 2/2/2003 | $19,624 | $12,772 |
| | | 2/3/2003 | $11,302 | $12,772 |

*Figure 231 CLOSINGBALANCEMONTH() always returns the value of its base measure on the last day of the month in the current filter context (We have used a Sales measure here to demonstrate, but in reality, these functions are more useful with things like Inventory or Cash Balance.)*

# DATEADD()

This function is also used as a <filter> argument to CALCULATE(), and shifts your date filter context forward or backward in time.

 DATEADD(<Date Column>, <number of intervals>, <interval type>)

- <Date Column> - the usual. Put your date column from your calendar table here.
- <Number of Intervals> - Set this to 1 to move one interval later in time, -1 to move back one, etc.
- <Interval Type> - Set this to Year, Quarter, Month, or Day – no quotes

Example measure that shows us last year's [Total Sales]:

```
[Total Sales DATEADD 1 Year Back] =
CALCULATE (
    [Total Sales],
    DATEADD ( Calendar[Date], -1, YEAR )
)
```

Here are its results for 2003 side-by-side with a pivot showing the original [Total Sales] measure for 2002:

| CalendarYear 2003 | | CalendarYear 2002 | |
|---|---|---|---|
| Month | Total Sales DATEADD 1 Year Back | Month | Total Sales |
| January | $596,747 | January | $596,747 |
| February | $550,817 | February | $550,817 |
| March | $644,135 | March | $644,135 |
| April | $663,692 | April | $663,692 |
| May | $673,556 | May | $673,556 |
| June | $676,764 | June | $676,764 |
| July | $500,365 | July | $500,365 |
| August | $546,001 | August | $546,001 |
| September | $350,467 | September | $350,467 |
| October | $415,390 | October | $415,390 |
| November | $335,095 | November | $335,095 |
| December | $577,314 | December | $577,314 |
| Grand Total | $6,530,344 | Grand Total | $6,530,344 |

Figure 232 DATEADD() version filtered to 2003 matches the original measure filtered to 2002

And now the same comparison, but with Quarter on Rows instead:

| CalendarYear 2003 | | CalendarYear 2002 | |
|---|---|---|---|
| Quarter | Total Sales DATEADD 1 Year Back | Quarter | Total Sales |
| 1 | $1,791,698 | 1 | $1,791,698 |
| 2 | $2,014,012 | 2 | $2,014,012 |
| 3 | $1,396,834 | 3 | $1,396,834 |
| 4 | $1,327,799 | 4 | $1,327,799 |
| Grand Total | $6,530,344 | Grand Total | $6,530,344 |

Figure 233 Same comparison, just with Quarter on Rows rather than Month. Again, perfect match.

# Growth Versus Last Year (Year-Over-Year, YOY, etc.)

One obvious application of DATEADD() and similar functions is the calculation of growth versus the prior year.

```
[Pct Sales Growth YOY] =
   ( [Total Sales] – [Total Sales DATEADD 1 Year Back] )
      / [Total Sales DATEADD 1 Year Back]
```

| CalendarYear 2003 | | | CalendarYear 2002 | |
|---|---|---|---|---|
| Month | Pct Sales Growth YOY | Total Sales | Month | Total Sales |
| January | -26.5 % | $438,865 | January | $596,747 |
| February | -11.2 % | $489,090 | February | $550,817 |
| March | -24.6 % | $485,575 | March | $644,135 |
| April | -23.7 % | $506,399 | April | $663,692 |
| May | -16.4 % | $562,773 | May | $673,556 |
| June | -18.0 % | $554,799 | June | $676,764 |
| July | 77.2 % | $886,669 | July | $500,365 |
| August | 55.2 % | $847,414 | August | $546,001 |
| September | 188.3 % | $1,010,258 | September | $350,467 |
| October | 160.1 % | $1,080,450 | October | $415,390 |
| November | 257.2 % | $1,196,981 | November | $335,095 |
| December | 200.0 % | $1,731,788 | December | $577,314 |
| Grand Total | 49.9 % | $9,791,060 | Grand Total | $6,530,344 |

Figure 234 [Pct Growth YOY] displayed for 2003 and compared to 2002 in the second pivot

# Quirks and Caveats

There are a few things you will discover about DATEADD() that might make you scratch your head a bit, so We'll give some advanced notice.

## You Must Have Contiguous Date Ranges on Your Pivot

If we filter a Quarter out of our pivot we will get an error:

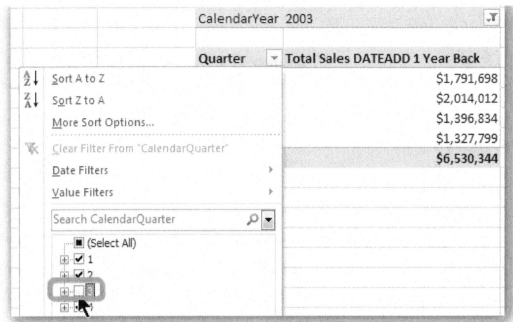

*Figure 235 Filtering Quarter 3 out of the pivot...*

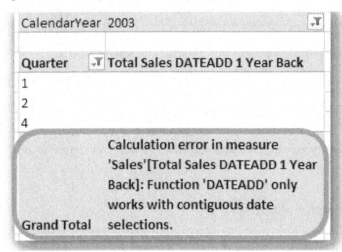

*Figure 236 ...yields an error with DATEADD()*

The same thing would happen if we were using Month on rows and filtered out one or more months.

> Note that the error occurs in the Grand Total cell. There is *nothing* wrong with each of the single-Quarter measure cell calculations, but when the Grand Total fails, the entire pivot fails. The filter context of the Grand Total cell is Quarter={1,2,4} and Year={2003}, and when DATEADD() goes back a year, that "skips" Quarter 3 of 2002, which DATEADD() cannot do.

> Merely hiding the Grand Total (using the pivot Design tab on the ribbon) will *not* fix this problem. The only way to fix this is to prevent the Grand Total from even being calculated in the first place, which we will explain in the chapter on IF().

# DATEADD() Has Special Handling for "Complete" Months/Quarters/Years

**This one and the next one are really subtle. If you struggle to understand, don't worry about it** – just remember that there's something special going on here, so that if/when you discover this on your own, you can come back here and re-read this section.

2004 is a leap year, in which February contains 29 days. Let's add a simple measure to the Calendar table that shows this:

```
[Number of Days] =
COUNTROWS ( Calendar )
```

Figure 237 29 days in Feb 2004

And now we will add the DATEADD() measure we created before, [Total Sales DATEADD 1 Year Back]:

| Year | 2004 | |
|------|------|--|

| Month | Number of Days | Total Sales DATEADD 1 Year Back |
|-------|----------------|----------------------------------|
| January | 31 | $438,865 |
| February | 29 | $489,090 |
| March | 31 | $485,575 |
| April | 30 | $506,399 |
| May | 31 | $562,773 |
| June | 30 | $554,799 |
| July | 31 | $886,669 |
| August | 31 | $847,414 |
| **Grand Total** | **244** | **$4,771,584** |

Figure 238 Question: does $489,090 represent 28 days of 2003 sales, or 29 days?

Let's compare that to a 2003 pivot for the "raw" [Total Sales] measure:

| lendarYear | 2004 | | | CalendarYear | 2003 | |
|------------|------|--|--|--------------|------|--|

| onth | Number of Days | Total Sales DATEADD 1 Year Back | Month | Total Sales | Number of Days |
|------|----------------|----------------------------------|-------|-------------|----------------|
| nuary | 31 | $438,865 | January | $438,865 | 31 |
| bruary | 29 | $489,090 | February | $489,090 | 28 |
| arch | 31 | $485,575 | March | $485,575 | 31 |
| pril | 30 | $506,399 | April | $506,399 | 30 |
| ay | 31 | $562,773 | May | $562,773 | 31 |

Figure 239 DATEADD() is returning 28 days' worth of Feb 2003 sales even though it starts out with a 29-day filter context in 2004!

# DATEADD() Lacks Intelligence for Weeks

| CalendarYear | 2004 | | | CalendarYear | 2003 | |
|--------------|------|--|--|--------------|------|--|

| WeekNum | Total Sales DATEADD 1 Year Back | WeekNum | Total Sales |
|---------|----------------------------------|---------|-------------|
| 1 | $45,668 | 1 | $64,297 |
| 2 | $100,546 | 2 | $95,893 |
| 3 | $107,535 | 3 | $106,530 |
| 4 | $101,609 | 4 | $94,935 |
| 5 | $83,508 | 5 | $95,348 |
| 6 | $135,289 | 6 | $134,367 |
| 7 | $118,548 | 7 | $119,924 |
| 8 | $132,961 | 8 | $135,850 |

Figure 240 With WeekNum on Rows, the DATEADD() measure does NOT match!

To see why the numbers don't match, we need to add Date to Rows as well:

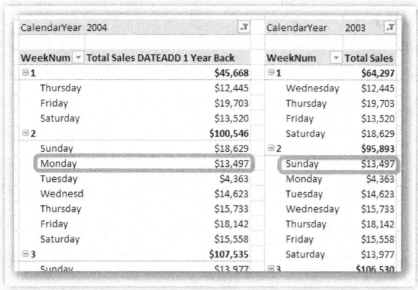

Figure 241 *Both pivots report Sunday through Monday, but the DATEADD() measure is returning 2003's Sunday sales in the context of 2004 Monday*

Stated another way, the weeks are misaligned by one day:

| CalendarYear 2004 | | CalendarYear | 2003 | |
|---|---|---|---|---|
| **WeekNum** ▼ | **Total Sales DATEADD 1 Year Back** | **WeekNum** ▼ | **Total Sales** | |
| ⊟1 | $45,668 | ⊟1 | $64,297 | |
| Thursday | $12,445 | Wednesday | $12,445 | |
| Friday | $19,703 | Thursday | $19,703 | |
| Saturday | $13,520 | Friday | $13,520 | |
| ⊟2 | $100,546 | Saturday | $18,629 | |
| Sunday | $18,629 | ⊟2 | $95,893 | |
| Monday | $13,497 | Sunday | $13,497 | |
| Tuesday | $4,363 | Monday | $4,363 | |
| Wednesd | $14,623 | Tuesday | $14,623 | |
| Thursday | $15,733 | Wednesday | $15,733 | |
| Friday | $18,142 | Thursday | $18,142 | |
| Saturday | $15,558 | Friday | $15,558 | |
| ⊟3 | $107,535 | Saturday | $13,977 | |
| Sunday | $13,977 | ⊟3 | $106,530 | |
| Monday | $13,255 | Sunday | $13,255 | |

Figure 242 **Why doesn't this work, if it works for Month and Quarter?** *Well for starters, 52 weeks in a year times 7 days per week = 364. So we are never going to get weeks quite right unless we change years to be 364 days long instead of 365 (which some custom calendars actually do).*

So the concept of "week" is defined only in our Calendar table, in the WeekNumOfYear column. Look at the pivots above – Week 1 of 2004 has only 3 days in it! And Week 1 of 2003 has only 4!

That's purely the "fault" of our Calendar table:

| D... ⌐ ▼ | DayNameOfWeek ▼ | WeekNumberOfYear ↕ | CalendarYear ⏷ |
|---|---|---|---|
| 1/1/2004 | Thursday | 1 | 2004 |
| 1/2/2004 | Friday | 1 | 2004 |
| 1/3/2004 | Saturday | 1 | 2004 |

Figure 243 *Our Calendar table DOES only have 3 days in it for Week 1 of 2004*

Whereas the time intelligence functions can intrinsically "know" what we mean by Month/Quarter/Year, they rely on the calendar table for all other concepts, so there isn't any "magic fixup" when we navigate using DATEADD() in a filter context involving weeks.

# SAMEPERIODLASTYEAR()

 SAMEPERIODLASTYEAR(<Date Column>)

This is a shortcut function that is just a wrapper to DATEADD(). It is 100% equivalent to DATEADD() with "-1, Year" as the last two arguments:

```
SAMEPERIODLASTYEAR ( Calendar[Date] )
```

Is exactly the same as:

```
DATEADD ( Calendar[Date], -1, YEAR )
```

# PARALLELPERIOD(), NEXTMONTH(), PREVIOUSYEAR(), etc.

## PARALLELPERIOD()

This one is *almost* a wrapper to DATEADD(), but it differs in one crucial way that is best shown by example.

 PARALLELPERIOD(<Date Column>, <number of intervals>, <interval type>)

Let's create an example measure:

```
[Total Sales PARALLELPERIOD Back 1 Year] =
CALCULATE (
    [Total Sales],
    PARALLELPERIOD ( Calendar[Date], -1, YEAR )
)
```

| CalendarYear | 2003 | | | CalendarYear | 2002 | |
|---|---|---|---|---|---|---|
| **Row Labels** | **Total Sales PARALLELPERIOD Back 1 Year** | | | **Month** | **Total Sales** | |
| January | $6,530,344 | | | January | $596,747 | |
| February | $6,530,344 | | | February | $550,817 | |
| March | $6,530,344 | | | March | $644,135 | |
| April | $6,530,344 | | | April | $663,692 | |
| May | $6,530,344 | | | May | $673,556 | |
| June | $6,530,344 | | | June | $676,764 | |
| July | $6,530,344 | | | July | $500,365 | |
| August | $6,530,344 | | | August | $546,001 | |
| September | $6,530,344 | | | September | $350,467 | |
| October | $6,530,344 | | | October | $415,390 | |
| November | $6,530,344 | | | November | $335,095 | |
| December | $6,530,344 | | | December | $577,314 | |
| **Grand Total** | **$6,530,344** | | | **Grand Total** | **$6,530,344** | |

*Figure 244 PARALLELPERIOD() always fetches the full year when you go back 1 year, no matter what "size" your filter context is (Month in this case).*

So PARALLELPERIOD() *navigates* just like DATEADD(), but when it gets to its "destination," it expands the filter context to the size of the specified <interval type> - Year, Quarter, or Month.

 Reminder: you don't have to remember all of the details of all of these functions. (We sure don't!) You just need to know that they exist, then be able to find the one that serves your current purpose, and quickly re-familiarize yourself as needed.

## NEXTMONTH(), PREVIOUSYEAR(), etc.

These functions are all just wrappers to PARALLELPERIOD() – they navigate and expand in exactly the same way.

```
[Total Sales NEXTMONTH] =
CALCULATE ( [Total Sales], NEXTMONTH ( Calendar[Date] ) )
```

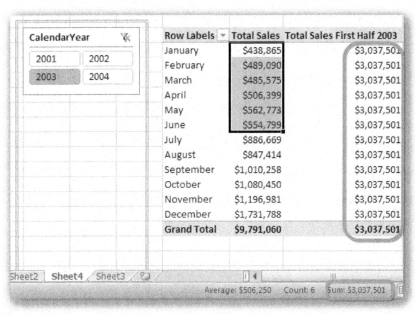

Figure 245 NEXTMONTH() always grabs the FULL next month, even if we start in the context of a single day.

# DATESBETWEEN()

Ah, we have a special place in our hearts for DATESBETWEEN(). Sometimes, you don't want anything special – you just want total control over the date range in a measure. And DATESBETWEEN() delivers just that.

 DATESBETWEEN(<date column>, <start date expr>, <end date expr>)

Let's start with a very simple example:

| Row Labels | Total Sales | Total Sales First Half 2003 |
|---|---|---|
| January | $438,865 | $3,037,501 |
| February | $489,090 | $3,037,501 |
| March | $485,575 | $3,037,501 |
| April | $506,399 | $3,037,501 |
| May | $562,773 | $3,037,501 |
| June | $554,799 | $3,037,501 |
| July | $886,669 | $3,037,501 |
| August | $847,414 | $3,037,501 |
| September | $1,010,258 | $3,037,501 |
| October | $1,080,450 | $3,037,501 |
| November | $1,196,981 | $3,037,501 |
| December | $1,731,788 | $3,037,501 |
| Grand Total | $9,791,060 | $3,037,501 |

CalendarYear: 2001, 2002, 2003, 2004

Sheet2 / Sheet4 / Sheet3

Average: $506,250    Count: 6    Sum: $3,037,501

Figure 246 Note how DATESBETWEEN() completely overrides existing filter context on the Calendar table, otherwise it would be blank for July-December (and for January-June would match [Total Sales] for each month)

## "Life to Date" Calculations

Earlier, we used DATESYTD() to calculate "year to date" sales, but what if you want a running total that does not reset at the start of each year, but instead just keeps piling up year after year?

Fortunately, DATESBETWEEN() lets us use expressions for the endpoint arguments:

```
[Total Sales Life to Date] =
CALCULATE (
    [Total Sales],
    DATESBETWEEN (
        Calendar[Date],
        "1/1/1900", LASTDATE ( Calendar[Date] )
    )
)
```

*Figure 247 "Life to Date" using DATESBETWEEN() matches grand total across 2001-2003, as expected*

*Figure 248 Expanding to Month level, "Life to Date" measure still returns expected results*

## Removing That Hardwired 1/1/1900

Yeah, that's ugly. Let's replace it with FIRSTDATE(ALL(Calendar[Date])):

```
[Total Sales Life to Date] =
CALCULATE (
    [Total Sales],
    DATESBETWEEN (
        Calendar[Date],
        FIRSTDATE ( ALL ( Calendar[Date] ) ),
        LASTDATE ( Calendar[Date] )
    )
)
```

**Why ALL(Calendar[Date])?** Because otherwise we'd just get the first date in the filter context, (which would be January 1, 2003 in the $10,235,582 cell highlighted in the pivot above). We need to apply ALL() in order to clear the current filter context and literally find the first date in the entire Calendar table.

> Note that we do *not* want ALL() on the LASTDATE() in the <end date> argument of DATESBETWEEN() in this case, otherwise it would always return sales for all time, and not sales up until the current filter context date.

## DATESBETWEEN() is Fantastic with Disconnected Tables Too!

You remember the Min/Max Threshold version of disconnected tables? You can do the same thing with dates, using a disconnected DateRange table, your normal Calendar table, and DATESBETWEEN().

We won't belabor that here, since it's a repetition of a familiar pattern, but for a detailed example, see
http://ppvt.pro/ABCampaign

# 15 - IF(), SWITCH(), BLANK(), and Other Conditional Fun

## Using IF() in Measures

It is time to introduce conditional/branching logic into our formulas. This starts out as simple as you would expect.

Consider our [Pct Sales Growth YOY] measure from last chapter:

```
[Pct Sales Growth YOY] =
  ( [Total Sales] - [Total Sales DATEADD 1 Year Back] )
     / [Total Sales DATEADD 1 Year Back]
```

We get an error because [Total Sales DATEADD 1 Year Back] is 0 for 2001 – there were no sales in 2000, so this is really a "div by 0" error.

 Technically speaking, [Total Sales DATEADD 1 Year Back] is *not* returning 0 for 2001, it is returning blank – when there are no rows in the source tables corresponding to the filter context, measures return blank. But when we divide by blank, that's the same as dividing by zero in terms of causing an error.

| Row Labels ▾ | Pct Sales Growth YOY |
|---|---|
| 2001 | #NUM! |
| 2002 | 99.9 % |
| 2003 | 49.9 % |
| 2004 | 104.8 % |
| Grand Total | 101.5 % |

*Figure 249 We get a #NUM error for 2001*

This is an easy fix – we just edit the formula, and wrap our original formula in an IF(): And the results:

| Row Labels ▾ | Pct Sales Growth YOY |
|---|---|
| 2001 | 0.0 % |
| 2002 | 99.9 % |
| 2003 | 49.9 % |
| 2004 | 104.8 % |
| Grand Total | 101.5 % |

*Figure 250 Now returns 0% instead of an error*

## The BLANK() Function

We can do better than 0% though can't we? 0% implies that we had 0 growth, when in reality, this calculation makes no sense at all for 2001. So rather than return 0, we can return the BLANK() function.

Let's edit the formula accordingly:

```
[Pct Sales Growth YOY] =
IF (
    [Total Sales DATEADD 1 Year Back] = 0,
    BLANK (),
    ( [Total Sales] - [Total Sales DATEADD 1 Year Back] )
        / [Total Sales DATEADD 1 Year Back]
)
```

And the results:

| Row Labels ▾ | Pct Sales Growth YOY |
|---|---|
| 2002 | 99.9 % |
| 2003 | 49.9 % |
| 2004 | 104.8 % |
| Grand Total | 101.5 % |

*Figure 251 Aha! Now 2001 is gone completely, nice!*

**Why does 2001 disappear from the pivot completely?** Because all displayed measures return BLANK() for 2001.

 This is a VERY helpful trick. Retuning BLANK() in certain situations will become one of your most relied-upon techniques.

If we add a measure that is not BLANK() for 2001, 2001 is displayed once again:

| Row Labels ▼ | Pct Sales Growth YOY | Total Sales |
|---|---|---|
| 2001 | | $3,266,374 |
| 2002 | 99.9 % | $6,530,344 |
| 2003 | 49.9 % | $9,791,060 |
| 2004 | 104.8 % | $9,770,900 |
| **Grand Total** | **101.5 %** | **$29,358,677** |

*Figure 252 2001 is displayed as long as any single measure returns a non-blank result*

**You can force 2001 to display, however, even if all measures are blank.** Under Pivot Options, on the Pivot Options tab, are the following two checkboxes:

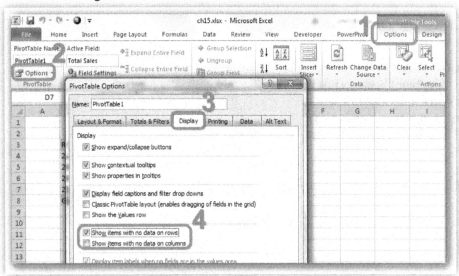

*Figure 253 Check that first checkbox...*

| Row Labels ▼ | Pct Sales Growth YOY |
|---|---|
| 2001 | |
| 2002 | 99.9 % |
| 2003 | 49.9 % |
| 2004 | 104.8 % |
| **Grand Total** | **101.5 %** |

*Figure 254 ...and 2001 will be displayed even when all measures are blank.*

# DIVIDE() Function

The DIVIDE() function was introduced in an update to Power Pivot v2 and has been our favorite since. Here is the function description:

DIVIDE(<numerator>, <denominator> [,<alternateresult>])
Safe Divide function with ability to handle divide by zero case
<alternateresult> is an optional argument and defaults to BLANK, which is good in most cases.

Here is how you can rewrite the measure we've been working on using DIVIDE.

```
[Pct Sales Growth YOY using DIVIDE] =
DIVIDE (
    [Total Sales] - [Total Sales DATEADD 1 Year Back],
    [Total Sales DATEADD 1 Year Back]
)
```

Elegant, right? And generates the same results.

| Row Labels ▼ | Pct Sales Growth YOY | Pct Sales Growth YOY using DIVIDE |
|---|---|---|
| 2001 | | |
| 2002 | 99.9 % | 99.9 % |
| 2003 | 49.9 % | 49.9 % |
| 2004 | 104.8 % | 104.8 % |
| **Grand Total** | **101.5 %** | **101.5 %** |

*Figure 255 DIVIDE() Function gets us the same result, but in an elegant formula*

The DIVIDE() version isn't just aesthetically pleasing, but even offers better performance than the earlier version of our measure. We now use it pretty much by default whenever division is required.

Keep in mind that the if..then..else pattern we developed prior to DIVIDE, is still valuable. And would come in handy in many scenarios, not just division by zero.

 **IF(<test>, <DAX expression>, BLANK())** is a valuable pattern you will find useful in many scenarios

# The ISBLANK() Function

Excel has this function too, of course, but it's worth bringing up here. When we test for "=0" as we did in the formulas above, and the measure returns BLANK(), the IF() evaluate to True.

We could have tested for ISBLANK() instead of "=0", but that would still leave us exposed to an error in the case where [Total Sales DATEADD 1 Year Back] returned a legitimate 0 (meaning, there were rows, but the sum of the SalesAmt column was 0 – rare but possible).

So most of the time, we just test for "=0." But when you want to distinguish between 0 and BLANK(), ISBLANK() is what you need.

# HASONEVALUE()

Another new function in Power Pivot V2. Primarily you can think of this as the "am I in a subtotal or grand total cell?" function, although it definitely comes in handy elsewhere too.

To demonstrate, first let us create the following measure:

```
[Subcategory pct of Category Sales] =
[Total Sales] /
CALCULATE ( [Total Sales],
ALL ( Products[SubCategory] ) )
```

And here it is with along with [Total Sales], and Category/Subcategory on Rows:

Those 100.0% subtotals and grand total are useless though. We'd love to suppress them.

To do this, we are going to detect when our filter context contains more than one Subcategory, because having more than one Subcategory is the definition of a subtotal/grand total cell for that field, as explained in the chapter on ALL().

| Row Labels ▼ | Total Sales | Subcat pct of Cat Sales |
|---|---|---|
| ⊟ **Accessories** | **$700,760** | **100.00 %** |
| Bike Racks | $39,360 | 5.62 % |
| Tires and Tubes | $245,529 | 35.04 % |
| ⊟ **Bikes** | **$28,318,145** | **100.00 %** |
| Mountain Bikes | $9,952,760 | 35.15 % |
| Road Bikes | $14,520,584 | 51.28 % |
| Touring Bikes | $3,844,801 | 13.58 % |
| ⊟ **Clothing** | **$339,773** | **100.00 %** |
| Caps | $19,688 | 5.79 % |
| Gloves | $35,021 | 10.31 % |
| Jerseys | $172,951 | 50.90 % |
| Shorts | $71,320 | 20.99 % |
| Socks | $5,106 | 1.50 % |
| Vests | $35,687 | 10.50 % |
| **Grand Total** | **$29,358,677** | **100.00 %** |

*Figure 256 Each Subcategory is calculated as a percentage of its parent Category, in terms of [Total Sales]*

So we edit our original measure to detect that condition, using the HASONEVALUE() function:

```
[Subcategory pct of Category Sales] =
IF (
    HASONEVALUE ( Products[SubCategory] ),
    [Total Sales] /
    CALCULATE ( [Total Sales],
            ALL ( Products[SubCategory] )
    ),
    BLANK ()
)
```

HASONEVALUE() is equivalent to IF(COUNTROWS(VALUES())=1 – we used to have to use this latter approach, but now in Power Pivot v2, HASONEVALUE() is much better.

Results:

| Row Labels | Total Sales | Subcat pct of Cat Sales |
|---|---|---|
| ⊟ Accessories | $700,760 | |
| Bike Racks | $39,360 | 5.62 % |
| Bike Stands | $39,591 | 5.65 % |
| Bottles and Cages | $56,798 | 8.11 % |
| Cleaners | $7,219 | 1.03 % |
| Fenders | $46,620 | 6.65 % |
| Helmets | $225,336 | 32.16 % |
| Hydration Packs | $40,308 | 5.75 % |
| Tires and Tubes | $245,529 | 35.04 % |
| ⊟ Bikes | $28,318,145 | |
| Mountain Bikes | $9,952,760 | 35.15 % |
| Road Bikes | $14,520,584 | 51.28 % |
| Touring Bikes | $3,844,801 | 13.58 % |
| ⊟ Clothing | $339,773 | |
| Caps | $19,688 | 5.79 % |
| Gloves | $35,021 | 10.31 % |
| Jerseys | $172,951 | 50.90 % |
| Shorts | $71,320 | 20.99 % |
| Socks | $5,106 | 1.50 % |
| Vests | $35,687 | 10.50 % |
| Grand Total | $29,358,677 | |

Figure 257 Subtotals and grand totals suppressed for just this measure, still "on" for [Total Sales]

 We could turn off Subtotals and/or Grand Totals via the Pivot Design tab on the ribbon, but that would turn off totals for [Total Sales] as well. We want to do this *just* for [Subcat pct of Cat Sales].

# IF() Based on Row/Column/Filter/Slicer Fields

Our first use of IF() in this chapter tested against the value of a measure. But what if we want to test where we "are" in the pivot in terms of filter context?

**For example, what if we want to calculate something a little differently for a specific country?**

We've added a new lookup table to our model, one named SalesTerritory. It contains a Country column, which we are displaying on Rows, along with our [Sales to Parents] measure:

| Country | Sales to Parents |
|---|---|
| Australia | $2,486,889 |
| Canada | $762,530 |
| France | $1,400,775 |
| Germany | $1,460,348 |
| United Kingdom | $1,666,415 |
| United States | $3,655,420 |

Figure 258 We don't trust that number for Canada...

All right, let's invent a problem. Pretend for a moment that we cannot trust the [NumberOfChildren] column in our Customers table for Canadian customers – something about the way we collect data in Canada makes that number not trustworthy. And that column is the basis for our [Sales to Parents] measure.

So for Canada, and Canada only, we want to substitute a different measure, [Sales to Married Couples], for that measure. (And of course, everyone in our organization is "on board" with this change – We're not deliberately misleading anyone!)

So, how do we detect when Country=Canada? We'll give you the measure formula first and then explain it.

```
[Sales to Parents Adj for Canada] =
IF (
    HASONEVALUE ( SalesTerritory[Country] ),
    IF (
        VALUES ( SalesTerritory[Country] ) = "Canada",
        [Sales to Married Couples],
        [Sales to Parents]
    ),
    BLANK ()
)
```

## The VALUES() Function

First, let's explain what this VALUES() function is all about. Quite simply, it returns the filter context as specified by the pivot. So sometimes it returns a single value for a column, and other times it returns multiple values (if you are in a total cell).

Examples:

| Country | ▼ | Sales to Parents |
|---|---|---|
| Australia | | $2,486,889 |
| Canada | | $762,530 |
| France | | $1,400,775 |
| Germany | | $1,460,348 |
| United Kingdom | | $1,666,415 |
| United States | | $3,655,420 |
| **Grand Total** | | **$11,432,377** |

Figure 259 For the highlighted measure cell, VALUES(SalesTerritory[Country]) returns "Canada"

| Country | ▼ | Sales to Parents |
|---|---|---|
| Australia | | $2,486,889 |
| Canada | | $762,530 |
| France | | $1,400,775 |
| Germany | | $1,460,348 |
| United Kingdom | | $1,666,415 |
| United States | | $3,655,420 |
| **Grand Total** | | **$11,432,377** |

Figure 260 In this case though, it returns multiple values: {"Australia"," Canada", "France"… , "United States"}

OK, now let's work from the inside out and explain the formula.

1. **IF(VALUES(SalesTerritory[Country])="Canada"** – we cannot directly test IF(SalesTerritory[Country]) – that violates the "no naked columns" rule of measures. And since Country is a text string, we need to use something other than MIN, MAX, etc., so we use VALUES().

2. **IF(HASONEVALUE(SalesTerritory[Country])** – If we perform an IF(VALUES()) ="Canada" test in a case where there is more than one value, we will get an error. So we need to "protect" our IF(VALUES()) test with the IF(HASONEVALUE()) test, and only let the IF(VALUES()) test "run" in cases where there is only one value.

OK, let's see the measure in action:

| Country | ▼ | Sales to Parents | Sales to Parents Adj for Canada |
|---|---|---|---|
| Australia | | $2,486,889 | $2,486,889 |
| Canada | | $762,530 | $1,078,215 |
| France | | $1,400,775 | $1,400,775 |
| Germany | | $1,460,348 | $1,460,348 |
| United Kingdom | | $1,666,415 | $1,666,415 |
| United States | | $3,655,420 | $3,655,420 |

Figure 261 Our special measure differs only for Canada, as desired.

# Using VALUES() for Columns That Are Not on the Pivot

You are *not* restricted to using VALUES() with columns that are on the pivot. In fact it is often quite useful to use VALUES() with a column that is *not* used.

For instance, let's look at this pivot that has two fields from the Products table on Rows (Category and Color), and the simple [Product Count] measure:

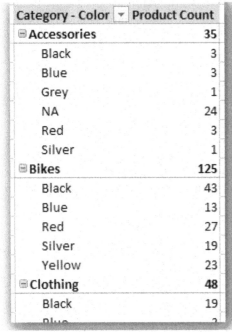

Now let's focus on a single cell:

Figure 263 For the highlighted measure cell, what does VALUES(Products[Color]) return?

Figure 262 Simple Products pivot

In this case, VALUES(Products[Color]) returns {"Black", "Blue", "Red", "Silver", "Yellow"}.

> Note how "Grey" and "NA" are *not* returned for this "Bikes" measure cell, but those two colors *are* returned for Accessories. This is because Category and Color (the fields on Rows) are both columns from the Products table, which means that a Category filter has an impact on what is valid for Color. Category="Bikes" filters the Products table, and there are no Bikes of Color "Grey" or "NA".
>
> The same sort of thing would be true if Color came from Products and Category came from a related table, one that had a Lookup Table role with respect to Products (since Lookup tables filter their partner Data tables).

Now, if we remove Color from the pivot, what does VALUES(Products[Color]) return?

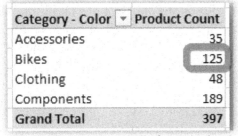

Figure 264 Same pivot cell after Color has been removed – what does VALUES(Products[Color]) return?

It returns exactly the same list as before: {"Black", "Blue", "Red", "Silver", "Yellow"}.

Whether Color was on the pivot or not, the cell we had highlighted did *not* have any direct filters applied for Color. The only Color filters were those implied by the Category filter context, which is still there.

> So if we had Calendar[Year] on the pivot in place of Products[Category], VALUES(Products[Color]) would return all colors, since Calendar and Products have no relationship between them.

## VALUES() Only Returns Unique Values

We had the [Product Count] measure on the pivot for a reason:

*Figure 265 There are 35 Products in the Accessories Category, which is 35 rows of the Products table, but only 6 different values for Color.*

So even though the filter context has 35 rows of the Products table "active" for the highlighted cell, COUNTROWS(VALUES(Products[Color])) would return 6.

To drive that home, let's do exactly that:

```
[Color Values] =
    COUNTROWS(VALUES(Products[Color]))
```

| Category - Color ⌄ | Product Count | Color Values |
| --- | --- | --- |
| ⊟ Accessories | 35 | 6 |
| Black | 3 | 1 |
| Blue | 3 | 1 |
| Grey | 1 | 1 |
| NA | 24 | 1 |
| Red | 3 | 1 |
| Silver | 1 | 1 |

*Figure 266 Proof that VALUES() only returns the unique values*

# SWITCH()

What if we want to do something different for multiple different countries though, and not just Canada? Nested IF()'s are one way of course, but the new function SWITCH() is *much* cleaner.

We will define a Calculated Column to see SWITCH in action but it can be used in measures in the same manner.

Here's an example where we are determining Continent based on the Country name in our Territory table:

```
=SWITCH([Country]
    , "United States", "North America"
    , "Canada", "North America"
    , "France", "Europe"
    , "Germany", "Europe"
    , "United Kingdom", "Europe"
    , "Rest of the World"
)
```

Let us show you the results and then come back to explain it:

| SalesTerritoryKey | Country | Continent |
|---|---|---|
| 1 | United States | North America |
| 2 | United States | North America |
| 3 | United States | North America |
| 4 | United States | North America |
| 5 | United States | North America |
| 6 | Canada | North America |
| 7 | France | Europe |
| 8 | Germany | Europe |
| 9 | Australia | Rest of the World |
| 10 | United Kingdom | Europe |
| 11 | NA | Rest of the World |

*Figure 267 Results of SWITCH() function*

Here's how SWITCH() works:

1. **Starting with the second argument, SWITCH()'s arguments operate in pairs** – if it matches "United States" it returns "North America, if it matches "France" it returns "Europe"
2. **If you end SWITCH() with an "odd" argument, that is treated as the "ELSE"** – the "Rest of the World" is by itself, not paired with another argument. So if the current value doesn't match any of the prior tests, "Rest of the World" will be returned.

## SWITCH TRUE()

SWITCH() can be even more versatile when TRUE() is passed as the first argument. Then it lets you specify a condition to match on, instead of an exact value.

For example, let's add another Calculated Column in the Products table to indicate the ListPrice range:

```
=SWITCH( TRUE()
    , [ListPrice] < 100, "$"
    , [ListPrice] < 500, "$$"
    , [ListPrice] < 1000, "$$$"
    , "$$$$"
)
```

And the results are:

| ProductKey | ProductName | ListPrice | ListPriceBucket |
|---|---|---|---|
| 463 | Half-Finger Glov... | $24.5 | $ |
| 465 | Half-Finger Glov... | $24.5 | $ |
| 467 | Half-Finger Glov... | $24.5 | $ |
| 391 | LL Fork | $148.2 | $$ |
| 412 | HL Mountain Fro... | $300.2 | $$ |
| 587 | Mountain-400-W... | $769.5 | $$$ |
| 588 | Mountain-400-W... | $769.5 | $$$ |
| 589 | Mountain-400-W... | $769.5 | $$$ |
| 590 | Mountain-400-W... | $769.5 | $$$ |
| 290 | HL Mountain Fra... | $1,364.5 | $$$$ |
| 291 | HL Mountain Fra... | $1,364.5 | $$$$ |

*Figure 268 SWITCH with TRUE() is even more versatile*

Here's how SWITCH() is working here:

1. Starting with the second argument, SWITCH()'s arguments operate in pairs, as before. However, here instead of matching a specific value, they are evaluating the condition; if true then that paired value is selected. E.g. if [List Price] < 100 is true, then "$" is returned

2. If you end SWITCH() with an "odd" argument, that is treated as the "ELSE", as before. In this case "$$$$" is by itself and is returned if none of the conditions match

3. **The order of conditions is important, since the first match would yield a result**. So if you specified [List Price] < 1000 as the first condition, that would be true for an item priced at $90 as well as $400, and "$$$" would be returned for each of those. Defeating what we're trying to do here.

See http://ppvt.pro/switchTrue for more on this.

> For file size reasons, sometimes it's better to create calculated columns outside of Power Pivot (ex: in a database or using Power Query) and then import them as part of the original table - as opposed to creating them as calculations within Power Pivot. But that's only sometimes - we write calculated columns in Power Pivot all the time without worry. See the Performance chapter for more on this.

# 16 - SUMX() and Other X ("Iterator") Functions

## Need to Force Totals to Add Up "Correctly?"

Remember our [Sales per Day] measure? Let's take another look at it:

| Year - ModelName | Sales per Day |
|---|---|
| ⊟ **2001** | **$18,046** |
| Mountain-100 | $6,104 |
| Road-150 | $14,533 |
| Road-650 | $963 |
| ⊟ **2002** | **$17,891** |
| Mountain-100 | $5,993 |
| Mountain-200 | $5,077 |
| Road-150 | $16,381 |
| Road-250 | $8,829 |
| Road-550-W | $1,475 |
| Road-650 | $1,329 |
| ⊟ **2003** | **$26,825** |
| All-Purpose Bike Stand | $210 |
| Bike Wash | $20 |
| Classic Vest | $111 |
| Cycling Cap | $44 |
| Fender Set - Mountain | $109 |

Smaller than sum of its children

These sum to a lot more than $17,891

*Figure 269 The subtotals do not match the sum of their parts*

As your measures get more sophisticated, this will happen a lot: you will get subtotals and grand totals that don't equal the sum (or even the average) of their children. (In this case, it's because [Sales per Day] has a different denominator for each ModelName of bike).

Of course, many times that is 100% desirable. If you have an average temperature for each of the 12 months of the year, for instance, averaging those 12 numbers will *not* give you the average temperature for the year, since each month consists of a different number of days.

But again, in sophisticated measures (and business contexts) sometimes the correct logic for the smallest granularity is not correct for the next level up.

**In other words, sometimes you need to *force* a total to equal the sum (or the average, etc.) of its children.**

**SUMX(), and other "X" functions like it, will help you do just that.**

## Anatomy of SUMX()

 SUMX(<table or table expression>, <arithmetic expression>)

That's it. Two arguments.

SUMX() operates as follows:

1. It steps through every single row in <table or table expression>, one at a time. You can pass a raw table name for this argument, or use a function that returns a table, such as VALUES() or FILTER(). The contents of <table or table expression> are subject to the filter context of the current measure cell. (This "stepping through" behavior is often described as "iterating.")
2. For each row, it evaluates <arithmetic expression> using the filter context of the current row.
3. It remembers the result of <arithmetic expression> from each row, and when done, it adds them all up.

# SUMX() in Action

Returning to the subtotals example, let's look at the pivot again:

Now we write a new measure:

```
[Sales per Day Totals Add Up] =
    SUMX ( VALUES ( Products[ModelName] ),
        [Sales per Day] )
)
```

Note that we used VALUES(Products[ModelName]) for the <table or table expression> argument. That lets us be very specific – we want this SUMX() to step through all of the unique values of ModelName from the current filter context. If we specified the entire Products table instead (and no VALUES function), SUMX() would step through every row of the Products table from the current filter context, which might be a different number of rows.

| Year - ModelName | Sales per Day |
|---|---|
| ⊟ 2001 | $18,046 |
| Mountain-100 | $6,104 |
| Road-150 | $14,533 |
| Road-650 | $963 |
| ⊟ 2002 | $17,891 |
| Mountain-100 | $5,993 |
| Mountain-200 | $5,077 |
| Road-150 | $16,381 |
| Road-250 | $8,829 |
| Road-550-W | $1,475 |
| Road-650 | $1,329 |
| ⊟ 2003 | $26,825 |

Figure 270 [Sales per Day] with Calendar[Year] and Products[ModelName] on Rows

Results:

| Year - ModelName | Sales per Day | Sales per Day Totals Add Up |
|---|---|---|
| ⊟ 2001 | $18,046 | $21,600 |
| Mountain-100 | $6,104 | $6,104 |
| Road-150 | $14,533 | $14,533 |
| Road-650 | $963 | $963 |
| ⊟ 2002 | $17,891 | $39,085 |
| Mountain-100 | $5,993 | $5,993 |
| Mountain-200 | $5,077 | $5,077 |
| Road-150 | $16,381 | $16,381 |
| Road-250 | $8,829 | $8,829 |
| Road-550-W | $1,475 | $1,475 |
| Road-650 | $1,329 | $1,329 |
| ⊟ 2003 | $26,825 | $41,754 |
| All-Purpose Bike Stand | $210 | $210 |
| Bike Wash | $20 | $20 |
| Classic Vest | $111 | $111 |
| Cycling Cap | $44 | $44 |
| Fender Set - Mountain | $109 | $109 |

Average: $6,514    Count: 6    Sum: $39,085

Figure 271 New measure: the totals are the sum of the individual models

## Detailed Stepthrough

Just to drive it home, let's walk through the evaluation of the measure above, for the highlighted cell in the pivot:

| Year - ModelName | Sales per Day | Sales per Day Totals Add Up |
|---|---|---|
| ⊟ 2001 | $18,046 | $21,600 |
| Mountain-100 | $6,104 | $6,104 |
| Road-150 | $14,533 | $14,533 |
| Road-650 | $963 | $963 |

Figure 272 We are going to step through how the SUMX() clause of the measure arrived at $21,600

Following the 3 points outlined in the "anatomy of SUMX()" section:

1. **SUMX() steps through every row in VALUES(Products[ModelName]).** The filter context provided by the pivot in this case is a completely unfiltered Products table because this cell is Year=2001, Products=All (it has no "coordinates" in the pivot from the Products table). So VALUES(Products[ModelName]) returns every single unique value of [ModelName] from the Products table.

How many values *is* that, actually? Let's check.

```
[ModelName Values] =
    COUNTROWS ( VALUES ( Products[ModelName] ) )
```

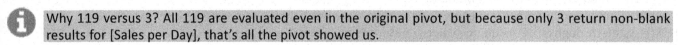

| Year - ModelName | Sales per Day | Sales per Day Totals Add Up | Model Name Values |
|---|---|---|---|
| ⊟ 2001 | $18,046 | $21,600 | 119 |
| All-Purpose Bike Stand | | | 1 |
| Bike Wash | | | 1 |
| Cable Lock | | | 1 |
| Chain | | | 1 |

*Figure 273 That is 119 values, even though we only see 3 on the pivot below 2001 in the prior screenshot!*

Why 119 versus 3? All 119 are evaluated even in the original pivot, but because only 3 return non-blank results for [Sales per Day], that's all the pivot showed us.

2. **For each of those 119 values, SUMX() evaluates the [Sales per Day] measure.** The Year=2001 filter context is maintained throughout this process, for every row. But the Products[ModelName] filter context changes every time SUMX() moves to the next of the 119 rows.

So it evaluates [Sales per Day] with filter context Year=2001, ModelName="All-Purpose Bike Stand", and that returns blank, because that model was not sold in 2001 (there are no rows in the Sales table with Year=2001, ModelName="All-Purpose Bike Stand".) Then it moves on to Year=2001, ModelName="Bike Wash", then Year=2001, ModelName="Cable Lock", etc.

Only three of those 119 rows in VALUES(Products[ModelName]) return non-blank results for [Sales per Day], and those are the three we saw displayed on the original pivot: "Mountain-100", "Road-150", and "Road-650".

3. **All 119 results of [Sales per Day] are then summed up.** 116 blank values sum to 0 of course, and then the other three sum to $21,600.

# MINX(), MAXX(), AVERAGEX()

These three operate in *precisely* the same manner as SUMX.

The only difference is in that last step – rather than summing up all of the results returned by each step, they then apply a different aggregation: MIN(), MAX(), or AVERAGE().

# FILTER()

FILTER could have been named FILTERX, since it's very much a part of the X function family. They key difference is that FILTER returns a table, instead of a single value like SUMX (or other X functions). However the workings of the two are quite similar. Here's their syntax side by side:

```
SUMX(<table or table expression>, <arithmetic expression>)

FILTER(<table or table expression>, <filter condition>)
```

Here's how the two work:

- Both functions go row by row over the <table> (first argument), in other words they iterate over the <table>.
- SUMX computes the <arithmetic expression>; FILTER evaluates the <filter condition> for each row
- In the end, SUMX sums up all the values computed at each row. FILTER gathers all the table rows which passed the <filter condition> and returns them as a table.

We hope you see the striking resemblance here.

### STDEVX.P(), STDEVX.S(), VARX.P(), VARX.S()

Again, these are exactly the same as all of the other "X" functions discussed so far, but we separated them out because of the ".P versus .S" flavors.

The difference between the P and S versions is precisely the same difference as that between the STDEVP() and ST-DEVS() functions in normal Excel. You use the P version when your data set represents the entire population of results, and the S function when all you have is a sample of the data.

It's a statistics thing, not a DAX thing.

# COUNTX() and COUNTAX()

Technically speaking, these are no different from the others mentioned so far. But there is a subtle difference when you think about it carefully.

Let's return to our SUMX() example from before. Remember the formula? It was:

```
SUMX ( VALUES ( Products[ModelName] ), [Sales per Day] )
```

And it iterated through 119 unique values of ModelName, of which only 3 had non-blank values for [Sales per Day].

If we replaced SUMX() with COUNTX(), what would we get for an answer?

We'd get 3, because COUNTX() does not "count" blanks.

So we can think of COUNTX() as being "COUNT *NONBLANK* X()" really.

## Why is This Different From COUNTROWS(), Then?

COUNTROWS() cannot take a measure as an argument, so it cannot be used to evaluate how many times that measure returns a non-blank value, which COUNTX() can do.

## COUNTAX() versus COUNTX()

COUNTAX() will also return 3 in this case, so it's really no different in the vast majority of cases. There is one specific kind of case where COUNTAX() returns something different – we will use that as an example at the end of this chapter.

 COUNTAX() treats the absence of rows, and blank results from a measure, *exactly* the same way as COUNTX(). The only place where COUNTAX() differs from COUNTX() is when you are counting text values in a column, and there are rows with text values of "" – rows that exist, but which contain an empty string. There will be an example of that at the end of this chapter.

# Using the X Functions on Fields That Aren't Displayed

In the one set of illustrations so far, you've seen SUMX() used to make totals add up "correctly."

But you can also use an X function to loop over a field that is *not* on the pivot, then report back on what it found.

Let's take the pivot we used for SUMX():

| Year - ModelName | Sales per Day | Sales per Day Totals Add Up |
|---|---|---|
| ⊟ 2001 | $18,046 | $21,600 |
| Mountain-100 | $6,104 | $6,104 |
| Road-150 | $14,533 | $14,533 |
| Road-650 | $963 | $963 |
| ⊟ 2002 | $17,891 | $39,085 |
| Mountain-100 | $5,993 | $5,993 |
| Mountain-200 | $5,077 | $5,077 |

*Figure 274 Where we left off with our completed SUMX() measure*

And let's add a new measure:

```
[Max Single-Country Sales] =
MAXX ( VALUES ( SalesTerritory[Country] ), [Total Sales] )
```

Results:

| Year - ModelName | Sales per Day | Sales per Day Totals Add Up | Max Single-Country Sales |
|---|---|---|---|
| ⊟ 2001 | $18,046 | $21,600 | $1,309,047 |
|    Mountain-100 | $6,104 | $6,104 | $304,749 |
|    Road-150 | $14,533 | $14,533 | $984,024 |
|    Road-650 | $963 | $963 | $27,265 |
| ⊟ 2002 | $17,891 | $39,085 | $2,154,285 |
|    Mountain-100 | $5,993 | $5,993 | $365,749 |
|    Mountain-200 | $5,077 | $5,077 | $286,231 |
|    Road-150 | $16,381 | $16,381 | $1,123,577 |
|    Road-250 | $8,829 | $8,829 | $524,360 |
|    Road-550-W | $1,475 | $1,475 | $49,021 |
|    Road-650 | $1,329 | $1,329 | $105,09. |

*Figure 275 Interesting new measure, but is it correct?*

Let's check by adding Country to the pivot:

| Year - ModelName | Sales per Day | Sales per Day Totals Add Up | Max Single-Country Sales |
|---|---|---|---|
| ⊟ 2001 | $18,046 | $21,600 | $1,309,047 |
| ⊟ Mountain-100 | $6,104 | $6,104 | $304,749 |
|    Australia | $4,233 | $4,233 | $304,749 |
|    Canada | $3,379 | $3,379 | $20,275 |
|    France | $3,383 | $3,383 | $30,450 |
|    Germany | $3,387 | $3,387 | $44,025 |
|    United Kingdom | $3,877 | $3,877 | $54,275 |
|    United States | $4,006 | $4,006 | $132,200 |
| ⊟ Road-150 | $14,533 | $14,533 | $984,024 |
|    Australia | $6,649 | $6,649 | $984,024 |
|    Canada | $4,055 | $4,055 | $121,661 |
|    France | $3,868 | $3,868 | $143,131 |
|    Germany | $3,959 | $3,959 | $186,070 |
|    United Kingdom | $4,026 | $4,026 | $225,431 |
|    United States | $6,920 | $6,920 | $941,085 |
| ⊟ Road-650 | $963 | $963 | $27,265 |
|    Australia | $780 | $780 | $20,274 |
|    Canada | $699 | $699 | $4,894 |
|    France | $699 | $699 | $6,991 |
|    Germany | $699 | $699 | $7,690 |
|    United Kingdom | $743 | $743 | $11,885 |
|    United States | $737 | $737 | $27,265 |

*Figure 276 It is indeed reporting the max single-country sales*

# But *Which* Country?

Since this is most "magical" when the Country field is *not* on the pivot, one of the most common questions we get is "OK but how can I display which Country was the max when Country is not on the pivot? Knowing which one is just as important as knowing the amount."

As of Power Pivot v2 there isn't a function that just *does* that for you.

We did write a post on this though, that won't fit here for space reasons. It uses the function FIRSTNONBLANK() – check it out here if you are interested: http://ppvt.pro/WhatDidXFind

# RANKX()

OK, this one is actually quite a bit different from the others even though its syntax is similar.

Let's do that whole "work backward from desired result" thing again:

| Customer FullName | Total Sales | Customer Sales Rank |
|---|---|---|
| Jordan Turner | $15,999 | 1 |
| Willie Xu | $13,490 | 2 |
| Nichole Nara | $13,295 | 3 |
| Kaitlyn Henderson | $13,294 | 4 |
| Margaret He | $13,269 | 5 |
| Randall Dominguez | $13,266 | 6 |
| Adriana Gonzalez | $13,243 | 7 |
| Rosa Hu | $13,216 | 8 |
| Brandi Gill | $13,196 | 9 |
| Brad She | $13,173 | 10 |
| Francisco Sara | $13,165 | 11 |
| Maurice Shan | $12,910 | 12 |
| Janet Munoz | $12,489 | 13 |

*Figure 277 We want a measure that ranks customers by [Total Sales]*

Here's the formula for that rank measure:

```
[Customer Sales Rank] =
RANKX ( ALL ( Customers[FullName] ), [Total Sales] )
```

## The Use of ALL()

The only difference we see so far is that we used ALL() instead of VALUES() in the first argument.

Why is that?

Because if we use VALUES(), we get 1's for everyone:

| Customer FullName | Total Sales | Customer Sales Rank |
|---|---|---|
| Bradley Kumar | $3,345 | 1 |
| Bradley Lal | $2,664 | 1 |
| Aaron Alexander | $70 | 1 |
| Bradley Luo | $3,400 | 1 |
| Aaron Baker | $1,751 | 1 |
| Bradley Nara | $5,898 | 1 |
| Aaron Butler | $15 | 1 |
| Bradley Pal | $124 | 1 |
| Aaron Carter | $40 | 1 |
| Bradley Rai | $79 | 1 |
| Aaron Coleman | $62 | 1 |

*Figure 278 If we replace ALL() with VALUES(), everybody's our #1 customer!*

OK, why is *that*?

Well it makes *some* sense actually – for each row of the pivot, there is only one value of Customer[FullName] – so the RANKX measure ranks each customer as if he/she were the only customer in the world ☺

So by applying ALL(), we rank each customer against everyone else. We guess that's intuitive, but the more we think about it, the more even *that* doesn't feel right.

The pragmatic thing to do here is not worry about it. Just use ALL() and be happy we have the function ☺

# Ties

Let's look at the bottom of that same pivot, with ALL() restored so not everyone is #1:

| | | |
|---|---|---|
| Xavier White | $4 | 18326 |
| Trisha Zhao | $4 | 18326 |
| Ronald Mehta | $4 | 18326 |
| Trevor Coleman | $4 | 18326 |
| Omar Zhao | $4 | 18326 |
| Shane Mehta | $4 | 18326 |
| Abigail Morris | $2 | 18390 |
| Abigail Bennett | $2 | 18390 |
| Alex Collins | $2 | 18390 |
| Brad Kumar | $2 | 18390 |
| Cody Sanders | $2 | 18390 |
| Dylan Taylor | $2 | 18390 |
| Hunter Miller | $2 | 18390 |
| Marcus Morgan | $2 | 18390 |
| Natalie Bryant | $2 | 18390 |
| Melanie Peterson | $2 | 18390 |
| Natalie Rivera | $2 | 18390 |
| **Grand Total** | **$29,358,677** | **1** |

There are 64 people tied with $4 of sales, so rank "skips" to 18,390

*Figure 279 By default, ties are handled like this, but you can override that with the fifth (and optional argument), by setting it to Dense*

# The Optional Parameters

RANKX() actually has five parameters instead of the two possessed by the other X functions, but the last three are optional:

 RANKX(<table or table expression>, <arithmetic expression>, <*optional* alternate arithmetic expression>, <*optional* sort order flag>, <*optional* tie-handling flag>

<optional alternate arithmetic expression> - The third argument to RANKX() may be the most mysterious thing in all of Power Pivot. If we weren't writing this book, we would happily continue to ignore that we don't understand it. We recommend always leaving it blank. Seriously. (But we will return to it in Chapter 17, because completely taking a "pass" on it doesn't feel right).

<optional sort order flag> -This allows you to control rank order (ascending/descending) by setting to 1 or 0. It defaults to 0 if you leave it blank, which ranks largest values highest.

<optional tie-handling flag> - This can be set to Skip or Dense. It defaults to Skip, which is the behavior seen in the previous picture. If we change it to Dense, this is what the ties look at near the bottom of the pivot:

```
RANKX ( ALL(Customers[FullName]), [Total Sales],,,DENSE )
```

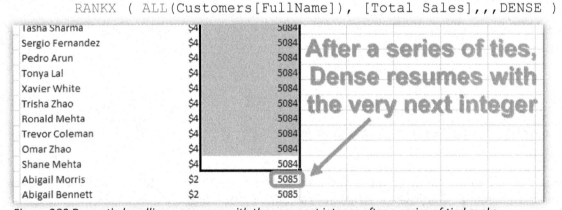

*Figure 280 Dense tie handling – resumes with the very next integer after a series of tied ranks*

# Duplicate FullNames?

Very dangerous, this one. If you have two customers with the same FullName, they will be combined into a single customer and ranked unfairly high by their combined sales.

So make sure you rank by a unique field. We recommend concatenating CustomerKey or something unique with Full-Name so that you can still recognize the customer by name, and still maintain uniqueness.

 For more fun with RANKX check out http://ppvt.pro/moreRANKX for ranking items within and across groups (e.g. Popsicles can be #1 selling item in Ice-Creams but be #23 in Desserts).

# TOPN()

Okay, you got us, **TOPN() is not an X function**. But RANKX and TOPN kinda play in the same sandbox. So we'll cover TOPN here.

 TOPN(<n_value>, <table>, <orderBy_expression>, [<order>],...)
Returns the top N rows of the specified table.

RANKX assigns a numeric rank. TOPN ranks the rows, but then filters them to the top N rows (N is user specified) and returns these set of rows. We think of RANKX when we actually need to see the rank of an item on a pivot. We think of TOPN when we need to filter down to top rows (say top products, top customers, top salesmen etc.), before we perform some calculation on these top rows. Let's see this in an example.

Here are our sales figures and the count of products we sold in 2002:

| CalendarYear | 2002 | |
|---|---|---|
| **MonthName** | **Total Sales** | **Product Sold Count** |
| January | $596,747 | 25 |
| February | $550,817 | 23 |
| March | $644,135 | 24 |
| April | $663,692 | 23 |
| May | $673,556 | 25 |
| June | $676,764 | 25 |
| July | $500,365 | 28 |
| August | $546,001 | 31 |
| September | $350,467 | 31 |
| October | $415,390 | 31 |
| November | $335,095 | 30 |
| December | $577,314 | 31 |
| **Grand Total** | **$6,530,344** | **56** |

*How top heavy are we?*

*Figure 281 2002 seems a fairly stable year for Sales*

We want to get a sense of how "top heavy" are we, in terms of products? Do a few top products comprise a majority of our sales? How has that changed over time? Let's take it from the TOPN (Get it? Sigh! The futility of nerd jokes in print). Here's our measure:

```
Sales for Top 5 Products =
CALCULATE (
    [Total Sales],
    TOPN ( 5, Products, [Total Sales] )
)
```

Let's look specifically at TOPN.

**1st argument: 5**. This just tells TOPN, what N is? Is it TOP5, TOP10 or TOP20? i.e. How many top rows are to be returned.

**2nd argument: Products**. This is the table from which TOPN rows are to be extracted.

 Note: For the 2nd argument, you are not restricted to passing in just table names which exist in your model. You can use any DAX expression that returns a table, such as VALUES(), FILTER() etc.

**3rd Argument: [Total Sales]**. This tells TOPN how to evaluate what is a "top" row? You want top products by sales, by cost, by margin or something else? So specify the appropriate measure here, which you want TOPN to use to rank your rows.

We'll add one more "derived" measure before we see our results (Ooh! We love reusing measures and hence all derived measures).

```
% Sales for Top 5 Products =
DIVIDE ( [Sales for Top 5 Products], [Total Sales] )
```

And here are our results:

| MonthName | Total Sales | Product Sold Count | Sales for Top 5 Products | % Sales for Top 5 Products |
|---|---|---|---|---|
| January | $596,747 | 25 | $458,019 | 77 % |
| February | $550,817 | 23 | $475,910 | 86 % |
| March | $644,135 | 24 | $497,380 | 77 % |
| April | $663,692 | 23 | $508,114 | 77 % |
| May | $673,556 | 25 | $500,958 | 74 % |
| June | $676,764 | 25 | $508,114 | 75 % |
| July | $500,365 | 28 | $244,771 | 49 % |
| August | $546,001 | 31 | $249,047 | 46 % |
| September | $350,467 | 31 | $173,914 | 50 % |
| October | $415,390 | 31 | $161,521 | 39 % |
| November | $335,095 | 30 | $153,434 | 46 % |
| December | $577,314 | 31 | $242,231 | 42 % |
| Grand Total | $6,530,344 | 56 | $2,948,494 | 45 % |

*Wow! July was a turning point!*

*Figure 282 TOPN really helps us understand what is going on with our business*

It is clear that we have lessened our reliance on just a top few products to generate a bulk of our sales. A good move by any company, especially fictitious ones like AdventureWorks.

# Non-Measure Second Arguments to the X Functions

So far, we've only used measures for that second argument to these X functions.

But actually this is one place where you can break the "no naked columns" rule. You actually can just put a column name in for that second argument. And SUMX() will happily sum it.

In fact, you can even put a calculated column style formula in there, like Customers[YearlyIncome] / Customers[NumberOfChildren], and that will also work.

## The COUNTAX() Mystery Solved!

**The ability to use a non-measure expression as that final argument helps us solve the COUNTAX() conundrum.** When you use a *measure* as the second argument, we do not believe there is *any* situation in which COUNTX() and COUNTAX() will return different results.

But COUNTAX() will let you use a text column as the second argument, whereas COUNTX(), if you use a column as the second argument, requires that it be numeric or date type.

So here's a silly little table we added to the Power Pivot window as a test:

*Figure 283 CountTest table – a testbed for COUNTAX()*

Here's a measure we wrote against it:

```
[COUNTAX Test] =
COUNTAX ( CountTest, CountTest[Column1]
)
```

And the results:

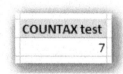

*Figure 284 The measure returns 7. From an 8-row table. So it didn't count the one row with a blank value, which is different from the absence of a row. Subtle!*

Change the COUNTAX() to COUNTX() and we get an error – COUNTX() refuses to accept a text column as the second argument.

So there you have it. The reason COUNTAX() exists.

(It's actually more useful in calculated columns than measures, so this wasn't really a "fair" test of its value).

# 17 - Multiple Data Tables

So far we have only been working with a single Data table – Sales. Data tables typically represent business processes, and in this case the Sales table represents the sales transactions. But clearly a real business would have more than one business process and they would be collecting data on each one of those. Let us introduce "Service Calls" as our next business process.

## Service Calls

In our scenario we have a central call center that receives service calls from all of our customers. We record the customer ID, the date of the call and the product about which they called. We also record the call duration (in minutes) for each call and a subjective assessment as to whether the resolution was positive, negative or neutral. This data is available to us at the end of each day in a CSV format shown as below.

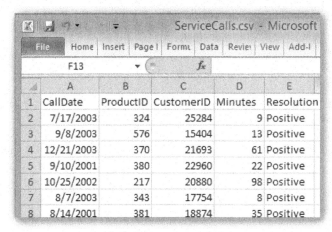

Figure 285 Service Calls data as recorded in our system

Let us bring in this data into our model.

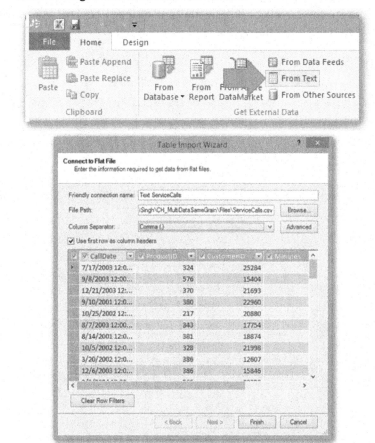

Figure 286 Use Get External Data to connect to the CSV file and import it into our data model

Now we have the ServiceCalls table within our model.

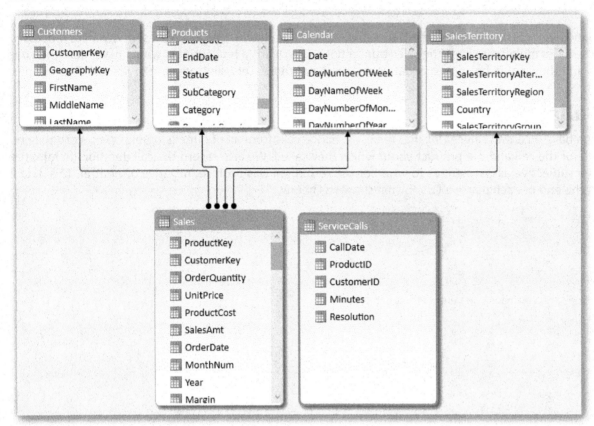

*Figure 287 ServiceCalls table imported into our data model*

For the next few steps, let's pretend that ServiceCalls is the only data table in our model.

We are well versed in the steps required to build such a data model: creating relationships and defining new measures (we love those measures, don't we!). So let's do that. Let's start with relationships:

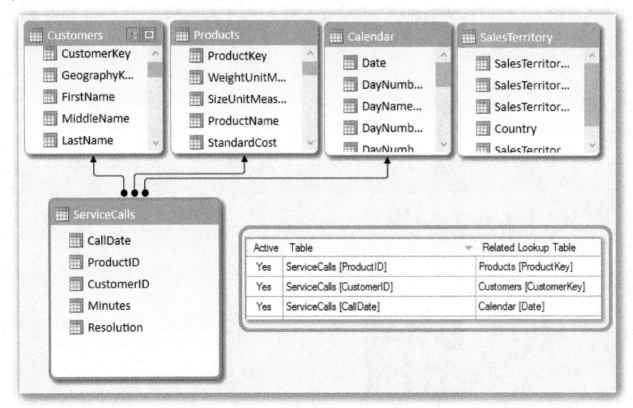

*Figure 288 Relationships created for the new ServiceCalls table*

Notice how we did NOT create relationships between Sales and ServiceCalls? This is an extremely important point: **YOU NEVER RELATE DATA TABLES TO ONE ANOTHER!** Power Pivot won't even let you, actually, because there are duplicates in each Data table's key/id columns. (For instance, we take multiple calls on a single day, and sell multiple products on a single day, so Sales and ServiceCalls each contain multiple rows for a given date.) This is one of the most common mistakes we see Excel pros making as they transition to Power Pivot, but the "antidote" is a simple rule: **The way to "splice" additional Data tables into a model is by relating them to a shared set of Lookup tables, NOT by attempting to relate Data tables directly to one another.**

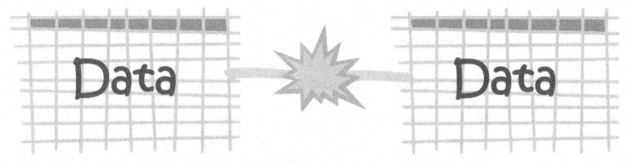

*Figure 289 NEVER attempt to relate Data tables to one another*

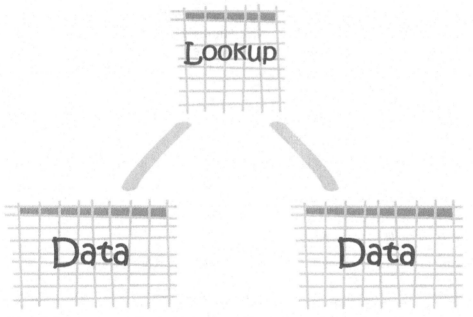

*Figure 290 Instead, we splice multiple Data tables into a model by relating them to one or more shared Lookup tables*

OK, terrific! Now that ServiceCalls is related to our Lookup tables, we are at par with the Sales table. Now we can define some basic measures:

```
[Calls] = COUNTROWS ( ServiceCalls )

[Total Call Minutes] = SUM ( ServiceCalls[Minutes] )

[Avg Call Length] = DIVIDE ( [Total Call Minutes],[Calls] )
```

Additionally, our Call Center Director has informed us that it costs us an average of **$1.75 per minute** for the service call, considering the personnel, telecommunication and other costs. We can then create a measure for [Cost of Calls]:

```
[Cost of Calls] = [Total Call Minutes] * 1.75
```

With measures and relationships defined, we can start quickly gleaning insight into our service calls in much the same way that we've been able to analyze our sales data:

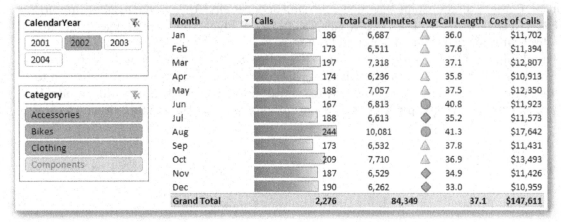

Figure 291 Our modified model now provides insight on our Service Calls business process

# Service Calls and Sales Mashup

**But if that were The Whole Story, we would not have an entire chapter dedicated to it!** Oh no, dear friends, the true magic is just beginning. What if we want to see our Sales metrics "side by side" with our Service Call metrics?

## In Traditional Excel

In traditional Excel, "side by side" analysis of multiple Data tables is... tedious. Clumsy. Depressing. It can wear you down in a big way. (We're talking about *data* here, and calling it depressing. But it's the truth.) In that old world, we could take a few approaches. A typical one is to show two pivot tables side by side. And we *could* do that with our Power Pivot model as well:

| CalendarYear | Cost of Calls | | CalendarYear | Total Sales |
|---|---|---|---|---|
| 2001 | $78,906 | | 2001 | $3,266,374 |
| 2002 | $147,611 | | 2002 | $6,530,344 |
| 2003 | $148,166 | | 2003 | $9,791,060 |
| 2004 | $99,152 | | 2004 | $9,770,900 |
| **Grand Total** | **$473,834** | | **Grand Total** | **$29,358,677** |

Figure 292 This traditional approach feels so caveman-like. We can do better.

This breaks down quickly as you build your pivots, for instance in cases where the labels do not line up.

| CalendarYear | 2004 | | CalendarYear | 2004 |
|---|---|---|---|---|
| **ProductName** | **Calls** | | **ProductName** | **Total Sales** |
| All-Purpose Bike Stand | 15 | | All-Purpose Bike Stand | $20,670 |
| Bike Wash - Dissolver | 15 | ? | AWC Logo Cap | $11,732 |
| Classic Vest, L | 9 | ? | Bike Wash - Dissolver | $4,174 |
| Classic Vest, S | 13 | | Classic Vest, L | $8,128 |
| Fender Set - Mountain | 7 | | Classic Vest, M | $8,065 |
| Half-Finger Gloves, L | 13 | | Classic Vest, S | $6,477 |
| Half-Finger Gloves, M | 9 | | Fender Set - Mountain | $27,211 |

Figure 293 Some elements may appear in one pivot but not the other

In traditional Excel, perhaps you'd then hide the pivots and start writing formulas that "peer" into the pivots, fetching values, and then using those formulas to construct a report sheet from scratch. But regardless of the approach, such side-by-side analysis of two disparate data sets in traditional Excel is labor-intensive.

Furthermore, whatever you build would be **tied to a specific shape of report**. For example if you build a report to compare Service Calls and Sales by Month and Product Category; if you are then asked to change that to show Product SubCategory – you would almost have to start from scratch to build this new report.

# Do Not "Flatten"

*Figure 294 Thou shalt not "flatten" data tables together into Frankentables* ☺

We have also seen an approach where the two Data tables are combined together in one flattened **Franken-Data** table. This is one of the places where Access is often used, for instance, or SQL queries if you're using a "real" database. (We've also seen Power Query used to perform this flattening.)

Flattening is an unnecessary step, and even worse, it requires you to "pre-aggregate" the data as part of the flattening process, which "destroys" a lot of useful detail. DON'T DO THIS! ☺ In our training classes we often say that for Excel users, **learning Power Pivot is more about *unlearning* than learning something new**. And one of those unlearning commandments is "**Thou shall no longer flatten tables together into franken-tables**". You should neither flatten Data and Lookup tables together, nor multiple Data tables into one. Multiple Data tables typically represent distinct business processes (think how different a Sales Transaction is to a Service Call) and do not belong mashed together in the same table.

## Measures from Different Data Tables in the Same Pivot!

By now, you have hopefully fallen in love with the **portability** of DAX measures and their "**define once, use anywhere**" capability, and also their "**re-arrange your pivots at will, and the measures will automatically adjust**" flexibility.

Well that portability now has another awesome benefit: instead of the side-by-side pivots approach, **we can just place both the Service Calls measures and the Sales measures in the same pivot!** Like this:

| CalendarYear | 2004 .T | |
| --- | --- | --- |
| **ProductName** ▼ | **Total Sales** | **Cost of Calls** |
| All-Purpose Bike Stand | $20,670 | $1,062 |
| AWC Logo Cap | $11,732 | |
| Bike Wash - Dissolver | $4,174 | $607 |
| Classic Vest, L | $8,128 | $635 |
| Classic Vest, M | $8,065 | |
| Classic Vest, S | $6,477 | $1,106 |
| Fender Set - Mountain | $27,211 | $382 |

Measures from two different data sets in the same pivot!!!

*Figure 295 Your old and tedious job of slaving in the data mines is over. Get ready for your new life!*

Whoa! That worked. And it's fully portable. Try changing the shape of the pivot:

Figure 296 Measures from different data sets adapt to the shape of our pivot

Were you surprised that this worked? Feels like magic, doesn't it? But there is fundamentally nothing new going on here. Everything is still governed by the same DAX rules that you have already learned. Remember rule #4 from the golden rules?

**4  Filters Follow the Relationship(s):** If the filtered tables (Calendar and Products) are Lookup tables, follow relationships to their related Data tables and filter those tables too. Only Data rows related to active Lookup rows will be active.

Figure 297 Filters flow downhill across relationships

The key here are the common Lookup tables - Lookup tables that connect to both data tables via relationships. And we know relationships flow downhill, so a filter on an uphill lookup table (e.g. Products or Calendar) will flow down to Data tables - **both** data tables in this case (Sales & Service Calls). Thus the measures give us the correct results in the combined pivot table.

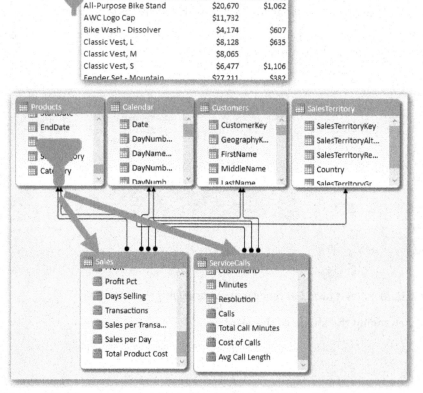

Figure 298 Filter on a Lookup table flows downhill to ALL related Data tables

That's worth re-emphasizing: a filtered Lookup table will "transmit" that filtering to ALL of its related Data tables. All of its outgoing "filter transmission wires" will be activated, if we allow ourselves to use that metaphor.

# Hybrid Measures

So, we can take any measure from any of these data tables, show them side-by-side in the same pivot, and slice and dice them using any attribute from a common lookup table. Awesome.

But sometimes we want to go even further, and **run a calculation *across* these two data sets**. For example, can we "improve" our existing [Profit] measure to also account for the cost of service calls?

$$\text{Profit} := [\text{Total Sales}] - [\text{Total Product Cost}]$$

| ProductName | Total Sales | Total Product Cost | Profit | Cost of Calls |
|---|---|---|---|---|
| All-Purpose Bike Stand | $20,670 | $7,731 | $12,939 | $1,062 |
| AWC Logo Cap | $11,732 | $9,034 | $2,698 | |
| Bike Wash - Dissolver | $4,174 | $1,561 | $2,613 | $607 |
| Classic Vest, L | $8,128 | $3,040 | $5,088 | $635 |
| Classic Vest, M | $8,065 | $3,016 | $5,048 | |
| Classic Vest, S | $6,477 | $2,422 | $4,055 | $1,106 |
| Fender Set - Mountain | $27,211 | $10,177 | $17,034 | $382 |

*Can our profit metric account for cost of Service Calls?*

*Figure 299 Can we write a measure that "hybridizes" data from two Data tables?*

Remember, this would use numbers from two different data tables. In traditional Excel, this would take the "labor-intensiveness" to an even-deeper level. But with Power Pivot, let's give it a try:

```
[Net Profit] = [Profit] - [Cost of Calls]
```

| ProductName | Profit | Cost of Calls | Net Profit |
|---|---|---|---|
| All-Purpose Bike Stand | $12,939 | $1,062 | $11,877 |
| AWC Logo Cap | $2,698 | | $2,698 |
| Bike Wash - Dissolver | $2,613 | $607 | $2,006 |
| Classic Vest, L | $5,088 | $635 | $4,453 |
| Classic Vest, M | $5,048 | | $5,048 |
| Classic Vest, S | $4,055 | $1,106 | $2,949 |
| Fender Set - Mountain | $17,034 | $382 | $16,653 |

*Figure 300 Our hybrid measure performs a calculation across measures from different Data tables*

**We have created a new species of measures, are you feeling all-powerful yet?** Now that we have our new measure, we do not need [Profit] and [Cost of Calls] displayed on the pivot. We can take them off and focus *just* on Net Profit. Or you can continue to show them side-by-side, totally your choice. You can even use another visualization tool to pull together a quick profit report.

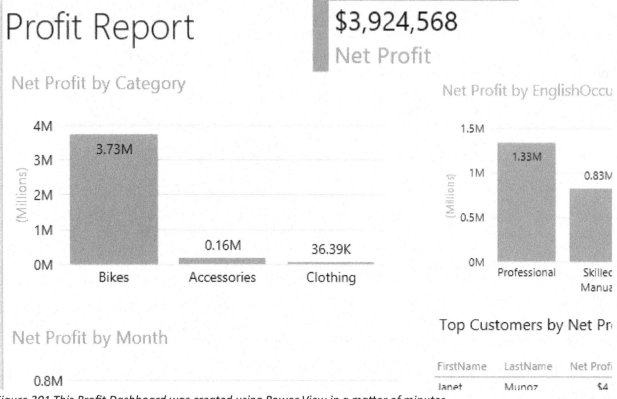

*Figure 301 This Profit Dashboard was created using Power View in a matter of minutes*

 **This is an important, let-that-sink-in moment.** Power Pivot is the heart of all the Power BI products, and relationships and measures are the core of Power Pivot. Harnessing their power, you are well on your way to mastering the world of data.

**The "rest" is easy.** Visualization – building reports and such – becomes cheap and nearly free! Using portable measures, you can slice and dice using any of the attributes available and quickly build any report.

**To quickly build a report/dashboard is one thing, but to quickly ADJUST is perhaps even MORE important.** How many times have you been asked to build a report, and then provided *precisely* what you were asked for, only to have the "requestor" immediately request a change? In the old days, that change (a "minor" one in the requestor's mind) often would take you as long as it took to build the original report!

**In the Power Pivot world, though, here's how that story will play out.** You will go back to your office, click one checkbox in the field list, and You. Are. Done. We like to say that you should then *wait 30 minutes* before providing the result, so that you maintain some sense of mystery and magic ☺. 30 minutes is AMAZING turnaround compared to the old days, but 10 seconds is almost too fast – it makes it seem trivial, and cheapens the smart investments you previously made in your data model. Use the 30-minute waiting period to do something else productive. You've earned it.

**We also encourage you to forgive the requestors** who change the requirements on you as soon as you deliver what they originally said they needed. This is a fundamental truth that we have learned the hard way: *human beings do not know what they need until they have seen what they asked for.* Accept and embrace this fact, the sooner the better. Our traditional tool sets were in outright conflict with this basic human behavior, but Power Pivot flows right along with us, in the way that we naturally think and operate. The difference could not be bigger.

# Multiple Data Tables Gotchas

There are a few rules and guidelines which you should be aware of when working with multiple data tables.

## Using Fields from Lookup Table vs. the Data Table

Let us look at our total sales and count of service calls by date. We can do so in separate pivots as shown below.

| Row Labels ▼ | Total Sales | | Row Labels ▼ | Calls |
|---|---|---|---|---|
| 7/1/2001 | $14,477 | | 7/1/2001 | 7 |
| 7/2/2001 | $13,932 | | 7/2/2001 | 4 |
| 7/3/2001 | $15,012 | | 7/3/2001 | 11 |
| 7/4/2001 | $7,157 | | 7/4/2001 | 4 |
| 7/5/2001 | $15,012 | | 7/5/2001 | 8 |
| 7/6/2001 | $14,313 | | 7/6/2001 | 14 |

*Figure 302 Both pivots work and return correct result*

But as we have seen earlier, you could put both measures side-by-side within the same pivot. You try to do that and get this result.

| Row Labels ▼ | Total Sales | Calls |
|---|---|---|
| 7/1/2001 | $14,477 | 7,374 |
| 7/2/2001 | $13,932 | 7,374 |
| 7/3/2001 | $15,012 | 7,374 |
| 7/4/2001 | $7,157 | 7,374 |
| 7/5/2001 | $15,012 | 7,374 |
| 7/6/2001 | $14,313 | 7,374 |
| 7/7/2001 | $7,856 | 7,374 |

*Figure 303 The [Calls] measure is not returning expected result*

The [Calls] measure is simply repeating the same number throughout – 7,374 which happens to be the grand total of all calls. Whatever happened to the promise of "define once, use anywhere"? Are you feeling let down? Let's peel the covers and see what is going on.

If we examine the pivot, we realize we have used the Sales[OrderDate] column (from a Data table) on our pivot Rows, instead of Calendar[Date] from the Calendar (Lookup) table. Why does this matter? Because relationships flow downhill, not uphill.

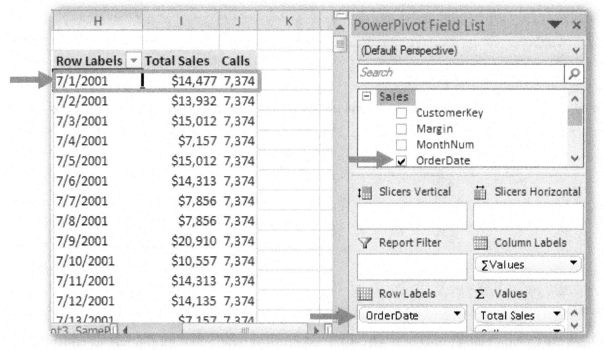

*Figure 304 We used a column from a Data table instead of a Lookup table*

The same golden rules we have covered apply to the calculation of any DAX measures, and "stepping through" that process should always be our first instinct when we get a confusing result. Let's step through the calculation for the row highlighted above. The incoming filter coordinates here are

```
Sales[OrderDate] = 7/1/2001
```

**Remember our insistence** on thinking about the Pivot Table Coordinates (Step 1 in the Golden Rules) as *Table[Column]* = *Value*. This is where it pays off. If you think of it generically as

```
Date = 7/1/2001
```

**That would not help you.** As humans we do tend to think this way, but with DAX it helps to think like the DAX engine. In DAX, Sales[OrderDate] is very different than Calendar[Date].

Next we follow the chain of steps in the golden rules. When we get to Step 4: Relationships flow downhill, we realize that our filter (Sales[OrderDate]) is on the Data table and would *not* flow uphill to the Calendar Lookup table. That means that the ServiceCalls table ends up with no filters applied in step 5 (the arithmetic step), and hence we get the grand total of all rows (7,374) returned in the pivot. The same happens for each row in the pivot table.

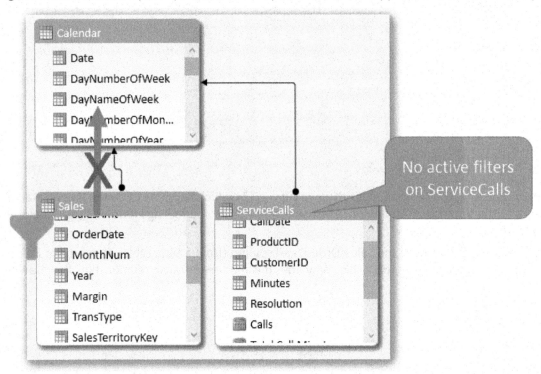

*Figure 305 Filters do not flow uphill across a relationship*

Now that we know what the issue is, the fix is easy. We will use the [Date] column from Calendar – our Lookup table.

| Calendar[Date] | Total Sales | Calls |
|---|---|---|
| 7/1/2001 | $14,477 | 7 |
| 7/2/2001 | $13,932 | 4 |
| 7/3/2001 | $15,012 | 11 |
| 7/4/2001 | $7,157 | 4 |
| 7/5/2001 | $15,012 | 8 |
| 7/6/2001 | $14,313 | 14 |
| 7/7/2001 | $7,856 | 4 |

*Figure 306 Measures show correctly with the Calendar[Date] field from the Lookup table*

 **Use fields from the Lookup Tables (and not the Data Tables) on Rows/Columns (and Filters/Slicers) when analyzing measures from different data tables.** This is a good rule of thumb. In fact, it's often good practice even in models that have only ONE data table.

The best way to avoid falling into this trap is to **hide the Data table columns**. This is easily done by right clicking and selecting '**Hide from Client Tools**'.

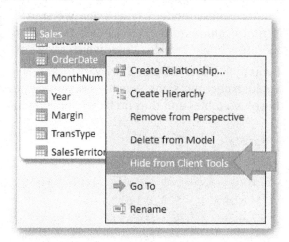

*Figure 307 Hide the column from Data Tables*

 What? You say your Data table had not only the Date column, but also Year, Quarter, and Month columns? Perhaps you *also* have these fields in your Calendar lookup table, but you just *like* having them around in the Data table as well. Or maybe you actually brought them into your Data table from the Lookup table using RELATED(). **Don't do that!** ☺ Don't keep copies of these columns, since they "bloat" your model and also tempt you into making unconscious mistakes.

Here are some good guidelines:

- **Ideally your Data tables should contain only** numeric "amount" columns (like quantity and amount paid), plus the "Key" or "ID" fields (Date, ProductKey, CustomerKey...) which are used to connect to Lookup tables.
- **All other columns should ideally "live" in related Lookup tables.** Yep, all of them.
- **One "check" we like to make is to visually scan Data tables for text columns.** Usually, text columns are not needed in Data tables, and when we see text, it's a clue that we could "outsource" such columns to a Lookup table.
- **So in an ideal Data table, you can hide ALL of the columns!** "Key" columns (that form relationships) are hide-able since you already have their "twins" in the Lookup tables. And your numeric amount columns are hide-able since you have defined 'Explicit' measures for them. If you don't quite reach this nirvana, don't sweat it – it's merely something to strive for, plus it illustrates some good concepts to think it through.

## Data Table Connected to Some but Not All Lookup Tables

You may have noticed that we have been diligently avoiding using the SalesTerritory table in any of our pivots in this chapter. We don't want it to feel left out, so here we go.

| Country | Calls |
|---------|-------|
| Australia | 7,374 |
| Canada | 7,374 |
| France | 7,374 |
| Germany | 7,374 |
| NA | 7,374 |
| United Kingdom | 7,374 |
| United States | 7,374 |
| **Grand Total** | **7,374** |

*Figure 308 Houston, we have a problem!*

Alas! The repeating number (Usually a red flag, but not ALLways! ☺ Get it? Sigh, hard to land ALL() function jokes in print). But did we expect anything less? After all the two tables are not related.

*Figure 309 SalesTerritory to ServiceCalls: Do I know you?*

SalesTerritory does not apply to our ServiceCalls data, neither in our data nor in our business processes. Thus there would never be a relationship between SalesTerritory and ServiceCalls, but it also wouldn't even make sense for us to want a report that broke support data out by territory.

If our business model changes and we started operating Service Centers based on SalesTerritory, and we added a Territory column to our ServiceCalls table in order to track that, then we would update our model. But right now we operate a single Service Center which serves all our customers.

If you pulled in a table of Star Wars locations in your data model and used that in a Pivot with a Sales measure, you would expect the same result – a repeating number (the grand total) since there would be no relationship between these two tables and thus no filters applied to Sales table.

| StarWars | Total Sales |
|---|---|
| Alderaan | $29,358,677 |
| Bespin | $29,358,677 |
| Coruscant | $29,358,677 |
| Dagobah | $29,358,677 |
| Endor | $29,358,677 |
| Hoth | $29,358,677 |
| Kamino | $29,358,677 |
| Kashyyyk | $29,358,677 |
| **Grand Total** | **$29,358,677** |

*Figure 310 Sales has no relation with Star Wars locations*

While the behavior is expected and correct, this is still something you need to be careful about.

 The modified general rule then becomes: **Use fields from the *shared* Lookup tables when analyzing measures from different data tables.**

## Staying Out of Trouble

You can get into trouble in a few ways, even though they all come back to the same underlying, mechanical fundamentals of the Golden Rules. The easiest would be if you use a column that does not apply and you get a repeating number. Fairly easy to spot.

| Country | Calls |
|---|---|
| Australia | 7,374 |
| Canada | 7,374 |
| France | 7,374 |
| Germany | 7,374 |
| NA | 7,374 |
| United Kingdom | 7,374 |
| United States | 7,374 |
| **Grand Total** | **7,374** |

*Figure 311 Repeating number pattern is easy to spot*

But what if you build a pivot as shown below. You add a filter – SalesTerritory[Country] = "Australia" but may not realize that the new filter only filtered [Total Sales] and [Calls] is unchanged (showing you a worldwide number). If you happen to send this report out to someone they would be totally unfamiliar with your model and would assume you are showing them numbers just for Australia. Refer back to the general rule to stay out of such trouble.

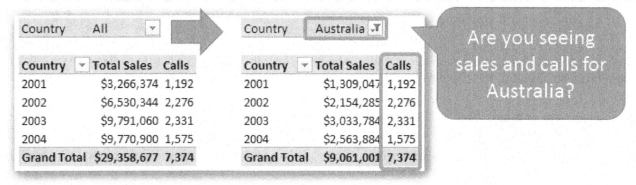

*Figure 312 Are we seeing numbers for Australia or Worldwide or both?*

**You have to exercise extra care when using Hybrid Measures**, such as our [Net Profit] measure. At first glance the pivot below raises no red flags (as there's no repeating number at least).

| Country | Total Sales | Profit | Net Profit |
|---|---|---|---|
| Australia | $9,061,001 | $3,685,855 | $3,212,022 |
| Canada | $1,977,845 | $829,922 | $356,088 |
| France | $2,644,018 | $1,086,265 | $612,431 |
| Germany | $2,894,312 | $1,187,371 | $713,537 |
| NA | | | ($473,834) |
| United Kingdom | $3,391,712 | $1,390,491 | $916,657 |
| United States | $9,389,790 | $3,900,981 | $3,427,147 |
| Grand Total | $29,358,677 | $12,080,884 | $11,607,050 |

*Figure 313 Looks can be deceiving, for hybrid measures: it's the inside that counts.*

Only when you remind yourself of the definition of the [Net Profit] measure and bring in the underlying measures, do you see what's going on.

$$[\text{Net Profit}] := [\text{Profit}] - [\text{Cost of Calls}]$$

| Country | Profit | Cost of Calls | Net Profit |
|---|---|---|---|
| Australia | $3,685,855 | $473,834 | $3,212,022 |
| Canada | $829,922 | $473,834 | $356,088 |
| France | $1,086,265 | $473,834 | $612,431 |
| Germany | $1,187,371 | $473,834 | $713,537 |
| NA | | $473,834 | ($473,834) |
| United Kingdom | $1,390,491 | $473,834 | $916,657 |
| United States | $3,900,981 | $473,834 | $3,427,147 |
| Grand Total | $12,080,884 | $473,834 | $11,607,050 |

*Figure 314 If two wrongs don't make a right, one wrong certainly does not make a right*

Now you can see that the [Profit] measure calculates correctly by Country, however [Cost of Calls] does not, since the ServiceCalls is not related to the SalesTerritory table. Therefore [Net Profit] also is returning a spurious number. Just refer back to the general rule and stay out of such trouble.

# 18 - Multiple Data Tables – Differing Granularity

It's time to have a responsible conversation about grains, and how "fat" are your data rows. Even if you're on a Paleo diet and have forsaken all grains, this chapter should go down easy. "Grain" defines what a single row in your data table represents.

- **In *more* granular data sets,** each row represents a relatively "small" slice of data. Highly granular data sets tend to contain more rows, and each row contains "small" numbers.

- **In *less* granular data sets,** each row represents a "fatter" chunk of data, and therefore these data sets tend to contain fewer rows.

- **We are deliberately using imprecise terms** like "more," "less," and "fewer," because there is no precise definition of high- and low-granularity. It truly is a relative concept that only matters in comparison: the only thing that's important is whether your multiple data tables *match* each other in terms of granularity.

- **If your data tables have the *same* granularity,** the previous chapter is all you need. But if they have differing granularities, well, welcome to this chapter ☺

 The most common example of a granularity difference occurs with respect to time. Example: in one data set, a single row may represent an individual transaction ("high" granularity), but in another, an entire week's worth of transactions are pre-aggregated into a single row ("low" granularity).

Pre-aggregation is not limited to time, however. For instance, one data set might contain rows for individual Locations, whereas another could be pre-aggregated to an entire Region (each row represents a collection of individual Locations).

Your grains will impact how your data model will be built. In general, the more granular the dataset, the more powerful and flexible your model can be, so at PowerPivotPro, we're always saying "give us the most granular you've got!" However, you may not always have this choice based on what data is made accessible to you. So let's review this using some examples.

## Example1: Budget versus Actuals

Here's a common problem: you have a Sales table, where each row represents an individual transaction. In our case that's about 60 thousand rows. But then you also have a Budget table, where each row is typically captured at a **coarser granularity**, and is much smaller in terms of row count.

For instance, here's a sample Budget table that we've imported into Power Pivot:

| CalendarYear | MonthNumberOfYear | SalesTerritoryRegion | Subcategory | Budgeted Sales |
|---|---|---|---|---|
| 2001 | 7 | Australia | Mountain Bikes | $71,510 |
| 2001 | 7 | Australia | Road Bikes | $190,248 |
| 2001 | 7 | Canada | Mountain Bikes | $4,183 |
| 2001 | 7 | Canada | Road Bikes | $15,429 |
| 2001 | 7 | France | Mountain Bikes | $7,916 |
| 2001 | 7 | France | Road Bikes | $31,825 |
| 2001 | 7 | Germany | Mountain Bikes | $4,384 |
| 2001 | 7 | Germany | Road Bikes | $36,068 |
| 2001 | 7 | Northwest | Mountain Bikes | $12,058 |
| 2001 | 7 | Northwest | Road Bikes | $49,089 |
| 2001 | 7 | Southwest | Mountain Bikes | $3,059 |
| 2001 | 7 | Southwest | Road Bikes | $59,190 |
| 2001 | 7 | United Kingdom | Mountain Bikes | $5,893 |
| 2001 | 7 | United Kingdom | Road Bikes | $28,572 |
| 2001 | 8 | Australia | Mountain Bikes | $54,200 |
| 2001 | 8 | Australia | Road Bikes | $163,254 |
| 2001 | 8 | Canada | Mountain Bikes | $8,031 |
| 2001 | 8 | Canada | Road Bikes | $22,168 |
| 2001 | 8 | France | Mountain Bikes | $8,196 |
| 2001 | 8 | France | Road Bikes | $10,289 |
| 2001 | 8 | Germany | Road Bikes | $46,872 |

CountTest | Customers | Sales | Products | Calendar | Exch Rates | MinListPrice | PriceTier | Budget | SalesTerritory | CompetitorSales

Record ◄ ◄ 1 of 1,877 ► ►◄

*Figure 315 Budget table: 1,877 rows at Year/Month/Territory/SubCategory granularity*

**And now the common question: how are our products selling compared to budget?**

# Difficult in Normal Excel

**Solving that problem in normal Excel is tedious.** The normal VLOOKUP() routine that we used in Excel for combining a Data table (like Sales) with a Lookup table (like Products) does not work in this case.

**The problem is essentially that Sales and Budget are** *both* **Data tables.** Which one would you VLOOKUP() "into" the other? Plus, each table has multiple rows that correspond to multiple rows in the other, so even if you decided which way VLOOKUP() should "flow," you wouldn't be able to successfully construct a single VLOOKUP() formula.

**A common solution, as we've seen earlier, involves creating** *two* **pivots – one to measure Sales, the other to measure Budget, and then writing formulas that index into each pivot** to form one unified "Sales vs. Budget" report. Takes awhile to get it right, and then when someone inevitably wants to see a slightly different report format or rollup level, it's almost as much work to modify as it was to create the first time!

# Much Faster *and* More Flexible in Power Pivot

Hey, we wouldn't be bringing it up if we didn't have a solution for you ☺

**The short version is that with Power Pivot, Sales and Budget can co-exist in the same pivot.** And you still don't need to combine them into one table.

# Creating Relationships – We Need Some New Lookup Tables

**The next piece of good news is that we can achieve everything we need with relationships.** No fancy disconnected tables or "dotted line" relationships through measures.

**But we do have a problem:** the Budget table refuses to relate to any of our Lookup tables.

For instance, let's try relating Budget to Products using the only Product-related column in Budget: the SubCategory column.

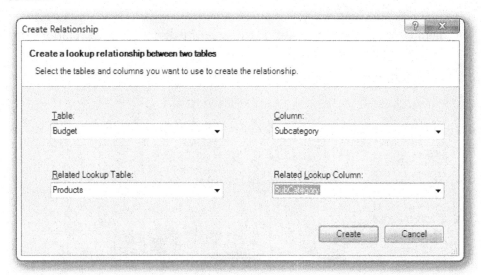

*Figure 316 Attempting to relate Budget to Products...*

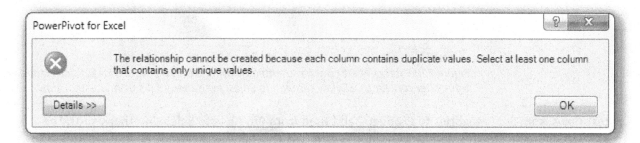

*Figure 317 ...results in the dreaded "many to many" error.*

Well that makes sense: each SubCategory value (like "Mountain Bikes") *does* appear many times in each table.

We have a mismatched granularity problem between Budget and the rest of our model that's existed so far. Which is why it's such a tough problem in normal Excel actually. So how do we solve it? We need a SubCategories Lookup table!

Then we relate it to Products *and* Budget tables, matching the SubCategory column in each.

So now our Diagram View looks like:

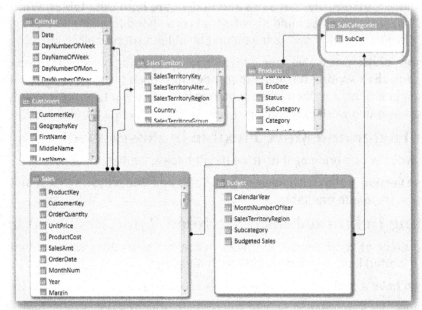

*Figure 319 Updated Diagram View – SubCategories table now acts as Lookup table to both Products and Budget tables*

**Remember, filter context "flows" in the *opposite* direction of the relationship arrows in Power Pivot 2010 and 2013. Let's visualize that:**

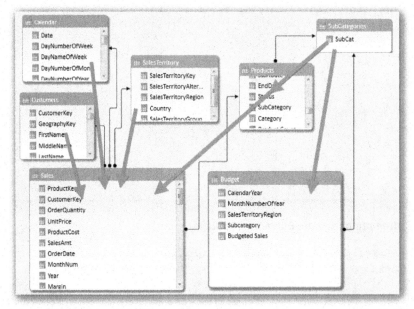

*Figure 320 Filter context flow represented by orange arrows. Note that SubCategories table filter context DOES flow through to Sales, even though it's a "multi-step" flow.*

 Filter context flows from SubCategories to Products, and then from Products to Sales. In other words, the SubCategories still influences Sales (in terms of filter context) as if SubCategories were directly related to Sales. Stated more generally, filter context is transitive: if table A is a Lookup table for table B, and table B is a Lookup table for table C, a filter on table A *will* impact table C.

*Figure 318 A single-column SubCategories table*

# Where Do We *Get* This New Lookup Table? Consider a Database or Power Query

**It's mighty tempting to create this SubCategories table via copy/paste. But this is another one of those places where sourcing your data using a Database or Power Query really shines.** You can automatically build a unique list of Sub-Category values, using a table or query in a database, or by transforming the data in Power Query (whose "Remove Duplicates" command may as well have been named "Make Lookup Table from a Data Table.") This is an absolute life-saver, since it saves you from manual update work in the future when you gain new SubCategories (or retire old ones).

 Note: Later in the Power Query chapter we will actually walk you through an example of creating a Lookup table.

**In absolute terms, it isn't a ton of manual effort** to update the SubCategories table that you created via copy/paste. So compared to the normal Excel way, it's not a big deal.

**But little manual stuff like that starts to stand out a *lot* more, once the other 95% of your spreadsheet life now lacks manual drudgery.**

**When you get to the point where an entire family of sophisticated Excel reports would just be running themselves every day if it weren't for this one manual step,** suddenly that one manual step becomes a big win to eliminate, whereas that same task would have been hardly noticeable in the old world of constant tedious effort.

## SalesTerritory is at Same Granularity Already

For SalesTerritory, we do *not* need to create a new Lookup table. SalesTerritory is the one place where Budget *does* match our existing granularity. So we just create the relationship for that one, no new table required.

## Repeating the "New Table" Process for Calendar

Budget's granularity in terms of time only goes down to Year/Month pairs. So again, we need a new lookup table at that same granularity.

Here is the newly-create YearMonths table:

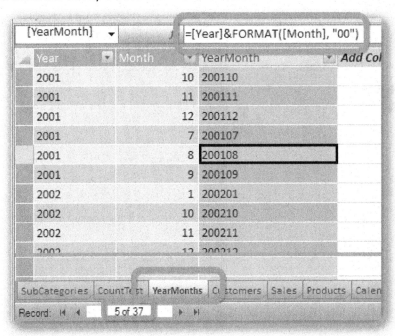

*Figure 321 The new YearMonths table. Note the rowcount of 37, and the calculated column we will use to create relationships.*

 That YearMonth calculated column is a pattern I (Rob) find myself repeating a lot. The FORMAT() function is used to add the extra zero in front of single-digit month numbers. That isn't strictly necessary here – I use it just to make Year/Month combos sort properly – but it's become such force of habit for me that I figured I would share it.

**We add that same sort of YearMonth calculated column to our Budget table, *and* our Calendar table, then create both relationships, yielding the following Diagram View:**

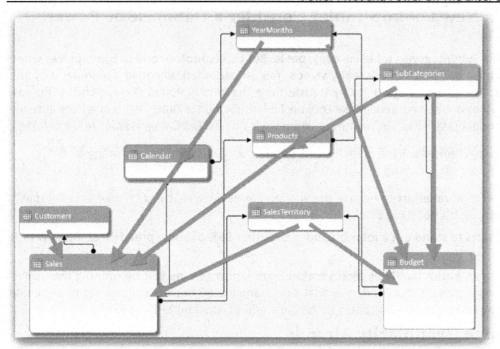

*Figure 322 Diagram View updated to show new tables, relationships, and filter context flow (orange arrows). Note that with this many tables, we have turned off the details on each table so that more can fit on a single screen.*

## Integrated Pivot

We can now construct a single pivot using measures from both Sales and Budget, as long as we *only* use fields from shared Lookup tables on Rows/Column/Filters/Slicers.

A "shared" Lookup table is a table that filters both of our Data tables.

In this case, there are three shared Lookup tables: YearMonths, SalesTerritory, and SubCategories, all marked with asterisks in this diagram:

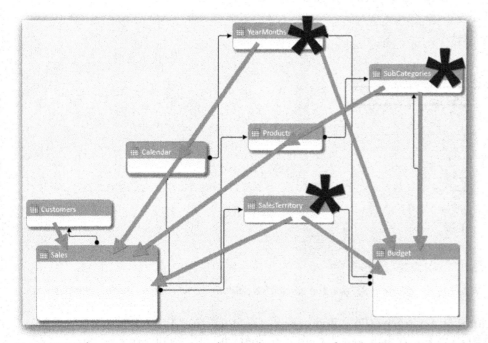

*Figure 323 When constructing a pivot that displays measures from both Budget and Sales, only the three tables marked with asterisks should be used on Rows/Columns/Filters/Slicers, because only those three filter both Sales and Budget.*

We have created a single, simple measure on the Budget table:

```
[Total Budgeted Sales] = SUM ( Budget[Budgeted Sales] )
```

Let's put that on a new pivot, along with [Total Sales] from the Sales table:

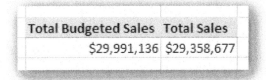

| Total Budgeted Sales | Total Sales |
|---|---|
| $29,991,136 | $29,358,677 |

*Figure 324 These measures come from different Data tables: Budget and Sales*

But the real test comes when we start adding fields to Rows, for instance. Here we have Year on rows:

| Row Labels ▼ | Total Budgeted Sales | Total Sales |
|---|---|---|
| 2001 | $3,236,761 | $3,266,374 |
| 2002 | $6,635,482 | $6,530,344 |
| 2003 | $10,001,112 | $9,791,060 |
| 2004 | $10,117,781 | $9,770,900 |
| Grand Total | $29,991,136 | $29,358,677 |

*Figure 325 Year on Rows, and both measures still work! But note that in this case, Year comes from the YearMonths table and NOT from the Calendar table!*

 Once you have the same sort of field (like Year) in more than one table in your model, you need to make sure you are using the right one for the measures in your pivot. The Calendar[Year] column will not work properly with your Budget measures, for instance. When we are diligent, we try to rename one set of fields using a sensible prefix/suffix so that we can easily differentiate the two different fields coming from different tables.

## Hybrid Measures with Data at Different Grain

This next part is either going to make you yawn and say "yeah, that's obvious" or make you scream "that is the most awesome thing I have EVER seen!" Or somewhere in between perhaps. We still get smiles on our faces every single time we do this.

**We can write new measures that reference (and compare) measures from these separate tables, Budget and Sales, in spite of their differing granularity.**

For instance:

```
[Sales vs. Budget] =
 ( [Total Sales] - [Total Budgeted Sales] )
     / [Total Budgeted Sales]
```

Results:

| Year ▼ | Total Budgeted Sales | Total Sales | Sales vs Budget |
|---|---|---|---|
| 2001 | $3,236,761 | $3,266,374 | 0.9 % |
| 2002 | $6,635,482 | $6,530,344 | -1.6 % |
| 2003 | $10,001,112 | $9,791,060 | -2.1 % |
| 2004 | $10,117,781 | $9,770,900 | -3.4 % |
| Grand Total | $29,991,136 | $29,358,677 | -2.1 % |

*Figure 326 [Sales versus Budget] in action. (We added the conditional formatting, that was not automatic).*

Now we can remove the original two measures, then pile some more fields onto Rows and Columns:

| Sales vs Budget | Column Labels ▾ | | | | |
|---|---|---|---|---|---|
| SubCat - Region ▾ | 2001 | | 2002 | | 2003 |
| ⊟ Mountain Bikes | 3.8 % | | -3.3 % | | -3.5 % |
| Australia | 8.4 % | | -8.6 % | | -6.3 % |
| Canada | -10.0 % | | 3.3 % | | -8.5 % |
| France | 0.5 % | | -4.6 % | | -4.7 % |
| Germany | -15.7 % | | 8.5 % | | -3.2 % |
| United Kingdom | 7.6 % | | 6.3 % | | -11.0 % |
| United States | 3.4 % | | -1.7 % | | 3.2 % |
| ⊟ Road Bikes | 0.3 % | | -1.0 % | | 0.1 % |
| Australia | -6.5 % | | -1.5 % | | -0.1 % |
| Canada | -3.1 % | | 0.7 % | | -6.2 % |
| France | -3.9 % | | -7.6 % | | 0.2 % |
| Germany | -10.8 % | | -3.7 % | | 2.4 % |
| United Kingdom | 1.1 % | | 4.0 % | | -4.9 % |
| United States | 12.7 % | | -0.0 % | | 3.9 % |
| ⊞ Bike Racks | | | | | 3.9 % |
| ⊞ Bike Stands | | | | | -4.7 % |
| ⊞ Bottles and Cages | | | | | -5.1 % |
| ⊞ Caps | | | | | -7.8 % |

*Figure 327 Sales vs. Budget, made criminally simple. Under- and Over- Performers just jump out at you. And this pivot can be rear-ranged/restructured at will – the formulas will just keep working, as long as you only use Lookup tables that filter both Data tables.*

# Example 2: Using that Mysterious RANKX() Third Argument

All right, this has become a matter of honor. The third argument will be put to good use. But we had to invent new data in order to put together a credible example.

First, here is the new data. Pretend we have acquired sales figures for our chief competitor, and how well their bikes have been selling over the past few years.

That is here in the CompetitorSales table:

| ModelName ▾ | Year 🔢 ▾ | SalesAmt ▾ |
|---|---|---|
| Trail 61 | 2001 | $4,428,670 |
| Trail 412 | 2001 | $608,628 |
| Road 187 | 2001 | $1,596,374 |
| Mountain 385 | 2001 | $4,938,898 |
| Trail 333 | 2001 | $1,655,169 |
| Mountain 175 | 2001 | $3,290,579 |
| Mountain 348 | 2001 | $4,487,781 |
| Mountain 127 | 2001 | $165,191 |
| Mountain 159 | 2001 | $1,040,273 |
| Trail 130 | 2001 | $1,612,589 |
| Trail 153 | 2001 | $842,439 |
| Mountain 403 | 2001 | $908,305 |
| Trail 493 | 2001 | $2,922,936 |
| Mountain 496 | 2001 | $1,928,876 |
| Trail 329 | 2001 | $1,174,214 |
| Trail 487 | 2001 | $725,476 |
| Mountain 225 | 2001 | $209,844 |

SubCategorie | CompetitorSales | CountTest | YearMonths | Cu

*Figure 328 CompetitorSales is just three columns: ModelName, Year, and SalesAmt*

## The Problem: Ranking MY Products Against Theirs!

So… what if we want to see how OUR products rank against our competitors in terms of sales?

**For example, if one of our models sold $3M worth of product, and their top three Models sold $4M, $3.5M, and $2.5M, that means our model would rank 3rd against their models.**

(Credit goes to Scott Senkeresty for breaking the logjam and suggesting a scenario in which the third argument could be used.)

## Year Granularity Mismatch Means a New Lookup Table

Just like in Sales vs. Budget, since we have a granularity mismatch, we need a new Lookup table. This time it's the simplest one yet: Years.

*Figure 329 The new Lookup table, Years*

Now we relate that to CompetitorSales, and also to Calendar (so we can filter Sales via "two-hop" relationship path), yielding the following table diagram:

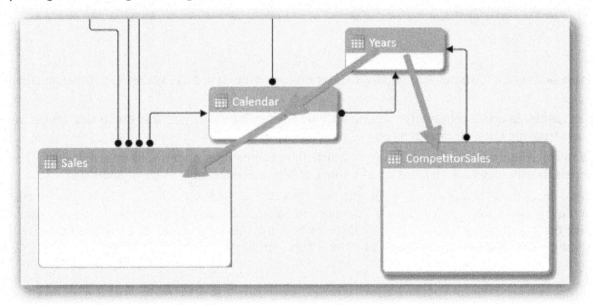

*Figure 330 Table diagram (other tables moved aside to highlight just this "corner" of the model)*

## Simple Measure

Now we add a very simple measure on the CompetitorSales table:

```
[Compete Sales] =
SUM ( CompetitorSales[SalesAmt] )
```

And here it is on a simple pivot:

| Model | ↓ | Compete Sales |
|---|---|---|
| Trail 412 | | $11,064,747 |
| Trail 153 | | $10,935,275 |
| Mountain 385 | | $10,773,383 |
| Trail 487 | | $10,328,574 |
| Trail 222 | | $9,966,929 |
| Trail 333 | | $9,955,816 |
| Trail 61 | | $9,925,752 |
| Mountain 175 | | $9,632,946 |
| Trail 493 | | $8,872,714 |
| Mountain 403 | | $8,648,188 |
| Mountain 496 | | $8,262,950 |
| Road 101 | | $8,220,904 |

*Figure 331 [Compete Sales] with CompetitorSales[ModelName] on Rows*

## Now the Absolutely Amazing "Cross-Rank" Measure

Back on the Sales table (or the Products table if you prefer):

```
[Model Sales Rank vs Competition] =
RANKX (
     VALUES ( CompetitorSales[ModelName] ),
     [Compete Sales],
     [Total Sales]
)
```

What does that formula *mean*? It starts out like it's going to just rank competitive products against each other and then takes a twist:

- **VALUES(CompetitorSales[ModelName])** – this means that the "entities" being ranked are in fact the unique ModelNames from the CompetitorSales table.

- **[Compete Sales]** – this means that the measure by which those competitive models will be ranked will be their own [Compete Sales] measure. So far, this is just normal, totally understandable usage of RANKX().

- **[Total Sales]** – but whoa! This means we're going to take the value of [Total Sales] in our current filter context (which on the left-side pivot, is a ModelName from *our* company), and insert it into the pecking order established by the first two arguments! Essentially, treat the value of this measure, in the current filter context, as if it were a participant in the normal evaluation of RANKX() as controlled by the first two arguments.

And results:

| My Products' Sales | | Model Sales Rank vs Competition | Their Sales | |
|---|---|---|---|---|
| Model | Total Sales | | Model | Compete Sales |
| Mountain-200 | $7,929,475 | 14 | Trail 412 | $11,064,747 |
| Road-150 | $5,549,897 | 19 | Trail 153 | $10,935,275 |
| Road-250 | $4,451,260 | 19 | Mountain 385 | $10,773,383 |
| Touring-1000 | $2,992,008 | 20 | Trail 487 | $10,328,574 |
| Road-350-W | $1,580,220 | 20 | Trail 222 | $9,966,929 |
| Road-550-W | $1,514,622 | 20 | Trail 333 | $9,955,816 |
| Mountain-100 | $1,341,121 | 20 | Trail 61 | $9,925,752 |
| Road-750 | $779,206 | 20 | Mountain 175 | $9,632,946 |
| Road-650 | $645,380 | 20 | Trail 493 | $8,872,714 |
| Touring-2000 | $451,924 | 20 | Mountain 403 | $8,648,188 |
| Mountain-400-W | $417,833 | 20 | Mountain 496 | $8,262,950 |
| Touring-3000 | $400,869 | 20 | Road 101 | $8,220,904 |
| Mountain-500 | $264,330 | 20 | Road 187 | $7,955,912 |
| Sport-100 | $225,336 | 20 | Mountain 127 | $7,296,954 |
| Long-Sleeve Logo Jersey | $86,783 | 20 | Mountain 348 | $6,882,475 |
| Short-Sleeve Classic Jersey | $86,168 | 20 | Mountain 225 | $6,549,169 |
| Women's Mountain Shorts | $71,320 | 20 | Trail 130 | $5,822,266 |

*Figure 332 New Cross-Rank measure compared to pivot displaying competitive sales. Our top product would indeed be behind their 13 best products, earning a rank of 14.*

## And Since Both Are Filtered by the Years Table...

We can add Years[Year] as a slicer to both pivots!

Let's see if it still works when we slice to a different year:

| Year | | | |
|---|---|---|---|
| 2001 | 2002 | 2003 | 2004 |

| My Products' Sales | | Model Sales Rank vs Competition | Their Sales | |
|---|---|---|---|---|
| Model | Total Sales | | Model | Compete Sales |
| Mountain-200 | $3,723,271 | 4 | Trail 487 | $4,506,831 |
| Road-250 | $2,144,214 | 9 | Trail 333 | $3,989,343 |
| Touring-1000 | $1,058,527 | 13 | Road 187 | $3,971,737 |
| Road-550-W | $676,096 | 16 | Trail 153 | $3,710,833 |
| Road-350-W | $540,915 | 17 | Trail 412 | $3,172,682 |
| Road-750 | $326,154 | 19 | Mountain 403 | $3,050,286 |
| Road-650 | $264,651 | 19 | Trail 493 | $2,982,821 |
| Touring-2000 | $195,591 | 20 | Trail 329 | $2,736,560 |
| Touring-3000 | $163,317 | 20 | Mountain 496 | $1,722,153 |
| Mountain-400-W | $159,284 | 20 | Trail 222 | $1,343,252 |
| Mountain-500 | $107,083 | 20 | Mountain 127 | $1,287,586 |
| Sport-100 | $92,584 | 20 | Mountain 348 | $1,085,922 |

*Figure 333 Shared Year slicer: measure still works*

Wow.

# 19 - Performance: Keep Things Running Fast

## How Important is Speed?

### "Now" Is Three Seconds in Length

**Let's start here. Research suggests that human beings perceive the moment of "now" to be three seconds in length.** Hugs are even typically three seconds! Think of it as the fundamental unit of human time – something that takes three seconds or less is happening "now," and something that lasts longer than that requires... waiting.

Sound squishy or touchy-feely to you? Well it's relevant to us data crunchers too, in a big way.

**Earlier this year, someone at Microsoft emailed and asked me (Rob) the following question:** "For large Power Pivot workbooks, how long do you think users will expect to wait when they click a slicer?"

**My answer:** "It must be fast, period. They don't care that there is a lot of data behind it. If it isn't fast, they won't engage. The limits of human patience are not the least bit sympathetic to our data volume or complexity problems."

**When we produce interactive reports or dashboards for consumption by the rest of our workgroup, we must keep in mind that the speed of interaction is critical. Anything longer than three seconds, and we risk losing the consumer altogether.**

 If you would like to read an interesting article on this "3 seconds" topic, see http://ppvt.pro/3srule

## What Happens When Something Takes Longer Than Three Seconds?

If a slicer click or related interaction takes too long, three things happen:

1. **The user's train of thought is broken while waiting on the click to complete.** Their mind wanders off topic and they often flip back over to email while they wait. They sometimes forget to come back.

They do not "commit" to the experience, do not get absorbed, and generally decide to remain "shallow" in their thoughts toward it.

2. **If they grow to expect "long" wait times, they will ultimately decide not to click at all.** If they know that conducting a slicer click exploration of the data is going to take 15 seconds a click, and they may have to execute 10 clicks over the course of their exploration, they simply decide not to do it at all.

Yeah, if they had invested that 2.5 minutes, they may have discovered something amazing or revolutionary in the data. Tough. Humans aren't built for that. They want their three seconds.

3. **Ultimately, and most importantly, your impact as a professional is severely diminished.** Putting together something amazing that no one uses is the same thing as doing nothing at all. Your work (and you) will be undervalued and viewed as expendable.

**So it is important to think of speed as an equal, a "peer," of the content you are delivering.** You *cannot* simply tell yourself, "I'm delivering a ton of great information, it's worth the wait for people when they click the slicer." Speed is just as important as having the right numbers.

**To underscore that point: it is better to produce something that delivers, say, 10 "points" of information that *everyone* is using than to deliver 50 "points" of information that only 10% of people use.** That's not just a point about speed of course – making the report visually clean and understandable is also important. And while we have many opinions about that stuff, we don't have space for it in this book. So we'll stick to performance.

## Slicers: The Biggest Culprit

**It may surprise you to learn that those innocuous, friendly little slicers on your report are usually far and away the most expensive parts of your report.**

Time to revisit those three terms we introduced in the FILTER() chapter:

**Performance:** the practice of keeping your reports fast for your users. For instance, if someone clicks a slicer and it takes 30 seconds for the pivot to update, we would refer to that as "poor performance." If it responds instantly, we might call that "excellent performance," or we might say that the pivot "performs well."

**Response time:** the amount of time it takes a report to respond to a user action and display the updated results. In the example above, we described a "response time" of 30 seconds as poor. Generally we try to keep response times to 3 seconds or less.

**Expensive:** an operation is said to be "expensive" if it consumes a lot of time and therefore impacts performance/response time. For instance, above we could have described <column> = <static value> tests as "inexpensive" for the DAX engine, and richer comparisons like <column> = <measure> as "potentially expensive."

## "Cross-Filtering" Behavior

You've probably seen cross-filtering in action but not given it much thought. Here's an example from the NFL (American football) data that we use occasionally on the blog:

*Figure 334 No selections made on slicers, but no player heavier than 330 pounds has ever caught a Touchdown (TD) Pass (at least not in this data set)*

Now we select two "tiles" in the top slicer – the ones at 320 and 340 pounds:

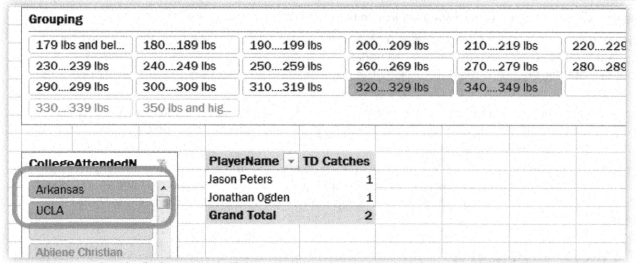

**Grouping**

| 179 lbs and bel... | 180....189 lbs | 190....199 lbs | 200....209 lbs | 210....219 lbs | 220....229 |
| 230....239 lbs | 240....249 lbs | 250....259 lbs | 260...269 lbs | 270....279 lbs | 280...289 |
| 290....299 lbs | 300....309 lbs | 310....319 lbs | 320...329 lbs | 340...349 lbs | |
| 330....339 lbs | 350 lbs and hig... | | | | |

| PlayerName | TD Catches |
| --- | --- |
| Jason Peters | 1 |
| Jonathan Ogden | 1 |
| **Grand Total** | **2** |

CollegeAttendedN

- Arkansas
- UCLA
- Abilene Christian

*Figure 335 Note that the "CollegeAttended" slicer now has only two selectable values – all other are disabled*

**Why has the CollegeAttended slicer "filter itself" if we have not made any selection on it?**

Well there are only two players in this data set weighing 320 pounds or more who have a TD Catch – Jason Peters and Jonathan Ogden, and they attended Arkansas and UCLA. The slicer is being helpful and showing you that clicking any other CollegeAttended will yield a completely blank pivot.

> If clicking a given "tile" in a slicer would yield a completely blank pivot (every measure returning blank), then that tile will be disabled. That's what we call "cross filtering," and it's a slicer behavior that is enabled for all slicers by default.

Cross-filtering can be, and usually is, a very helpful feature.

## Cross-Filtering is Expensive in Terms of Performance

But it's also a LOT of work for the Power Pivot engine. Here, we add another measure to the previous pivot, without changing our slicer selections at all:

**Grouping**

| 179 lbs and bel... | 180....189 lbs | 190....199 lbs | 200....209 lbs | 210....219 lbs | 220....229 l |
| 230....239 lbs | 240....249 lbs | 250....259 lbs | 260...269 lbs | 270....279 lbs | 280...289 l |
| 290....299 lbs | 300....309 lbs | 310....319 lbs | 320...329 lbs | 340...349 lbs | |
| 330....339 lbs | 350 lbs and hig... | | | | |

| PlayerName | TD Catches | Total Catches |
| --- | --- | --- |
| Fred Miller | | 1 |
| Jason Peters | 1 | 2 |
| Jonathan Ogden | 1 | 1 |
| Robert Hicks | | 1 |
| **Grand Total** | **2** | **5** |

CollegeAttendedN...

- Arkansas
- Baylor
- Mississippi State
- UCLA
- Abilene Christian

*Figure 336 Added one measure, [Total Catches], and now two more Colleges are clickable*

See that? So the slicers are not just sensitive to each other, they are also sensitive to the measures on the pivot. That means the measures have to be evaluated for each of the Colleges in the slicer (even though we have clicked none) to see if *either* measure would return a value for *each* tile!

In order to enable or disable tiles in a slicer, the cross-filtering behavior actually *re-runs the entire pivot behind the scenes*, as if the tiles in the slicer were on Rows (or Columns)! Those rows of the "behind the scenes" pivot that returned at least one non-blank value are the tiles that will be displayed as clickable.

That "behind the scenes" process is repeated for *every* slicer connected to your pivot, *every* time the report consumer clicks something.

**So the short version is this: every slicer you add is just as expensive as adding an entire new pivot.** A single pivot with five slicers, in other words, will be about as slow as six pivots. Let that sink in.

# Mitigating the Effects of Cross-Filtering

So, what do we do about this? A few possibilities:

1. **Do nothing.** If you're still under 3 seconds, you may not need to worry.
2. **Use fewer slicers.** Always worth considering since they eat so much screen real estate anyway. If a particular slicer is unlikely to be used most of the time, and is there "just in case the consumer needs it," you might consider creating a completely separate report to address that use case.
3. **Turn off cross-filtering for some slicers**. This is simple to do, the question is more about when to do it – for which slicers? Let's cover the "how" first.

## How to Turn off Cross-Filtering

1. **Select a slicer.** We do this by clicking somewhere in the label area of the slicer, typically. The key is to get the slicer Options tab to show up in the ribbon:

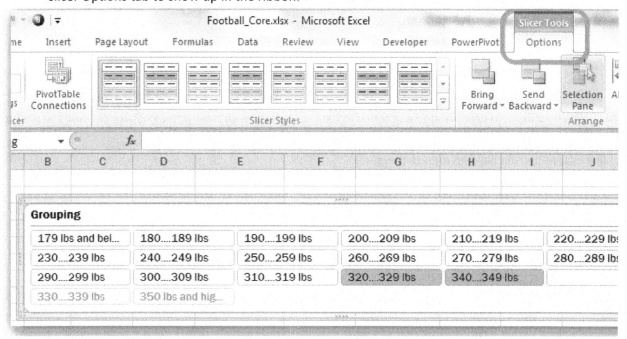

*Figure 337 Select a slicer in the sheet itself (not the field list), and this ribbon tab will appear*

2. **Click the Slicer Settings button** on that ribbon tab:

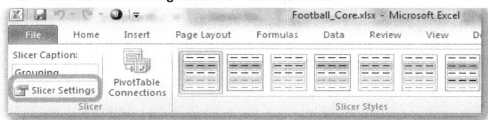

*Figure 338 Click this button*

3. **On the resulting dialog, uncheck** this checkbox:

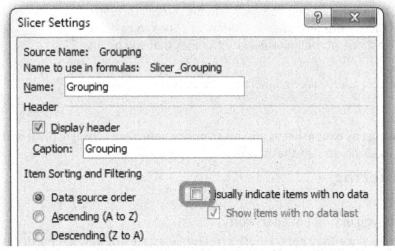

*Figure 339 Unchecking this checkbox turns off cross-filtering for this slicer*

## Turning off Cross-Filtering Only Impacts *that* Slicer

To see what we mean by this, check out the slicer after cross-filtering has been turned off:

| Grouping | | | | | |
| --- | --- | --- | --- | --- | --- |
| 179 lbs and bel... | 180...189 lbs | 190...199 lbs | 200...209 lbs | 210...219 lbs | 220...229 lb |
| 230...239 lbs | 240...249 lbs | 250...259 lbs | 260...269 lbs | 270...279 lbs | 280...289 lb |
| 290...299 lbs | 300...309 lbs | 310...319 lbs | 320...329 lbs | 330...339 lbs | 340...349 lb |
| 350 lbs and hig... | | | | | |

*Figure 340 The highlighted tile used to be disabled and sorted to the end, but now with cross-filtering off, it's enabled and back to its original position*

OK, so disabling cross-filter *did* have an impact there.

But now look at the *other* slicer:

*Figure 341 The other slicer is STILL only showing four enabled tiles*

So this means this slicer is still affected by the other. For instance, let's clear the selection on the first slicer and see what happens:

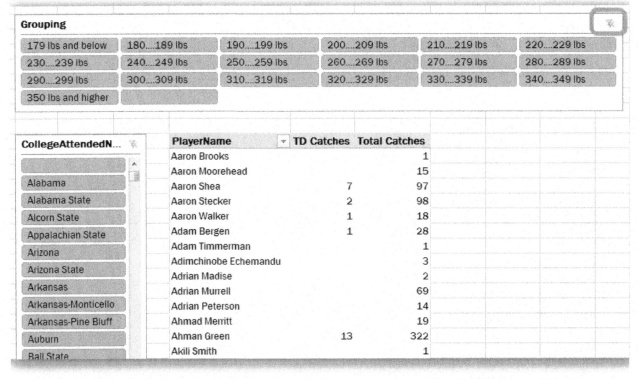

Figure 342 Even though Slicer 1 has cross filtering turned off, selections made in Slicer 1 STILL impact Slicer 2

A slicer with cross-filtering turned off still impacts all other slicers. Disabling cross-filter only impacts whether that slicer is impacted by other slicers. Think of this as turning off "incoming" filtering for that slicer, rather than "outgoing" filtering.

## Slicers For Which You Should Turn Cross-Filtering Off

At a high level there are three kinds of slicers for which we feel pretty good about disabling cross filtering:

1. **Slicers for which all tiles almost always have data.** If all or most tiles are always going to be active anyway, why have cross-filtering chewing up response time? One common example of this is Calendar/Time related slicers. You generally have data for every month for instance (if not you may want to consider trimming your Calendar table).

2. **Slicers with very few tiles.** The cross-filtering feature is most useful for keeping the consumer from having to scroll the slicer, looking for the tile they want to select. So if there are only four tiles, and there is no scrollbar to worry about, that slicer jumps out at us as a candidate.

3. **Slicers that form the "top" of a hierarchy.** If you have three slicers – one for Country, one for State, and one for City, the consumer tends to make a choice on Country, then State, and then City (assuming they need to filter that deep). It's pretty critical that State and City slicers retain cross-filtering (for the long scrolling reason), but disabling it for Country does not compromise that. Plus, the topmost slicer in a hierarchy tends to have the fewest tiles too.

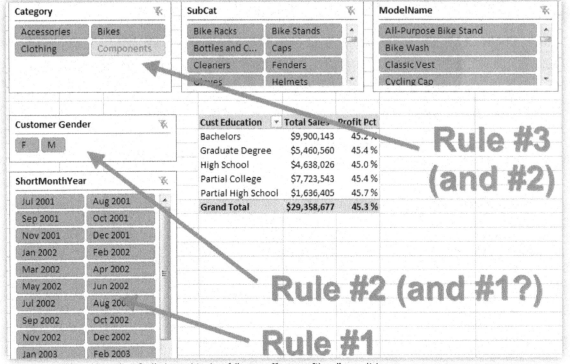

*Figure 343 An example of all three kinds of "turn off cross-filter" candidates*

OK, that's the easiest/most obvious thing to look at if/when a report is slow. Let's move on to data shaping.

# The Shape of Your Source Tables Is Also Important

The shape (and characteristics) of your source tables can also have a tremendous impact on performance. In this section we will list some of our most impactful tips. Some of these changes are easy to make, and others require more up-front planning.

## Narrower Tables are Better

- **Remove columns you aren't going to use.** Leave them out when importing or delete unneeded columns from existing tables.

- **Move as many columns as you can from Data tables to Lookup tables.** The "narrower is better" rule applies more forcefully to tables that have higher row counts. So if you can move a row from a Data table to a Lookup table, even if it means creating a new Lookup table, it is very often worth doing so.

Here's a quick example:

| StoreID | Date | TotalSales | City | State | ZIP |
|---|---|---|---|---|---|
| 174 | 4/1/201... | 33376 | Duvall | WA | 98019 |
| 187 | 4/1/201... | 89909 | Kirkland | WA | 98033 |
| 205 | 4/1/201... | 44317 | Kirkland | WA | 98033 |
| 276 | 4/1/201... | 74610 | Bellevue | WA | 98005 |
| 302 | 4/1/201... | 53480 | Redmo... | WA | 98052 |
| 309 | 4/1/201... | 29123 | Redmo... | WA | 98052 |
| 323 | 4/1/201... | 91802 | Redmo... | WA | 98052 |
| 325 | 4/1/201... | 52957 | Kirkland | WA | 98034 |
| 377 | 4/1/201... | 70203 | Kirkland | WA | 98033 |
| 400 | 4/1/201... | 34442 | Bellevue | WA | 98004 |
| 407 | 4/1/201... | 10768 | Bellevue | WA | 98004 |

*Figure 344 A fragment of a Sales table. Note how every time we have 98033 for ZIPCode, City=Kirkland and State=WA*

We don't need all three columns (City/State/ZIP) in this Sales table – ZIP is all we need in order to precisely "pin down" City and State. So we can move City and State to another table:

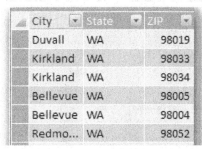

*Figure 345 Our new Locations table (could also sensibly have been named ZIPCodes)*

And remove City and State columns from Sales:

| StoreID | Date | TotalSales | ZIP |
|---|---|---|---|
| 174 | 4/1/201... | 33376 | 98019 |
| 187 | 4/1/201... | 89909 | 98033 |
| 205 | 4/1/201... | 44317 | 98033 |
| 276 | 4/1/201... | 74610 | 98005 |
| 302 | 4/1/201... | 53480 | 98052 |
| 309 | 4/1/201... | 29123 | 98052 |
| 323 | 4/1/201... | 91802 | 98052 |
| 325 | 4/1/201... | 52957 | 98034 |
| 377 | 4/1/201... | 70203 | 98033 |
| 400 | 4/1/201... | 34442 | 98004 |
| 407 | 4/1/201... | 10768 | 98004 |
| 467 | 4/1/201... | 59412 | 98053 |
| 542 | 4/1/201... | 69295 | 98053 |
| 651 | 4/1/201... | 79463 | 98004 |

*Figure 346 City and State columns removed from Sales table*

Then we relate Sales to Locations:

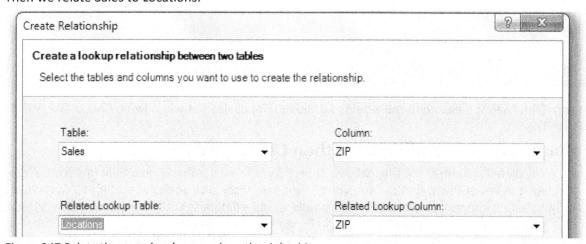

*Figure 347 Relate them, and we've now done the right thing*

- **Sometimes it may even be worth "pivoting" the source data before import (moving columns to rows).** Power Query has the UNPIVOT transformation, that can turn a wide and short table into a tall and narrow table. If you are working with a Database, you can also use the SQL UNPIVOT command. This sometimes can make a big difference, and other times have no impact, so it requires some experimentation.

Here's an example of a "wide" Sales table:

| Date | TotalSales | Normal Sales | Promo Sales | Returns | Rebates | Margin | Discounts |
|------|-----------|--------------|-------------|---------|---------|--------|-----------|
| 174 4/1/201... | 33376 | 43204 | 24086 | 37931 | 34375 | 28185 | 26023 |
| 187 4/1/201... | 89909 | 42600 | 21669 | 22323 | 44419 | 23394 | 26730 |
| 205 4/1/201... | 44317 | 22952 | 35902 | 40079 | 28999 | 34696 | 24511 |
| 377 4/1/201... | 70203 | 28269 | 25455 | 43945 | 25594 | 25531 | 20542 |
| 400 4/1/201... | 34442 | 28631 | 20924 | 21041 | 44641 | 34339 | 39198 |
| 407 4/1/201... | 10768 | 49734 | 44222 | 46381 | 25651 | 48936 | 28179 |
| 467 4/1/201... | 59412 | 28251 | 33842 | 44064 | 40492 | 45455 | 32095 |
| 542 4/1/201... | 69295 | 36118 | 48611 | 40257 | 37022 | 42440 | 29791 |

*Figure 348 Many numerical columns: a "wide" table (9 columns, 1M rows)*

Here's that same table "unpivoted" to be tall and narrow:

| StoreID | Date | AmtType | Amt |
|---------|------|---------|-----|
| 174 | 4/1/201... | 1 | 33376 |
| 187 | 4/1/201... | 1 | 89909 |
| 205 | 4/1/201... | 1 | 44317 |
| 377 | 4/1/201... | 1 | 70203 |
| 400 | 4/1/201... | 1 | 34442 |
| 407 | 4/1/201... | 1 | 10768 |
| 467 | 4/1/201... | 1 | 59412 |
| 542 | 4/1/201... | 1 | 69295 |
| 651 | 4/1/201... | 1 | 79463 |
| 787 | 4/1/201... | 1 | 18329 |
| 893 | 4/1/201... | 1 | 27108 |
| 174 | 4/1/201... | 2 | 43204 |
| 187 | 4/1/201... | 2 | 42600 |
| 205 | 4/1/201... | 2 | 22952 |
| 377 | 4/1/201... | 2 | 28269 |
| 400 | 4/1/201... | 2 | 28631 |
| 407 | 4/1/201... | 2 | 49734 |
| 467 | 4/1/201... | 2 | 28251 |
| 542 | 4/1/201 | 2 | 36118 |

*Figure 349 Table has been reduced to 4 columns, but now 7M rows*

Then, rather than your [Total Sales] measure formula being SUM(Sales[TotalSales]), it will now be CALCULATE(SUM(Sales[Amt]), AmtType=1).

## Imported Columns Are Generally Better than Calculated Columns

If you can implement a calculated column in the original data source (typically a database), and then import that column rather than calculate it in Power Pivot, that can surprisingly improve slicer click performance. If you can, implement a calculated column before importing to Power Pivot (typically within a database OR by using Power Query), and then bring in that new source column rather than calculate it in Power Pivot. That can surprisingly improve slicer click performance. (Imported columns are compressed more efficiently, leading to smaller file sizes, lower RAM consumption, and usually better slicer click performance).

A few notes on this:

- **Again, the more rows in the table, the more impactful this change can be.** We don't worry about it in small Lookup tables for instance.

- **If the calculated column is commonly used on Rows/Columns/Slicers, that is more impactful than a numeric column.** Converting a column like "Category" from calculated to imported will yield a bigger performance improvement, for instance, than "QuantitySold," which is typically just used as the basis for a SUM() measure.

(But if you've moved all of your Row/Column/Slicer/Filter fields to smaller Lookup tables as recommended earlier in the book, this sort of change would be happening in a smaller table anyway and may not be much help.)

- **If the calculated column is the basis for a relationship, that is more impactful.** This is basically an extension of the previous bullet, since a relationship column is used to link a Lookup table to its Data table, and the Lookup table's columns are used on Rows/Columns/Slicers/Filters. So if nearly every column in your Data and Lookup tables is imported, but you created a single calculated column in your Data table so that you could link it to the Lookup table, you're likely paying most of the calculated column penalty despite your efforts elsewhere.

## "Star Schema" is Generally Better than "Snowflake Schema"

Longtime database folks already know what we are talking about. Everyone else has no idea, so the following explanation is for you ☺

Snowflake schema = multiple levels of Lookup tables.
Star schema = one level of Lookup tables.

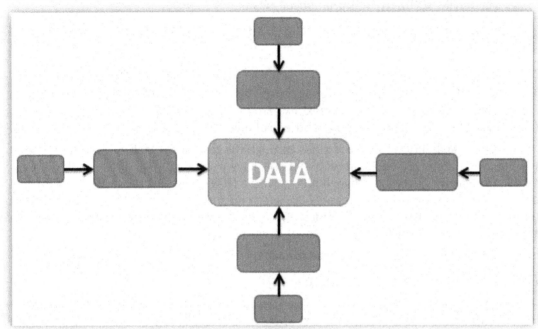

Figure 350 Snowflake schema: multiple levels of Lookup tables

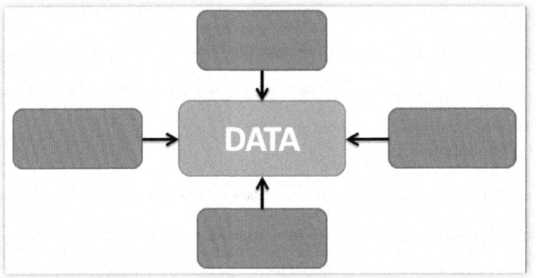

Figure 351 Star schema: if you can "squash" chained lookup tables into single, larger tables, that often can improve performance (yes even though it makes the tables wider – the most important table to keep narrow is the Data table)

Note: in the chapter on Multiple Data Tables (such as Budget versus Sales), it was explained that sometimes you cannot avoid multi-hop Lookup table arrangements. That's fine. Just don't go crazy and create lots of chained Lookup tables because you *can* – do it only when you have to. And if your reports exhibit good response times already, you can ignore this guideline altogether ☺

# Measure Performance

We could write many chapters on this, and they still wouldn't be enough. In fact, others such as Marco Russo, Alberto Ferrari, and Chris Webb are the "go to" people when it comes to measure tuning and performance. We learn from them all the time – we don't claim to be the world's greatest at DAX. (Our knack is more for explaining it and prioritizing what you need to know first). Their blogs and books are definitely worth checking out if you find yourself "outgrowing" this book ☺

But there are a few quick tips worth sharing.

## DISTINCTCOUNT() is Much Faster than COUNTROWS(DISTINCT())

In v1, we had to use COUNTROWS(DISTINCT()), because we lacked a DISTINCTCOUNT() function.

Now though you should always use DISTINCTCOUNT(). It is *dramatically* faster.

## FILTER() Should Only Be Used Against Lookup Tables and Other "Small" Columns

This tip has been mentioned before, but the reason behind it has not. Here it is, as briefly as possible.

A "raw" <filter> argument to CALCULATE() has the ability to inspect large "blocks" of rows all at once to see whether those rows should be active according to a specified filter context like Products[Color]="Blue". That is what makes a raw <filter> so blindingly fast to evaluate, even against tens or hundreds of millions of rows of data!

FILTER() lacks that "block inspection" capability, and *always* steps through the rows in its <table> argument *one at a time.* A raw CALCULATE() <filter> that scans 100 million rows might only have to look at 1,000 different blocks in order to decide which of the 100 million rows should be active. But if you use a FILTER() against those same 100 million rows, it may have to make 100 million inspections rather than 1,000, which means it could be 100,000 times slower! In practice DAX uses various optimization and caching techniques, thus your results would vary based on your data model and complexity of the measure.

However, as a general rule, **with FILTER(), smaller tables are your friend.**

## Remember That the "X" Functions Are Loops

**If you have a SUMX() measure in your pivot, for instance, remember that it looks at every row in the <table> argument one at a time, just like FILTER().** Sometimes it's easy to forget how much work SUMX() and similar functions are doing behind the scenes.

It's especially easy to forget how much work is going on if the column or table from the <table> argument is not displayed on the pivot. (It's not actually slower, it's just that you don't *see* what it's looping through.)

**In our experience, a single X function is rarely a problem. But when you start "nesting" loops inside of other loops, things can get crazy in a hurry.**

For instance, one time we wrote a measure that was essentially a SUMX() of a MAXX() – our formula was something like:

```
SUMX(<table with 1k rows>, [Another Measure])
```

But the formula for [Another Measure] was:

```
MAXX(<table with 1k rows>, <simple SUM measure>)
```

**You see where this is going. We had a 1,000 row loop inside another 1,000 row loop, so our measure was doing 1 million loops for every single measure cell in the pivot!** That was... not fast.

**Similarly, if you have an X function measure as part of the <rich filter> argument inside a FILTER() function, you can again get into nested loops just like this** – the FILTER() might step through 1,000 rows, evaluating a 1,000-loop SUMX() at each step, resulting in 1 million loops for each measure cell in the pivot.

We have given you a lot of ways you should shape your data to optimize performance, let's talk about a tool that can help you do that.

# 20 - Power Query to the Rescue

**Databases are a "luxurious" data source.** The data that we've been loading into Power Pivot throughout this book originated from a very clean sample data set provided by Microsoft. We then made some adjustments and additions to make said data suitable for the purposes in this book.

That's a key characteristic of databases: human beings put effort into them so that the data is clean, complete, and optimized for how it's going to be used.

So if most of your data for analysis comes from a database, that's great news! And even better if you are on good terms with the Database Administrator (DBA) who runs said database. If you have "bad" data, the DBA is usually able to clean that up and turn it into "good" data before it gets loaded into Power Pivot.

*Figure 352 If you have a DBA (Database Administrator) – love them, hug them, thank them. And then ask them nicely to clean and re-shape data for your purposes.*

**But outside of Database Land, Real Data is… Messy.** Sadly, most of the world does NOT get their data from databases. Most of the world is up to its eyeballs in text files and Excel files, and *those* are the source of data for analysis and reporting.

In fact, even in cases where you *do* have a database, *and* a friendly DBA, *some* of your data is still likely coming from those sorts of Wild West sources. After all, the Export to Excel button is the 3rd most common button in all traditional data and BI applications (after OK and Cancel of course), and those buttons produce these sorts of files.

(This is deliciously ironic of course – all of those tools that were supposed to be the "be all, end all" for reporting and analysis – well, they fail, in practice, 99 times out of 100. So then we just use those expensive and bloated systems' Export to Excel buttons as data sources for the *real* work, which always happens in Excel, and now also in Power Pivot and Power BI. Such is the world of data, everywhere.)

Yes, real data is often split across numerous files when you really want it in a single file. Real data is strung across columns when you really need it in rows. Real data comes in a flat table when you really need separate data and lookup tables.

*Figure 353 Most people, sadly, live outside of Database Fairy Tale Land. They live in the Messy Real World of Data.*

**So, this chapter is *not* for those of us who reside full-time in Database Land.** If you live in Database Land, and have a friendly DBA who will clean and shape all of your data for you, fantastic, skip to the next chapter!

**This chapter is for the rest of us.** When you need to clean and re-shape data out here in the Messy Real World of data dumps and exports, responsible data ninjas reach for Power Query.

# Power Query: Bring Order to Messy Data

Power Query lets you clean, shape and transform your data while still retaining the ability of one click or automated refresh. Gone are the 23 manual steps you did in Excel and could never really remember.

Here are some reasons we love Power Query:

- **Perfect Complement to Power Pivot:** Power Pivot has very limited means to clean, shape and transform data (hence the earlier reliance on databases). Thus Power Query as an Excel Add-In (also integrated with Power BI Desktop) becomes the perfect complement to Power Pivot.

- **Easy to learn, but also incredibly deep:** Okay, the instant love comes from the "easy to learn" part. It is incredibly easy to start with. The interface is very intuitive with most actions driven by the friendly and familiar Office ribbon interface. But you are not limited to the buttons on the ribbon – there is an entire language lurking under the surface, ready to do your bidding.

Power Query has so much to offer that you could write a whole book about it. In fact, we recommend "M Is for (Data) Monkey" by the wizards Ken Puls and Miguel Escobar: http://ppvt.pro/DataMonkey

*Figure 354 If you seek an entire book on Power Query and M, look no further than this cleverly-titled tome*

So, while we clearly don't have the space to include an entire second book in these pages, we *will* cover the highest-value and easiest-to-learn techniques here.

You can view this as an introduction, or you can view it as "All I Ever Needed to Know About Power Query, I Learned In Kindergarten." And this chapter, dear friends, is Power Query Kindergarten.

Power Query (within Excel and Power BI Desktop) is currently receiving updates on a monthly basis. That means you can expect new and improved functionality going forward. That also means that the interface might look *slightly* different than the screenshots you see here. Usually this should at worst be a case of renaming or reshuffling. Power Query has stabilized enough that we expect the core functionality covered here to remain the same.

We have used Excel 2013 screenshots in this chapter. Sample files are available in Excel 2013 format and PBIX (Power BI Desktop) format.

With all that said, let's dive into the key examples.

# #1 - Appending Files to Create a Single Power Pivot Table

## Scenario

You would like to create a Product Lookup table. However the challenge is that your company has three manufacturing plants and each manufactures a *distinct* set of products. You receive a separate Product file from each plant, and you would like to combine these files into a single table before feeding them into Power Pivot. Furthermore, you would ideally like this to be automatic, so the next time you get new files, a single click will process the whole kit and caboodle. (Or better yet, schedule an automatic refresh – the mythical Zero Click Solution spoken of in hushed tones around campfires late at night.)

And just to make things a bit more difficult, let's say that the Product files from each plant are published to a website:

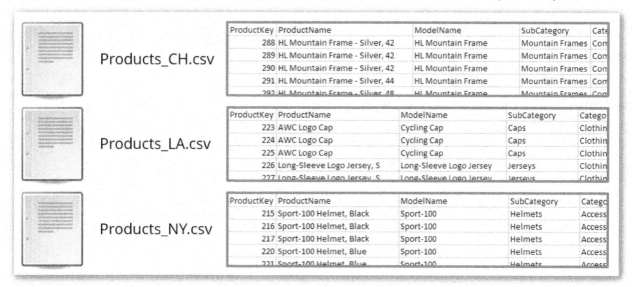

Figure 355 *Need to combine three CSV files of identical structures – located on a website*

You don't need to download the CSV files to your computer! You can leave the files where they are and build a completely automatic system—one that requires *zero* manual intervention on an ongoing basis.

## Connecting to One of the CSV Files

Once Power Query is downloaded and installed, you get a Power Query ribbon tab, which has a "From Web" button on it:

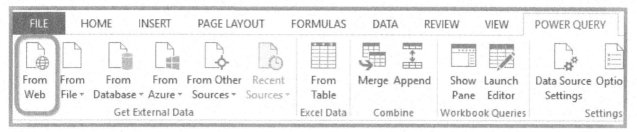

Figure 356 *You start by clicking the "From Web" button on the Power Query ribbon tab (Excel 2013 version pictured)*

After you click this From Web button on the Power Query ribbon tab, enter the URL for one of the CSV Files:

*Figure 357 Don't download the CSV – just link to it on the website!*

You now get a pop-up query window with its own ribbon:

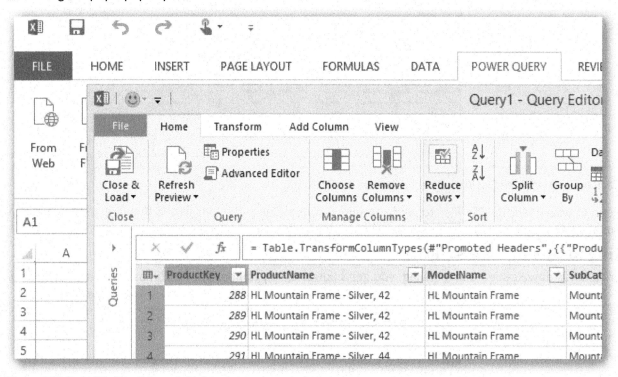

*Figure 358 Ooh. We like ribbons full of tools.*

## Adding a Custom Column to "Tag" This File

Next, you need to add a column to "tag" this file as containing the products from Chicago plant. Click Add Custom Column, specify the column name and enter a static formula (="CH"):

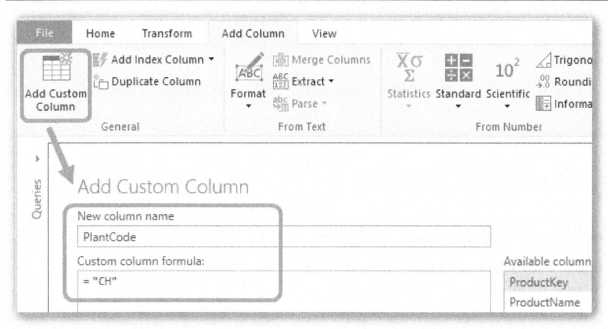

*Figure 359 Creating a Custom Column in Power Query – there's a lot more you could do here using Power Query formulas*

Once you hit OK you should see the results:

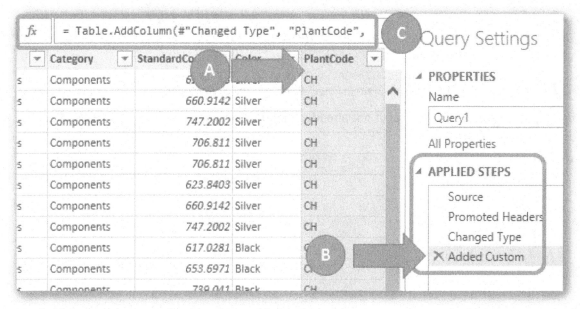

*Figure 360 Our new custom column has been added to the results*

Notice the following:

a) **The custom column** gets added in the Power Query result

b) **The Applied Steps** show a new step for the 'Added Custom' Column. Notice it shows a catalog of all Power Query Steps taken so far. This represents the core ability of Power Query, to record and replay all data transformation steps you take. Thus enabling one-click or automated refresh. All in a human friendly interface.

c) **The formula bar** shows the M language formula for this step. Power Query has its own formula language known as 'M'. The formula bar gives you a glimpse into the world of M. However, you don't need to learn or understand M in order to use Power Query via its powerful ribbon tools.

Then you rename this query and click Close & Load:

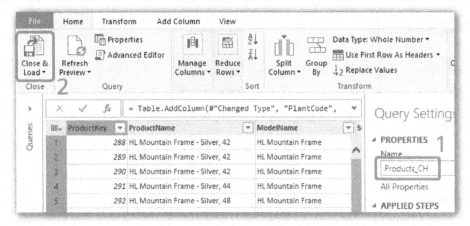

Figure 361 Rename this query to be Products_CH, and click Close & Load

## Loading the Data into Power Pivot

The steps above "land" the data in Excel:

| | A | B | C | D |
|---|---|---|---|---|
| 1 | ProductKey | ProductName | ModelName | SubCategory |
| 2 | 288 | HL Mountain Frame - Silver, 42 | HL Mountain Frame | Mountain Frames |
| 3 | 289 | HL Mountain Frame - Silver, 42 | HL Mountain Frame | Mountain Frames |
| 4 | 290 | HL Mountain Frame - Silver, 42 | HL Mountain Frame | Mountain Frames |
| 5 | 291 | HL Mountain Frame - Silver, 44 | HL Mountain Frame | Mountain Frames |
| 6 | 292 | HL Mountain Frame - Silver, 48 | HL Mountain Frame | Mountain Frames |
| 7 | 293 | HL Mountain Frame - Silver, 46 | HL Mountain Frame | Mountain Frames |

Figure 362 This is not QUITE what you want. You want the data in Power Pivot, aka the Data Model.

No sweat. You just bring up the Query Pane in Excel (if not already visible) then right click and choose 'Load To…':

Figure 363 Load To lets you change the 'target' where Power Query data gets loaded

We find the Load To dialog box one of the confusing ones in Power Query but here is what you need to select in order to get the desired result:

- Only Create Connection: This essentially tells Power Query not to load it in Excel
- Add this data to the Date Model: This tells Power Query to load the data into Power Pivot

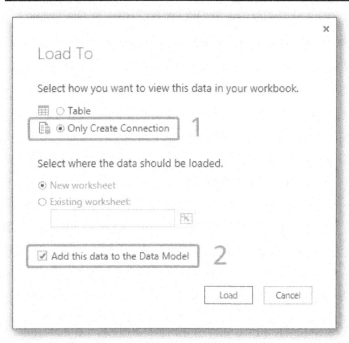

Figure 364 The above combination loads the data in Power Pivot but not in Excel

You may see a warning as below, essentially warning that the data would be removed from Excel, just click Continue.

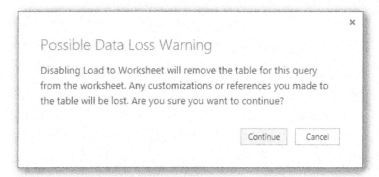

Figure 365 Click Continue to proceed with the data load if you see this warning

Now you see the data in the Power Pivot window instead of in Excel:

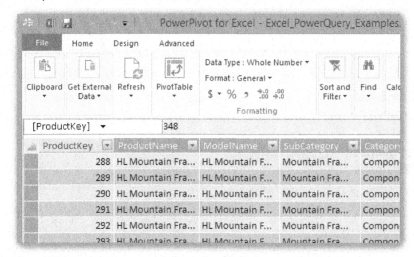

Figure 366 Power Query loads data directly to Power Pivot

 The ability to send Power Query data directly to Power Pivot only exists Excel 2013 onwards. For Excel 2010, you could load the data to Excel and click 'Create Linked Table' to send it to Power Pivot. (Or go into Power Pivot, open Existing Connections, and use will see one created by Power Query. Open that one.)

## Connecting to the Second CSV File

To connect to the second CSV file, you use the same steps as for the first one, but with a different URL:

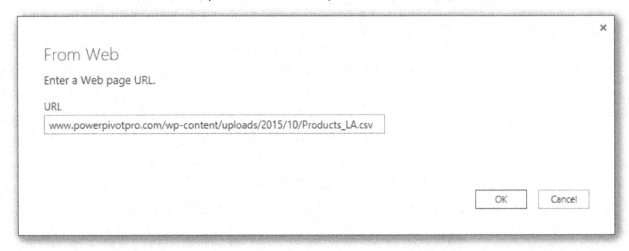

*Figure 367 From Web again, but now a different URL*

You repeat all of the steps from the first CSV, but this time, you assign our Custom Column (PlantCode) a static value of "LA" rather than "CH", and a different Query name:

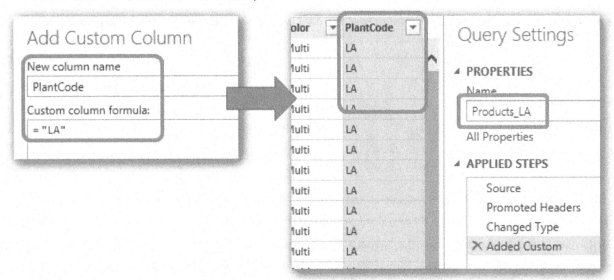

*Figure 368 Same steps as before, but different custom column value and query name.*

## Connecting to the Third CSV File

As you might guess, connecting to the third CSV file is just like connecting to the first two, but with "NY" instead of "LA" or "CH" in the custom column and query name.

After you connect to the third file, you have three queries defined in the workbook. The Workbook Queries pane now shows all three CSV queries:

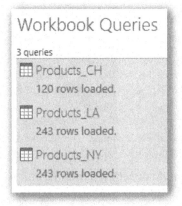

*Figure 369 The Workbook Queries pane now shows all three CSV queries*

## Time for the Append!

Now, back on the Excel Power Query ribbon, you click Append:

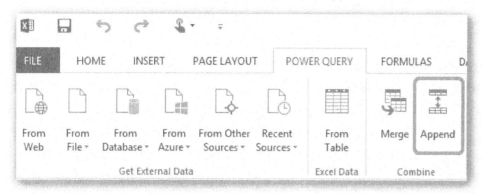

*Figure 370 Launch the Append dialog*

In the Append dialog, you specify Products_CH and Products_LA:

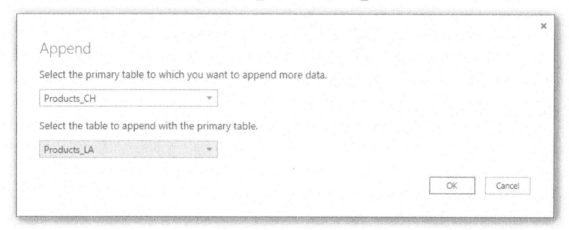

*Figure 371 The Append dialog lets you choose only two tables/queries, but that's okay for now.*

Next, Power Query asks you about privacy. Since these CSV files are on a 100% public website, you can select Public:

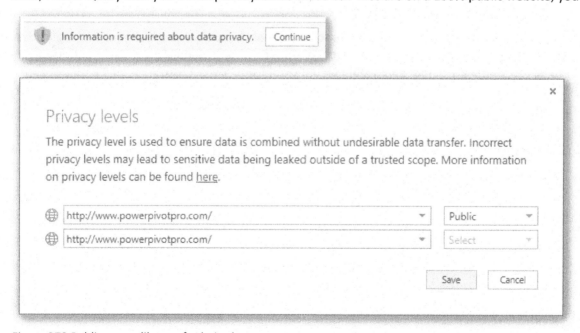

*Figure 372 Public seems like a safe choice here.*

 In Power Query option settings, you can choose to ignore the Privacy levels thereby suppressing this warning. However only do so once you understand the implications. See http://ppvt.pro/pqPrivacy for more.

Rename the query as Products, but also check out the Power Query formula bar:

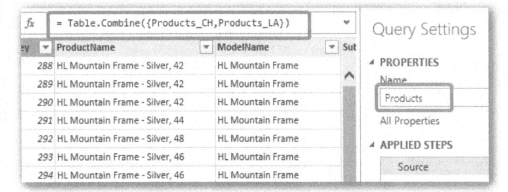

*Figure 373 The formula bar shows Table.Combine, an M function in use. Can you modify that directly?*

Can you modify the formula in the formula bar directly and add Products_NY? Yes, you absolutely can edit the formula yourself, and create a 3-table append all in one step:

*Figure 374 Edit the formula manually to add the third table/query to the Append!*

## "Keeping" Only the Appended Query

You now have four tables in the Power Pivot window: the three original CSV queries, plus the Append result:

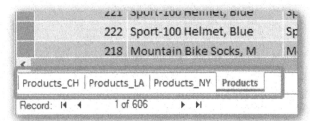

*Figure 375 Four tables, but we really only need the one combined/appended table.*

Although you have four tables, you really only need the one combined/appended table. Fixing the needless duplication is no problem. Just revisit the three original queries and uncheck 'Add this data to the Data Model'. Click continue if you see any Data Loss warning, just warning you that data would be removed from Power Pivot.

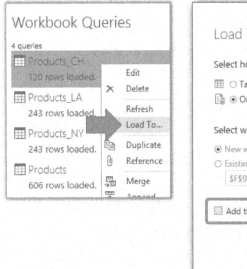
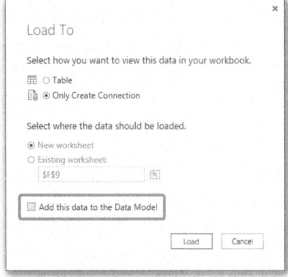

*Figure 376 For all three original queries, uncheck both boxes, then Load.*

Now you get just one table in Power Pivot, and YES, it does contain all three tables combined:

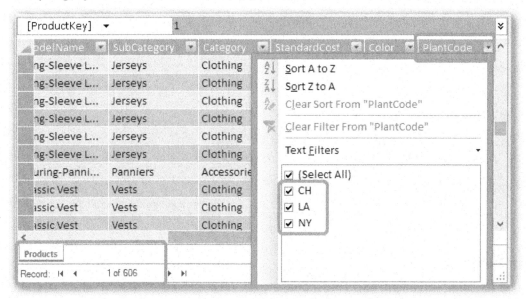

*Figure 377 Only our Products table shows up in Power Pivot*

Notice that there is now only one tab in Power Pivot. It has 606 rows, which is all three CSV files combined. And the PlantCode column, which did *not* exist in any of the CSV files, is present in the result, with all three different values for PlantCode (CH, LA, NY).

 **Load To... Dialog Box**: If you select 'Only Create Connection' and leave unchecked 'Add this data to the Data Model', the data is not loaded anywhere and the query is labeled 'Connection Only'. Which may seem useless, but as you have seen, is in fact quite useful in defining *interim* queries in Power Query which you later combine, merge or operate upon. Also note that Power Query Options let you change the default Load To behavior and enable a 'Fast Data Load' option.

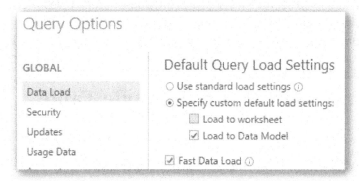

*Figure 378 Power Query Options let you change the default Load To and enable Fast Data Load*

## Testing Refresh

With only the final result table "landing" in Power Pivot, will Refresh know what to do? Test it to find out:

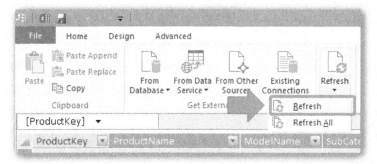

*Figure 379 The Append table is active and you click Refresh – not even Refresh All. Will it successfully re-run the three "child" queries, fetching all three CSV files and then appending them together?*

Yes, yes it does:

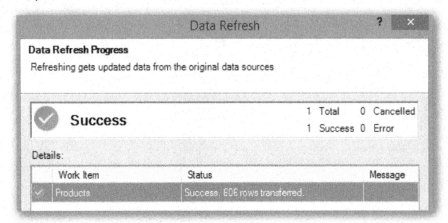

*Figure 380 Success. This is sweet.*

## Why This Is a Major Benefit

This trick in Power Query makes for some very happy Excel pros for a few reasons:

1. **You don't have to import the CSV files as three different tables,** and worry about how you would connect these to your other tables. Or struggle with writing duplicate measures against each one (like [Product Count CH], [Product Count LA], etc.), and then add them all together to form something like [Total Product Count]. Writing four times the formulas is never fun, convenient, or maintainable.

2. **You don't have to perform manual steps every time you want to refresh.** You can refresh your data with just one click (click Refresh or Refresh All). You can even schedule an automated refresh using PowerBI.com or Power Update (see http://ppvt.pro/pwrupdate).

3. **Despite both of those advantages, you can still do this 100% on our own**, in Excel, without having to recruit the help of a database to get it done. Until now, if you wanted to combine files *and* have autorefresh, you needed a database "intermediary" standing between your workbook and the data sources (the CSV files). And that usually meant both a hardware investment (a database server that is always on) *and* a human investment (a database pro to set it all up). And this is often neither practical nor possible. Now you can avoid all that.

4. **This trick is *not* limited to CSV files.** Any of the *many* sources that Power Query supports can be appended like this. If the files on your website were XML or Excel, or even a *mixture* of types, or if some of the files were on the web and some on a network drive, this would all still work.

# #2 - Combine Multiple Files from a Folder into a Single Table

## Scenario

You would like to create a single table containing all of your sales data. However the challenge is that you receive the sales data broken out by year and month in individual files (or even worse: a new file per day or week).

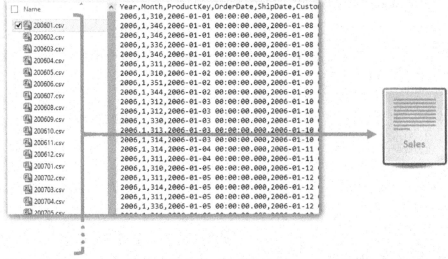

*Figure 381 Need to combine multiple files in a folder into a single Sales table*

You would like to easily combine these files, *including any new files created in that folder over time*, so that you can get the latest sales data with a single-click or an automated refresh.

## From Folder

From the Power Query ribbon you click From File > From Folder:

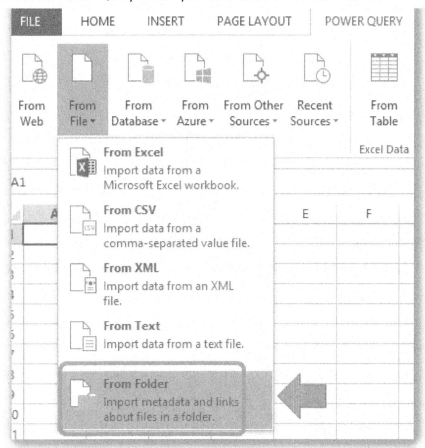

*Figure 382 You then specify the path for the folder where the files are located and click OK. This could be a network folder or even an FTP or a SharePoint folder that you have mapped to a drive.*

*Figure 383 The Power Query window may leave you disappointed at first, but be patient...*

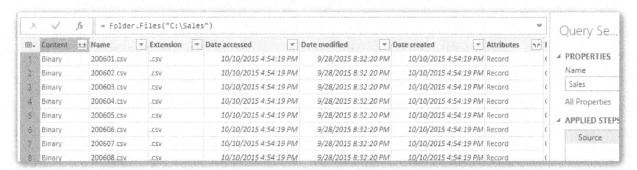

*Figure 384 Power Query is simply showing the list of files. How do you get to their content?*

## Combine CSV Files

The trick is using what we call the action button. Take a look at the buttons next to the column names at the top. Most columns have a filter button, which is useful as it provides you various filter options to apply on that column. But notice how the button in the Content column looks different. These are what we call action buttons as they do something cool when you click them.

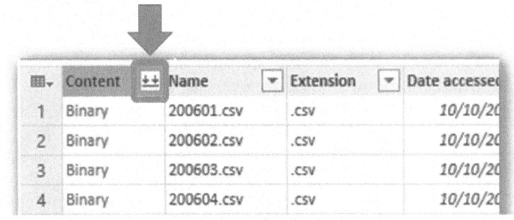

*Figure 385 Click the button next to the Content column heading*

Clicking the action button adds several steps: Combined Binaries, Imported CSV, Changed Type. Now it looks quite promising.

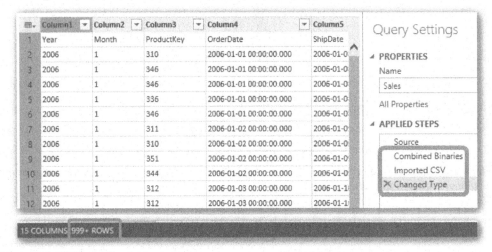

*Figure 386 All files in the folder have been imported and combined*

## First Row As Headers

You still have a few steps to take in order to load the final data. Notice the column headers say Column1, Column2, etc. Let's fix that by choosing 'Use First Row As Headers' from the Power Query ribbon:

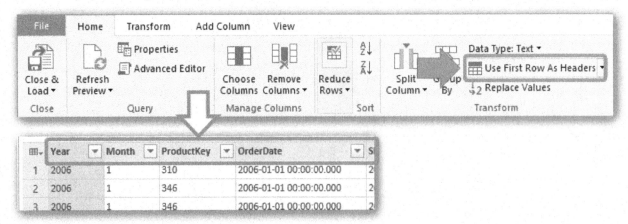

*Figure 387 Year, Month, ProductKey etc. show up as proper column headers*

# Change Data Type and Remove Errors

If you select the Year column, you will notice in the Power Query ribbon that the Data Type is set to *Text*. You can click on the Data Type dropdown and select the appropriate data type.

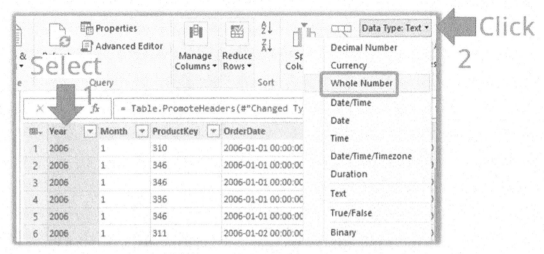

*Figure 388 Power Query is good at detecting appropriate Data Type for each column, however you can also choose the Data Type yourself when needed*

If you scroll down you will notice that there are rows which now show an *Error* for the Year column. This row is actually the header row coming in from each of our CSV file. Since each of our underlying CSV file has column headers, the headers are also interspersed in the combined data table – blech! To filter these out, you can simply click the 'Remove Errors' button on the Power Query ribbon:

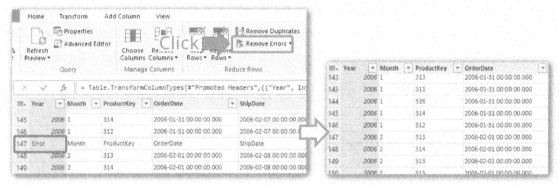

*Figure 389 Click Remove Errors to remove the header rows within the combine data table*

With that taken care of, check the data type for the other columns and change where needed. After that, click the dropdown on the 'Close & Load' button and click 'Close & Load To'. This will bring up the Load To dialog box, where you choose to load the table to the Data Model (Power Pivot) only.

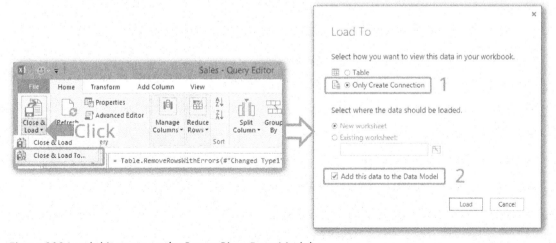

*Figure 390 Load this query to the Power Pivot Data Model*

All the CSV files will be combined and loaded up into a single Sales table:

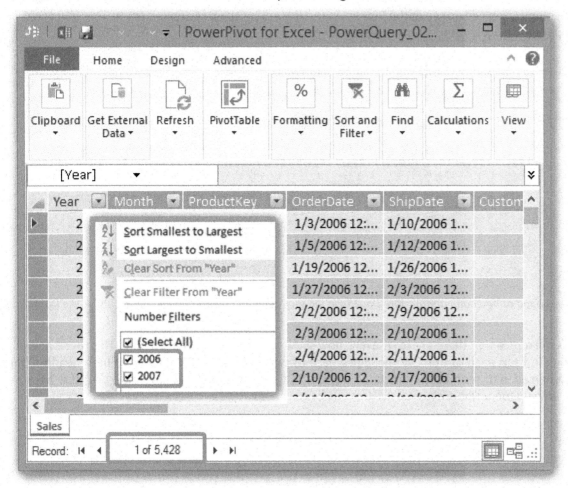

*Figure 391 24 different files covering the period of two years have been combined into a single table*

## Testing Refresh

What if additional files were dropped in that folder? Will Refresh pick them up automatically? Let's test it to find out. In our case we'll place new files for the year 2008 in the folder.

Yes, yes it does:

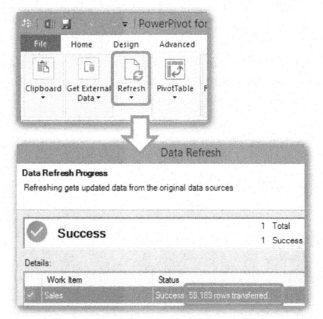

*Figure 392 New files received in the folder. Will Power Query automatically pick up these files?*

*Figure 393 Sweet Success. This is getting to our heads now.*

## Why This Is a Major Benefit

Here is why we love this Power Query trick:

1. **You can combine an unlimited number of files in a folder.** For a few files, you can use the append approach covered earlier. But for large number of files, especially when the exact number of files is unknown and can vary over time, this approach combines all files in one. And delivers the one-click and automated refresh possible with Power Query.

2. **You can write all your Power Pivot measures easily against a single table.** With the multiple Product table, there was the option, albeit painful, to bring in the files separately and define a measure on each file. Bringing in files individually is not even an option if you have monthly/weekly/daily files you need to combine. The "From Folder" option is the one to choose.

3. **This is easier and more human friendly than writing a macro.** Excel ninjas at times scoff at Power Query, alluding that they already know ten different ways to do the same tasks in Excel. Well that's great, but inevitably at some time whatever you build in Excel – you would transition it to someone else. Power Query makes the transition dead simple. It is self-documenting. Anyone can just go into Power Query, and step through the Applied Steps one by one to see the transformations being applied. And if one of the steps is erroring out, it is super easy to locate the erroneous step and fix it. **Power Query works for Excel ninjas as well as novices.** How cool is that!

# #3 – Adding Custom Columns to Your Lookup Tables

## Scenario

You would like to add one, or a few custom columns, to your Lookup tables. You have read the advice (in the Performance chapter) that "imported columns are generally better than calculated columns". However for this data source you do not have the support of a Database Administrator who could help you add these columns.

For this scenario, you would like to add a simple "PriceBucket" column to your Products table to bucket them as - $ (Inexpensive), $$ (Moderate), $$$ (High-End), $$$$ (Premium).

| Product Name | StandardCost | Color | ListPrice | PriceBucket |
|---|---|---|---|---|
| Touring-1000 Blue, 50 | 1481.9379 | Blue | 2384.07 | $$$$ |
| Touring-1000 Blue, 46 | 1481.9379 | Blue | 2384.07 | $$$$ |
| Touring-3000 Yellow, 58 | 461.4448 | Yellow | 742.35 | $$$ |
| Touring-2000 Blue, 46 | 755.1508 | Blue | 1214.85 | $$$$ |
| ML Mountain Handlebars | 27.4925 | NA | 61.92 | $ |
| LL Mountain Handlebars | 17.978 | NA | 40.4909 | $ |
| LL Mountain Handlebars | 19.7758 | NA | 44.54 | $ |
| HL Mountain Handlebars | 48.5453 | NA | 109.3364 | $$ |

*Figure 394 Add a Custom Column for PriceBucket*

You could do this yourself using Power Query.

## Get Data

We'll use a jumpstart here and start with our basic tables loaded already. These are simply pulled in from our original AdventureWorks Access database, via Power Query with some basic transformations.

*Figure 395 Our basic tables have already been pulled in*

# Add Custom Column

On the 'Add Column' tab in the ribbon, you have plenty of options to add custom columns simply by clicking a ribbon button.

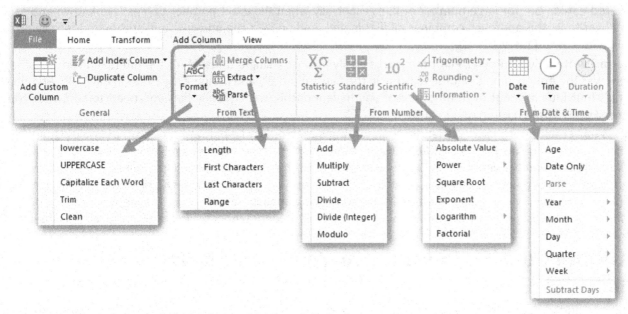

Figure 396 Plenty of options to Add Column with just a click of a button

 Note: The specific set of options that are enabled, versus others that are disabled are based on the data type of the column you have clicked and selected in Power Query. Therefore you should first click and select the column you are looking to use; in some cases you may also need to change the data type of your column (can be done from Power Query Home tab).

However, for our scenario, we need some specific logic, thus we will click the 'Add Custom Column' button.

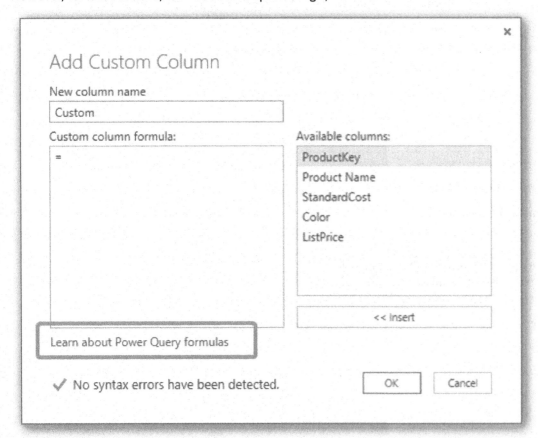

Figure 397 Click to add a custom column

## Define Custom Formula

You would get the same Add Custom Column window that we have seen before. But this time, we are doing something fancier than adding a static value. For help you can click on the 'Learn about Power Query formulas' link or grab your copy of "M Is for (Data) Monkey" which you always keep handy ☺

Here is our final formula:

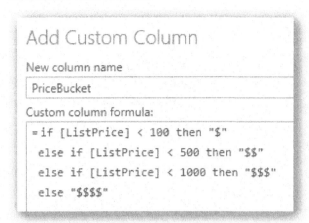

**Add Custom Column**

New column name

PriceBucket

Custom column formula:

```
= if [ListPrice] < 100 then "$"
  else if [ListPrice] < 500 then "$$"
  else if [ListPrice] < 1000 then "$$$"
  else "$$$$"
```

*Figure 398 Our Custom Column formula*

Fairly straightforward, but know that you have a lot of power available to you here as you tap into the M language.

After you load your table into Power Pivot, the new custom column can be used to slice and dice your measures as you please.

| Produc... | StandardCost | Color | ListPrice | Product Name | PriceBucket |
|---|---|---|---|---|---|
| 410 | 26.9708 | Black | 60.745 | LL Mountain Fro... | $ |
| 412 | 133.2955 | Black | 300.215 | HL Mountain Fro... | $$ |
| 416 | 96.7964 | Black | 218.01 | Touring Front W... | $$ |
| 419 | 38.9588 | Black | 87.745 | LL Mountain Rea... | $ |
| 420 | 104.7951 | Black | 236.025 | ML Mountain Re... | $$ |
| 421 | 145.2835 | Black | 327.215 | HL Mountain Re... | $$ |

| PriceBucket | Total Sales | OrderCount |
|---|---|---|
| $ | $961,582 | 20,886 |
| $$ | $78,951 | 577 |
| $$$ | $2,507,617 | 3,857 |
| $$$$ | $25,810,527 | 11,348 |
| **Grand Total** | **$29,358,677** | **27,659** |

*Figure 399 Our PriceBucket custom column in action inside a pivot table*

## Why This Is so Amazing

Power Query becomes the one-stop-shop for all data cleaning-shaping-transforming needs. Custom Column falls squarely in that area, and once you get a little comfortable with the M language, you would be using Power Query to add all your custom columns.

We certainly prefer to do that now in Power Query and not have to worry about Calculated Columns in Power Pivot.

# #4 - Using Power Query to "Unpivot" a Table

## Scenario

Even if you are not familiar with the term 'Unpivot', you will recognize the problem when you see it. This is one of the most common *and* most frustrating data shaping tasks on the planet. Let's say you have a table of Budget data that looks like this:

Data arranged in columns

| | A | B | C | D | E | F | G | H | I | J | K | L | M | N | O | P |
|---|---|---|---|---|---|---|---|---|---|---|---|---|---|---|---|---|
| 1 | Region | Market | MODEL | Jan-15 | Feb-15 | Mar-15 | Apr-15 | May-15 | Jun-15 | Jul-15 | Aug-15 | Sep-15 | Oct-15 | Nov-15 | Dec-15 | Grand Total |
| 2 | Central | Chicago | 2500C | 76,773 | 94,829 | 52,161 | 65,506 | 53,200 | 45,553 | 37,906 | 30,259 | 22,612 | 14,966 | 7,319 | 328 | $501,412 |
| 3 | Central | Cleveland | 2500C | 38,536 | 149,568 | 61,596 | 79,023 | 90,653 | 93,902 | 97,251 | 100,600 | 103,949 | 107,298 | 110,646 | 113,995 | $1,146,916 |
| 4 | Central | Milwaukee | 2500C | 104,585 | 109,731 | 97,999 | 102,231 | 98,938 | 97,059 | 95,179 | 93,300 | 91,420 | 89,541 | 87,662 | 85,782 | $1,153,427 |
| 5 | East | Boston | 2500C | 148,008 | 67,982 | 58,262 | 119,091 | 74,218 | 64,571 | 54,924 | 45,277 | 35,630 | 25,983 | 16,335 | 6,688 | $716,968 |
| 6 | East | New York | 2500C | 102,970 | 125,118 | 97,509 | 95,336 | 92,606 | 87,554 | 82,503 | 77,452 | 72,401 | 67,350 | 62,299 | 57,248 | $1,020,346 |
| 7 | East | Philadelphia | 2500C | 100,098 | 47,251 | 117,404 | 114,636 | 123,289 | 134,666 | 146,042 | 157,419 | 168,796 | 180,173 | 191,549 | 202,926 | $1,684,249 |
| 8 | South | Austin | 2500C | 64,428 | 78,201 | 116,905 | 31,790 | 58,029 | 52,108 | 46,187 | 40,266 | 34,345 | 28,424 | 22,503 | 16,582 | $589,764 |
| 9 | South | Dallas | 2500C | 140,945 | 59,309 | 34,965 | 123,407 | 70,417 | 62,721 | 55,025 | 47,330 | 39,634 | 31,938 | 24,242 | 16,546 | $706,480 |
| 10 | South | Houston | 2500C | 113,503 | 45,711 | 126,919 | 84,061 | 90,769 | 90,057 | 89,345 | 88,634 | 87,922 | 87,210 | 86,498 | 85,786 | $1,076,416 |
| 11 | West | Los Angeles | 2500C | 58,400 | 98,389 | 69,750 | 146,082 | 151,757 | 175,198 | 198,638 | 222,079 | 245,520 | 268,961 | 292,401 | 315,842 | $2,243,017 |
| 12 | West | San Francisco | 2500C | 67,295 | 53,376 | 37,238 | 30,613 | 15,585 | 2,966 | 9,652 | 22,271 | 34,889 | 47,508 | 60,126 | 72,744 | $454,262 |
| 13 | West | Seattle | 2500C | 140,135 | 88,710 | 79,771 | 68,225 | 38,043 | 15,576 | 6,891 | 29,358 | 51,825 | 74,292 | 96,758 | 119,225 | $808,808 |
| 14 | Central | Chicago | 3500C | 68,238 | 48,589 | 134,258 | 56,975 | 89,985 | 95,173 | 100,361 | 105,549 | 110,737 | 115,925 | 121,113 | 126,301 | $1,173,204 |
| 15 | Central | Cleveland | 3500C | 41,539 | 109,826 | 139,315 | 81,102 | 129,990 | 144,808 | 159,626 | 174,443 | 189,261 | 204,079 | 218,897 | 233,715 | $1,826,600 |

*Figure 400 Data arranged in columns instead of rows*

This is a very common shape – data arranged in columns - especially from exported data. You see, a lot of exports are exports from "reports" – things that were meant to be The Last Word on a topic, but don't get the job done. And much like we often like to put dates on columns of our pivots, these reports are designed to be friendly to the human eyeball. But Power Pivot isn't an eyeball. It's a hardcore data crunching machine, and it prefers dates captured in rows instead of across multiple columns.

Data arranged in row

| Region | Market | MODEL | MonthYear | Budget |
|---|---|---|---|---|
| Central | Chicago | 2500C | Jan-15 | $76,773 |
| Central | Chicago | 2500C | Feb-15 | $94,829 |
| Central | Chicago | 2500C | Mar-15 | $52,161 |
| Central | Chicago | 2500C | Apr-15 | $65,506 |
| Central | Chicago | 2500C | May-15 | $53,200 |
| Central | Chicago | 2500C | Jun-15 | $45,553 |
| Central | Chicago | 2500C | Jul-15 | $37,906 |
| Central | Chicago | 2500C | Aug-15 | $30,259 |
| Central | Chicago | 2500C | Sep-15 | $22,612 |
| Central | Chicago | 2500C | Oct-15 | $14,966 |
| Central | Chicago | 2500C | Nov-15 | $7,319 |
| Central | Chicago | 2500C | Dec-15 | $328 |
| Central | Cleveland | 2500C | Jan-15 | $38,536 |
| Central | Cleveland | 2500C | Feb-15 | $149,568 |

*Figure 401 Desired End-Result after reshaping, data in rows*

When you have date-related columns in your source data, you *really* should turn those into a single date column, turning the "wide and short" table into a "narrow and tall" table.

Date columns like this are very inconvenient in Power Pivot. They force you to write measures for each month, for instance ([Jan Sales], [Feb Sales], etc.) *and* make it impossible to perform time-series analysis using things like DATEADD, DATESYTD, and The Greatest Formula in the World (covered in a later chapter).

So how would you re-shape this table into something that is much more Power Pivot friendly? Again, Power Query to the rescue.

## Get Data from Excel

This time, the source data lives in an Excel (.XLSX) file. Select *From File > From Excel* and then select your XLSX file. Once file is selected, you are presented with a list of all the tables available in that workbook (in this case, it's just the Budget worksheet). Select the Budget worksheet and click Edit.

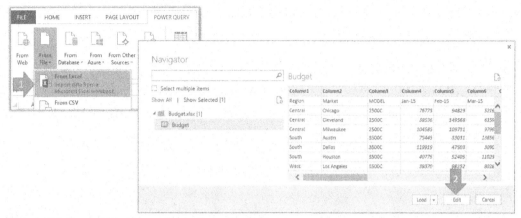

*Figure 402 Connecting Power Query to an Excel file*

## Header Row Handling and Remove Column

This will launch the Power Query editor window. Initially, Power Query treats the first row of the table as data rather than as a header row. No problem: Just click the Use First Row as Headers button to take care of the header row issue once and for all.

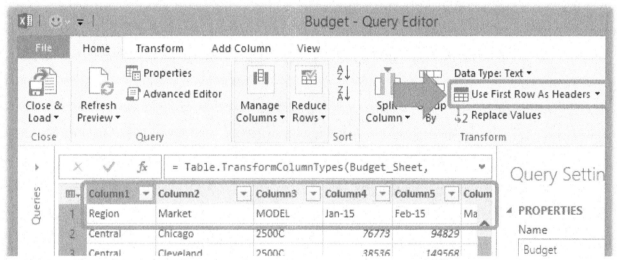

*Figure 403 Click the highlighted button to use first row as headers*

Notice the Grand Total column at the very end. That column is redundant since we already have data at the month level which we can add up to get the Grand Total. Thus select the column and click Remove Columns button.

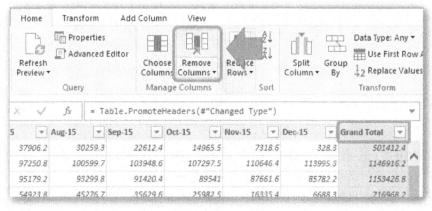

*Figure 404 Remove unnecessary columns*

# Unpivot!

The Unpivot operation (moving data from columns to rows) is found under the Transform tab on the ribbon. Here you can select all the month columns and click *Unpivot*. But as a shortcut, we can select the columns to the left of the Month columns (Region, Market, Model) and then click *Unpivot Other Columns*.

(*Note*: To select multiple columns, hold down Ctrl key and click the column headers)

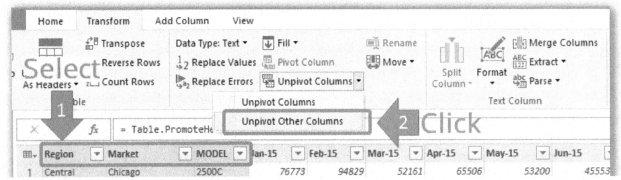

*Figure 405 Unpivot Other Columns*

And here's the result:

Unpivoting complete!

| | Region | Market | MODEL | Attribute | Value |
|---|--------|--------|-------|-----------|-------|
| 1 | Central | Chicago | 2500C | Jan-15 | 76773 |
| 2 | Central | Chicago | 2500C | Feb-15 | 94829 |
| 3 | Central | Chicago | 2500C | Mar-15 | 52161 |
| 4 | Central | Chicago | 2500C | Apr-15 | 65506 |
| 5 | Central | Chicago | 2500C | May-15 | 53200 |
| 6 | Central | Chicago | 2500C | Jun-15 | 45553.1 |
| 7 | Central | Chicago | 2500C | Jul-15 | 37906.2 |
| 8 | Central | Chicago | 2500C | Aug-15 | 30259.3 |
| 9 | Central | Chicago | 2500C | Sep-15 | 22612.4 |
| 10 | Central | Chicago | 2500C | Oct-15 | 14965.5 |
| 11 | Central | Chicago | 2500C | Nov-15 | 7318.6 |
| 12 | Central | Chicago | 2500C | Dec-15 | 328.3 |
| 13 | Central | Cleveland | 2500C | Jan-15 | 38536 |
| 14 | Central | Cleveland | 2500C | Feb-15 | 149568 |

*Figure 406 Unpivoting moved the data from column to rows*

The advantage of the "Unpivot Other Columns" approach (over just "Unpivot") is that you can deal with an arbitrary number of columns. If the same file later picks up new columns for the year 2016, guess what, Power Query will still be able to reshape the whole data if you used Unpivot Other Columns.

Unpivot Other Columns would elegantly handle growth in columns

| Region | Market | Jan-15 | Feb-15 | Mar-15 | Apr-15 | May-15 | Jun-15 | Jul-15 | Aug-15 | Sep-15 | Oct-15 | Nov-15 | Dec-15 | Jan-16 | Feb-16 | Mar-1 |
|--------|--------|--------|--------|--------|--------|--------|--------|--------|--------|--------|--------|--------|--------|--------|--------|-------|
| Central | Chicago | 76,773 | 94,829 | 52,161 | 65,506 | 53,200 | 45,553 | 37,906 | 30,259 | 22,612 | 14,966 | 7,319 | 328 | 69,096 | 104,312 | 52,16 |
| Central | Cleveland | 38,536 | 149,568 | 61,596 | 79,023 | 90,553 | 93,902 | 97,251 | 100,600 | 103,949 | 107,298 | 110,646 | 113,995 | 34,682 | 164,525 | 67,75 |
| Central | Milwaukee | 104,585 | 109,731 | 97,999 | 102,231 | 98,938 | 97,059 | 95,179 | 93,300 | 91,420 | 89,541 | 87,662 | 85,782 | 104,585 | 120,704 | 88,19 |
| East | Boston | 148,008 | 67,982 | 58,262 | 119,091 | 74,218 | 64,571 | 54,924 | 45,277 | 35,630 | 25,983 | 16,335 | 6,688 | 162,809 | 67,982 | 58,26 |
| East | New York | 102,970 | 125,118 | 97,509 | 95,336 | 92,606 | 87,554 | 82,503 | 77,452 | 72,401 | 67,350 | 62,299 | 57,248 | 113,267 | 125,118 | 97,50 |
| East | Philadelphia | 100,098 | 47,251 | 117,404 | 114,636 | 123,289 | 134,666 | 146,042 | 157,419 | 168,796 | 180,173 | 191,549 | 202,926 | 110,108 | 47,251 | 105,66 |
| South | Austin | 64,428 | 78,201 | 116,905 | 31,790 | 58,029 | 52,108 | 46,187 | 40,266 | 34,345 | 28,424 | 22,503 | 16,582 | 70,871 | 78,201 | 116,90 |
| South | Dallas | 140,945 | 59,309 | 34,965 | 123,407 | 70,417 | 62,721 | 55,025 | 47,330 | 39,634 | 31,938 | 24,242 | 16,546 | 140,945 | 53,378 | 34,96 |
| South | Houston | 113,503 | 45,711 | 126,919 | 84,061 | 90,769 | 90,057 | 89,345 | 88,634 | 87,922 | 87,210 | 86,498 | 85,786 | 124,853 | 50,282 | 114,22 |
| West | Los Angeles | 58,400 | 98,389 | 69,750 | 146,082 | 151,757 | 175,198 | 198,638 | 222,079 | 245,520 | 268,961 | 292,401 | 315,842 | 58,400 | 88,550 | 69,75 |
| West | San Francisco | 67,295 | 53,376 | 37,238 | 30,613 | 15,585 | 2,966 | 9,652 | 22,271 | 34,889 | 47,508 | 60,126 | 72,744 | 60,566 | 58,714 | 40,96 |
| West | Seattle | 140,135 | 88,710 | 79,771 | 68,225 | 38,043 | 15,576 | 6,891 | 29,358 | 51,825 | 74,292 | 96,758 | 119,225 | 140,135 | 79,839 | 79,77 |
| Central | Chicago | 68,238 | 48,589 | 134,258 | 56,975 | 89,985 | 95,173 | 100,361 | 105,549 | 110,737 | 115,925 | 121,113 | 126,301 | 75,062 | 53,448 | 134,2 |
| Central | Cleveland | 41,639 | 109,826 | 139,315 | 81,102 | 129,990 | 144,808 | 159,625 | 174,443 | 189,261 | 204,079 | 218,897 | 233,715 | 37,385 | 109,826 | 139,3 |

*Figure 407 Unpivot Other Columns will still correctly reshape all our data as columns get added*

## Rename and Change Type

Just a few final steps. Unpivot gave us an "Attribute" column that is our desired Month column, and a "Value" column with the Budget data. Right click and rename the Attribute column and change the data type of Value column to currency, yielding:

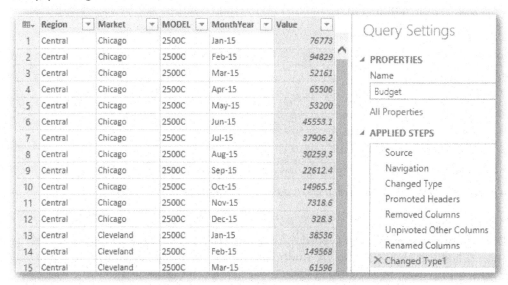

*Figure 408 Bingo.*

Load it to Power Pivot Data Model, similar to earlier examples and we're done:

*Figure 409 We have the right shape, with the right columns, and 576 rows (our original "wide" data set had only 48 rows, but far more columns).*

And oh yeah – when you click Refresh, it all just works.

## Why This Is a Major Benefit

**Not only is unpivoting good for our formulas**, but it means you can write a single Sales measure instead of 12, and time intelligence calculations are possible – but it is *also* good for file size and speed. One of the topics covered in "Performance" chapter is precisely this "unpivot" operation, and its tremendous benefits.

Now you can set up this Unpivot query one time, and every time you click Refresh (or a scheduled refresh runs), the right thing just happens.

Note from Avi: Before Power Query, I used to use SQL statements (in a database) to Unpivot data, but each time I had to crack open my SQL book to look up the – not so simple – syntax. Now, I just love being able to do it in Power Query with a single click!

 **Note**: Kinda funny isn't it – in a world of Pivots, one of the most useful tools is called "Unpivot." And then you use it to feed data into...Power Pivot.

# #5 - Using Power Query to Create a Lookup Table from a Table

## Scenario

You want to create separate Data and Lookup tables in your Power Pivot Data Model as per the best practices. However you often receive a single *flattened* table, with elements of both data and lookup tables.

| Bookings | | | | | |
|---|---|---|---|---|---|
| Date | CustomerKey | FullName | Phone | AddressLine1 | Amount |
| 7/22/2001 | 11000 | Jon Yang | 1 (11) 500 555-0162 | 3761 N. 14th St | $3,400 |
| 7/22/2003 | 11000 | Jon Yang | 1 (11) 500 555-0162 | 3761 N. 14th St | $2,342 |
| 11/4/2003 | 11000 | Jon Yang | 1 (11) 500 555-0162 | 3761 N. 14th St | $2,507 |
| 7/18/2001 | 11001 | Eugene Huang | 1 (11) 500 555-0110 | 2243 W St. | $3,375 |
| 7/20/2003 | 11001 | Eugene Huang | 1 (11) 500 555-0110 | 2243 W St. | $2,420 |
| 6/12/2004 | 11001 | Eugene Huang | 1 (11) 500 555-0110 | 2243 W St. | $589 |

*Figure 410 Bookings - Is this a Data table? Or is it a Data Table with a Lookup table hiding inside of it?*

**Reminder: Why We Need Lookup Tables**

In our chapter on relationships and performance, we covered the many benefits of separate Data and Lookup tables. Performance, file size, and the ability to analyze multiple data tables in the same pivot (such as Budget and Actuals) all are greatly improved by separating your Lookup and Data tables.

**Each row in the Bookings table captures three essential pieces of information**: When, Who, and How Much. A single column (Date, CustomerKey, and Amount, respectively) is responsible for capturing each piece of information. This is the kind of information that data tables are meant to capture. So far, so good.

**But the table *also* contains additional information about each customer** – FullName, Phone, and Address. This is overkill; there is no need for each of the first three rows, for instance, to tell us that customer 11000 lives at 3761 N. 14th St. If we know it's customer 11000, we could *look up* their address in a separate table!

**That is the sort of information that is better captured in Lookup tables**, and ideally, we would "outsource" those columns (FullName, Phone, and Address) to precisely such a table.

Here is your desired end result:

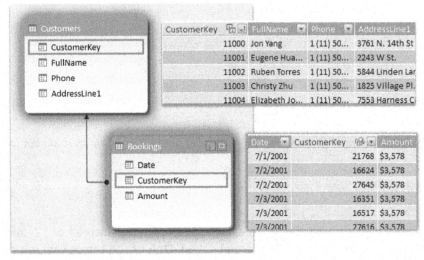

*Figure 411 Bookings and Customers as separate Data and Lookup tables*

Let's see how we can do this using Power Query so that our Data and Lookup tables are always accurate and stay up-to-date with a one-click or automated refresh.

**One-click or Automated Refresh**: We keep saying this again and again, and for good reason. You may be thinking, what's the big deal – I can do these steps in plain old Excel in less than five minutes. The five minutes, doesn't seem much when you are spending hours, if not days, slaving away to put together reports. But with all the Power BI tools, when nearly everything is automated, a five-minute manual step will start to chafe at you. And once you do go to automated refresh, you will never want to go back!

## Create Lookup Table

Our Booking table lives in Access, so in the Power Query ribbon select 'From Access', then select the Bookings table and click Edit (to launch the Power Query Editor):

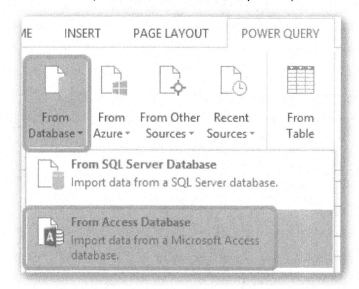

Figure 412 Our Booking table lives in Access, so that's the Power Query button we are going to press.

Now we remove the columns that we do not want in our new Customers table. Date and Amount are not relevant in a table that describes each Customer, so we ctrl-click those two column headers to select them, then right click and choose Remove Columns:

Figure 413 Ctrl-click the two columns we don't need, then right click to Remove them

We will sort by CustomerKey, by selecting that column and clicking the Sort A-Z button. This step is purely for demonstration, so we can easily show you the effect of the next step (Remove Duplicates). This step is *not* needed to build Lookup tables.

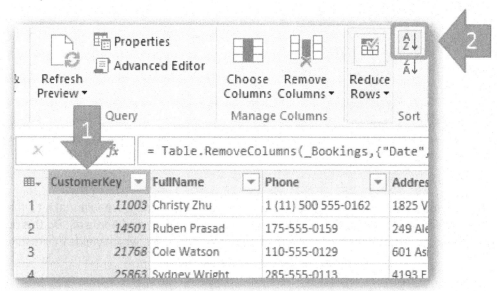

Figure 414 Sort by CustomerKey, just so we can observe the effects of the next step

Now we just select the CustomerKey column and click Remove Duplicates:

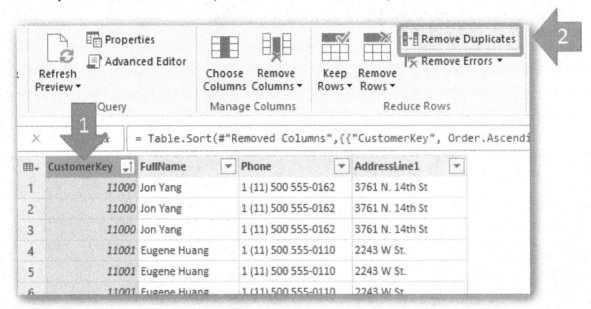

*Figure 415 To get a single row for each CustomerKey, we simply remove the duplicates!*

As a last step, we rename this query to be Customers, and then continue on and load it to the Power Pivot data model. You can see that the CustomerKey is now unique, with duplicates removed.

| CustomerKey | FullName | Phone | AddressLine1 |
|---|---|---|---|
| 11000 | Jon Yang | 1 (11) 500 555-0162 | 3761 N. 14th St |
| 11001 | Eugene Huang | 1 (11) 500 555-0110 | 2243 W St. |
| 11002 | Ruben Torres | 1 (11) 500 555-0184 | 5844 Linden Land |
| 11003 | Christy Zhu | 1 (11) 500 555-0162 | 1825 Village Pl. |
| 11004 | Elizabeth Johnson | 1 (11) 500 555-0131 | 7553 Harness Circle |
| 11005 | Julio Ruiz | 1 (11) 500 555-0151 | 7305 Humphrey Driv |

**Query Settings**

◢ PROPERTIES

Name

Customers

All Properties

*Figure 416 Change query name and load to Data Model only*

Let's look at our freshly-minted Customers table in Power Pivot:

| CustomerKey | FullName | Phone | AddressLine1 |
|---|---|---|---|
| 11000 | Jon Yang | 1 (11) 50... | 3761 N. 14th St |
| 11001 | Eugene Hua... | 1 (11) 50... | 2243 W St. |
| 11002 | Ruben Torres | 1 (11) 50... | 5844 Linden Lar |
| 11003 | Christy Zhu | 1 (11) 50... | 1825 Village Pl. |
| 11004 | Elizabeth Jo... | 1 (11) 50... | 7553 Harness Ci |

*Figure 417 It's sorted by CustomerKey. Each key appears just once, but we still have their properties columns like FullName, Address, and Phone! Perfect!*

## Create Data Table

Now we can go back and import the original Data table (Bookings). This time, the only change we will make to the "raw" Booking table is to remove those excess customer property columns (FullName, Phone, and Address). Do this by selecting those columns and clicking the Remove Columns button on the Power Query ribbon, which yields this result:

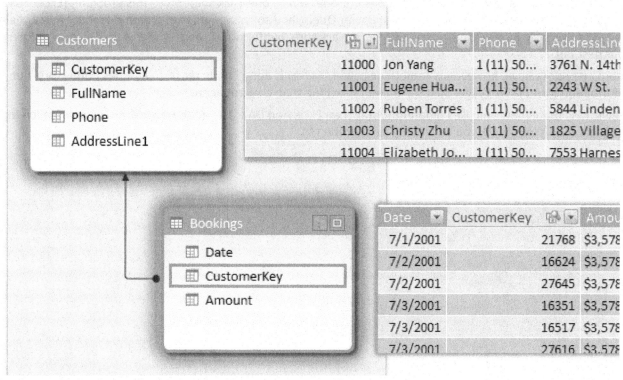

*Figure 418 The Bookings data table, with the customer properties removed (via the ribbon button)*

Continue on and load the table into Power Pivot.

## Relating the Two Tables

Now that we have both our Data (Bookings) and Lookup (Customers) table, we can easily relate them in Power Pivot via the CustomerKey. Thus getting our final result:

*Figure 419 Linking our Data and Lookup tables in Power Pivot*

## Why This Is so Amazing

Before Power Query, back before the earth cooled, yes, there were other ways to create Lookup tables from similar data sets.

You could do this in plain old Excel, by using manual steps to create a unique list of CustomerKey and customer attributes, and importing that into Power Pivot. But that requires manual effort each time we want to refresh and import the latest Bookings data. New customers are likely to be appearing in the data all the time, and our manually-created Lookup table will constantly fall out of date.

You also could build such a Lookup table in the original source database (or ask nicely for someone else to do that for you). That's a fabulous solution – when it's actually an option. You don't always have access to a database (and/or the skills to operate one).

**With Power Query**, in just a few simple steps you can do yourself, you have a refreshable, self-maintaining lookup/data table pair. An elegant solution to a very common data transformation problem.

# #6 - Creating a Calendar Table: Advanced Power Query

Power Pivot needs a Calendar table like Rob needs coffee: when deprived of this essential ingredient, both are still useful to an extent, but fall short of their potential...and sometimes return incorrect or confusing answers.

<pause for sip of coffee>

Of course, creating a Calendar table involves all the same problems as creating a Lookup table; after all, Calendar table is merely a special *kind* of Lookup table! If you manually create a Calendar table, you have to update it frequently to include more recent dates (and sometimes "drop" older dates from the past), OR you have to be okay with a Calendar table that extends "into the future" – which can pollute your slicers and pivots with needless date values AND make some of your calculations do funny things in the most recent (incomplete) month.

Trust us on this, it's less hassle to have a Calendar table that is "in lockstep" with your Data table(s) – one that starts on the first date for which you have data, and ends on the last date for which you have data.

To have that "lockstep" Calendar, you have the same choices as above: manual (repeatedly), or database. And now, Power Query.

## "Wait, I Don't See a 'Make Calendar' Button!"

Yes, as of version 2.26 in late 2015, Power Query does *not* offer a nice one-click solution to this problem. (Excel 2016 Power Pivot does offer something, but not as part of Power Query, and so far we find the "create calendar" functionality in Excel 2016 to be lacking. It will improve over time, we are sure, but for now... we still need something, and Power Query is our best bet).

What Power Query *does* have, however, is something called "M." M is not a character from a James Bond story, but a data transformation formula language. So it's even more exciting than a secret agent.

The bad news: M is brand new and uses different syntax than Excel and DAX. The good news: if you've been following the Power Query examples above, you've already been writing M.

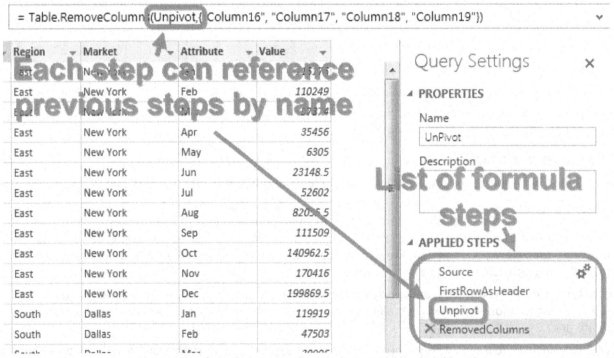

*Figure 420 The language you see in the formula bar is M that was generated by the ribbon buttons. A query can contain multiple formula steps, and each step can reference previous steps by name.*

So the ribbon buttons on the Power Query ribbon tab are similar to the Macro Recorder for VBA macros – they help you write M without *knowing* M, but then you can edit the M by hand if you want.

 **Note**: We won't lie to you. We did *not* know how to write the M formulas to generate a "lockstep" Calendar table. But we did know who to ask at Microsoft, and they happily sent us the M we needed.

## Steps

Within the Excel Power Query ribbon, click From Other Sources > Blank Query.

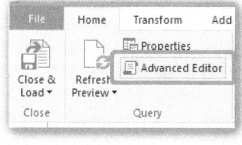

*Figure 422 Now select and remove all text within the Advanced Editor window and paste the M language code as below (available with the file downloads for this book):*

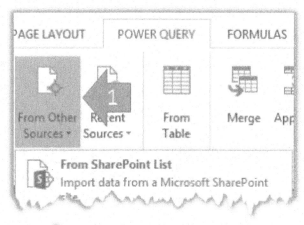

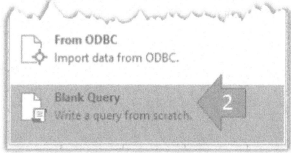

*Figure 421 This, as expected, brings up a blank query. Change the name of the query to Calendar, then click on the Advanced Editor, button.*

```
let
ChangedType = Table.TransformColumnTypes(Bookings,{{"Date", type date}}),
MaxDate = Record.Field(Table.Max(ChangedType, "Date"),"Date"),
MinDate = Record.Field(Table.Min(ChangedType, "Date"),"Date"),
DaysElapsed = Number.From(MaxDate-MinDate),
DatesList = List.Dates(MinDate, DaysElapsed+1,Duration.From(1)),
RawDatesTable = Table.FromList(DatesList, Splitter.SplitByNothing(),
{"Date"}, null, ExtraValues.Error),
ChangedType1 = Table.TransformColumnTypes(RawDatesTable,{{"Date", type
date}}),
InsertedDay = Table.AddColumn(ChangedType1, "Day", each Date.Day([Date]),
type number),
InsertedMonth = Table.AddColumn(InsertedDay, "Month", each
Date.Month([Date]), type number),
InsertedYear = Table.AddColumn(InsertedMonth, "Year", each Date.Year([Date]),
type number)
in
    InsertedYear
```

This code snippet can be found in the accompanying book files and assumes that you have an original table named Bookings, and it contains a column named Date. (The places where those names appear in the formulas above are highlighted in color. So that you can see where to change them in order to match your own data set.)

Click done on the Advanced Editor window (make sure there were no syntax errors detected):

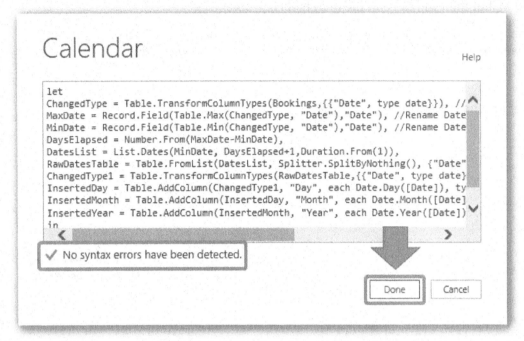

*Figure 423 You can paste or edit M code within the Advanced Editor window*

This should yield our final result, which you can load to Power Pivot data model:

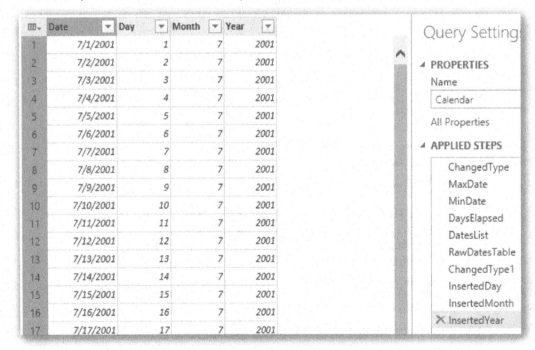

*Figure 424 Our final calendar table generated using M code*

# Why This Is a Major Benefit

This showcases the possibilities in Power Query, with the use of its M language. Here we get an auto-generated Calendar table, in Power Pivot, that starts on our oldest date from the data table and continues up to (and including) the most recent date in our data table. Each date appears only once, and NO dates are skipped. Those are all important qualities of a Calendar table. And, of course, all of this updates automatically and properly every time we click Refresh (or with a scheduled refresh).

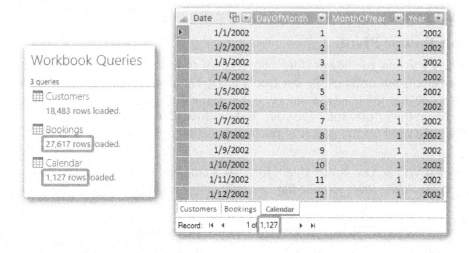

Figure 425 Power Query used our original Bookings table (27,617 rows) to produce a Calendar table (1,127 rows) – one instance of each date, with no gaps.

**You can also insert additional columns as needed in your Calendar table**, just by using the ribbon buttons. Select your Date column, and in the Add Columns ribbon tab, click Date, then choose your transformation (e.g. Day of Week).

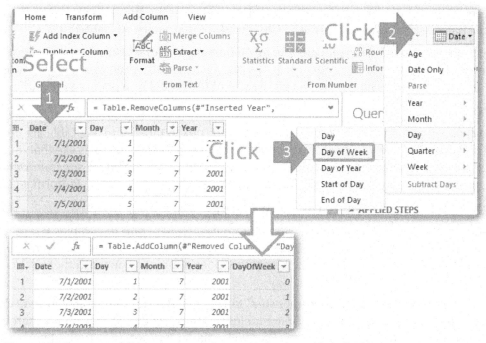

Figure 426 Creating additional columns in your Calendar table is fairly easy

**You can insert new M formula steps** easily wherever the ribbon interface falls short of what you need. This opens your world to all the richness the M language has to offer. Just click the "fx" button and type in your M formula in the formula bar.

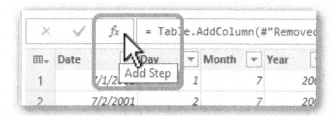

Figure 427 You can also edit the M code for any step, even the steps generated by clicking the ribbon buttons. Just click in the formula bar to start editing. Or if you are feeling brave, click on the Advanced Editor button (as we did to paste our Calendar code) to edit all your steps at once.

# How NOT to Use Power Query

## Don't Use Power Query Without Power Pivot

You may encounter a few one-off tasks where you *only* use Power Query, but when it comes to building any scalable, durable, agile BI/Reporting system, Power Pivot is *not* optional. Power Query is a great tool but it does not replace Power Pivot. A well-built Power Pivot data model has the ability to answer not only the questions that you are asking right now, but also the questions you may ask in the future. You have your "Define Once, Use Everywhere" measures which you can slice-and-dice any which way you want via the power of relationships. You do not get that with Power Query alone.

Power Query and Power Pivot complement each other. Use Power Query to clean, shape and transform your data before it lands in your data model. Continue to use Power Pivot to build data models, define relationships and a treasure trove of measures.

## Don't Use Power Query Calculations as a Substitute for DAX Measures

This one is essentially a continuation of the previous one. Once you get the hang of M, Power Query's calculation engine starts to tempt you – maybe you should not *just* clean and shape data with it, but *also* start to crunch numbers... you know, actually produce the final reports. We've seen a number of our clients doing this.

Using M / Power Query to add calculated columns is awesome, and is something we highly recommend if you have sufficient M skill.

But using M as a substitute for DAX measures is a mistake. Measures are more dynamic – they automatically adjust and recalculate in response to Slicers, Filters, and different-shaped pivots. DAX measures are the "portable formulas." M only re-calcs when you reload the data. And for aggregations like SUM, etc., DAX is far more efficient/fast.

Some egregious examples we have seen include, **using Power Query to add a Cumulative Total column, or using Power Query to perform Time Intelligence calculation** (Year over Year etc.). At a recent client visit, when we replaced these Power Query custom columns with Power Pivot measures we reduced the size of the model by a phenomenal 90%!

## Don't Use Power Query to Flatten Tables

From previous chapters you already know that flat tables which "blend" Data and Lookup tables into one table are *not* the ideal shape for Power Pivot. Yes, Power Query *would* make it easier to merge Data and Lookup tables like that. But you know better by now. Resist the temptation. You will get maximum value from your data model via separate Data and Lookup tables. If still in doubt, reread the chapters on Multiple Tables and Relationships, and also on Performance.

## Don't Use Power Query to Mash Two Data Tables Together

We advised against this in the Multiple Data Tables chapter, and will reiterate it here. Separate data tables typically capture data from separate business processes. For example, the budget setting process is very different than how your sales transactions occur. Just because you need to analyze them together does not mean you mash them in to a single table.

Again, Power Query makes it very easy to produce such "franken-monster" tables, but that doesn't mean you *should*. Follow the best practices we have laid out in this book, leave your Data tables separate, tie them together via shared Lookup tables, and then bust out some serious Measures on them. That will yield a far more flexible and powerful model than any "frankentables" you might be tempted to create in Power Query.

You have now met Power Query, one of the "newer" tools in the Power BI family. It's time now to meet another member; one of the latest additions - Power BI Desktop.

# 21 - Power BI Desktop

## Meet the New Kid On the Block

**And the new kid has all the fancy toys:**

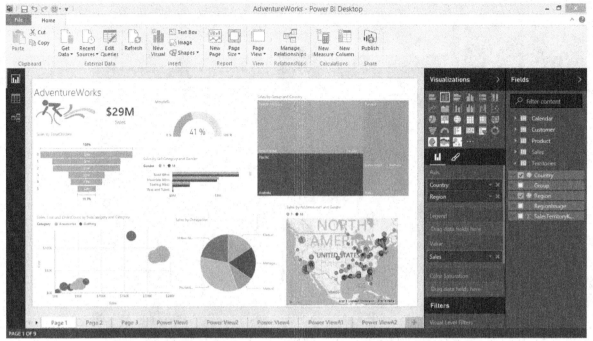

*Figure 428 Power BI Desktop (Report mode)*

Get ready for some shock and awe before we dive into the details. Here is some of what Power BI Desktop has to offer. And remember, all of this is at your fingertips TODAY without learning anything new - it's the same engines!

## Tons of Visualizations

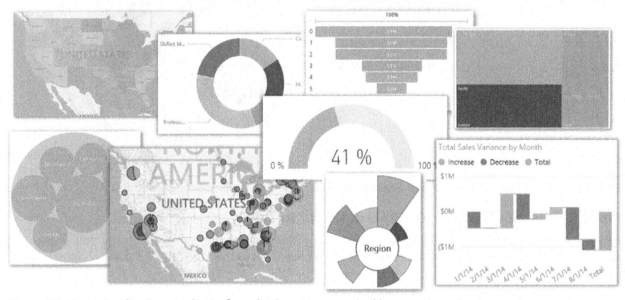

*Figure 429 Many visualizations to choose from, heck you can even build your custom visuals*

# Creating Reports is Easy as 1-2-3

Easily add visuals to your report:

1.  Choose your visualization
2.  Drag and Drop fields from your field list
3.  Pump up your visuals using all the customization options

*Figure 430 Create your visuals using the familiar field list (similar to the one you see when creating pivot tables)*

## Fully-Interactive Reports Make Your Data Come to Life

Reports are fully interactive, offering cross-filtering by clicking any element and drill-down across multiple levels. You also have options to deploy your reports to web or mobile (we'll cover that in the "YouTube for Data" chapter).

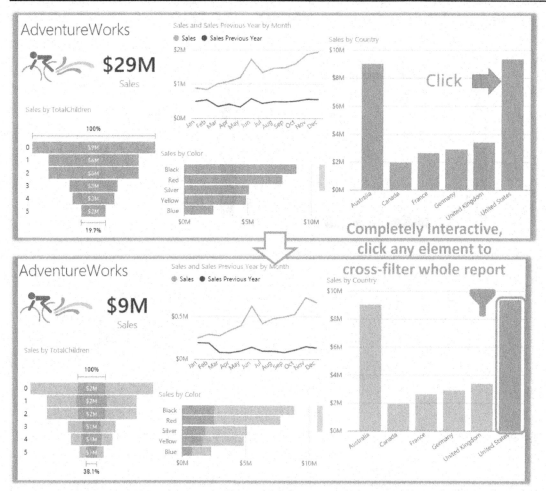

Figure 431 Click on any element to cross-filter your report - it's like everything is a slicer!

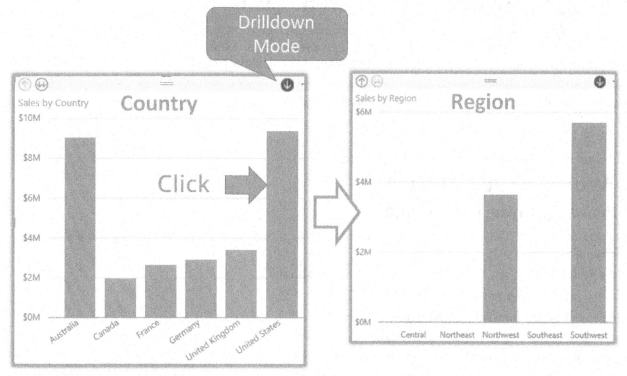

Figure 432 Drilldown to multiple levels

### Power Pivot, Power Query and Power View++ All in One Package

This isn't just about pretty visuals, Power BI Desktop actually has Power Pivot and Power Query all rolled in with the visualization piece. **Beauty with Brains!**

*Figure 433 Power BI Desktop has all the strength of Power Pivot and Power Query inside*

### Download Today!

Best of all, Power BI Desktop is available to download for free from Microsoft ([http://ppvt.pro/pbiDownload](http://ppvt.pro/pbiDownload)).

# Remember: Same Engines, Different Visuals

In one of the early chapters of this book, we outlined how Power BI Desktop fits into the overall picture, and how it relates to Excel, Power Pivot, and Power Query. The short version of that is "Power BI Desktop contains the same PP and PQ engines, and is merely a different container with a different visualization layer."

To demonstrate that "same engines" compatibility, we are going to intersperse Desktop examples into the rest of the book. (In parallel with Excel-based examples, because we think the Excel-based versions of these engines are still *very* important).

And it doesn't seem "fair" to start using Desktop examples without some words of introduction. But since Desktop is so similar to Excel-based Power BI, it won't take very long ☺

# A Few Words of Perspective

## You're Probably Going to Use Both

Who is going to use Power BI Desktop versus Excel-based Power BI? More specifically, what should *you* decide to do? Which one should *you* use?

First rule here is, don't sweat it. Let this question answer itself naturally.

Let's break the world into four groups of people:

1.  People who exclusively use Excel-based Power BI tools
2.  People who exclusively use Power BI Desktop
3.  People who use *both* flavors, Excel-based *and* Desktop
4.  Unfortunate souls who use *neither* – because they haven't heard of them or because they are forced to use some other, incredibly clumsy toolset

Most of you reading this are in the process of escaping group #4, or have recently completed your escape ☺

New "escapees" then overwhelmingly find themselves in group #1, because the Excel versions are the most naturally inviting.

A handful find themselves in group #2, because they were explicitly looking for a BI tool rather than an Excel turbo-charger. Nothing wrong with that of course, it's legitimate. It's just that this is not the majority of humans.

But guess what? We think that, over time, **the largest group, by far, will be group #3.**

You will probably wind up using both. Maybe not soon, but eventually.

Because they share the same engines, you can move between them with very little trouble. And there are things that you can do in one that you can't do in the other.

That even starts with how to "sell" these tools to your organization.

## The "Sales Pitch" – Show Excel-Based to the Analysts, Desktop to Execs

That's an important point, so let's stop and call it out...

If you are trying to gain buy-in for the Power BI toolset at your company, let us recommend the following two-pronged "sales" approach:

- **When you are pitching the tools to "analyst" types who use Excel** (the "producers" of analytics), show them the Excel-based versions as their "gateway drug." They don't want to be pitched on a brand new container/app like Desktop. They are programmed to resist it, and for good reason – they've been burned repeatedly by other "miracle" tools that were supposed to replace Excel, and every time, those tools have failed them. Much better to tell them that "Excel has become way more powerful, let me show you."

- **When you are pitching to executives and other "consumers" of analytics,** consider showing them the Power BI Desktop visuals. A polished demo of something that uses data that is relevant to them, in that environment, tends to be very compelling. (Better yet, use the PowerBI.com web renderings or mobile apps, to be discussed in the chapter on YouTube for Data.) Don't show these people formulas, relationships, or any of that "behind the scenes" stuff. Show them finished awesomeness, and that will win you the buy-in your need in order to continue your important work – with formulas and relationships of course ☺

# The "Tour"

OK, as promised, we will now give you a brief introduction to the tool (caveat: the interface is changing rapidly so things may have moved around by the time you're reading this). The easiest way to learn is to download Desktop for free, from Microsoft (http://ppvt.pro/pbiDownload) and try it out for yourself.

## Missing Terminology

As we pointed out earlier, Power BI Desktop has moved away from the Power* names, using new terms as below:

- Power Query => Get Data
- Power Pivot => Data Model
- Power View => Reports

This takes the focus away from the tools and onto the task you need to perform. And since Power BI Desktop has broken out of the mold of Excel, instead of the add-in feel, you have a well-blended experience: the function-ality of Power Pivot, Power Query and a much-improved version of Power View all in one neat little package, de-spite the cosmetic changing of names. Let's dig in.

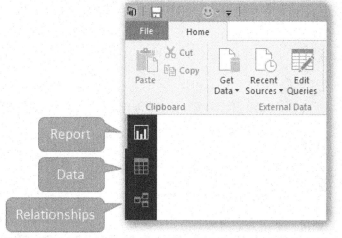

*Figure 434 Click to switch to Report, Data or Relationship modes*

## The Different Modes

Power BI Desktop has three modes: **Report, Data** and **Relationships** that you can toggle through based on the task you are focusing on.

The report mode was the first screenshot in the chapter, and is where you share and present information to consumers (much like the role played by the Excel grid and charts in Power Pivot).

Here are the Data and Relationship modes:

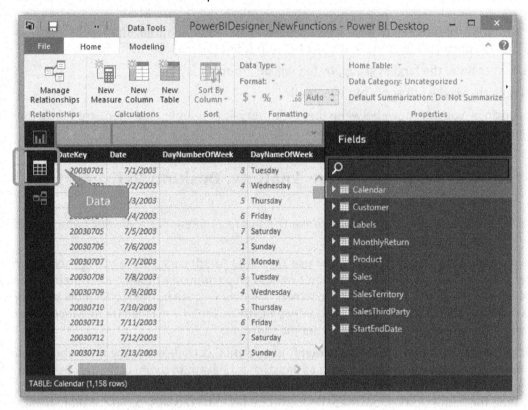

Figure 435 Data mode in Power BI Desktop – looks a lot like the Power Pivot data model window.

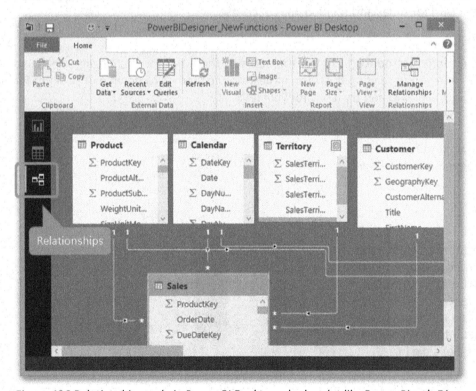

Figure 436 Relationship mode in Power BI Desktop – looks a lot like Power Pivot's Diagram View.

# Get Data (a.k.a. Power Query)

The Get Data button is the way to pull all data into the Power BI Desktop. Those familiar with Power Query will find the interface very similar. And those totally new will still find it fairly intuitive and easy to use.

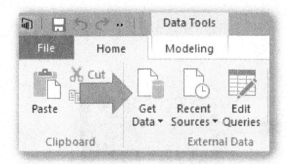

Figure 437 Click Get Data to start pulling data into your model

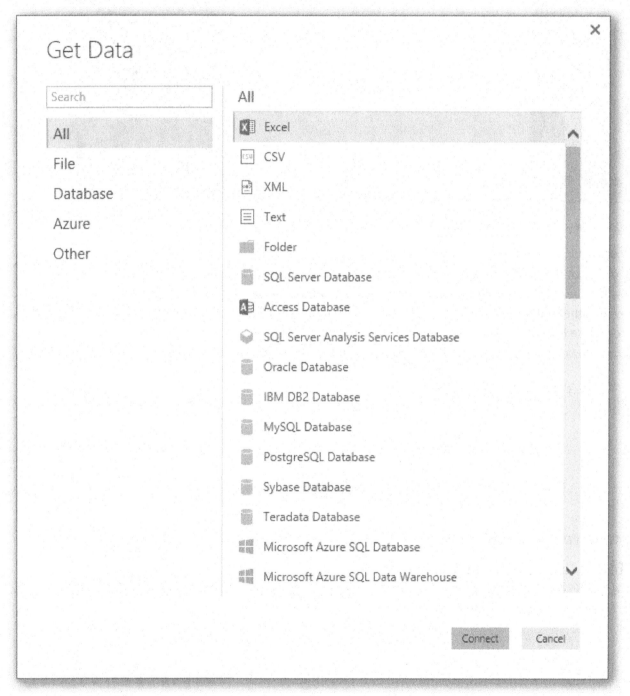

Figure 438 The list of options look familiar to those in Power Query

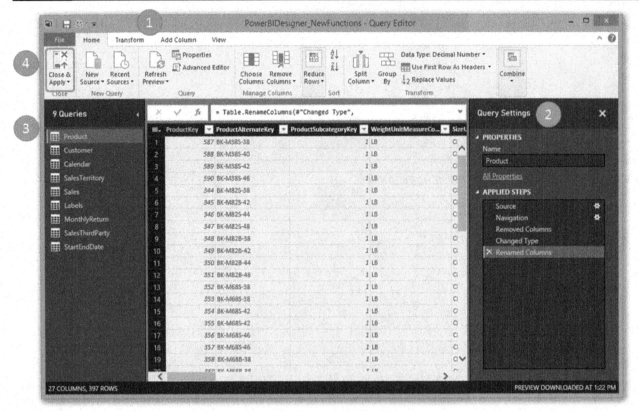

*Figure 439 Query Interface lets you shape and transform the data you bring in to your model*

Once you connect to your data you can:

1.  Use the options on the ribbon to shape and transform your data as needed
2.  Specify Query Settings such as Name and review/edit applied steps
3.  Review other queries if you have brought in multiple tables into your model
4.  Click 'Close & Apply' to load the data into your model

From the main Power BI Desktop window you can click Edit Queries to launch the "Power Query" window again.

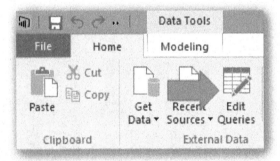

*Figure 440 Click Edit Queries to launch the "Power Query" window again*

## Data Model (a.k.a. Power Pivot)

You will not find a Power Pivot or Data Model button in Desktop. But the 'Home' and 'Modeling' tabs on the ribbon have most of what we need (The 'Modeling' tab is currently shown only in 'Data' mode).

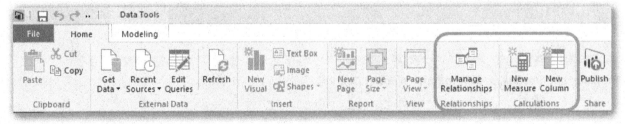

*Figure 441 Manage relationships and create new measures, what more do we need ☺*

*Figure 442 Few more options on the Modeling tab*

**Manage Relationships**: This looks similar to manage relationships in Power Pivot for Excel, except for the Advanced Options available (covered in the chapter on "Complicated" Relationships). You can also create relationships by dragging and dropping in the Power BI Desktop relationship mode - which acts similar to the Power Pivot diagram view.

*Figure 443 Manage Relationships in Power BI Desktop*

**Create New Measures**: You can use the 'New Measure' button on the Home tab on the ribbon. However, we often find ourselves right clicking in the field list and selecting 'New Measure', since we want to make sure our measure is placed in the right table.

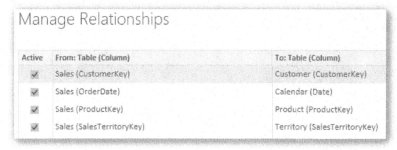

*Figure 445 Define your measure in the formula bar that pops up using the same DAX syntax you have been using with Power Pivot*

**Create Calculated Columns**: Creating calculated column is equally easy. Just right click and select 'New Column'.

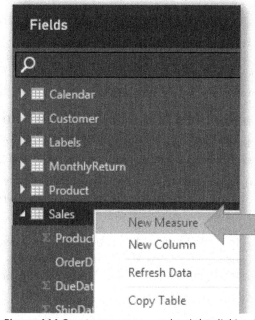

*Figure 444 Create new measure by right clicking in the Fields list*

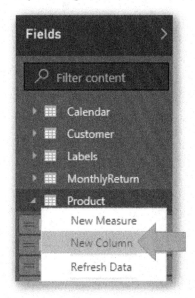

*Figure 446 Adding a calculated column*

Specify the DAX formula for the calculated column, just as you would in Power Pivot.

```
ListPriceBucket = SWITCH( TRUE()
, [ListPrice] < 100, "$"
, [ListPrice] < 500, "$$"
, [ListPrice] < 1000, "$$$"
, "$$$$"
)
```

*Figure 447 DAX formula for calculated column*

Here is our new calculated column, as seen in the Data mode

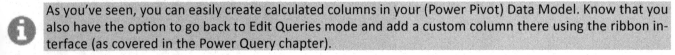

| ProductKey | ProductName | ListPrice | ProductCategory | ListPriceBucket |
|---|---|---|---|---|
| 307 | HL Mountain Frame - Silve | 1204.3248 | Components | $$$$ |
| 308 | HL Mountain Frame - Silve | 1240.4545 | Components | $$$$ |
| 309 | HL Mountain Frame - Silve | 1364.5 | Components | $$$$ |
| 524 | LL Mountain Frame - Silve | 264.05 | Components | $$ |
| 525 | LL Mountain Frame - Silve | 264.05 | Components | $$ |
| 526 | LL Mountain Frame - Silve | 264.05 | Components | $$ |
| 527 | LL Mountain Frame - Silve | 264.05 | Components | $$ |
| 551 | LL Mountain Frame - Silve | 264.05 | Components | $$ |
| 211 | HL Road Frame - Red, 58 | | Components | $ |

*Figure 448 Our newly minted calculated column*

ℹ As you've seen, you can easily create calculated columns in your (Power Pivot) Data Model. Know that you also have the option to go back to Edit Queries mode and add a custom column there using the ribbon interface (as covered in the Power Query chapter).

## Reports (a.k.a. Power View, but Much Better!)

Building reports in Desktop will feel similar to Power View, if you are one of the small minority who tried out Power View before Microsoft called a "do over" and started developing Power BI Desktop instead.

But if you have never used Power View, you will still find Reports (in Power BI Desktop) easy to learn. Essentially you pick elements from the Fields list (just like when building an Excel Pivot Table) then choose your visualization- there are many available with more on the way.

ℹ In fact Microsoft has promised a new visualization "Every Single Week". Power BI now also allows users to use **custom visuals** from a library of visuals developed by Microsoft as well as the Power BI community. Read http://ppvt.pro/morevisuals for the announcement.

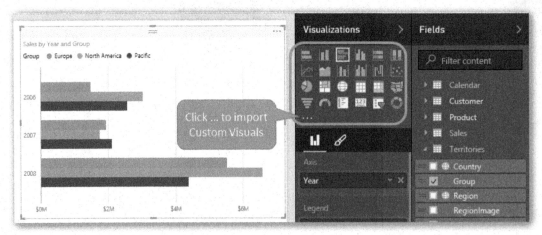

*Figure 449 Choose your visualization in Power BI Desktop*

You also have lots of ways to customize your visuals. Of course you can drag and drop the fields that you want to see in your visual. But you can also fine tune the colors, the x/y-axis, data labels, background and other settings.

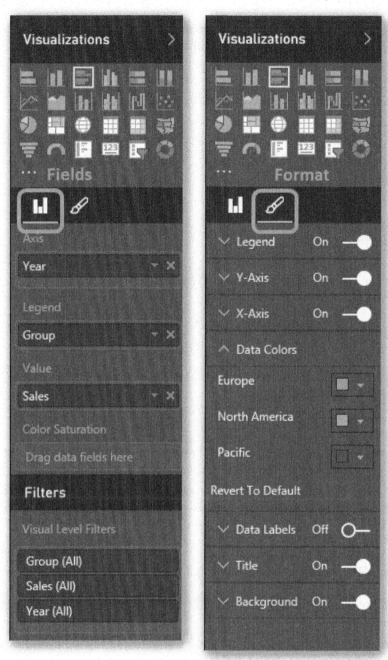

*Figure 450 Lots of ways to customize the Fields and Formats for your visuals*

# Import Existing Excel Power Pivot Models!

This one is important enough to be called out:

 **If you have existing Excel Power Pivot models, you can easily import them** into Power BI Desktop (just select File > Import > Excel Workbook Contents). This imports elements including Power Query, Power Pivot and Power View sheets. See http://ppvt.pro/importExcel for more details.

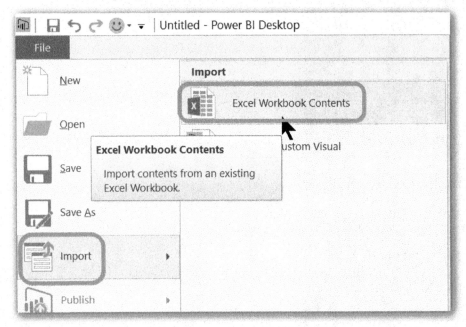

*Figure 451 This should really say "Import Power Pivot Model from Excel Workbook" (but it also imports Power Query queries and Power View display sheets).*

**Remember, Power BI Desktop uses the same data engines** as the "Power engines" we've been learning in Excel! Power Pivot and Power Query are included in Desktop, even though they aren't given those names.

**So, this "import" is really just Desktop "stealing"** all of the tables, formulas, relationships, and queries from an existing Power Pivot workbook. It is *not* even correct to call this a conversion, because the languages (DAX and M) are unchanged.

# Sharing Power BI Desktop Files

As of writing, you can publish your Power BI Desktop files only to PowerBI.com. (That may change in the future).

 You could also share the Power BI Desktop (.pbix) file itself, but given how it's geared towards "authors" it makes for a poor experience for "end-users"

Now that we have made friends with some of the new members in Power BI family, it's time to go back to Power Pivot (the DAX Engine) and dive into some deeper topics. But never fear! Power BI Desktop WILL make many more appearances in this book, especially (but not only) in the "YouTube for Data" chapter.

# 22 - "Complicated" Relationships

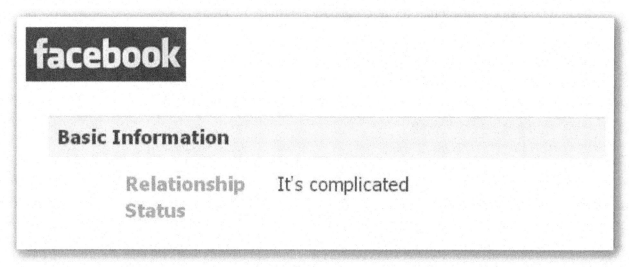

Figure 452 It's OK. It happens sometimes, and we are here to help.

In DAX, as in life, relationships are very important. (We often joke about how we are here to help you with your relationship problems – nerdy and corny, yes, but it always draws laughs).

And in DAX, as in life, some relationships are more, um, complicated than others.

## Multiple Relationships Between the Same Two Tables

Consider the *Sales* table and the *Calendar* table; we already have a relationship between these two tables as shown below using columns

```
Sales[OrderDate] -> Calendar[Date]
```

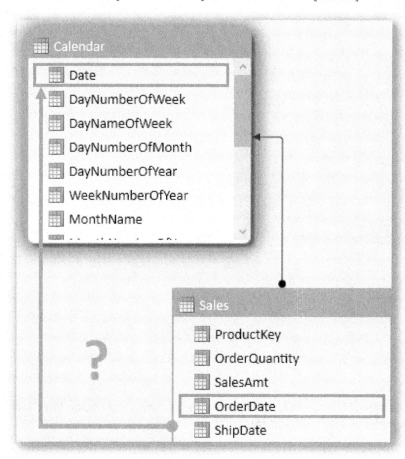

Figure 453 Can these two tables have more than one relationship to each other?

Order date is not the only date field we have in our Sales table. We also have a *ShipDate*. What if we sometimes wanted to analyze our sales data by *ShipDate*?

How do we handle that? Do we create another relationship between these two tables? Would that even work? Let's give it a try.

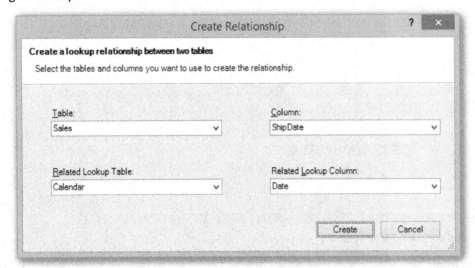

*Figure 454 Attempting to create relationship between Sales[ShipDate] -> Calendar[Date]*

Maybe you were expecting an error when you clicked the create button on the dialog box above. But it actually does work, sort of.

You notice, in the diagram below, that the newly created relationship is represented by a dotted line instead of a solid line.

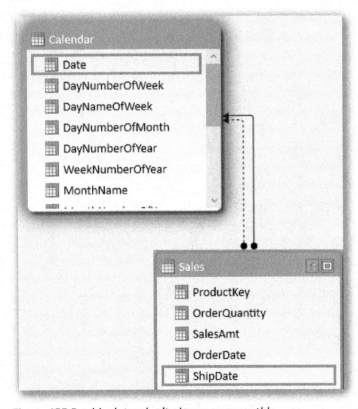

*Figure 455 Double dates don't always go smoothly*

It is easier to understand what's going on if we open the *Manage Relationships* dialog box from the Design tab. Note the *Active* column for the two relationships between Sales and Calendar table.

While one says Active=Yes, for the other Active=No.

*Figure 456 Only one relationship can be active between two tables at any given time*

Turns out, at any given time, only one relationship can be active between any two tables. So how do we solve for the scenario where we want to analyze the Sales data by *ShipDate*?

Well, we could flip the *Active* relationship, by editing it from the *Manage Relationship* dialog box.

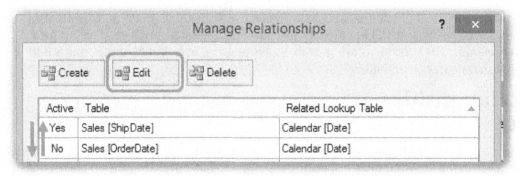

*Figure 457 Edit relationships, to change the one that is active*

If you had a pivot table showing [Total Sales] by Calendar Year and Month Name, here is how it would change as you change the relationship that is active.

*Figure 458 Pivot shows Total Sales based on Order Date or Ship Date based on the active relationship*

Note the change in July numbers; looks like some items ordered in July 2001 were not shipped in the same month.

Now of course, this would be a very clumsy approach even for you (model author), let alone the end-users. So let's explore some more elegant options to do the same.

# USERELATIONSHIP()

CALCULATE is a magical function and it comes to our rescue one more time. We started using CALCULATE with very simple arguments like Sales[Year]=2002. But the example below shows yet another power that CALCULATE can wield. We write a new measure as below:-

```
[Total Sales by Ship Date] =
CALCULATE (
    [Total Sales],
    USERELATIONSHIP ( Sales[ShipDate], Calendar[Date] )
)
```

Now we can put both [Total Sales] and [Total Sales by Ship Date] measures on the same pivot.

| Row Labels | Total Sales | Total Sales by Ship Date |
|---|---|---|
| ⊟ 2001 | $3,266,374 | $3,105,587 |
| July | $473,388 | $349,490 |
| August | $506,192 | $518,096 |
| September | $473,943 | $481,550 |
| October | $513,329 | $509,319 |
| November | $543,993 | $532,655 |
| December | $755,528 | $714,476 |

*Figure 459 Total Sales by OrderDate and by ShipDate, both on the same pivot*

When you need it, this is a powerful weapon indeed.

Yes, you will need to "clone" some or all of your existing Sales measures (just those that you plan to also display by ShipDate) using CALCULATE and USERELATIONSHIP. But that's a small price to pay for such smooth integration. And remember, DAX formulas are portable – write once, use everywhere – so it's not like you will need to repeat that process indefinitely.

# Many to Many Relationships

## First, a Bad Example

We currently have *Sales[OrderDate]* connected to *Calendar[Date]*. This is a "one to many" relationship. The *Calendar* table represents the 'one' side, since in the *Calendar* table a specific date only appears once. The *Sales* table represents the 'many' side of the relationship, because in the Sales table, each date appears more than once. (Since we hopefully make more than one sale on any given date).

This "one to many" flavor of relationship is the default kind of relationship in DAX, and it's the only kind we've been dealing with thus far.

Now let's do something silly. We also have a date field in the *Customers* table, the customer *BirthDate*. Would we be able to create a relationship between *Sales[OrderDate]* and *Customer[BirthDate]*?

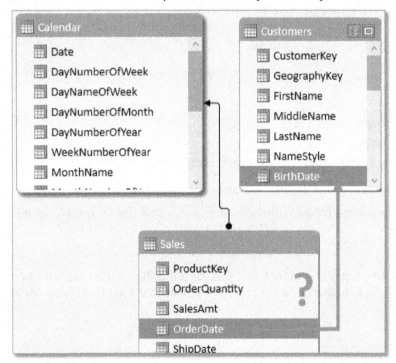

*Figure 460 Would Power Pivot allow us to relate Sales[OrderDate] -> Customers[BirthDate]?*

Note that, while *Sales[OrderDate]* has repeated values, so does the *Customers[BirthDate]*.

Figure 461 We have many repeated values for both columns

Let us go ahead and attempt to create this relationship.

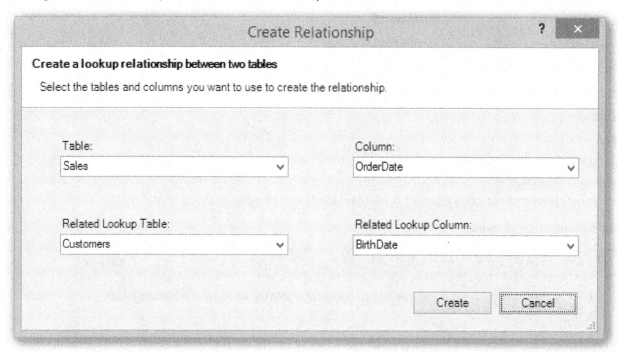

Figure 462 Attempt to create relationship

We promptly get an error as below.

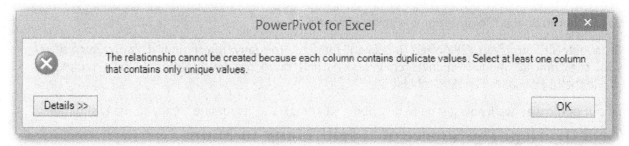

Figure 463 Error Message: The relationship cannot be created because each column contains duplicate values. Select at least one column that contains only unique values.

This is one of those Microsoft error messages which is easy to understand: Power Pivot would not let us create a relationship because there are repeated (duplicate) values on each side.

It's almost as if Power Pivot knows that what we're trying to do here makes no sense at all.

 It's worth stressing, again, that this example is NOT realistic, as it makes ZERO sense to ever relate Customer BirthDate to a transaction date. We chose it just to illustrate that we get an error.

So if we ignore this comically contrived example, what IS a good example?

# Another Bad Example

But wait, first we want to share *another* bad example!

Remember how we said, in our first chapter on Multiple Data Tables, that you should NEVER try to relate two Data tables to one another?

Heck, let's live dangerously and try it, just for grins.

Pretend we just imported ServiceCalls for the first time, and rather than relating it to the Lookup tables, we try creating a relationship between it and Sales, on OrderDate and CallDate:

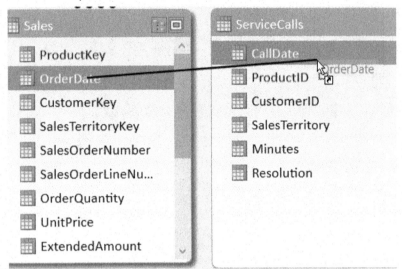

Figure 464 Let's try relating two Data tables together, because we like error messages

This gives us the same error of course:

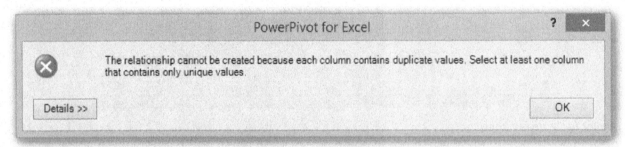

Figure 465 Same error when we try relating Data tables to each other

So why did we bother to do this? To drive home a point, of course.

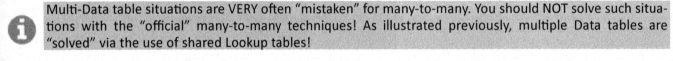

Multi-Data table situations are VERY often "mistaken" for many-to-many. You should NOT solve such situations with the "official" many-to-many techniques! As illustrated previously, multiple Data tables are "solved" via the use of shared Lookup tables!

OK, with that out of the way, we'll now get on to describing what makes a "legitimate" many-to-many situation.

# Real-World Overlap: The Source of "Legit" Many-to-Many

In our experience, true many-to-many usually "happens" in your Lookup tables themselves. It can be spotted, in other words, even if you completely ignore your Data tables.

Many-to-many, or M2M as the cool kids call it, comes down to how your business (or the real world) is organized, and specifically to the concept of membership:

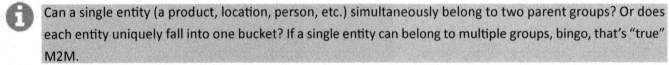

Can a single entity (a product, location, person, etc.) simultaneously belong to two parent groups? Or does each entity uniquely fall into one bucket? If a single entity can belong to multiple groups, bingo, that's "true" M2M.

And we don't mean cases like a particular product belonging to Color=Blue and Category=Bikes. Those are different columns. Only single columns count. So if a single product can be Category=Bikes *and* Category=EcoVehicles, *then* you have true M2M.

Here, let's illustrate with a sketch, cuz we like sketches:

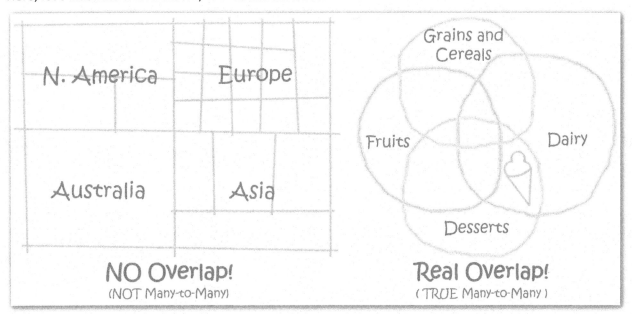

*Figure 466 Countries and/or regions each fall into exactly one continent. But ice cream can be simultaneously categorized as Dairy and Dessert!*

This leads to a Lookup table (Foods) that contains *two* rows for a single food:

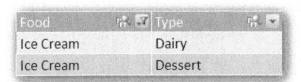

| Food | Type |
|------|------|
| Ice Cream | Dairy |
| Ice Cream | Dessert |

*Figure 467 We now have duplicates in our LOOKUP table, and that's a problem – we won't be able to relate it to a Data table because of those dupes!*

So, um... now what?

If you tried to create a relationship between your Data table (Sales) and this "broken" Lookup table, it would fail as expected. Here are both tables

Data Table (Sales)

| Date | Food | Units |
|------|------|-------|
| 1/8/2013 | Ice Cream | 189 |
| 1/9/2013 | Cake | 14 |
| 1/10/2013 | Grapefruit | 182 |
| 1/11/2013 | Cake | 181 |
| 1/12/2013 | Yogurt | 153 |
| 1/13/2013 | Cake | 170 |
| 1/14/2013 | Ice Cream | 140 |
| 1/15/2013 | Apples | 185 |
| 1/16/2013 | Grapefruit | 117 |
| 1/17/2013 | Dinner Rolls | 53 |

Lookup Table? (Food)

| Food | Category | Calories | Serving Size |
|------|----------|----------|--------------|
| Yogurt | Dairy | 145 | 8 oz |
| Milk | Dairy | 150 | 1 cup |
| Sandwich Bread | Grains and ... | 65 | 1 slice |
| Dinner Rolls | Grains and ... | 85 | 1 roll |
| Ice Cream | Dairy | 270 | 1 cup |
| Ice Cream | Dessert | 270 | 1 cup |
| Pie | Dessert | 355 | 1 piece |
| Danish | Dessert | 235 | 1 pastry |
| Danish | Breakfast | 235 | 1 pastry |
| Corn Flakes | Grains and ... | 110 | 1 oz |

*Figure 468 Our Lookup Table has multiple rows for the same food*

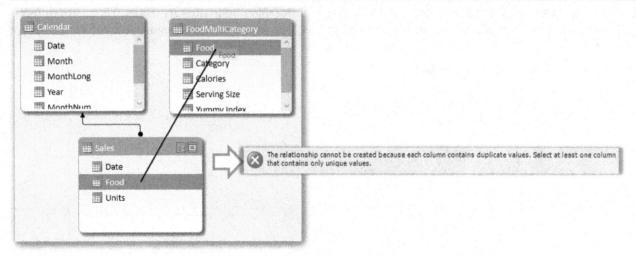

*Figure 469 If you tried creating a relationship, you would get the expected error*

First thing we need to do is to remove the multiple rows in our lookup table; for that we will separate the "Category" column (the multiple piece) from the Foods table. That will let us relate our Sales and Food table.

Food                                                          Category

| Food | Calories | Serving Size | Yummy Index |
|------|----------|--------------|-------------|
| Yogurt | 145 | 8 oz | Yum! |
| Milk | 150 | 1 cup | Meh |
| Sandwich Bread | 65 | 1 slice | Meh |
| Dinner Rolls | 85 | 1 roll | Meh |
| Ice Cream | 270 | 1 cup | Yum! |
| Pie | 355 | 1 piece | Yum! |
| Danish | 235 | 1 pastry | Yum! |

| Category |
|----------|
| Dairy |
| Grains and Cereals |
| Dessert |
| Breakfast |
| Fruit |

*Figure 470 Separate Category from Food to get a clean Lookup table*

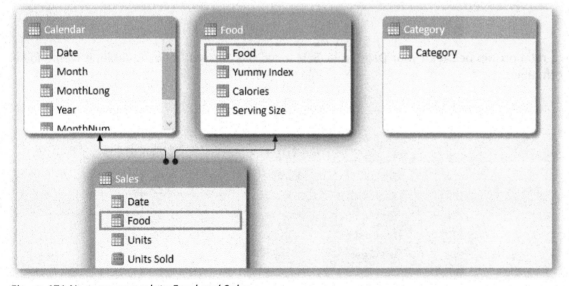

*Figure 471 Now you can relate Food and Sales*

But our Category table is sitting all by itself, feeling lonely. They way to connect Food and Category, is via a "Bridge" table.

# "Bridge" Table

A many-to-many relationship between two entities can be handled using a bridge table. For example the Food and Category tables need a bridge table as below.

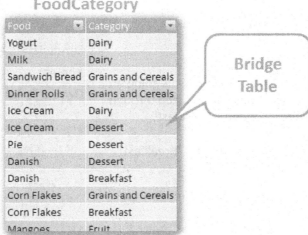

*Figure 472 Many to Many relationship is mapped via a bridge table*

*FoodCategory* (the bridge table) lists, for each food, all of the categories to which that food belongs - one row per "parent" category for that food.

Now we can go ahead and create relationships as shown below, between

```
FoodCategory[Food] -> Food[Food]

FoodCategory[Category] -> Category[Category]
```

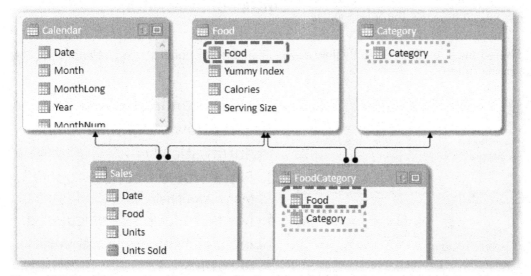

*Figure 473 FoodCategory can be connected to Food and Category via a standard relationship*

But trouble looms ahead. Let's define a basic measure

```
Units Sold = SUM ( Sales[Units] )
```

Nothing earth shattering here, and it all works as expected.

Now let's see if we can analyze this by FoodCategory. As soon as we drag in something from the Category table in the pivot, we see that things aren't quite right. (Even if we were to try the bridge table FoodCategory[Category] column, we'd get the same result.)

| Category[Category] ▼ | Units Sold |
|---|---|
| Breakfast | 3,355,276 |
| Dairy | 3,355,276 |
| Dessert | 3,355,276 |
| Fruit | 3,355,276 |
| Grains and Cereals | 3,355,276 |
| **Grand Total** | **3,355,276** |

*Figure 475 The same number repeats for all categories*

Clearly that is not the right result. Let's break down what is going on here by following the steps in the Golden Rules. We will step through using the highlighted cell, Units Sold for Category "Breakfast".

**Step 1**. Detect Pivot Coordinates: *Category[Category]* = "Breakfast"

**Step 2**. Apply filters from CALCULATE: N/A

**Step 3**. Apply filters to respective tables: Apply filter to *Category* table

**Step 4**. Flow relationships downhill (Lookup to Data table): Since *Category* is filtered in step 3 and *Category* is the Lookup table for *FoodCategory* (which is acting as a Data table for this relationship), the filter flows downhill and is applied as shown to *FoodCategory*.

**Step 5 & 6**: Evaluate the arithmetic and return result to Pivot:
Units Sold = SUM (Sales[Units)

**Wait a minute...the *Sales* table never got filtered in any of the steps above!** So SUM( Sales[Units] ) would return the sum of *all* rows in the Sales table; 3,355,276. And the same number repeats for each Units Sold cell, with the same answer each time, since the *Sales* table never gets filtered.

| Food | ▼ | Units Sold |
|---|---|---|
| Apples | | 267,142 |
| Cake | | 264,219 |
| Cheese | | 254,759 |
| Corn Flakes | | 260,968 |
| Danish | | 262,406 |
| Dinner Rolls | | 258,099 |
| Grapefruit | | 244,543 |
| Ice Cream | | 265,646 |
| Mangoes | | 257,215 |
| Milk | | 257,363 |
| Pie | | 243,664 |
| Sandwich Bread | | 262,775 |
| Yogurt | | 256,477 |
| **Grand Total** | | **3,355,276** |

*Figure 474 Standard measures work as expected*

| Category |
|---|
| Breakfast |

| Food | | Category | |
|---|---|---|---|
| Danish | | Breakfast | |
| Corn Flakes | | Breakfast | |
| Mangoes | | Breakfast | |
| Grapefruit | | Breakfast | |

*Figure 476 FoodCategory filtered to FoodCategory[Category]="Breakfast"*

The *Sales* table does not get filtered since relationships only flow downhill, and never uphill across a relationship. The image below summarizes our predicament.

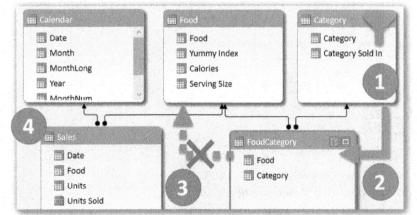

1. Filters coming from this table
2. Filter flows *"downhill"* automatically
3. Filter would not flow *"uphill"* (not without help ☺)
4. Measure *[Units Sold]* calculated in Sales table which never gets filtered

*Figure 477 Filters flow "downhill" across relationships, not "uphill"*

Turns out there is a really simple way to force the filters to flow "uphill". Simple to write down, not simple to come up with. It took some genius work on the part of greats like Jeffrey Wang and Gerhard Brueckl to come up with this. But we can simply put it to good use.

To write a new measure, which forces the relationship to flow "uphill", we can simply write using the pattern below:

```
Units Sold by Category =
CALCULATE ( [Units Sold], FoodCategory )
```

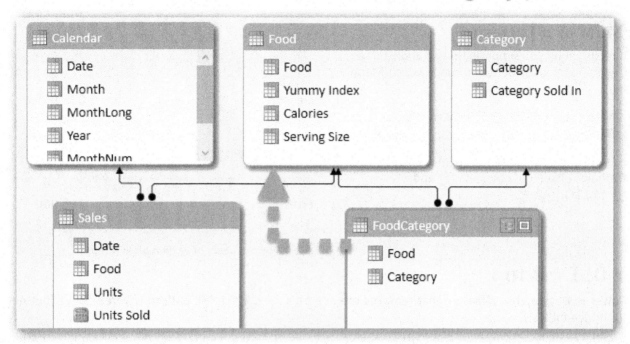

*Figure 478 If the force (of CALCULATE) is with you, you can force a relationship "uphill"*

> ℹ️ Using the "downstream" table (Bridge Table) as a filter argument in CALCULATE forces the filters to flow "uphill" across the relationship

See the end result below with our new measure working as expected:

| Category[Category] | Units Sold by Category |
|---|---|
| Breakfast | 1,025,132 |
| Dairy | 1,034,245 |
| Dessert | 1,035,935 |
| Fruit | 768,900 |
| Grains and Cereals | 1,046,061 |
| **Grand Total** | **3,355,276** |

Average: 982,055   Count: 5   Sum: 4,910,273

*Figure 479 Our new measure shows the right results*

Do note that if you sum up the individual rows, they do NOT add up to the Grand Total. This is easily explained when we add Food to the pivot as well.

Remember Ice Cream had a dual identity; we wanted it categorized as Dairy *and* Dessert. And indeed our Food-Category table maps Ice Cream to Dairy and Dessert. Thus Ice Cream shows in both places. The same is true for other foods mapped to multiple categories. Hence the values shown for Category are correct (as per our mapping), but if you add them up, you would end up double-counting your values. But the Grand Total cell does the right thing and shows you the **correct** total units sold (without any double-counting)!

## Apply M2M as a Pattern

We would recommend you simply learn and apply this as a pattern, wherever you encounter a true Many-to-Many relationship:

 **M2M Measure = CALCULATE ( [Measure], BridgeTable )**

For the truly curious you can dig through articles by Jeffrey and Gerhard: http://ppvt.pro/jeffLink and http://ppvt.pro/GERHARD1.

| Category --> Food | Units Sold by Category |
|---|---|
| ⊟ **Breakfast** | **1,025,132** |
| Corn Flakes | 260,968 |
| Danish | 262,406 |
| Grapefruit | 244,543 |
| Mangoes | 257,215 |
| ⊟ **Dairy** | **1,034,245** |
| Cheese | 254,759 |
| Ice Cream | 265,646 |
| Milk | 257,363 |
| Yogurt | 256,477 |
| ⊟ **Dessert** | **1,035,935** |
| Cake | 264,219 |
| Danish | 262,406 |
| Ice Cream | 265,646 |
| Pie | 243,664 |
| ⊟ **Fruit** | **768,900** |
| Apples | 267,142 |

*Figure 480 One can never have enough Ice Cream*

# Power BI Desktop

Surprise! Power BI Desktop has a feature that removes the need for the CALCULATE pattern covered above (but not the need for bridge tables!)

First let's load the same *Food, Category, FoodCategory* tables in Power BI Desktop and create the same simple measure as before:

```
Units Sold = SUM ( Sales[Units] )
```

The measure happily works, even when you drag Category on the Pivot table. No alteration or additional work required!

| Category | Units Sold |
|---|---|
| Breakfast | 1,025,132 |
| Dairy | 1,034,245 |
| Dessert | 1,035,935 |
| Fruit | 768,900 |
| Grains and Cereals | 1,046,061 |
| **Total** | **3,355,276** |

Units Sold by Category

| Category | Food | Units Sold |
|---|---|---|
| Breakfast | Corn Flakes | 260,968 |
| | Danish | 262,406 |
| | Grapefruit | 244,543 |
| | Mangoes | 257,215 |
| | **Total** | **1,025,132** |
| Dairy | Cheese | 254,759 |
| | Ice Cream | 265,646 |
| | Milk | 257,363 |
| | Yogurt | 256,477 |
| | **Total** | **1,034,245** |
| Dessert | Cake | 264,219 |
| | Danish | 262,406 |
| | Ice Cream | 265,646 |
| | Pie | 243,664 |
| | **Total** | **1,035,935** |
| Fruit | Apples | 267,142 |

*Figure 481 In Power BI Desktop, regular formulas can work across our many-to-many relationship without any additional changes*

The secret is uncovered when you examine the relationships with the bridge table. When you open the relationship view, you'll notice that the arrows are bi-directional – indicating that filters flow uphill as well as downhill!

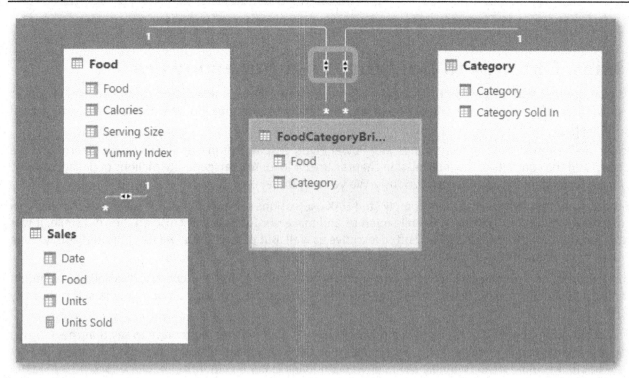

*Figure 482 Filters flow both in both directions across these relationships!*

You can change this behavior if you like by clicking *Manage Relationships* and then editing the relationship.

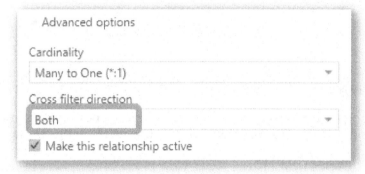

*Figure 483 Manage Relationship > Edit Relationship > Advanced lets you control the filtering direction (Cross Filter Direction can be set to 'Single' or 'Both')*

How did this relationship get set to "Both" directions? Actually, during data import, Power BI automatically detected that this was a Bridge table situation, and did it for us. This makes the filters flow both ways across the relationship (downhill and uphill in our terminology). Hence solving our many-to-many scenario, without any additional DAX work required on our side.

# 23 - Row and Filter Context Demystified

## The Basics: Gateway to Doubling Your Superpowers

For the first year or two of our respective DAX careers, we must admit that we kinda feared these two sets of words: Row Context vs. Filter Context. (Actually, Filter Context was mostly non-mysterious, but Row Context ironically proved to be more difficult).

And to be clear, we were still doing *fantastic things* with Power Pivot, despite that mystery! That whole "learning curve similar to Excel," and the contents of the Intermission chapter, are no joke. You can generate millions of dollars of value per year without understanding this chapter. Seriously. We've been there.

But during those early days, writing the more complicated DAX expressions sometimes felt like pulling the handle on a Vegas slot machine. Would the Context Gods smile upon us and make our formula work? When they did smile, it was quite literally "jackpot" – a satisfying result and often lucrative as well. But at least once, we lost *days* trying to write a single formula, so the point of this chapter is to spare you experiences like those.

After months and years of continuously becoming exponentially more adept at the Dax Kwon Do martial arts, we found ourselves on a "plateau" for awhile. It was weird. For the first time, our powers weren't doubling in strength every three months.

But then, this chapter happened. OK, this chapter didn't exist back then, so it's more accurate to say that *the things in this chapter were the missing ingredient in our own brains*. Once this all crystallized – especially the Exceptions later in this chapter – boom, we were off and running again, powers doubling every few months like clockwork.

So, that's how you should view this chapter. Optional, especially in the early going, but when you are ready, grasshopper, THIS is how you snatch the pebble from our hand.

## The Simple Definitions

As it happens, both of these are straightforward concepts that we can "defang" for you today. We can define them, for starters, as below:

> Row Context = Current Row
> Filter Context = Filter Coordinates Coming from the Pivot

*Note*: Yes, we have covered Filter Context extensively in prior chapters. This is necessary in order to properly contrast it with Row Context, and to explain all the deliciously-powerful exceptions that make us cackle like mad scientists today.

## Row Context: The Key Ingredient of Calc Columns

Row Context is simply the knowledge of **current row**. Power Pivot, unlike Excel, does not have the A1 style reference (rows are not numbered), but it does have the current row. The row context (current row) is automatically defined for Calculated Columns. Let's hear that again:

> Row Context (current row) is automatically defined for Calculated Columns

That is why, you can define a Calculated Column, Amount Due, as below

```
[Unit Price] * [Quantity]
```

When we refer to [Unit Price] or [Quantity] there is no ambiguity, we are referring to these values in the current row.

| Unit Price | Quantity | Amount Due | |
|---|---|---|---|
| 21.98 | 1 | 21.98 | |
| 21.98 | 1 | 21.98 | |
| 21.98 | 1 | 21.98 | ← Current Row |
| 24.99 | 1 | 24.99 | |
| 4.99 | 1 | 4.99 | |

*fx* =[Unit Price] * [Quantity]

*Figure 484 Row Context is automatically defined for Calculated Columns*

Keep in mind, you cannot refer to the Next Row or Previous row (no A1 style reference) without resorting to some trickery (See http://ppvt.pro/CurRowNextRow). But you do have the current row and that enables you to write "single row at a time" calculated columns.

## There's No Row Context in Measures!

What about in a Measure though? Do we have a Row Context there? Attempting to write a measure using the same formula as the Calculated Column above yields an error. We know this already from the 'No *Naked Columns* in Measures' rule outlined earlier.

```
[Total Amount Due] =
[Unit Price] * [OrderQuantity]
```

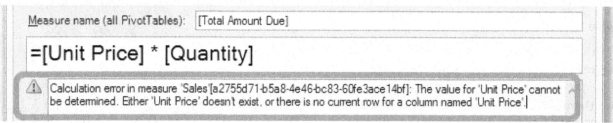

*Figure 485 No "Naked Columns" in Measures*

**In a Measure, we do NOT have a Row Context** (we have no sense of a current row).

Think of it this way: in a measure, the DAX engine always assumes that multiple rows are "left standing" after the filter engine does its work. And how can [Unit Price] be "reduced" to a single value if there are multiple rows of it?

 This is why measures always require an aggregation function: to "collapse" multiple rows of values into a single value. In a calc column, however, a "naked" column reference is legal, because we have a Row Context (aka the current row), and therefore have no need for "collapsing" multiple values into one.

## Filter Context: The Key Ingredient of Measures

Consider the Excel table below, you can see that for the rows shown, the Calorie column adds up to 756.

Now, let us filter the table to Category = "Drinks" as below.

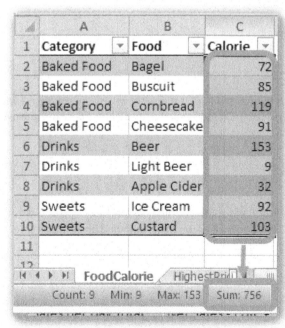

*Figure 486 All rows sum up to a total of 756*

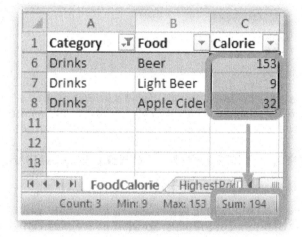

*Figure 487 Now the rows are filtered to Category = "Drinks"*

Now you can see Calorie column adds up to 194.

You can state this as:
a) The Sum of Calorie for Drinks is 194.
b) The Sum of Calorie for the current Filter Context, Food-Calorie[Category] = "Drinks" is 194

a) Is how a human might speak, b) is closer to DAX talk. But what it boils down to, Filter Context is nothing but the set of rows that you have filtered down to. Your filter context originates from the coordinates coming in from the Pivot Table (row/column/filters). Which can then flow downhill across relationships and be altered by CALCULATE. But none of this is any more complicated than the simple filter we chose in the Excel table above.

Filter Context is the set of coordinates coming from the pivot for the current measure cell being calculated. Those coordinates, in turn, result in a filtered set of rows upon which the arithmetic ultimately runs.

## There's No Filter Context in Calc Columns!

Above we explained that Measures lack a Row Context. Well, Calc Columns return the favor and lack a Filter Context!

To illustrate, let's go into our Sales table and write a calc column with the following formula:

```
[My Calc Column] =
SUM ( Sales[Freight] )
```

And see what we get:

This is actually three lessons in one, so let's spell them out very carefully:

1. **Aggregation functions like SUM always ignore Row Context**, and operate against the Filter Context instead.

2. **But there is NO Filter Context** in a Calc Column. That doesn't mean we get no data, however. In fact quite the opposite…

3. **No Filter Context is the same as "the absence of filters."** So the aggregation function (SUM) ends up "operating on" the *entire* [Freight] column – *all* of the rows get added up!

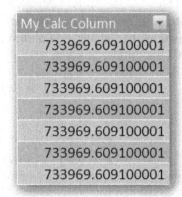

*Figure 488 We get the same answer for every row of the calc column when using an aggregation function like SUM*

 We are reasonably positive that you skimmed those three points ☺. Go back and re-read them until it all makes sense, because they are CRUCIAL to the additional superpowers conveyed by this chapter. We'll wait right here.

## Recap So Far

**Row Context**                      **Filter Context**

*Figure 489 Row Context is literally always a SINGLE row, and a Row Context is "present" in Calc Column formulas. By contrast, Filter Context is the set of coordinates coming from the pivot, and usually results in MULTIPLE rows being active. Filter Context is present in Measure formulas. These concepts are therefore almost perfect opposites.*

# Interaction with Relationships

## Relationships and Filter Context

As we've seen repeatedly in our Golden Rules, filter context flows downhill via relationships. Again filter context is simply a set of filters/coordinates. So what do we mean when we say 'Filter context flows downhill via the relationship'?

Let us understand with an example, again with the caveat that this is a review:

*Figure 490 SalesTerritory Table is filtered to [Country] = "United States"*

This filters the SalesTerritory table. But the SalesTerritory and Sales tables are related.

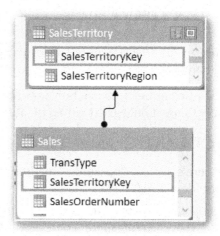

The filter on SalesTerritory will flow down to the Sales table, by virtue of the relationship, aka the filter transmission wire. That "wire" is attached via the **key columns connecting the two tables**. The SalesTerritory[Country] = "United States" filter, filters the column:-

SalesTerritory[SalesTerritoryKey] = { 1, 2, 3, 4, 5}

Due to the relationship the Sales table is then also filtered down to

Sales[SalesTerritoryKey] = { 1, 2, 3, 4, 5}

*Figure 491 SalesTerritory and Sales are related*

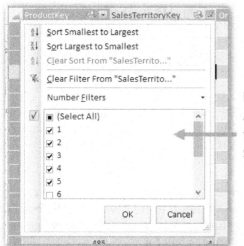

Filter flows down via the relationship. Almost as if the Sales Table itself was filtered to
Sales[SalesTerritoryKey] = {1, 2, 3, 4, 5}

*Figure 492 Filter Context flows down via a relationship*

This is a simple example. But even for complex scenarios, the mechanism remains the same.

 Filter context flows downhill by default. But can also be forced to **flow uphill** via advanced tricks, such as in the chapter on many to many relationships, in which we used CALCULATE to perform this special magic.

## Relationships and Row context

What about relationships and row context? Well, those two aren't on speaking terms. They do not talk to each other.

Seriously, there's no interaction whatsoever between relationships and row context (except when you use relationship-aware functions like RELATED of course). Row context does not affect, nor is it affected by, relationships.

Again, with the exception of RELATED and RELATEDTABLE, Row Context does not interact with relationships at all – relationships are only "used" in Filter Context situations.

# Exceptions and Overrides!

## Iterator Functions Create Row Context During Measure Calculation

Aha! We told you there were some delicious exceptions! Welcome to the first such juicy morsel: You can "manufacture" a Row Context, in a measure, when using Iterator functions.

 The X functions (like SUMX, RANKX, etc.) and the FILTER function are special. They are *iterators* that step through the <table> you give them - *one row at a time*. So, *within* these functions, you DO have a Row Context, and do NOT require aggregation functions around column references!

For example, inside the SUMX function, we can reference columns as values, without aggregation functions:

```
[Total Amount Due] =
SUMX ( Sales, Sales[Unit Price] * Sales[Quantity] )
```

And that works just fine. So if you need to perform row-wise calculations within a measure, the X functions are the way to do it.

**Similarly, inside a FILTER function, you can perform any math you want** using "naked" column references. This comes in very handy at times where you want to keep rows where "two times column A is greater than column B" for instance.

 But using an iterator function does NOT suddenly create a Row Context for the *entire* measure formula. The Row Context only exists within the iterator function itself.

## CALCULATE Creates Filter Context in Calc Columns

Yep, there's a tricky "backdoor" method for this as well, and it comes back to our old friend CALCULATE.

That's right, our favorite function does more than allow us to manipulate filter context. It even *creates* filter contexts where there previously were none.

**The CALCULATE function transforms the current Row Context into a Filter Context.** "What the heck," you say? Yeah. It's probably easier to just show you. So let's return to that previous example, where we had a SUM() inside a calc column:

And this time, let's wrap the SUM inside a CALCULATE:

```
= CALCULATE ( SUM ( Sales[Freight] ) )
```

If you were to write a measure as above, using CALCULATE with no filter arguments, you would feel silly. But for a calculated column, this serves a very useful function. CALCULATE takes the current Row Context and "pretends" that it was actually a Filter Context.

| My Calc Column |
|---|
| 733969.609100001 |
| 733969.609100001 |
| 733969.609100001 |
| 733969.609100001 |
| 733969.609100001 |
| 733969.609100001 |
| 733969.609100001 |

*Figure 493 SUM(Sales[Freight]) in a calc column yields the same number for every row.*

Which gives us this result:

| Freight | My Calc Column |
|---|---|
| 59.6018 | 59.6018 |
| 57.9998 | 57.9998 |
| 84.9998 | 84.9998 |
| 0.7248 | 0.7248 |
| 0.5495 | 0.5495 |
| 0.1248 | 0.1248 |
| 0.8748 | 0.8748 |

*Figure 494 Wahoo! A calc column that precisely duplicates the Freight column we already had!*

OK, so that is *also* not terribly useful, is it? More interesting than the same value on every row, but still doesn't provide us with actual useful results. So let's change examples to one where it *is* helpful.

### We can use CALCULATE to "follow" relationships in calc columns

Instead of a calc column in the Sales table, let's go to one of our Lookup tables, like Products, and write one there:

| ProductSales] ▾ | | $f_x$ =CALCULATE(SUM(Sales[SalesAmt])) | |
|---|---|---|---|
| ProductKey | | ProductSales | StandardC |
| 211 | | | |
| 210 | | | |
| 480 | | $7,307.39 | |
| 529 | | $9,480.24 | |
| 477 | | $21,177.56 | |
| 528 | | $15,444.05 | |
| 530 | | $7,425.12 | |
| 484 | | $7,218.60 | |

*Figure 495 Ooh! Now, in our Lookup table's calc column, we get the sum of all MATCHING rows from the Data table (Sales).*

Why is that? Because Filter Context does flow across relationships.

So, if you ever want to get a "subtotal" type of calc column in a Lookup table, look no further than CALCULATE.

 Note that we typically do *not* need such subtotal columns in our Lookup tables, as we dynamically calculate subtotals in pivots using measures. The "valid" reason to do something like this is so that you can then *group* your Products, for instance, into buckets like "Top Sellers," "Mid Sellers," etc. – in other words, we typically aren't interested in the subtotal number *itself* as a calc column, but we use the number as an *input* to another calculation (one that buckets the rows into groups, that we subsequently use on Rows, Columns, Filters or Slicer, or potentially as a filter clause in CALCULATE... you get the idea.)

## Using Measures Within a Row Context: a Genuine Curveball

We have long had a [Total Sales] measure defined:

```
Total Sales =
SUM ( Sales[SalesAmt] )
```

So, what happens if we define a calc column in the Products table as below:-

```
= [Total Sales]
```

Check out the results:

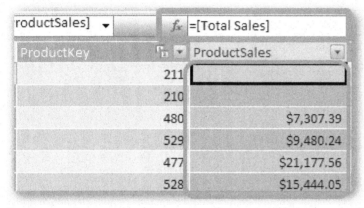

*Figure 496 Using a Measure produces surprisingly "correct" results*

So what happened to row context not interacting with relationships? Well, whenever you reference a measure, the DAX engine pretends you had wrapped a CALCULATE around it. Thus, when operating in a Row Context (in a Calculated Column or inside an iterator function like FILTER), if you reference a Measure, it will act as if it had been wrapped in a CALCULATE. i.e. the Row Context will be transitioned to a Filter Context.

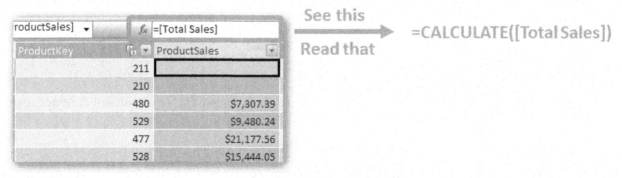

*Figure 497 Measure references always act as if wrapped inside a CALCULATE*

 Whenever you reference a measure in a calc column (or inside an iterator function), there is an implied CALCULATE wrapped around it. This will frustrate you to no end, for instance, if you've been pulling your hair out for days, wondering why your FILTER function is behaving very strangely. In fact, that is the #1 place that this "implied CALCULATE" will burn you. In fact, let's look at precisely such an example...

# Putting It All Together: Review Example

We already have a measure defined to count transactions

```
Transactions =
COUNTROWS ( Sales )
```

Let us define a new measure to count transaction only for our highest priced items (the highest price point in our Products table happens to be $3578.27)

```
Transaction for Highest Price = CALCULATE (
    COUNTROWS (Sales),
    FILTER (
        Products,
        Products[ListPrice] = MAX ( Products[ListPrice] )
    )
)
```

We can see that the measure works

| Row Labels | Transactions | Transaction for Highest Price | | OrderDate | ProductKey | ListPrice | Transactions |
|---|---|---|---|---|---|---|---|
| 7/1/2001 | 5 | 1 | | 7/1/2001 | 310 | 3578.27 | 1 |
| 7/2/2001 | 4 | 2 | | | 336 | 699.0982 | 1 |
| 7/3/2001 | 5 | 4 | | | 346 | 3399.99 | 3 |
| 7/4/2001 | 2 | 2 | | 7/2/2001 | 310 | 3578.27 | 1 |
| 7/5/2001 | 5 | 4 | | | 311 | 3578.27 | 1 |
| 7/6/2001 | 4 | 4 | | | 344 | 3399.99 | 1 |
| 7/7/2001 | 3 | 2 | | | 351 | 3374.99 | 1 |
| 7/8/2001 | 3 | 2 | | 7/3/2001 | 312 | 3578.27 | 2 |
| 7/9/2001 | 6 | 3 | | | 313 | 3578.27 | 1 |
| 7/10/2001 | 3 | 2 | | | 314 | 3578.27 | 1 |
| 7/11/2001 | 4 | 4 | | | 330 | 699.0982 | 1 |

*Figure 498 Measure returns the desired result*

As a best practice, we often encourage you to

- Build Measures step by step
- Reuse Measures whenever possible

In that spirit, what if we altered the measure as below, defining an intermediate measure and reusing the same.

```
Highest Price = MAX ( Products[ListPrice] )
Transaction for Highest Price BROKEN = CALCULATE (
    COUNTROWS (Sales),
    FILTER (
        Products,
        Products[ListPrice] =[Highest Price]
    )
)
```

Okay, we might have given it away by the name of the measure, but see for yourself. Our new measure does not seem to work, even though it seems logically similar.

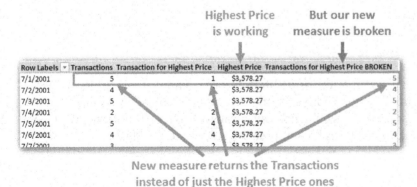

*Figure 499 New measure does not work even though "logically similar"*

In our opinion, this is the least sensible thing in the entire DAX language – the one place where a measure name returns a different result than the underlying formula. (Hey, it's an *amazing* language, and it's remarkable that it manages to be as *complete* as it is, with so few warts. This one stands out primarily as a byproduct of that near-perfection, because "lesser" languages have far more head-scratching examples, not to mention absolute breakdowns.)

Let's evaluate the measure with DAX eyes. We will number the lines so we can easily reference them.

```
1. Transaction for Highest Price BROKEN = CALCULATE(
2. COUNTROWS(Sales),
3. FILTER(
4.   Products,
5.   Products[ListPrice] =[Highest Price]
6. )
7. )
```

FILTER on line 3 is an Iterator (closely related to SUMX and all the other X functions), and we know what iterators are useful for – manufacturing a row context within measures. They iterate row by row over a given table and thus give us a current row (row context).

On line 5, we used a measure ([Highest Price]) where we have a row context (thanks to our iterator FILTER). Remember how to read measures when there is a row context in play? You imagine it wrapped inside a CALCULATE, transitioning the row context to a filter context.

Let us follow the path for a single pivot row Sales[OrderDate] = 7/1/2001 and compute our new measure [Transaction for Highest Price BROKEN] :

1. FILTER iterates through the Products table. The complete Products table, by the way. Remember filter context does not flow uphill, so Sales[OrderDate] = 7/1/2001 in no way filters down the Products table.

2. But since COUNTROWS(Sales) will only return a value where ProductKey exists in the Sales table, for our purposes we will focus on the ProductKey sold on 7/1/2001 = { 336, 310, 346 }

3. For ProductKey = 336, FILTER evaluates the condition
   Products[ListPrice] =[Highest Price]

4. Products[ListPrice] = $699.09 We have a row context, thanks to the iterator, thus a naked column reference is perfectly legit.

5. [Highest Price], being a measure reference, operates as if it is wrapped inside CALCULATE. Thus the row context (Product[ProductKey] = 336) is transitioned to a filter context. What would the below measure evaluate to with this filter context?
   Filter Context: Product[ProductKey] = 336
   Highest Price= MAX(Products[ListPrice])
   You guessed it, $699.09

6. So how does the filter condition evaluate for row ProductKey = 336
   Products[ListPrice] =[Highest Price]
   $699.09 = $699.09
   Evaluates to TRUE!

7. It is (hopefully) apparent at this point that the filter condition will evaluate to TRUE for every single Product. Since both sides of the comparison would always evaluate to the same value.

8. Thus our FILTER in this case does not provide any additional filters. The only filter would be the ones coming from the original pivot (Sales[OrderDate] = 7/1/2001). So our broken measure works the same as COUNTROWS(Sales) and always returns the same number as our [Transactions] measure

## Why Did Our Original Measure Work to Begin With?

```
Transaction for Highest Price = CALCULATE(
    COUNTROWS(Sales),
    FILTER(
        Products,
        Products[ListPrice] = MAX ( Products[ListPrice] )
    )
)
```

Do you recall the result we got when we defined a Calculated Column in Product table as

```
= SUM ( Sales[SalesAmt] )
```

We got the same repeating number in each row – the sum of **all** the Sales table rows, since there was no filter context in place.

Our MAX(Products[ListPrice]) meets the same fate. Since there is No filter context around the Products table, it always returns the maximum List Price across all products, which is $3578.27, shared by multiple products, all of which make it through our FILTER.

| [MaxListPrice] ▼ | *fx* =MAX(Products[ListPrice]) | |
|---|---|---|
| ProductKey ⁿᵤ ▼ | ProductSales ▼ | MaxListPrice ▼ |
| 211 | | $3,578.27 |
| 210 | | $3,578.27 |
| 480 | $7,307.39 | $3,578.27 |
| 529 | $9,480.24 | $3,578.27 |
| 477 | $21,177.56 | $3,578.27 |
| 528 | $15,444.05 | $3,578.27 |
| 530 | $7,425.12 | $3,578.27 |
| 484 | $7,218.60 | $3,578.27 |

*Figure 500 Without Row Context transition Filter Context returns all rows in original Filter Context*

Take a deep breath and realize that none of the steps involved are complicated. It is just the interaction amongst all of them applied in totality that is "hard" to grasp. Re-read the above, mechanically, and it will eventually "gel."

## Recap Within the Context of FILTER()

It is worthwhile to recap how row and filter context applies to the arguments of the FILTER function.

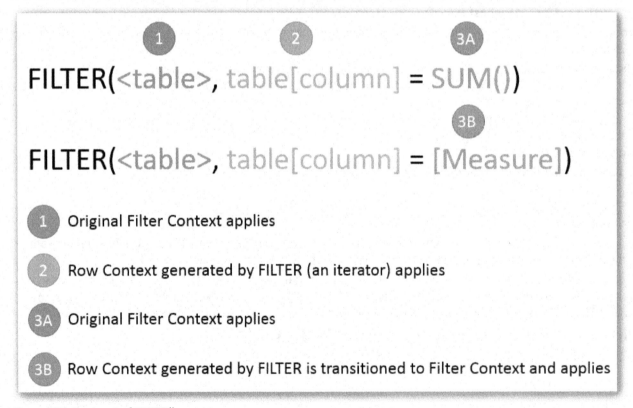

FILTER(&lt;table&gt;, table[column] = SUM())

FILTER(&lt;table&gt;, table[column] = [Measure])

1   Original Filter Context applies

2   Row Context generated by FILTER (an iterator) applies

3A   Original Filter Context applies

3B   Row Context generated by FILTER is transitioned to Filter Context and applies

*Figure 501 Anatomy of FILTER()*

**First Argument: <table>**
Can be a table name (e.g. Products) or a table expression using any function that returns a table (e.g. ALL(Products)). The original filter context (incoming from the pivot) applies to this table. Unless, of course, you override it using ALL().

**Second Argument: <condition>**

Within this argument, here's how each of the following expressions will evaluate:

- **table[column]** – a column reference uses the Row Context generated by FILTER (an iterator). Note that typically a "Naked" table[column] reference (without any aggregation functions around it) is not allowed in a measure, since measures lack a Row Context. But since FILTER is an iterator, it steps through row by row (of the table in the first argument) and generates a row context for us at each step of that iteration.

- **SUM() or other aggregation formula** – always refers to the Filter Context, and ignores Row Context – even the Row Context created by FILTER. The only Filter Context that is available is the one that comes from the pivot, so that's what the SUM will reference.

- **CALCULATE(SUM())** – the Row Context created by each iteration of the FILTER function will be transformed into a Filter Context, and the SUM will then operate off of that, respecting the Row Context, following relationships, etc.

- **[Measure]** – Will behave exactly the same as CALCULATE(SUM()), or CALCULATE of any other aggregation function, because measure references *imply* a CALCULATE.

## In Case of Emergency...

Ever heard the phrase, "percussive maintenance?" It's the fancy way of saying "if something isn't working, pound on it with your fist and see if that fixes it." This is one of those old clichés that's going out of style, because primarily, we used to pound our fists on tv's back in the day – and today's tv's don't exactly respond to it.

So let's try a more modern equivalent: "reboots are magic fixes." How many times have you rebooted a computer, a smart phone, or an application hoping that a problem magically vanishes? And how many times has it worked? (Quite frequently – that's our answer to both questions).

Well, if this chapter has left your head spinning, don't fret.

When something mysterious starts happening, there's no shame in semi-randomly trying these fixes:

1. Wrapping an aggregation function in a CALCULATE.
2. Replacing a measure reference with its underlying formula.

Even we occasionally find ourselves applying one of these techniques semi-blindly, without bothering to think it through. DAX is pretty cool like that, because once a formula works, it doesn't randomly stop working. We encourage you not to feel any shame from such heroics ☺

# Key Points from This Chapter

- Row Context is the knowledge of the Current Row

- Filter Context is the set of filter coordinates coming from the pivot

- Measures do not have a Row Context
  But we can manufacture Row Context in Measures, using Iterator functions (X functions and FILTER).

- Calculated Columns do not have a Filter Context
  But we can create one, using CALCULATE. CALCULATE transitions the current Row Context into a Filter Context, which adds to existing Filter Context. The key implication being that relationships, and the "filter transmission" they provide, will be respected within that calculation.

- Measure references used within a Row Context behave as if they were wrapped inside a CALCULATE, thus transitioning the existing Row Context to a Filter Context.

# 24 - CALCULATE and FILTER – More Nuances

Continuing the theme of "you already have superpowers, so consider this chapter optional or something you save for later…"

## CALCULATE Filter Arguments Override Pivot Filters

We already covered this in Chapter 8 on CALCULATE, but let's revisit that in some new light. This time, we will use a visual approach that has helped us grasp the concept. Let's say we have a measure defined as:-

```
[Red Bikes bought by Females] =
CALCULATE (
    SUM ( Sales[OrderQuantity] ),
    Products[Color] = "Red",
    Products[Category] = "Bikes",
    Customers[Gender] = "F"
)
```

We have a pivot table as shown below where we have pivot filters on Product[Color] and Customer[Gender] and Calendar[CalendarYear] on rows:

Let us try to understand the filters in play for the high-lighted cell.

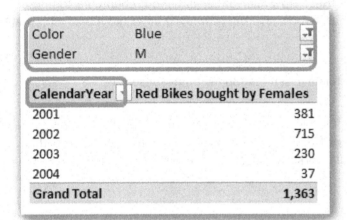

Figure 502 Pivot Table coordinates provide the initial filter context

Figure 503 CALCULATE and Pivot filter on the same fields, who wins?

The pivot table coordinates (filters) coming from the pivot can be seen as a set of blocks, with each block representing a table[column] filter. This is the original (incoming) set of filters for the highlighted cell:-

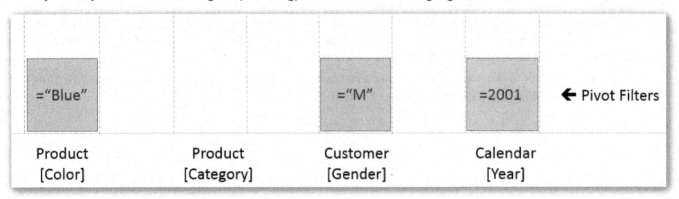

Figure 504 Incoming filters from the Pivot Table

Now, let's layer on the filters added by CALCULATE.

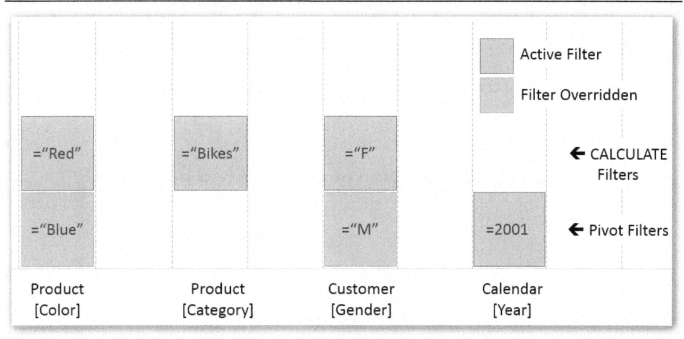

*Figure 505 CALCULATE Filters can override the Filters coming from Pivot Table*

Now you see, **when they both operate on the EXACT SAME table[column], the CALCULATE filters hide (override) the incoming filters**, like Product[Color] and Customer[Gender]. Otherwise, CALCULATE filters simply ADD to the filter context, like Product[Category]. The original filters which do not conflict with CALCULATE filters pass through untouched, like Calendar[Year] in this case.

Now let's take another look at the CALCULATE filter arguments.

# The "Secret" Second Purpose of ALL(), FILTER(), Etc.

## CALCULATE's Definition Gives Us a Hint!

If we check the syntax of the CALCULATE function, here is what it has to say about the filter arguments.

> CALCULATE(<expression>,<filter1>,<filter2>...)
> filter1, filter2...      A comma separated list of True/False expressions or **tables**

In the CALCULATE chapter we started by using simple True/False expressions as filter arguments, such as

```
CALCULATE ( [Total Sales], Sales[Year] = 2002 )
```

> A True/False Expression for CALCULATE is of the form
> Table[Column] <op> *fixed value*
> Where <op> is a comparison operator like = > < <= <= <>

But then, we quickly started *also* passing functions like ALL(), FILTER(), DATESYTD() etc. as filter arguments to CALCULATE. Those functions are definitely not True/False expressions, so are they... tables??

Let's focus specifically on ALL() for a moment.

## ALL() Is the "Remove Filters" Function, but it's Also a Table!

Our good friend ALL() – we first learned it as the "remove filters" function. And when we pass it as an argument to CALCULATE, that is precisely what it does.

But ALL(), like any superhero, has a secret second identity.

Let's take a look at another old friend, COUNTROWS. Its only argument is described merely as "<table>" – the same exact description of what CALCULATE can take as filter arguments!

So... can we pass ALL() as an argument to COUNTROWS? You bet we can! And also DATESBETWEEN and VALUES, just to name two...

```
[Count Days All Calendar] =
COUNTROWS ( ALL ( Calendar ) )
```

```
[Count Me Some Days] =
COUNTROWS (
    DATESBETWEEN ( Calendar[Date], "2/1/2002", "3/1/2002" )
)

[Count All Months] =
COUNTROWS ( ALL ( Calendar[MonthName] ) )

[Count Included Months] =
COUNTROWS ( VALUES ( Calendar[MonthName] ) )
```

| Row Labels | Count Days | Count Days All Calendar | Count Me Some Days | Count All Months | Count Included Months |
|---|---|---|---|---|---|
| ⊟ 2001 | 184 | 1,158 | 29 | 12 | 6 |
| Q3 | 92 | 1,158 | 29 | 12 | 3 |
| Q4 | 92 | 1,158 | 29 | 12 | 3 |
| ⊟ 2002 | 365 | 1,158 | 29 | 12 | 12 |
| Q1 | 90 | 1,158 | 29 | 12 | 3 |
| Q2 | 91 | 1,158 | 29 | 12 | 3 |
| Q3 | 92 | 1,158 | 29 | 12 | 3 |

*Figure 506 COUNTROWS accepts <table> as argument, thus can be used with Table functions*

## There Are *Dozens* of These Dual-Purpose Functions!

All of these functions – ALL, FILTER, TOPN, DATESBETWEEN, DATEADD, DATESYTD, VALUES, and many others – return a table, and thus can be used anywhere DAX asks us for a table (such as COUNTROWS in this case).

That is *in addition* to being usable as a <filter> argument to CALCULATE. For that reason, we like to refer to all of these functions as dual-purpose.

You could rewrite the first formula (or all the rest) using CALCULATE instead, as below:-

```
[Count Days All Calendar using CALCULATE] =
CALCULATE ( COUNTROWS ( Calendar ), ALL ( Calendar ) )
```

| Row Labels | Count Days All Calendar | Count Days All Calendar using CALCULATE |
|---|---|---|
| 2001 | 1,158 | 1,158 |
| 2002 | 1,158 | 1,158 |
| 2003 | 1,158 | 1,158 |
| 2004 | 1,158 | 1,158 |
| **Grand Total** | **1,158** | **1,158** |

*Figure 507 Two ways to get the same result: Use ALL as table argument or filter argument*

 Nearly all of the "special" functions that we can pass as <filter> arguments to CALCULATE can also be used wherever DAX asks us for a <table>. The only exception we are aware of is USERELATIONSHIP, which can only be used as a <filter>, and not as a <table>.

### Could Have Been Separate Functions?

To help explain this dual-purpose concept, we often tell students that Microsoft *could* have created separate functions for each purpose, like ALLFILTER and ALLTABLE, and only allowed us to use them one place each (the former as a <filter> to CALCULATE, and the latter as a <table>), but rather than "pollute" the function list by nearly doubling it in length, they allowed us to use the functions either place.

(DAX purists may disagree with this notion, and say they always see them as table functions, period, which is fine too. It's just a teaching trick that people seem to find helpful).

## Nesting Table Functions Inside One Another

It's time to have some fun with all of this new knowledge. In most examples so far we have seen FILTER restrict, or filter down, the set of rows that we were operating upon. But can you use FILTER to *un*filter, thus including *more* rows in the calculation than were originally "requested" by the pivot?

Look at this silly measure:

```
[Transactions Silly] =
CALCULATE ( [Transactions], FILTER ( Products, 1 ) )
```

| Row Labels ▼ | Transactions | Transactions Silly |
|---|---|---|
| Accessories | 36,092 | 36,092 |
| Bikes | 15,205 | 15,205 |
| Clothing | 9,101 | 9,101 |
| Components | | |
| Grand Total | 60,398 | 60,398 |

*Figure 508 Since 1 is always True, FILTER is not really filtering here – every row passes the test*

The FILTER function here is really not doing anything. It starts with the Product table (the first argument to FILTER, the current filter context applies here) iterates over that, and since the condition (1, the second argument to FILTER) is always true, it returns all the rows that it started with. So it does not alter the result in any way.

Moving on, it turns out that FILTER accepts <table> as its first argument:

 FILTER(<**table**>,<filter>)

So we can pass a table function in as the first argument to FILTER, which is itself a table function! This represents a significant expansion of your powers once you digest it.

## FILTER Can *Unfilter*?

Since ALL is a table function, let's give it a try:-

```
[Transactions All Products] =
CALCULATE ( [Transactions], FILTER ( ALL ( Products ), 1 ) )
```

Look at the result; that did indeed clear the filter on Product table in our pivot.

| Row Labels ▼ | Transactions | Transactions Silly | Transactions All Products |
|---|---|---|---|
| Accessories | 36,092 | 36,092 | 60,398 |
| Bikes | 15,205 | 15,205 | 60,398 |
| Clothing | 9,101 | 9,101 | 60,398 |
| Components | | | 60,398 |
| Grand Total | 60,398 | 60,398 | 60,398 |

*Figure 509 FILTER can unfilter? Now the force is truly with us!*

Let's break this down into steps, working from the inside out:

1.  ALL(Products) temporarily creates a virtual copy of the Products table with all filters removed. So this temporary table (that exists in the computer's memory only during the calculation of this formula) contains the entire Products table, regardless of the initial filter context specified by the pivot.

2.  FILTER(ALL(Products),1) then steps through that temporary table, one row at a time, and evaluates the True/False expression. Since that expression is a hard-coded 1, it's always True, which means every row in that temporary table is kept. Since the temporary table started out with every row from Products, FILTER returns another temporary table, also with every row of Products in it.

3.  Finally, since FILTER (step 2) was used as a <filter> argument to CALCULATE, and such <filter> arguments override the ones coming in from the pivot, we get the Transaction count for *all* products on each row.

So there you go, we have just used FILTER to *un*filter.

# Putting it All Together

Let's go way back to the very first example of CALCULATE() that we wrote

```
[2002 Sales] =
CALCULATE ( [Total Sales], Sales[Year] = 2002 )
```

Now that we know that, for CALCULATE we can either pass a True/False expression or a table as a filter argument; **can we rewrite the measure above by using a table expression?** (Why would we care about rewriting it thus? Hold your peace on that one, we'll come to that).

Let's try that same thing with FILTER() instead, which would return a filtered table:

```
[2002 Sales] =
CALCULATE (
    [Total Sales],
    FILTER ( Sales, Sales[Year] = 2002 )
)
```

| Row Labels ▼ | Total Sales | 2002 Sales | 2002 Sales via FILTER |
|---|---|---|---|
| 2001 | $3,266,374 | $6,530,344 | |
| 2002 | $6,530,344 | $6,530,344 | $6,530,344 |
| 2003 | $9,791,060 | $6,530,344 | |
| 2004 | $9,770,900 | $6,530,344 | |
| Grand Total | $29,358,677 | $6,530,344 | $6,530,344 |

*Figure 510 Our first try with FILTER did not produce matching results*

You can see, the results are not quite alike. The two measures produce different results in the pivot shown. Why?

Because CALCULATE overrides or ignores the incoming pivot filter. Thus at each row it ignores the incoming filter of Year=2001, Year=2002, Year=2003, Year=2004 and applies its own filter Year=2002.

We need to replicate the same behavior in our FILTER version and write the measure as below

```
[2002 Sales via FILTER ALL Sales Year] =
CALCULATE (
    [Total Sales],
    FILTER ( ALL ( Sales[Year] ), Sales[Year] = 2002 )
)
```

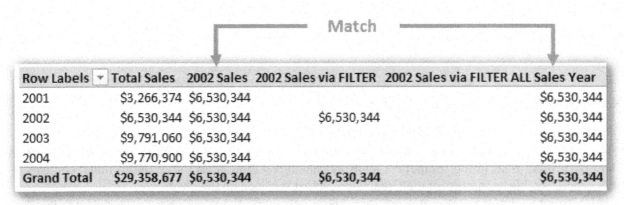

| Row Labels ▼ | Total Sales | 2002 Sales | 2002 Sales via FILTER | 2002 Sales via FILTER ALL Sales Year |
|---|---|---|---|---|
| 2001 | $3,266,374 | $6,530,344 | | $6,530,344 |
| 2002 | $6,530,344 | $6,530,344 | $6,530,344 | $6,530,344 |
| 2003 | $9,791,060 | $6,530,344 | | $6,530,344 |
| 2004 | $9,770,900 | $6,530,344 | | $6,530,344 |
| Grand Total | $29,358,677 | $6,530,344 | $6,530,344 | $6,530,344 |

*Figure 511 Our second try with FILTER matches perfectly*

Terrific! We have been able to rewrite our original measure faithfully using a FILTER table expression.

 This, in itself, is not useful, because hey, we achieved the same result much more efficiently with the simple True/False <filter> from before. Our intent is merely to illustrate a concept, and set the stage for other things. The ability to nest table functions inside other table functions turns out to be incredibly powerful, as is the ability to nimbly flip back and forth between using them as <table>'s, and using them as <filter>'s.

# 25 - Time Intelligence with Custom Calendars: Greatest Formula in the World

## Perhaps Our Favorite Thing in DAX

**Working with custom calendars in DAX has become something that we'd almost do for free, it's so much fun. Specifically, it just feels *powerful*, like you can do just about anything.**

That said, it took us a little while to discover the magic formula. It took some experimentation. But you won't have to do any of that – we will give you the secret, and explain how it works.

It also provides a platform to apply some of the things we have learned about CALCULATE and FILTER.

## Custom Calendars

There can be many types of custom calendars, such as Retail, Academic, Farming, Sport Season etc. Here is an example of the 4-5-4 Calendar published by the National Retail Federation.

*Figure 512 Sample Custom Calendar as used in Retail Source: NRF.com*

We will use a "4/4/5" calendar, but the concepts learned and measures used will be easily portable to any custom calendar.

## The Periods Table - a "4/4/5" Example

Let's say our company operates on the "4/4/5" calendar, which is very common in retail. "4/4/5" refers to the number of weeks in each period, where a period is *roughly* a month. These calendars rotate through four quarters in a year, each consisting 13 total weeks.

Here's an example – a Periods table imported into Power Pivot:

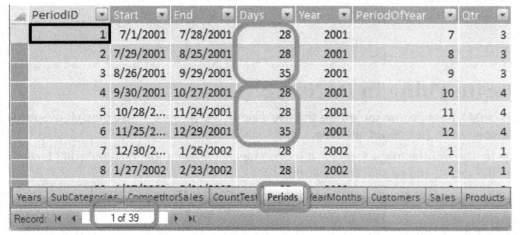

*Figure 513 Periods table – 39 rows spanning from 7/1/2001 to 9/25/2004 – note the repeating 28/28/35 pattern, which is 4/4/5 weeks*

## How This Changes Things: We Need to "Write" Our Own Time Intelligence Functions

**The critical point is not merely the existence of this table. The "wrinkle" here is that all "sales for period X" reports, as well as all comparisons of growth – versus last year, versus prior periods – must be performed according to the periods defined in this table.** Likewise, all "year to date" and similar calculations must respect this table.

The "smarter" time intelligence functions like DATESYTD(), DATEADD(), and SAMEPERIODLASTYEAR() – the ones with built-in knowledge of the standard calendar – will **not** work properly in this regard.

So we will need to essentially write our own versions of those functions from scratch, using other more primitive functions like FILTER(), ALL(), and DATESBETWEEN().

# Connecting the Periods Table

To connect our Periods table, we will add a PeriodID column to our existing Calendar table, so that we can connect these tables together.

| Date | PeriodID | DayNumberOfWeek | DayName |
|---|---|---|---|
| 7/26/2001 | 1 | 5 | Thursday |
| 7/27/2001 | 1 | 6 | Friday |
| 7/28/2001 | 1 | 7 | Saturday |
| 7/29/2001 | 2 | 1 | Sunday |
| 7/30/2001 | 2 | 2 | Monday |
| 7/31/2001 | 2 | 3 | Tuesday |
| 8/1/2001 | 2 | 4 | Wednesc |

*Figure 514 Add PeriodID in our regular Calendar Table*

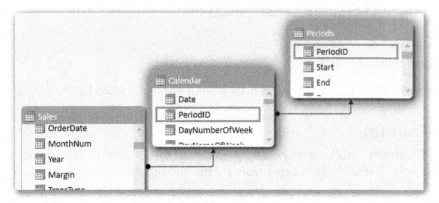

*Figure 515 PeriodID would let us connect Periods table to Calendar which is connected to Sales*

An alternate approach would be to build your Custom Calendar (Periods) table at a daily grain and connect it directly to our data table (Sales). Either approach is acceptable and the formulas we write would work in either case.

# Simple "Sales in Period" Measure

Let's start with the basics. We want a pivot that shows something like this:

| Periods[Year] > Qtr > Period | Sales in Period |
|---|---|
| ⊟ 2001 | $3,219,717 |
| ⊟ Q3 | $1,417,740 |
| P7 | $426,286 |
| P8 | $448,953 |
| P9 | $542,501 |
| ⊟ Q4 | $1,801,977 |
| P10 | $481,475 |
| P11 | $516,537 |
| P12 | $803,964 |
| ⊟ 2002 | $6,526,854 |
| ⊟ Q1 | $1,824,424 |
| P1 | $552,898 |
| P2 | $534,463 |
| P3 | $737,062 |
| ⊟ Q2 | $2,009,710 |
| P4 | $582,060 |
| P5 | $687,716 |
| P6 | $739,934 |

*Figure 516 Simplest pivot: just display sales data according to the custom Periods table (the 4/4/5 calendar)*

This is pretty straightforward actually, since we can use our existing measure [Total Sales] for this purpose without making any changes.

```
[Total Sales] =
SUM ( Sales[SalesAmt] )
```

**This just works**, since filters flow downhill via relationship across any number of levels. Thus, for example, filters on Periods[Year] will flow down to Calendar table, and will then flow down to Sales table.

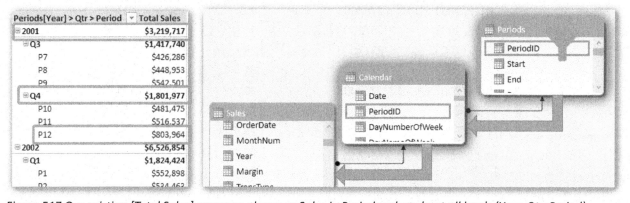

*Figure 517 Our existing [Total Sales] measure, shows us Sales in Period and works at all levels (Year, Qtr, Period)*

To help you visualize how the filters are flowing, let us add a few measures as below, and add them to our pivot.

```
[PeriodStartDate] =
FIRSTDATE ( Periods[Start] )
```

```
[PeriodEndDate] =
LASTDATE ( Periods[End] )
```

| Periods[Year] > Qtr > Period ▼ | PeriodStartDate | PeriodEndDate | Total Sales |
|---|---|---|---|
| ⊟2001 | 7/1/2001 | 12/29/2001 | $3,219,717 |
| ⊟Q3 | 7/1/2001 | 9/29/2001 | $1,417,740 |
| P7 | 7/1/2001 | 7/28/2001 | $426,286 |
| P8 | 7/29/2001 | 8/25/2001 | $448,953 |
| P9 | 8/26/2001 | 9/29/2001 | $542,501 |
| ⊟Q4 | 9/30/2001 | 12/29/2001 | $1,801,977 |
| P10 | 9/30/2001 | 10/27/2001 | $481,475 |
| P11 | 10/28/2001 | 11/24/2001 | $516,537 |

*Figure 518 Our new measures added to the pivot*

Here you can see, how for the 2001-Q3-P8 period the Calendar table would be filtered to dates between 7/29/2015 and 8/25/2015, which in turn would filter the Sales table. Thus, finally returning the total sales just for that period.

# Another Familiar Concept: Sales per Day

Let's add a simple measure to show us the total number of days in the selected period range.

```
Days in Period =
SUM ( Periods[Days] )
```

Let's add this new measure to our pivot and add some conditional formatting.

| Year > Qtr > Period ▼ | PeriodStartDate | PeriodEndDate | Days in Period | Total Sales |
|---|---|---|---|---|
| ⊟2003 | 12/29/2002 | 12/27/2003 | 364 | $9,614,218 |
| ⊟Q1 | 12/29/2002 | 3/29/2003 | 91 | $1,421,937 |
| P1 | 12/29/2002 | 1/25/2003 | 28 | $411,802 |
| P2 | 1/26/2003 | 2/22/2003 | 28 | $485,488 |
| P3 | 2/23/2003 | 3/29/2003 | 35 | $524,647 |
| ⊟Q2 | 3/30/2003 | 6/28/2003 | 91 | $1,632,944 |
| P4 | 3/30/2003 | 4/26/2003 | 28 | $483,894 |
| P5 | 4/27/2003 | 5/24/2003 | 28 | $488,796 |
| P6 | 5/25/2003 | 6/28/2003 | 35 | $660,254 |
| ⊟Q3 | 6/29/2003 | 9/27/2003 | 91 | $2,701,763 |
| P7 | 6/29/2003 | 7/26/2003 | 28 | $777,371 |
| P8 | 7/27/2003 | 8/23/2003 | 28 | $747,270 |
| P9 | 8/24/2003 | 9/27/2003 | 35 | $1,177,122 |
| ⊟Q4 | 9/28/2003 | 12/27/2003 | 91 | $3,857,574 |
| P10 | 9/28/2003 | 10/25/2003 | 28 | $943,911 |
| P11 | 10/26/2003 | 11/22/2003 | 28 | $1,048,462 |
| P12 | 11/23/2003 | 12/27/2003 | 35 | $1,865,201 |
| ⊟2004 | 12/28/2003 | 12/25/2004 | 364 | $9,997,888 |

*Figure 519 Note the "bump" in the third period of each quarter for days and sales, due to the 4/4/5 structure*

Since our periods are of varying sizes, in order to fairly compare "**apples to apples**" we should have a measure that compares sales per day (or per week).

We write our new measure that calculates sales per day in each period as below, by simply reusing our existing measures:

```
[Sales per Day in Period] =
DIVIDE ( [Total Sales], [Days in Period] )
```

| Year > Qtr > Period | Days in Period | Total Sales | | Sales per Day in Period | |
|---|---|---|---|---|---|
| ⊟ 2003 | 364 | $9,614,218 | | | $26,413 |
| ⊟ Q1 | 91 | $1,421,937 | | | $15,626 |
| P1 | 28 | $411,802 | | | $14,707 |
| P2 | 28 | $485,488 | | | $17,339 |
| P3 | 35 | $524,647 | | | $14,990 |
| ⊟ Q2 | 91 | $1,632,944 | | | $17,944 |
| P4 | 28 | $483,894 | | | $17,282 |
| P5 | 28 | $488,796 | | | $17,457 |
| P6 | 35 | $660,254 | | | $18,864 |
| ⊟ Q3 | 91 | $2,701,763 | | | $29,690 |
| P7 | 28 | $777,371 | | | $27,763 |
| P8 | 28 | $747,270 | | | $26,688 |
| P9 | 35 | $1,177,122 | | | $33,632 |
| ⊟ Q4 | 91 | $3,857,574 | | | $42,391 |
| P10 | 28 | $943,911 | | | $33,711 |
| P11 | 28 | $1,048,462 | | | $37,445 |
| P12 | 35 | $1,865,201 | | | $53,291 |
| ⊟ 2004 | 364 | $9,997,888 | | | $27,467 |

*Figure 520 [Sales per Day in Period] – note how the length of each period does not determine the size of its value. We can now compare "apples to apples" – for "4 versus 4 versus 5" Period but also versus Quarter and Year.*

# First New Concept: Sales per Day in Prior Period

## Getting Organized First

First let's add a PeriodYear column to the Periods table, so that we have a unique label for each period regardless of what year it is in:

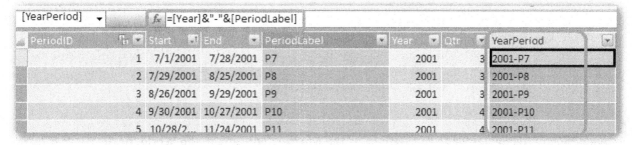

| PeriodID | Start | End | PeriodLabel | Year | Qtr | YearPeriod | |
|---|---|---|---|---|---|---|---|
| 1 | 7/1/2001 | 7/28/2001 | P7 | 2001 | 3 | 2001-P7 | |
| 2 | 7/29/2001 | 8/25/2001 | P8 | 2001 | 3 | 2001-P8 | |
| 3 | 8/26/2001 | 9/29/2001 | P9 | 2001 | 3 | 2001-P9 | |
| 4 | 9/30/2001 | 10/27/2001 | P10 | 2001 | 4 | 2001-P10 | |
| 5 | 10/28/2... | 11/24/2001 | P11 | 2001 | 4 | 2001-P11 | |

[YearPeriod]    $f_x$ =[Year]&"-"&[PeriodLabel]

*Figure 521 Unique label for periods, across years*

Use the Sort by Column setting to make sure it sorts correctly, instead of the default alphabetical sort (which would be unpleasant).

*Figure 522 Use Sort By Column to make sure our new label sorts correctly in pivots*

And here is our new column in a pivot:

| PeriodYear | Sales per Day in Period |
|---|---|
| 2001-P7 | $15,224 |
| 2001-P8 | $16,034 |
| 2001-P9 | $15,500 |
| 2001-P10 | $17,196 |
| 2001-P11 | $18,448 |
| 2001-P12 | $22,970 |
| 2002-P1 | $19,746 |
| 2002-P2 | $19,088 |
| 2002-P3 | $21,059 |
| 2002-P4 | $20,788 |
| 2002-P5 | $24,561 |
| 2002-P6 | $21,141 |
| 2002-P7 | $16,402 |
| 2002-P8 | $17,049 |
| 2002-P9 | $12,911 |
| 2002-P10 | $13,704 |

*Figure 523 PeriodYear on Rows, [Sales per Day in Period] on Values*

## Desired Results

In the context of that pivot, here is what we want to end up with:

| YearPeriod | Sales per Day in Period | Prior Period Sales per Day |
|---|---|---|
| 2001-P7 | $15,224 | |
| 2001-P8 | $16,034 | $15,224 |
| 2001-P9 | $15,500 | $16,034 |
| 2001-P10 | $17,196 | $15,500 |
| 2001-P11 | $18,448 | $17,196 |
| 2001-P12 | $22,970 | $18,448 |
| 2002-P1 | $19,746 | $22,970 |
| 2002-P2 | $19,088 | $19,746 |
| 2002-P3 | $21,059 | $19,088 |
| 2002-P4 | $20,788 | $21,059 |
| 2002-P5 | $24,561 | $20,788 |
| 2002-P6 | $21,141 | $24,561 |

*Figure 524 This is what we want: a measure that returns the [Sales per Day in Period] value for the immediately prior period.*

# The Greatest Formula in the World

Let's take the "work backwards" theme one step further and just reveal the formula, before we come back and explain it:

```
[Prior Period Sales per Day] =
CALCULATE (
    [Sales per Day in Period],
    FILTER (
        ALL ( Periods )
        , Periods[PeriodID]
            = MAX ( Periods[PeriodID] ) - 1
    )
)
```

On our blog, we only half-jokingly refer to this pattern as the Greatest Formula in the World, or GFITW. It is *by far* the #1 pattern you need to know when dealing with custom calendars and its application goes far beyond as well.

**As you get comfortable with the GFITW, some of you may prefer to treat it as just that: a pattern that you can adapt to your needs.** It's not *strictly* necessary that you understand in depth *why* it works, at least not immediately. (We certainly have copied a few normal Excel formulas and macros off the web in our day that we didn't fully understand at the time, no shame in it right?)

So for a moment let's just boil it down to the pattern itself:

**The GFITW Pattern – adapt and reuse this for all your custom calendar needs!**

```
CALCULATE(<base measure>,
        FILTER(ALL(<custom periods table>)
            , <row test with navigation arithmetic>
            )
        )
```

Got it? Now to explain how it works, starting from a high level and then getting progressively more detailed.

# "Clear Filters Then Re-Filter" – Another Name for GFITW

**At a high level, here's the way to understand GFITW: you clear *all* existing time-related filter context, then filter it back down to a *new* filter context. That new filter context is one that you control, typically using math that navigates backward in your custom calendar table. For this reason, you can also think of GFITW as "Clear filters, then re-filter."**

Another way to say it: first you clear all time-related filter context, yielding a completely "blank slate." Once that is done, you can reconstruct a brand new filter context, from scratch, without worrying about interference from the original filter context.

With that understanding, it's not hard to "parse" the GFITW into its component parts:

- **FILTER(ALL(<custom periods table>)...** - the ALL() insider the FILTER(), is part of the "Clear" phase. As we've seen it in action in the previous chapter.

- **FILTER(... <row test with navigation arithmetic>)** – this is the "re-filter" phase, the part where you build up a new filter context from scratch, using whatever logic is required.

Let's step through it using the cell below as the example we are trying to calculate

| YearPeriod | Sales per Day in Period | Prior Period Sales per Day |
|---|---|---|
| 2001-P7 | $15,224 | |
| 2001-P8 | $16,034 | $15,224 |
| 2001-P9 | $15,500 | $16,034 |
| 2001-P10 | $17,196 | $15,500 |

*Figure 525 Let's step through our GFITW measure for the highlighted cell*

## Clear Filter

We want to step through the Periods table row by row and select only the rows that we need for 'Prior Period' calculation. We are using FILTER for that purpose, which does just that.

However, if we passed the first argument to FILTER as below...

```
FILTER ( Periods, <row test> )
```

...the Periods table is subject to the original pivot filters, and by default is still filtered to Period[YearPeriod] = "2001-P8". By definition, though, we need to "get" P7's sales, and this pre-existing P8 filter will prevent that.

| YearPeriod | Sales per Day in Period | Prior Period Sales per Day |
|---|---|---|
| 2001-P7 | $15,224 | |
| 2001-P8 | $16,034 | $15,224 |
| 2001-P9 | $15,500 | $16,034 |
| 2001-P10 | $17,196 | $15,500 |

*Figure 526 The original filter context needs to be cleared before we proceed further*

But if we clear that initial filter, we will be able to subsequently iterate through the complete Periods table, so that we can precisely select the Periods row (or rows) that we need.

So we use ALL() when passing the first argument to FILTER:

```
FILTER ( ALL(Periods), <row test> )
```

This gives us a clean slate to operate in the next step.

## Re-Filter: Navigation Arithmetic

Now that we are stepping through the complete Periods table, let's see how we select only the rows we need.

Here is the entire FILTER() that we used in our [Prior Period Sales per Day] GFITW measure:

```
FILTER (
    ALL ( Periods )
    , Periods[PeriodID]
        = MAX ( Periods[PeriodID] ) - 1
)
```

The part of the GFITW pattern that we call "navigation arithmetic" is the second argument:

```
Periods[PeriodID] = MAX ( Periods[PeriodID] ) - 1
```

How does that work?

At first, it seems kinda strange: how can there be a row where PeriodID equals itself minus one? The answer lies in another important detail of the FILTER() function.

## Table[Column] Uses Row Context Generated by FILTER

Periods[PeriodID] is a "Naked" column reference, which we first learned is not to be used inside a measure (because there is no concept of current row inside a measure). Then how is Periods[PeriodID] working in our measure? Well, because FILTER, being a row-by-row iterator, has created a current row (row context) for us. Thus Periods[PeriodID] refers to the specific Periods row that FILTER is stepping through. And remember, it steps through the entire Periods table since we used ALL(Periods) as the first argument to FILTER.

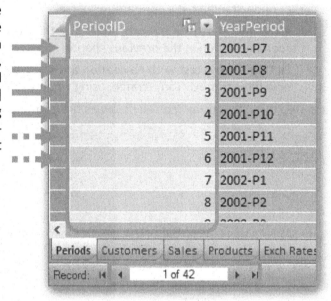

*Figure 527 Periods[PeriodID] refers one-by-one to each row as FILTER steps through the entire Periods table*

So that's what we are testing in our comparison, but what are we comparing it to?

## MAX() Operates Over a Filter Context

MAX() - or we could have used MIN() – is an aggregation function and operates over a filter context. "Which filter context?" you ask. Well, there is only one, the original pivot filter context. FILTER just generates a Row Context, it doesn't touch Filter Context in any way. Thus the original filters coming in from our pivot table still apply within our MAX().

For the cell we are using as an example, the filter context is Period[YearPeriod] = "2001-P8". Which means MAX(Periods[PeriodID]) would return PeriodID = 2.

| PeriodID | Start | End | YearPeriod | |
|---|---|---|---|---|
| 1 | 7/1/2001 | 7/28/2001 | 2001-P7 | |
| 2 | 7/29/2001 | 8/25/2001 | 2001-P8 | |
| 3 | 8/26/2001 | 9/29/2001 | 2001-P9 | |
| 4 | 9/30/2001 | 10/27/2001 | 2001-P10 | |

*Figure 528 Filter YearPeriod=2001-P8 yields PeriodID = 2*

And since the comparison is to MAX(...) - 1...

```
MAX ( Periods[PeriodID] ) - 1
```

We are essentially looking for Periods[PeriodID] = 1. Which is the correct prior period in our case.

> Subtracting 1 from the PeriodID in this case yields the previous period, because the Periods have consecutive PeriodID values.

To drive things home, let's look at the anatomy of this FILTER statement

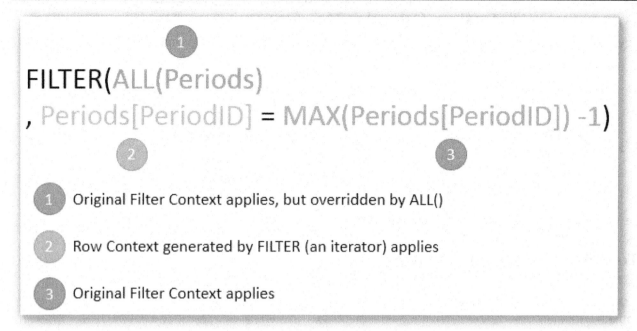

FILTER(ALL(Periods)
, Periods[PeriodID] = MAX(Periods[PeriodID]) -1)

**1** Original Filter Context applies, but overridden by ALL()

**2** Row Context generated by FILTER (an iterator) applies

**3** Original Filter Context applies

*Figure 529 Anatomy of FILTER statement used for GFITW*

## In Your Periods Table, You Always Need a Numeric PeriodID Column or Equivalent

Since our navigation always comes down to some sort of math, you absolutely need a PeriodID column; one that:

- Contains a unique number for each row
- Increases as time goes on
- Has consecutive numbers for periods that are consecutive in time

**Pretty simple – if you don't have a column on which you can perform sensible arithmetic, you aren't going to be able to navigate.**

# More GFITW measures – Year Over Year and Year To Date

Let's do a few more custom calendar measures. But before that let's define a convenience measure

```
Sales in Period =
[Total Sales]
```

This simply reuses our [Total Sales] measure, but gives us a convenient, easier to remember measure when we are working with our custom calendar.

## Prior Period Sales

Let's define this one before we build the other measures. For prior period sales, you can copy/paste the GFITW pattern from [Prior Period Sales per Day] measure, and simply substitute the <base measure> to be [Sales in Period]. Here is the measure with changed part highlighted:

```
[Prior Period Sales] =
CALCULATE (
  [Sales in Period],
  FILTER (
    ALL ( Periods )
    Periods[PeriodID]
      = MAX ( Periods[PeriodID] ) - 1
  )
)
```

| YearPeriod | Sales in Period | Prior Period Sales |
|---|---|---|
| 2001-P7 | $426,286 | |
| 2001-P8 | $448,953 | $426,286 |
| 2001-P9 | $542,501 | $448,953 |
| 2001-P10 | $481,475 | $542,501 |
| 2001-P11 | $516,537 | $481,475 |
| 2001-P12 | $803,964 | $516,537 |
| 2002-P1 | $552,898 | $803,964 |
| 2002-P2 | $534,463 | $552,898 |

*Figure 530 Prior Period Sales using the GFITW pattern*

# Year Over Year (YOY) Custom Calendar Measure

This one again applies the GFITW pattern, and only differs in terms of the navigation arithmetic.

```
[YOY Period Sales] =
CALCULATE (
 [Sales in Period],
 FILTER (
  ALL ( Periods ),
  Periods[PeriodID]
   = MAX ( Periods[PeriodID] ) - 12
 )
)
```

Really the only thing changed here is that we are sub-tracting 12 rather than 1.

# Year To Date (YTD) Measure with Custom Calendar

Let's get right to it. First, we add a new column to our Periods table:

Here are the results:

| YearPeriod | Sales in Period | YOY Period Sales |
|---|---|---|
| 2001-P7 | $426,286 | |
| 2001-P8 | $448,953 | |
| 2001-P9 | $542,501 | |
| 2001-P10 | $481,475 | |
| 2001-P11 | $516,537 | |
| 2001-P12 | $803,964 | |
| 2002-P1 | $552,898 | |
| 2002-P2 | $534,463 | |
| 2002-P3 | $737,062 | |
| 2002-P4 | $582,060 | |
| 2002-P5 | $687,716 | |
| 2002-P6 | $739,934 | |
| 2002-P7 | $459,261 | $426,286 |
| 2002-P8 | $477,370 | $448,953 |

*Figure 531 [YOY Period Sales] goes back 12 periods.*

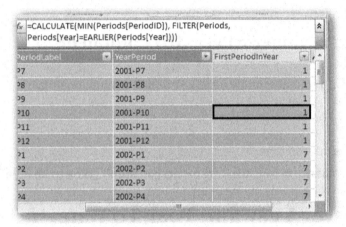

*Figure 532 We will explain this calculated column formula in the chapter on advanced calculated columns. For now, just focus on how it is used in the measure.*

> **ℹ** Again, if you have a database as your data source, and the skill (or assistance) to manipulate it, this is the sort of column that we highly recommend be implemented in the database rather than in a DAX column. Another option you have now is to leverage Power Query when sourcing this table and adding a custom column using Power Query.

And now, the measure; the same GFITW pattern with updated navigation arithmetic:

```
YTD Period Sales =
CALCULATE (
    [Sales in Period],
    FILTER (
        ALL ( Periods ),
        Periods[PeriodID]
          <= MAX ( Periods[PeriodID] )
        && Periods[PeriodID]
          >= MAX ( Periods[FirstPeriodInYear] )
    )
)
```

And the results:

| YearPeriod | Sales in Period | YOY Period Sales | YTD Period Sales |
|---|---|---|---|
| 2001-P7 | $426,286 | | $426,286 |
| 2001-P8 | $448,953 | | $875,239 |
| 2001-P9 | $542,501 | | $1,417,740 |
| 2001-P10 | $481,475 | | $1,899,215 |
| 2001-P11 | $516,537 | | $2,415,752 |
| 2001-P12 | $803,964 | | $3,219,717 |
| 2002-P1 | $552,898 | | $552,898 |
| 2002-P2 | $534,463 | | $1,087,361 |
| 2002-P3 | $737,062 | | $1,824,424 |
| 2002-P4 | $582,060 | | $2,406,483 |
| 2002-P5 | $687,716 | | $3,094,199 |
| 2002-P6 | $739,934 | | $3,834,133 |
| 2002-P7 | $459,261 | $426,286 | $4,293,395 |
| 2002-P8 | $477,370 | $448,953 | $4,770,765 |
| 2002-P9 | $451,886 | $542,501 | $5,222,651 |
| 2002-P10 | $383,725 | $481,475 | $5,606,376 |
| 2002-P11 | $297,905 | $516,537 | $5,904,281 |
| 2002-P12 | $622,573 | $803,964 | $6,526,854 |
| 2003-P1 | $411,802 | $552,898 | $411,802 |
| 2003-P2 | $485,488 | $534,463 | $897,290 |

*Figure 533 YTD Period Sales measure with custom calendar – good stuff.*

Here is an example to show you how the navigation arithmetic is working, for the highlighted cell. First the incoming filter context is essentially YearPeriod = "2001-P11". Next this yields us 5 and 1 as the MAX([PeriodID]) and the MAX-([FirstPeriodInYear]) values. Then FILTER iterates over the Periods table and just helps us select the periods between 1 and 5.

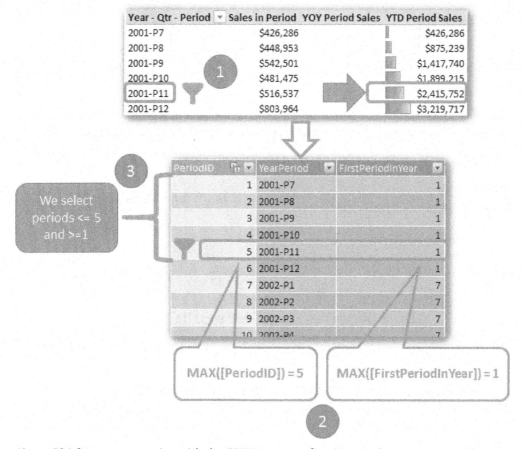

*Figure 534 Once you get going with the GFITW pattern, figuring out the navigation arithmetic is straight-forward, even fun!*

# Fixing Measures to Work at Total Level

Measures written as above for custom calendars can display some unexpected results when the pivot, instead of looking at a single "Period", is showing a sub-total or grand-total across Year/Quarters. This is because the logic we have used is very specific and operates at a period level. But you can easily make some small fixes to make your measures work again at totals/subtotals.

## Suppressing Prior Period for Totals

Notice that our [Prior Period Sales] measure displays meaningless value for the year subtotal.

| Year | YearPeriod | Sales in Period | Prior Period Sales |
|------|------------|-----------------|--------------------|
| ⊟ 2002 | 2002-P1 | $552,898 | $803,964 |
|      | 2002-P2 | $534,463 | $552,898 |
|      | 2002-P3 | $737,062 | $534,463 |
|      | 2002-P4 | $582,060 | $737,062 |
|      | 2002-P5 | $687,716 | $582,060 |
|      | 2002-P6 | $739,934 | $687,716 |
|      | 2002-P7 | $459,261 | $739,934 |
|      | 2002-P8 | $477,370 | $459,261 |
|      | 2002-P9 | $451,886 | $477,370 |
|      | 2002-P10 | $383,725 | $451,886 |
|      | 2002-P11 | $297,905 | $383,725 |
|      | 2002-P12 | $622,573 | $297,905 |
| **2002 Total** | | **$6,526,854** | **$297,905** |
| ⊟ 2003 | 2003-P1 | $411,802 | $622,573 |

Figure 535 Prior Period Sales is showing a meaningless value for Subtotal/Total

For now, let's say that "Prior Period Sales" only needs to be shown when a single period is being shown. There would be cases, such as this, where a measure does not make sense in a total/subtotal setting, and it is best simply suppressed.

 We will see an alternate way to address Prior Period Sales in a later section

Here is how we would rewrite our measure:

```
Prior Period Sales Total Suppressed =
IF (
    HASONEVALUE ( Periods[PeriodID] ),
    CALCULATE (
        [Sales in Period],
        FILTER (
            ALL ( Periods ),
            Periods[PeriodID] = MAX ( Periods[PeriodID] ) - 1 )
    )
    , BLANK()
)
```

Essentially, we have wrapped our earlier measure inside a HASONEVALUE() test. If PeriodID has only one value, we show our measure, else it returns a blank.

| Year | QtrLabel | Period | Sales In Period | Prior Period Sales | Prior Period Sales Total Suppressed |
|---|---|---|---|---|---|
| ⊟2002 | ⊟Q1 | P1 | $552,898 | $803,964 | $803,964 |
| | | P2 | $534,463 | $552,898 | $552,898 |
| | | P3 | $737,062 | $534,463 | $534,463 |
| | Q1 Total | | $1,824,424 | $534,463 | |
| | ⊟Q2 | P4 | $582,060 | $737,062 | $737,062 |
| | | P5 | $687,716 | $582,060 | $582,060 |
| | | P6 | $739,934 | $687,716 | $687,716 |
| | Q2 Total | | $2,009,710 | $687,716 | |
| | ⊟Q3 | P7 | $459,261 | $739,934 | $739,934 |
| | | P8 | $477,370 | $459,261 | $459,261 |
| | | P9 | $451,886 | $477,370 | $477,370 |
| | Q3 Total | | $1,388,518 | $477,370 | |
| | ⊟Q4 | P10 | $383,725 | $451,886 | $451,886 |
| | | P11 | $297,905 | $383,725 | $383,725 |
| | | P12 | $622,573 | $297,905 | $297,905 |
| | Q4 Total | | $1,304,203 | $297,905 | |
| 2002 Total | | | $6,526,854 | $297,905 | |
| ⊟2003 | ⊟Q1 | P1 | $411,802 | $622,573 | $622,573 |
| | | P2 | $485,488 | $411,802 | $411,802 |

Measure Suppressed

*Figure 536 HASONEVALUE test suppresses the measure for totals/subtotals*

## Fixing YOY to Work at Total Level

The [YoY Period Sales] measure also does not work correctly at subtotal/total level:

| Year | YearPeriod | Sales in Period | YOY Period Sales |
|---|---|---|---|
| | 2003-P10 | $943,911 | $383,725 |
| | 2003-P11 | $1,048,462 | $297,905 |
| | 2003-P12 | $1,865,201 | $622,573 |
| **2003 Total** | | **$9,614,218** | **$622,573** |
| ⊟**2004** | 2004-P1 | $1,261,841 | $411,802 |

???

*Figure 537 Can we make [YOY Period Sales] work at the totals level?*

Here is the formula again with the section relevant to our discussion highlighted in bold

```
[YOY Period Sales] =
CALCULATE (
    [Sales in Period],
    FILTER (
        ALL ( Periods ),
        Periods[PeriodID]
            = MAX ( Periods[PeriodID] ) - 12
    )
)
```

First let us try to determine why the measure is not working for the subtotal cell we highlighted. Do you remember how to debug your measures? Think like the DAX engine. And to do that you follow the **Golden Rules** outlined in an earlier chapter.

**Step 1**: Detect Pivot Coordinates: For the cell we highlighted, incoming filters are Periods[Year] = 2003

**Step 2**: CALCULATE alters filter context: This is where we are doing the heavy lifting using the FILTER function. FILTER function is an iterator and would iterate over all periods and evaluate the condition specified. Let's focus on this portion of our formula:

```
= MAX ( Periods[PeriodID] ) - 12
```

MAX is an aggregation function and our filter context (coming from Step 1) would apply here. So what is the MAX(Periods[PeriodID]) for Year 2003?

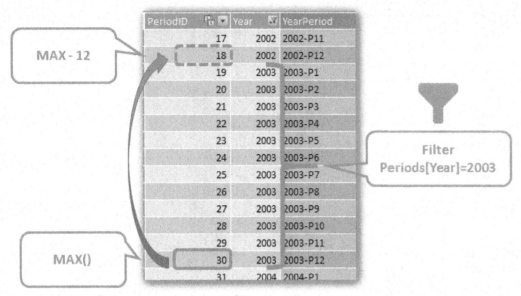

*Figure 538 MAX() operates on our current filter context*

For our Periods table, that returns PeriodID=30. If we subtract 12 from that, we get 30 -12 = 18. PeriodID 18 in our table represents YearPeriod = 2002-P12. And that is what our pivot table is showing.

| Year | YearPeriod | Sales in Period | YOY Period Sales |
|---|---|---|---|
|  | 2002-P11 | $297,905 | $516,537 |
|  | 2002-P12 | $622,573 | $803,964 |
| 2002 Total |  | $6,526,854 | $803,964 |
| 2003 | 2003-P1 | $411,802 | $552,898 |
|  | 2003-P2 | $485,488 | $534,463 |
|  | 2003-P3 | $524,647 | $737,062 |
|  | 2003-P4 | $483,894 | $582,060 |
|  | 2003-P5 | $488,796 | $687,716 |
|  | 2003-P6 | $660,254 | $739,934 |
|  | 2003-P7 | $777,371 | $459,261 |
|  | 2003-P8 | $747,270 | $477,370 |
|  | 2003-P9 | $1,177,122 | $451,886 |
|  | 2003-P10 | $943,911 | $383,725 |
|  | 2003-P11 | $1,048,462 | $297,905 |
|  | 2003-P12 | $1,865,201 | $622,573 |
| 2003 Total |  | $9,614,218 | $622,573 |
| 2004 | 2004-P1 | $1,261,841 | $411,802 |

*Figure 539 Golden rules help us understand the behavior of our formula*

## The Fix

Great, so now we understand why our measure is not working. If you think about it, the right way to shift to prior year would be to take whatever is the incoming time period (could be at Year/Quarter/Period level) and **shift the WHOLE time period back by 12 "periods".**

The best way to do that is to subtract 12 from the beginning of the current time frame *and* 12 from the end of it. So we subtract 12 from the MIN() and 12 from the MAX() of the PeriodID, and select only Periods that fall between that range.

 In the single-period case, the beginning and the end are the same PeriodID, so nothing actually changes there. Only when multiple periods are selected, as is the case in a total cell, does this change in formula make a difference. In that case the whole time range is shifted 12 periods back.

Here is our new measure:

```
YoY Period Sales Totals Fixed =
CALCULATE (
    [Sales in Period],
    FILTER (
        ALL ( Periods ),
        Periods[PeriodID]
            >= MIN ( Periods[PeriodID] ) - 12
            && Periods[PeriodID]
                <= MAX ( Periods[PeriodID] ) - 12
    )
)
```

This shifts the time period back by 12 periods, and works at all levels – Year/Quarter/Period.

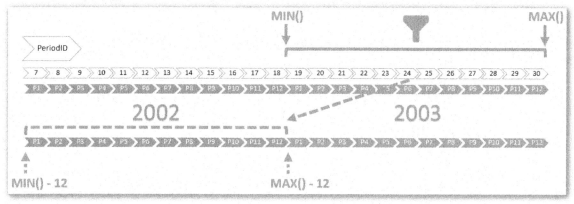

*Figure 540 Our new measure shifts back the time period by 12 months...*

| Year | QtrLabel | PeriodLabel | Sales in Period | YOY Period Sales | YoY Period Sales Totals Fixed |
|---|---|---|---|---|---|
| ⊟2002 | ⊞Q1 | | $1,824,424 | | |
| | ⊞Q2 | | $2,009,710 | | |
| | ⊟Q3 | P7 | $459,261 | $426,286 | $426,286 |
| | | P8 | $477,370 | $448,953 | $448,953 |
| | | P9 | $451,886 | $542,501 | $542,501 |
| | Q3 Total | | $1,388,518 | $542,501 | $1,417,740 |
| | ⊟Q4 | P10 | $383,725 | $481,475 | $481,475 |
| | | P11 | $297,905 | $516,537 | $516,537 |
| | | P12 | $622,573 | $803,964 | $803,964 |
| | Q4 Total | | $1,304,203 | $803,964 | $1,801,977 |
| 2002 Total | | | $6,526,854 | $803,964 | $3,219,717 |
| ⊟2003 | ⊞Q1 | | $1,421,937 | $737,062 | $1,824,424 |
| | ⊞Q2 | | $1,632,944 | $739,934 | $2,009,710 |
| | ⊟Q3 | P7 | $777,371 | $459,261 | $459,261 |
| | | P8 | $747,270 | $477,370 | $477,370 |
| | | P9 | $1,177,122 | $451,886 | $451,886 |
| | Q3 Total | | $2,701,763 | $451,886 | $1,388,518 |
| | ⊟Q4 | P10 | $943,911 | $383,725 | $383,725 |
| | | P11 | $1,048,462 | $297,905 | $297,905 |
| | | P12 | $1,865,201 | $622,573 | $622,573 |
| | Q4 Total | | $3,857,574 | $622,573 | $1,304,203 |
| 2003 Total | | | $9,614,218 | $622,573 | $6,526,854 |

*Figure 541 ...and works at Year, Quarter or Period level*

We can now also copy/paste that formula above and change the base measure to create a YOY version of [Sales per Day in Period]. The measure:

```
YoY Period Sales per Day =
CALCULATE (
    [Sales per Day in Period],
    FILTER (
        ALL ( Periods ),
        Periods[PeriodID]
            >= MIN ( Periods[PeriodID] ) - 12
            && Periods[PeriodID]
                <= MAX ( Periods[PeriodID] ) - 12
    )
)
```

The result:

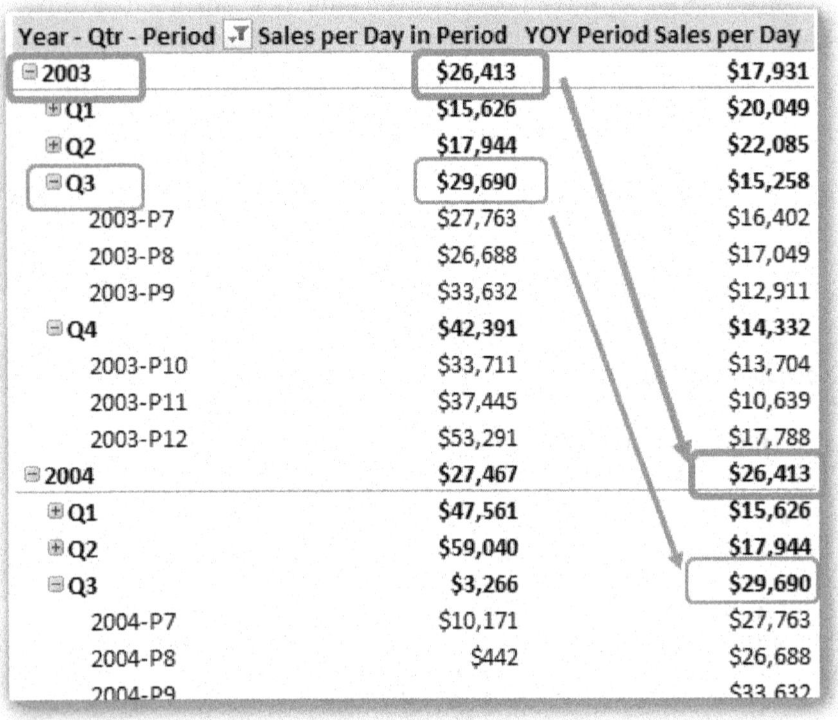

| Year - Qtr - Period | Sales per Day in Period | YOY Period Sales per Day |
|---|---|---|
| ⊟ 2003 | $26,413 | $17,931 |
| ⊞ Q1 | $15,626 | $20,049 |
| ⊞ Q2 | $17,944 | $22,085 |
| ⊟ Q3 | $29,690 | $15,258 |
| 2003-P7 | $27,763 | $16,402 |
| 2003-P8 | $26,688 | $17,049 |
| 2003-P9 | $33,632 | $12,911 |
| ⊟ Q4 | $42,391 | $14,332 |
| 2003-P10 | $33,711 | $13,704 |
| 2003-P11 | $37,445 | $10,639 |
| 2003-P12 | $53,291 | $17,788 |
| ⊟ 2004 | $27,467 | $26,413 |
| ⊞ Q1 | $47,561 | $15,626 |
| ⊞ Q2 | $59,040 | $17,944 |
| ⊟ Q3 | $3,266 | $29,690 |
| 2004-P7 | $10,171 | $27,763 |
| 2004-P8 | $442 | $26,688 |
| 2004-P9 | | $33,632 |

Figure 542 Sales per day version of the YOY measure, more useful for "apples to apples" comparisons

## Fixing Prior Period to Work on Totals, Too

For our first pass at the [Prior Period Sales] measure we simply suppressed the measure (returned blank), when we detected more than one PeriodID. But let's take it a step further and try to show the [Prior Period Sales] for the "corresponding" period. This is trickier than YOY – if the current total cell is a Quarter, we need to shift back 3 periods. But if the current total cell is a Year, we need to shift back 12. Here is our measure:

```
[Prior Period Sales Fixed] =
CALCULATE (
    [Sales in Period],
    FILTER (
        ALL ( Periods ),
        Periods[PeriodID]
            >= MIN ( Periods[PeriodID] ) - COUNTROWS ( Periods )
        && Periods[PeriodID]
            <= MAX ( Periods[PeriodID] ) - COUNTROWS ( Periods )
    )
)
```

So rather than subtracting a fixed number, like 12 for YOY, we subtract COUNTROWS(Periods), which is the number of currently selected periods; in other words, the "size" of the current time selection.

Results:

| Row Labels | Sales in Period | Prior Period Sales | Prior Period Sales Total Suppressed | Prior Period Sales Fixed |
|---|---|---|---|---|
| ⊟ 2002 | $6,526,854 | $297,905 | | $3,219,717 |
| ⊞ Q1 | $1,824,424 | $534,463 | | $1,801,977 |
| ⊞ Q2 | $2,009,710 | $607,716 | | $1,824,424 |
| ⊟ Q3 | $1,388,518 | $477,370 | | $2,009,710 |
| P7 | $459,261 | $739,934 | $739,934 | $739,934 |
| P8 | $477,370 | $459,261 | $459,261 | $459,261 |
| P9 | $451,886 | $477,370 | $477,370 | $477,370 |
| ⊟ Q4 | $1,304,203 | $297,905 | | $1,388,518 |
| P10 | $383,725 | $451,886 | $451,886 | $451,886 |
| P11 | $297,905 | $383,725 | $383,725 | $383,725 |
| P12 | $622,573 | $297,905 | $297,905 | $297,905 |
| ⊟ 2003 | $9,614,218 | $1,048,462 | | $6,526,854 |
| ⊞ Q1 | $1,421,937 | $485,488 | | $1,304,203 |
| ⊞ Q2 | $1,632,944 | $488,796 | | $1,421,937 |
| ⊟ Q3 | $2,701,763 | $747,270 | | $1,632,944 |
| P7 | $777,371 | $660,254 | $660,254 | $660,254 |
| P8 | $747,270 | $777,371 | $777,371 | $777,371 |
| P9 | $1,177,122 | $747,270 | $747,270 | $747,270 |

*Figure 543 Prior Period: Now matches at Period, Qtr, and Year levels. What can we say? Third time is a charm* ☺

Note: We are keeping all versions of this measure to be able to show how they are operating differently and generating different results. For your own models, only keep the latest version of the formula shown

# The Usual "Percent Growth" Formulas

Now you can do the usual "new minus old, divided by old" trick to get the growth percentage. You can do so with any measure, we'll use sales per day as an example. We already have the [Sales per Day in Period] and the [YOY Period Sales per Day] measures defined. We'll reuse these measures to define year-over-year growth and growth percentage.

 **Best Practice**: We've said so before and we'll say again, **reuse your measures**, wherever you can, and to define "derived" measures, rather than redefining the same formula in your new measure

Our measures:

```
Sales per Day in Period YoY Growth =
[Sales per Day in Period] - [YOY Period Sales per Day]


Sales per Day in Period YoY Growth % =
DIVIDE ( [Sales per Day in Period YoY Growth],
    [YOY Period Sales per Day] )
```

And results:

| Year - Qtr - Period | Sales per Day in Period | YOY Period Sales per Day | Sales per Day in Period YoY Growth | Sales per Day in Period YoY Growth % |
|---|---|---|---|---|
| ⊟ 2002 | $17,931 | $17,691 | $240 | 1 % |
| ⊞ Q1 | $20,049 | | $20,049 | |
| ⊞ Q2 | $22,085 | | $22,085 | |
| ⊟ Q3 | $15,258 | $15,580 | ($321) | -2 % |
| P7 | $16,402 | $15,224 | $1,178 | 8 % |
| P8 | $17,049 | $16,034 | $1,015 | 6 % |
| P9 | $12,911 | $15,500 | ($2,589) | -17 % |
| ⊟ Q4 | $14,332 | $19,802 | ($5,470) | -28 % |
| P10 | $13,704 | $17,196 | ($3,491) | -20 % |
| P11 | $10,639 | $18,448 | ($7,808) | -42 % |
| P12 | $17,788 | $22,970 | ($5,183) | -23 % |
| ⊟ 2003 | $26,413 | $17,931 | $8,482 | 47 % |
| ⊞ Q1 | $15,626 | $20,049 | ($4,423) | -22 % |
| ⊞ Q2 | $17,944 | $22,085 | ($4,140) | -19 % |
| ⊟ Q3 | $29,690 | $15,258 | $14,431 | 95 % |
| P7 | $27,763 | $16,402 | $11,361 | 69 % |
| P8 | $26,688 | $17,049 | $9,639 | 57 % |
| P9 | $33,622 | $12,911 | $20,711 | 160 % |

*Figure 544 Percent growth is as simple a calc as it always was, even though its component measures are quite sophisticated*

# 26 - Advanced Calculated Columns

## Perspective: Calculated Columns Are Not DAX's Strength!

**We are not saying that DAX is *bad* at calculated columns.** We are just saying that *Measures* are the magic in DAX, which is why we've spent the vast majority of the book on measures. We've always had calculated columns in "normal" Excel, so there can't be *too* much special about DAX columns, right?

### OK, Power Pivot Calc Columns *Are* a Strength in Some Ways.

**Well, even we have to stop for a moment and say: we've never had the ability to write a calc column against a 141 million row table now have we?**

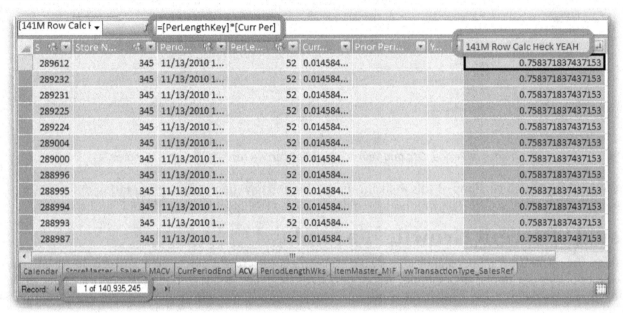

*Figure 545 Calculated column written against a table with 141 million rows in it! (And this wasn't some beast of a computer - we did this on a featherweight, 4 GB RAM Ultrabook that cost $899 retail when purchased in January 2012! Requires 64-bit of course.)*

**OK, so we'll refine our point: *other than* the benefits provided by massive data capacity, seamless refresh, named reference, and relationships, Power Pivot calculated columns are nothing new to us** ☺

## But More Difficult in Some Cases

Actually, to be completely honest, Power Pivot calculated columns are a bit *more* difficult than normal Excel columns, at least in some circumstances, because Power Pivot lacks "A1" style reference.

In completely "row-wise" calcs, like [Column1] * [Column2], Power Pivot is no more difficult than normal Excel. But when you want to do something like "sum all the rows in this table where the [ProductID] is the same as this current row," it gets a bit trickier.

 We're *not* criticizing Power Pivot for lacking A1-style reference. No, that was absolutely the correct decision. We just want to set your expectations – sometimes you will have to work a little harder in a Power Pivot calc column than you would in an Excel calc column, but even then, only when your calc goes beyond a single row.

Anyway, we'll get to that. But first, some simple stuff that just didn't fit anywhere else.

## Start Out With "Not so Advanced"

OK, there are a couple of calculated column quick topics we'd like to cover that don't really deserve the label "advanced," but should be covered *somewhere*.

## Grouping Columns

We've seen a quick example of *grouping columns* in SWITCH...TRUE, but let's cover it in some more detail. Our favorite example of *grouping columns* is the Sales by Temperature, aka "Temperature Mashup" demo. In that demo, we import a table of temperature (weather) data, relate it to the Sales table, and then report [Sales per Day] broken out by temperature:

OK, we obviously do NOT care to see temperature ranges broken out by a tenth of a degree. We want to group them into more useful ranges.

You can do this with a calculated column. In the demo, here's the formula we use in the Temperature table:

```
= SWITCH (
    TRUE (),
    [Avg Temp] < 40, "Cold",
    [Avg Temp] < 55, "Cool",
    [Avg Temp] < 70, "Warm",
    "Hot"
)
```

| Temperature | Sales per Day |
| --- | --- |
| 14 | $3,543 |
| 15.8 | $4,677 |
| 19.4 | $3,558 |
| 25.4 | $98 |
| 25.8 | $4,630 |
| 26.6 | $2,785 |
| 27.5 | $5,956 |
| 28 | $87 |
| 29.3 | $5,329 |
| 30.2 | $3,951 |
| 31.9 | $38 |
| 32.3 | $7 |
| 33.3 | $7,640 |
| 33.7 | $4,486 |
| 33.8 | $4,303 |
| 35.6 | $3,228 |
| 36.1 | $6,559 |

*Figure 546 Sales per Day with Temperature on Rows, but the temperature is very precise*

Here's what it looks like in the Temperature table as a calc column:

```
fx  =SWITCH(TRUE()
    , [Avg Temp] < 40, "Cold"
    , [Avg Temp] < 55, "Cool"
    , [Avg Temp] < 70, "Warm"
    , "Hot"
)
```

| Region | Month | MonthNumber | Avg Temp | TempRange |
| --- | --- | --- | --- | --- |
| Northeast | Jan | 1 | 26.3 | Cold |
| Northeast | Feb | 2 | 25.4 | Cold |
| Northeast | Mar | 3 | 31.4 | Cold |
| Northeast | Apr | 4 | 48.1 | Cool |
| Northeast | May | 5 | 52.8 | Cool |
| Northeast | June | 6 | 66.8 | Warm |
| Northeast | Jul | 7 | 70.4 | Hot |
| Northeast | Aug | 8 | 66 | Warm |

*Figure 547 Grouping column in the Temperature table*

And here's what it looks like used on Rows instead of the Avg Temp column:

| Temperature | Sales per Day |
| --- | --- |
| Cold | $13,527 |
| Cool | $9,485 |
| Hot | $6,662 |
| Warm | $14,739 |
| **Grand Total** | **$26,120** |

*Figure 548 TempRange on Rows – MUCH better*

 We've used many kinds of formulas along these lines – ROUND() has been a very popular function for us in this regard, for instance.

To see the whole "Temperature Mashup" demo end to end that first debuted in 2009 (!), visit http://ppvt.pro/TempMash

# Unique Columns for Sorting

Did you notice that the sort order is "off" in that Temperature report? Here is current and the desired order:

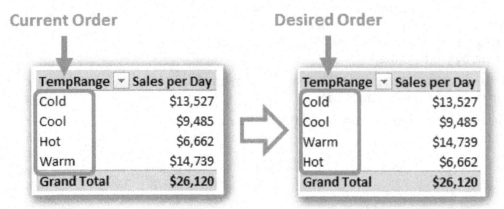

Figure 549 We would prefer the sort order to be Cold, Cool, Warm, Hot

OK, so let's use the Sort by Column feature, and use AvgTemp to sort the TempRange column:

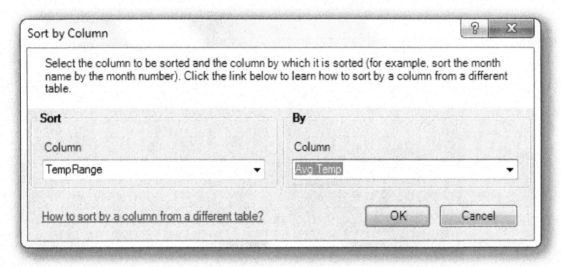

Figure 550 Attempting to use AvgTemp as the Sort By Column for TempRange

This yields an error:

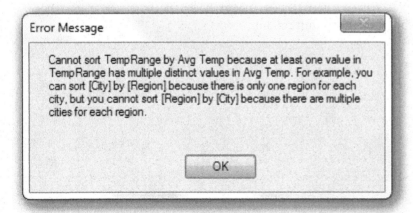

Figure 551 It does not like Green Eggs and Ham – not in a box, not with a fox. OK and it also doesn't like AvgTemp as a Sort By Column.

I (Rob) guess it *could* have used AvgTemp, since no single AvgTemp corresponds to two different TempRange values (48.1 for instance *always* maps to "Cool"), but Power Pivot doesn't want to trust me. It wants each value of TempRange to have a *single* value in the Sort By Column, and as a former (and sometimes current) software engineer myself, I can understand why it doesn't want to trust me ☺

So in this case, a SWITCH() does the trick –giving us a column with values 1-4:

```
= SWITCH (
    TRUE (),
    [Avg Temp] < 40, 1,
    [Avg Temp] < 55, 2,
    [Avg Temp] < 70, 3,
    4
)
```

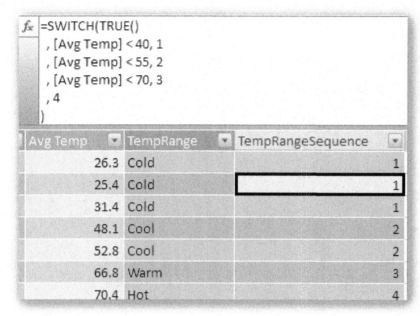

*Figure 552 A valid candidate for a sorting column – this one works*

Setting TempRange column to sort by TempRangeSequence column would give us the desired result.

## Another Sort by Column Example

For a slightly more sophisticated problem, consider the "QtrYear-Label" column in our Periods table:

We deliberately positioned it next to the PeriodID column so you could see that we have the same "matches multiple" problem here as the one we had in the Temperature example. Each Qtr-YearLabel value matches multiple PeriodID, thus we would not be able to sort QtrYearLabel using PeriodID.

We need to create a calculated column that we can use as a Sort-By. But a SWITCH() isn't going to save us this time. We need to do some math. Here's a pattern that we use over and over again:

```
([Year] * 4) + [Qtr]
```

OK, in pattern form that is:

```
(<Year Column> *
  <number of periods per year>) +
  <period column>
```

Where "period" can be quarter (of which there are 4 per year), month (12), week (52), semester (2), whatever

| PeriodID | QtrYearLabel |
|---|---|
| 7 | Q1 2002 |
| 8 | Q1 2002 |
| 9 | Q1 2002 |
| 19 | Q1 2003 |
| 20 | Q1 2003 |
| 21 | Q1 2003 |
| 31 | Q1 2004 |
| 32 | Q1 2004 |
| 33 | Q1 2004 |
| 10 | Q2 2002 |
| 11 | Q2 2002 |
| 12 | Q2 2002 |
| 22 | Q2 2003 |
| 23 | Q2 2003 |
| 24 | Q2 2003 |
| 34 | Q2 2004 |

*Figure 553 QtrYearLabel – note how each value matches multiple PeriodID values*

That gives us:

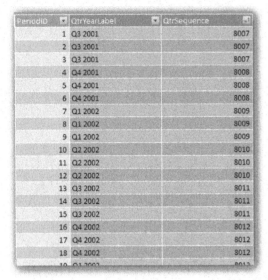

*Figure 554 Unique sort id/sequence column for our QtrYearLabel column*

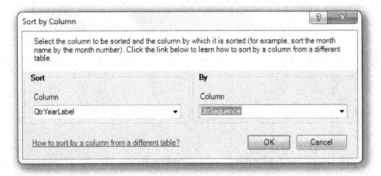

*Figure 555 And this one works*

# Now For the Advanced Examples

## Summing up in a Lookup Table

**Let's say you wanted to create a Total Sales column in your Products table, reflecting the sales for each Product.**

First, Rob might scold you. That's what measures are for! Why would you summarize a value in your Lookup table? But then Rob would calm down and admit that there are definitely cases where you might *occasionally* need to do this ☺

We have in fact, already defined this in the chapter on Row Filter context. Here it is again:

```
= CALCULATE ( SUM ( Sales[SalesAmt] ) )
```

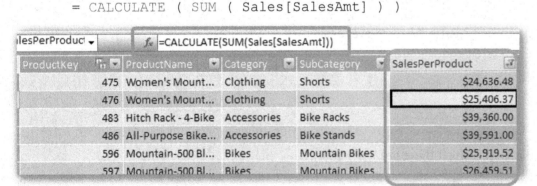

*Figure 556 CALCULATE changes Row to a Filter Context giving us the Total Sales for each Product*

But what if we wanted to do something different? Let's say we wanted to **create a Total Sales column, reflecting the sales for the category that the Product belongs to**. This is slightly tricky terrain, but let's plow through.

# Use of the EARLIER() Function

**Ah, the EARLIER() function. It was two years before we understood how/when to use it.** Only in recent years has it felt comfortable. But we are slow learners (well, Rob is at least), so your mileage may vary.

**And again, there are patterns for its use, and that's really all you are going to need, at least for a long time.**

**Here is the end result we are looking for, showing on each row the total sales from all products with a matching category:**

| ProductKey | ProductName | Category | SalesPerProduct | TotalCategorySales |
|---|---|---|---|---|
| 480 | Patch Kit/8 Patch... | Accessories | $7,307.39 | $700,759.96 |
| 529 | Road Tire Tube | Accessories | $9,480.24 | $700,759.96 |
| 477 | Water Bottle - 30... | Accessories | $21,177.56 | $700,759.96 |
| 528 | Mountain Tire Tu... | Accessories | $15,444.05 | $700,759.96 |
| 530 | Touring Tire Tube | Accessories | $7,425.12 | $700,759.96 |
| 484 | Bike Wash - Diss... | Accessories | $7,218.60 | $700,759.96 |
| 479 | Road Bottle Cage | Accessories | $15,390.88 | $700,759.96 |
| 478 | Mountain Bottle ... | Accessories | $20,229.75 | $700,759.96 |
| 538 | LL Road Tire | Accessories | $22,435.56 | $700,759.96 |
| 485 | Fender Set - Mo... | Accessories | $46,619.58 | $700,759.96 |
| 535 | LL Mountain Tire | Accessories | $21,541.38 | $700,759.96 |

*Figure 557 Every row with Category=Accessories sums to the same amount, which is the sum of all Accessories Sales Amount*

| ProductKey | ProductName | Category | SalesPerProduct | TotalCategorySales |
|---|---|---|---|---|
| 596 | Mountain-500 Bl... | Bikes | $25,919.52 | $28,318,144.65 |
| 597 | Mountain-500 Bl... | Bikes | $26,459.51 | $28,318,144.65 |
| 598 | Mountain-500 Bl... | Bikes | $31,319.42 | $28,318,144.65 |
| 599 | Mountain-500 Bl... | Bikes | $30,239.44 | $28,318,144.65 |
| 600 | Mountain-500 Bl... | Bikes | $22,139.59 | $28,318,144.65 |
| 584 | Road-750 Black, 58 | Bikes | $180,356.66 | $28,318,144.65 |
| 604 | Road-750 Black, 44 | Bikes | $194,396.40 | $28,318,144.65 |
| 605 | Road-750 Black, 48 | Bikes | $196,016.37 | $28,318,144.65 |
| 606 | Road-750 Black, 52 | Bikes | $208,436.14 | $28,318,144.65 |
| 591 | Mountain-500 Sil... | Bikes | $25,424.55 | $28,318,144.65 |
| 592 | Mountain-500 Sil... | Bikes | $25,424.55 | $28,318,144.65 |

*Figure 558 Filtered to Bikes*

**OK, here's the formula:**

```
1. =CALCULATE (
2.    SUM (Sales[SalesAmt]),
3.    FILTER (
4.        Products,
5.        Products[Category] = EARLIER (Products[Category])
6.    )
7. )
```

The only difference from our previous formula (for calc column *SalesPerProduct*) is the FILTER clause passed in the second argument to CALCULATE. Some salient points before we move on to look at EARLIER in line 5:

- Without the second FILTER argument, CALCULATE would transition the current row context into a filter context, and we would essentially get the same result as SalesPerProduct which we have seen before
- The second FILTER argument overrides that and lets us handpick the set of rows we want to use
- Note that, inside FILTER on line 4, we do not need to specify ALL(Products), just Products. Refer back to Figure 501 which explains that for FILTER's first table argument, the original filter context applies. And for a Calculated Column there is no filter context to begin with. Thus there is no need to clear any filters by using ALL().
- If you ignore the EARLIER function, we seem to be comparing Products[Category] to Products[Category]?! What gives? How many Products[Category] are there?

# EARLIER() in Action

Products[Category], being a naked column reference, refers to the Products[Category] in the row context. But how many row contexts are there? Well, as it turns out, in our case there are two row contexts:

1. Initial Row Context for the Calculated Column
2. Row Context generated by FILTER as it iterates over the Products table

If we are attempting to calculate TotalCategorySales say, for the row with ProductKey=597, then the image below shows the row contexts in play:

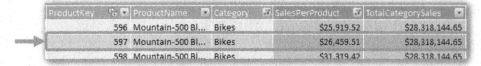

*Figure 559 FILTER creates a new "inner" row context, thus we end up with two row contexts in play*

As FILTER iterates over the Products table, it evaluates the condition for each row, and if TRUE, would include that row in the table it returns. Let's catch FILTER in action as it's doing this for a specific row, ProductKey=475 in our case.

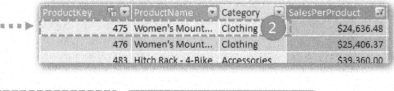

*Figure 560 EARLIER helps us navigate to the "outer" row context*

When we are at row ProductKey=475, we want to compare the Products[Category] for that row (our current row context, since we're inside FILTER) with the Products[Category] of the initial row. The EARLIER() function accomplishes that for us, by going back one level to the previous (earlier) row context that existed.

In this comparison, current row Products[Category] = "Clothing', whereas EARLIER(Products[Category]) = "Bikes" thus this row would not be returned by FILTER. But as FILTER moves through the Products table it would collect and return all rows with Products[Category] = "Bikes".

**If all of that didn't sink in, don't sweat it. Freely apply this as a pattern, your results will be equally awesome**. Let the understanding grow over time as you keep working with these patterns. If you look carefully, the pattern we just developed is strikingly similar to the GFITW, with some adaptations for it to work in Calculated Column.

**GFITW Pattern Modified for Calc Column**: Use when you need to calculate over all rows in the table, but comparing it to some value in the current row

```
CALCULATE(<base calculation>,
          FILTER(<table>),
                 <row test condition using EARLIER>
                 )
          )
```

Simple row test condition would look like

```
table[column] = EARLIER(table[column])
```

Where you see "=" you can use any comparison operator: =, >, <, <=, >=, <>
You can also combine multiple conditions using && (logical AND) or || (logical OR)

## An Even More Advanced Example

We had to include this one, both because it shows a few twists on the previous technique, and because it is one of the coolest, most inspiring examples of the potential we all now have as Excel Pros.

Rob has a neighbor who's a neuroscientist. In his field, he's kind of a big deal, like Will Ferrell in the movie "Anchorman." His name is Dan Wesson, he runs a research lab at Case Western Reserve University (CWRU), and his lab has been on CNN thanks to some exciting developments in Alzheimer's research that he spearheaded. (See? People know him).

This is a well-funded lab with all kinds of expensive equipment. It's an impressive place – we've toured it. Dan even has individual software packages that cost $10,000 for a single seat!

**And oh yeah, with our help, Dan has converted most of his data analysis over to Power Pivot. You know, the next generation of spreadsheet. That thing that costs approximately $10,000 *less* than his other software. That's right, Excel Pros – we even do Alzheimer's research!**

Here are a few of our favorite pictures of all time:

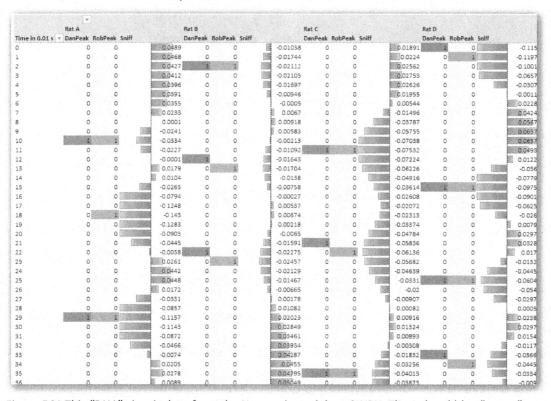

*Figure 561 This "DNA" view is data from the Neuroscience lab at CWRU. The red and blue "waves" are rats inhaling and exhaling – red is inhale, blue is exhale, and each row represents 1/100 of a second!*

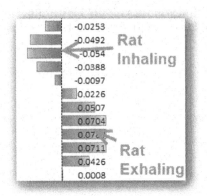

*Figure 562 Zoomed in on one of the inhale/exhale waves.*

Now here's the one that makes us the happiest:

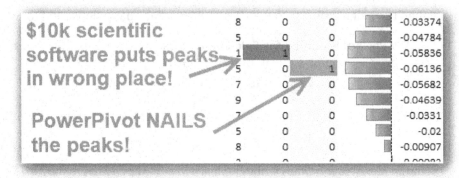

*Figure 563 Detecting the peak of each inhale event is very important to Dan's work. Look where the $10,000, purpose-built scientific software places the peaks versus where Power Pivot puts them!*

**That "peak detection" is just a calc column. Here's what the data looks like:**

**The most critical component of detecting an inhale peak is finding the most negative value in any given time-frame. Think of it as like a moving average, except that it's a moving minimum!**

| Time | Rat | Value |
|---|---|---|
| 0 | E | 0.0189 |
| 0.01 | E | 0.02238 |
| 0.02 | E | 0.02561 |
| 0.03 | E | 0.02752 |
| 0.04 | E | 0.02627 |
| 0.05 | E | 0.01959 |
| 0.06 | E | 0.00553 |
| 0.07 | E | -0.01486 |
| 0.08 | E | -0.03775 |
| 0.09 | E | -0.05746 |
| 0.1 | E | -0.07033 |
| 0.11 | E | -0.07531 |

*Figure 564 Time (in hundredths of a second), RatID, and Value - negative for inhale, positive for exhale. The bigger the absolute value, the more forceful the inhale/exhale.*

And here's our calc column formula for moving minimum:

```
1.  =CALCULATE(MIN(Data[value]),
2.      FILTER(Data,
3.          Data[Rat]=EARLIER(Data[Rat]) &&
4.          Data[TimeID] <= EARLIER(Data[TimeID]) +5 &&
5.          Data[TimeID] >= EARLIER(Data[TimeID]) -5
6.      )
7.  )
```

Hey, it's the same "GFITW Pattern for Calc Column" reapplied. Just like the first example we showed you for the EARLIER() function. But there are a few wrinkles:

- **Multiple conditions** – don't let this scare you. You can do as many as you want and combine them in using && (logical AND), as we have, or using || (logical OR).

- **The first condition set** – (Line 3) is just like our previous example. Only rows for the current rat should be counted, otherwise we're looking at someone else's breathing ☺

- **The second condition set is kinda cool** – (Line 4 and 5) it basically says "only count the five rows that happened sequentially before me, and the five rows that happened right after me." So we end up looking at a window in time that is 11 rows "long," which is actually 0.11 seconds.

The net result of the formula is that it tells us the smallest value in the current 11-row window.

From there, other calc columns can detect if the current row's Value column matches the new 11-row minimum column, in which case we're probably looking at a peak inhale.

See http://ppvt.pro/PkSniff for the full blog post; the formula shared in this book supersedes the one used in the blog post, since we have refined the formula over time as we gained deeper understanding of DAX ☺

If you're interested in reading more about this project, see:

http://ppvt.pro/Peak2Freq - where we move on to use our peak calc columns to produce frequency and amplitude measures.

http://ppvt.pro/FzzyTime - where we correlate the inhale/exhale data with events in another table that cannot be directly related (more calc column wizardry ensues)

# Calculated Columns are Static

In the intro to calculated column, we mentioned that there are only two events which trigger the calculation/recalculation of a Calculated Column

- Definition or Redefinition: When you define (or edit) the formula for the calculated column and hit enter, the column values are recalculated
- Data Refresh: When the Power Pivot table holding the calculated column is refreshed the column values are recalculated.

The computed values for each row are then stored within the data model along with the other columns, back to the file.

**In contrast, for Measures, the actual values are never stored and are always calculated "dynamically" based on the pivot that you build.**

Let's see this in a pivot, showing

1. **Calculated Column SalesPerProduct**=CALCULATE(SUM(Sales[SalesAmt]))
2. **Measure [Total Sales]** = SUM(Sales[SalesAmt])
3. **Measure [SalesPerProduct Measure]**=CALCULATE(SUM(Sales[SalesAmt]))

We threw in the third one to be clear that the behavior you would see has nothing to do with CALCULATE, and everything to do with Calculated Columns vs. Measures. Thus #3 has the exact formula as #1. Although the CALCULATE in a measure, without any filter arguments isn't any different than #2 ☺

Starting off with a basic pivot, all three seem to be providing the same result.

| | | Calc Column | Measure | Measure |
|---|---|---|---|---|
| ProductKey ⤓ | ProductName | SalesPerProduct ▾ | Total Sales | SalesPerProduct Measure |
| 312 | Road-150 Red, 48 | $1,205,877 | $1,205,877 | $1,205,877 |
| 310 | Road-150 Red, 62 | $1,202,299 | $1,202,299 | $1,202,299 |
| 313 | Road-150 Red, 52 | $1,080,638 | $1,080,638 | $1,080,638 |
| 314 | Road-150 Red, 56 | $1,055,590 | $1,055,590 | $1,055,590 |
| 311 | Road-150 Red, 44 | $1,005,494 | $1,005,494 | $1,005,494 |

*Figure 565 Similarities between Calc Column and Measures are only skin deep*

But as soon as we add a filter to CalendarYear, by using a slicer, we can see that while the calculated column values remain unchanged, measures are recalculated based on the Pivot Table filters:

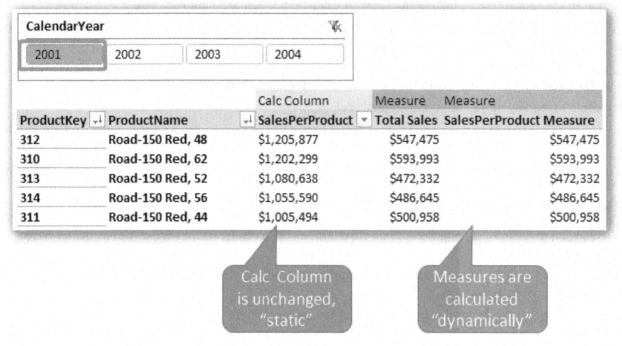

*Figure 566 Calc Columns are "static", Measures are "dynamic"*

You can think of the Calculated Column values as being stamped on to the respective rows, and behaving more like others columns coming from your data source i.e. the value stamped is not going to change based on any input coming from your pivot table.

# Memory and CPU Consumption During Recalculation of Complex Calc Columns

Calculated Columns do have a memory footprint which can impact the "runtime" performance i.e. displaying results in a Pivot Table. We discussed the implications of calculated columns in the Performance chapter.

However, there is another penalty that you incur with calculated columns, when you refresh your data. That is the penalty of all your calculated columns being recomputed. Usually this is a non-issue: most calculated columns do not take that long to compute and likely you are running an automated refresh of your model during after-hours, thus a delay isn't really a big deal. Therefore as long as "runtime" performance is fine, this is not a concern.

However certain kinds of calculated columns can eat a truly staggering amount of RAM when they're running. **Take our "moving minimum" example** from the peak detection scenario above for instance. That formula is written to only look at the previous five rows and the next five rows, plus the current row. **So we're only inspecting 11 rows at a time.**

**But to find those 11 rows to inspect, Power Pivot starts from scratch and goes looking through the *entire* table, one row at a time, and deciding whether each row belongs in that current window of 11.**

In normal Excel, relative reference takes care of this – Excel literally goes and looks five rows up and five rows down. It does *not* have to scan the entire worksheet, row by row, in order to find the right 11 rows. When it comes to "look at the rows close to me," Power Pivot is just fundamentally less intelligent than normal Excel. That's a consequence of lacking A1-style reference, which we've said before is a necessary evil in order to get a truly robust environment.

We'll leave you with one last observation on this topic: if you have one million rows in your table, that means scanning a million rows to calculate just a single row of the calc column. And since there are a million rows to calc, you have a million loops, each of which is a million rows of loop in itself. That's literally a *trillion* comparisons! Not only does that take a lot of time and processor power, but it takes a lot of RAM too.

Ultimately, with Dan's project, we had to abandon using Power Pivot calc columns for peak detection and implement the same "moving minimum" formula in SQL Server. That inhale/exhale table of his grew to be over 100 million rows! **But we still use Power Pivot for all of the measures and reporting, which after all is Power Pivot's strength.**

# 27 - New DAX Functions... and Variables!

## Amazing Since 2010, and STILL Improving

The DAX language (and the engine that goes with it) arrived on the scene in 2010 in a stunningly complete state. Unlike most "brand new" products, the DAX language offered tremendous breadth *and* depth in its very first release. That was no accident: the engineering team behind DAX had more than a decade of experience developing and refining a precursor language (called MDX). We, the users of DAX, therefore benefited tremendously from all of that experience, and there were very few places where "DAX v1" left us unsatisfied.

But Microsoft has continued to add to the language anyway, which is awesome ☺

Excel 2016 and Power BI Desktop both offer a number of new functions to make your life easier. In this chapter, we will highlight a few of our favorites.

## Important Note: Excel 2016+ and Power BI Desktop Only!

Yes, we just *hinted at* this in the immediately-preceding paragraph, but it needs to be called out in bright, blazing letters:

 **Everything** in this chapter will ONLY work in Excel 2016 or newer, or in Power BI Desktop! **Nothing** in this chapter will work in Excel 2010 or Excel 2013!

*Figure 567 This is the sort of error message you will see if you try to use these new functions in Excel 2010 or Excel 2013 Power Pivot*

## New Functions – Some Highlights

### DATEDIFF()

 DATEDIFF(<start_date>, <end_date>, <interval>)
<interval> can be: Second, Minute, Hour, Day, Week, Month, Quarter, Year

Example: We can define a calculated column, to determine the product lifespan in months, as below

```
ProductLifeSpan (Months) =
DATEDIFF ( 'Product'[StartDate], 'Product'[EndDate], MONTH )
```

| ProductName | StartDate | EndDate | ProductLifeSpan (Months) |
|---|---|---|---|
| All-Purpose Bike Stand | 7/1/2003 | | |
| AWC Logo Cap | 7/1/2001 | 6/30/2002 | 11 |
| AWC Logo Cap | 7/1/2002 | 6/30/2003 | 11 |
| AWC Logo Cap | 7/1/2003 | | |
| Bike Wash - Dissolver | 7/1/2003 | | |

*Figure 568 DATEDIFF makes it easy to calculate a date or time span*

This function should be useful in quite a few scenarios involving date/time span calculation.

Sometimes we twist ourselves in knots, thinking what the right answer should be, given specific dates. We like how the documentation explains what the return value is going to be:

 DATEDIFF Return Value: The count of interval boundaries crossed between two dates

So if you look at the month of January 2015 and the week boundary (Sunday is the default start of the week)...

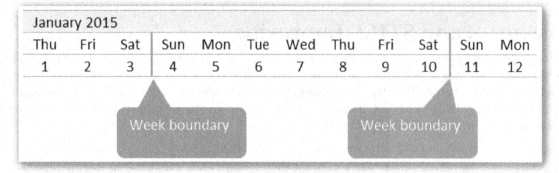

*Figure 569 Sunday marks the start of a week or week boundary*

...the DATEDIFF results shown below will all make sense:

| StartDate | EndDate | DateDiff (Weeks) |
|-----------|---------|------------------|
| 1/1/2015 | 1/3/2015 | 0 |
| 1/1/2015 | 1/4/2015 | 1 |
| 1/1/2015 | 1/5/2015 | 1 |
| 1/1/2015 | 1/10/2015 | 1 |
| 1/1/2015 | 1/11/2015 | 2 |
| 1/1/2015 | 1/12/2015 | 2 |

*Figure 570 DATEDIFF returns the count of interval boundaries crossed*

# MEDIAN() and PERCENTILE

Median and Percentile used to be fairly difficult to calculate in DAX (Percentile was covered in a three part article, see http://ppvt.pro/percentile). But now you can simply use the new functions.

**Median:**

 MEDIAN(<column>)

Example:

```
Median Sales =
MEDIAN ( Sales[SalesAmount] )
```

| Date | Total Sales | Average Sales | Median Sales |
|------|-------------|---------------|--------------|
| 12/1/2001 | $17,688 | $3,538 | $3,578 |
| 12/2/2001 | $25,544 | $3,193 | $3,578 |
| 12/3/2001 | $35,401 | $3,540 | $3,578 |
| 12/4/2001 | $14,834 | $2,967 | $3,578 |
| 12/5/2001 | $21,063 | $3,511 | $3,578 |

| Date | SalesOrderNumber | SalesAmount |
|------|------------------|-------------|
| 12/1/2001 | SO44807 | 3,374.99 |
| 12/1/2001 | SO44803 | 3,578.27 |
| 12/1/2001 | SO44804 | 3,578.27 |
| 12/1/2001 | SO44805 | 3,578.27 |
| 12/1/2001 | SO44806 | 3,578.27 |

*Figure 571 Note how Average and Median are distinct values*

**Percentile:**

Percentile comes in a pair of functions

PERCENTILE.INC(<column>, <k>)

PERCENTILE.EXC(<column>, <k>)

These are similar to the PERCENTILE.INC AND PERCENTILE.EXC functions in Excel.

Example:

```
Percentile50 =
PERCENTILE.INC ( Sales[SalesAmount], 0.50 )

Percentile90 =
PERCENTILE.INC ( Sales[SalesAmount], 0.90 )
```

| CalendarYear | Total Sales | Average Sales | Median Sales | Percentile50 | Percentile90 |
|---|---|---|---|---|---|
| 2001 | $3,266,374 | $3,224 | $3,578 | $3,578 | $3,578 |
| 2002 | $6,530,344 | $2,439 | $2,182 | $2,182 | $3,578 |
| 2003 | $9,791,060 | $401 | $30 | $30 | $2,071 |
| 2004 | $9,770,900 | $303 | $25 | $25 | $1,215 |

*Figure 572 Showing the 50th Percentile (same as Median) and 90th Percentile*

Notice the drop in 50th and 90th percentile Sales amount in year 2003, 2004. That is due to lower priced categories that AdventureWorks started selling those years (accessories and clothing, besides bikes). You have to admire the bold move there by the company.

## PRODUCT()

Being able to multiply values in a column was missing previously (see http://ppvt.pro/PRODUCTX for the kinds of workarounds that were required).

The calculation of cumulative returns is probably the most-common example of when we need this.

Let us say our dataset consists of monthly returns for the S&P 500:

| Year | Month | S&P 500 Return | Factor |
|---|---|---|---|
| 2012 | Jan | 4.36% | 1.0436 |
| 2012 | Feb | 4.06% | 1.0406 |
| 2012 | Mar | 3.13% | 1.0313 |
| 2012 | Apr | -0.75% | 0.9925 |
| 2012 | May | -6.27% | 0.9373 |
| 2012 | Jun | 3.96% | 1.0396 |

*Figure 573 Monthly returns for S&P 500*

If monthly return for month 1 was R1, for month 2 it was R2 and so on, the annual rate of return would be computed as:

```
(1+R1) x (1+R2)...(1+R12)   -   1
```

We already have the value 1+R stored in the column '*Factor*'. Thus we can define our measure as:

```
Annual Return =
PRODUCT ( MonthlyReturn[Factor] ) - 1
```

| Year | Month | Return | Factor | | Year | Annual Return |
|------|-------|--------|--------|--|------|---------------|
| 2013 | Jan | 5.04 % | 1.0504 | | 2013 | 29.61 % |
| 2013 | Feb | 1.11 % | 1.0111 | | Total | 29.61 % |
| 2013 | Mar | 3.60 % | 1.0360 | | | |
| 2013 | Apr | 1.81 % | 1.0181 | | | |
| 2013 | May | 2.08 % | 1.0208 | | | |
| 2013 | Jun | -1.50 % | 0.9850 | | | |
| 2013 | Jul | 4.95 % | 1.0495 | | | |
| 2013 | Aug | -3.13 % | 0.9687 | | | |
| 2013 | Sep | 2.97 % | 1.0297 | | | |
| 2013 | Oct | 4.46 % | 1.0446 | | | |
| 2013 | Nov | 2.80 % | 1.0280 | | | |
| 2013 | Dec | 2.36 % | 1.0236 | | | |

*Figure 574 Annual Rate of return calculated from Monthly Returns*

A very official and reliable source confirms that our results are accurate. The slight difference in decimal points is due to the fact that our monthly source data was rounded at the 2nd decimal place.

| Year ⬍ | Change in Index ⬍ |
|--------|-------------------|
| 2013 | 29.60% |

*Figure 575 Wikipedia confirms the veracity of our results*

# GEOMEAN() and GEOMEANX()

There are several measures of central tendency, such as median, arithmetic mean and geometric mean. In some scenarios geometric mean is more effective than the arithmetic mean. Geometric mean is the preferred approach (over arithmetic mean) when values are percentages (e.g. rate of return) or at different scales (e.g. movie ratings and movie box office total).

For our dataset we want to calculate the arithmetic and geometric mean of our annual returns over several years. For this we would use the X version of GEOMEAN function, which lets us iterate over the Years and calculate the mean returns.

Example:

```
Annual Return Arithmetic Mean =
AVERAGEX ( VALUES ( MonthlyReturn[Year] ), [Annual Return] )

Annual Return Geometric Mean =
GEOMEANX ( VALUES ( MonthlyReturn[Year] ), [Annual Return] )
```

| Year | Annual Return Arithmetic Mean | Annual Return Geometric Mean |
|------|-------------------------------|------------------------------|
| 2012 | 13.40 % | 13.40 % |
| 2013 | 29.61 % | 29.61 % |
| 2014 | 11.38 % | 11.38 % |
| Total | 18.13 % | 16.53 % |
| | Arithmetic Mean | Geometric Mean |

*Figure 576 Notice how the Geometric Mean and Arithmetic Mean are different*

This article provides more information about geometric mean: http://ppvt.pro/geomeanMath.

## Other Corresponding X Functions

We used GEOMEANX earlier. We will just point out that MEDIAN, PERCENTILE and PRODUCT each have their X function equivalents, namely:

MEDIANX, PERCENTILEX.INC, PERCENTILEX.EXC, PRODUCTX

Just like SUMX, these "X" functions all give you the ability to operate over Measure values (as opposed to values in a column, to which the non-X functions are limited), and to carefully control the <table> over which the calculation operates – including temporary tables created by table functions like ALL and FILTER! (As described in the chapter on CALCULATE and FILTER – More Nuances).

 **We suspect that the "X" versions of these functions will be just as useful** to you as the "non-X" versions, if not more so, since the X versions can be used to find the median of a set of measure values (or product of them, or where a single measure value "ranks" percentile-wise), and not just operating on values in a column. So make sure you check those out!

## CONCATENATEX: The Most Interesting Function in the World?

"I don't always need to concatenate a variable number of text values together in a DAX formula, but when I do, I require CONCATENATEX."

-Rob Collie

Here is a *very* special one:

 **CONCATENATEX**(<table>, <expression>, [delimiter])

CONCATENATEX is worth its weight in gold when you need it. This is another function we have been wanting for a while (See http://ppvt.pro/containsx). Let's put CONCATENATEX to some good use.

Example:

We will build this one in two steps.
**Step 1**: First we define a Top N measure to show us the Sales for our Top 3 products as below (note that TOPN is not a new function and is also available in Excel 2010 and 2013).

```
Top 3 Products Sales =
CALCULATE (
    [Total Sales],
    TOPN ( 3, Product, [Total Sales] )
)
```

**Step 2**: Next we want to actually list the Top 3 Products. We can do so by combining the power of TOPN with our new function CONCATENATEX as below (numbered to aid with explanation later):

```
1. Top 3 Products Names =
2. CONCATENATEX(
3. TOPN(3, Product, [Total Sales])
4. ,Product[ProductName]
5. , ", "
6. ,[Total Sales]
7. ,DESC
8. )
```

Let us show you the results first:

| CalendarYear | Month | Total Sales | Top 3 Products Sales | Top 3 Products Names |
|---|---|---|---|---|
| 2001 | Jul | $473,388 | $261,214 | Road-150 Red, 48, Road-150 Red, 44, Road-150 Red, 62 |
| 2001 | Aug | $506,192 | $271,949 | Road-150 Red, 62, Road-150 Red, 56, Road-150 Red, 52 |
| 2001 | Sep | $473,943 | $279,105 | Road-150 Red, 48, Road-150 Red, 52, Road-150 Red, 62 |
| 2001 | Oct | $513,329 | $264,792 | Road-150 Red, 62, Road-150 Red, 56, Road-150 Red, 48 |

*Figure 577 CONCATENATEX lets us show the names of the Top 3 Products*

| CalendarYear | Month | ProductKey | ProductName | Total Sales |
|---|---|---|---|---|
| 2001 | Jul | 312 | Road-150 Red, 48 | $100,192 |
| 2001 | Jul | 311 | Road-150 Red, 44 | $82,300 |
| 2001 | Jul | 310 | Road-150 Red, 62 | $78,722 |
| 2001 | Jul | 314 | Road-150 Red, 56 | $53,674 |

*Figure 578 We can validate the top 3 products for 2001 July*

Here is the complete syntax of the function (we had skipped some optional arguments earlier):

 CONCATENATEX(<table>, <expression>, [delimiter], [orderby_expression1], [order1]...)

**<table>** (Line 3): Like the other X functions, it takes a table as its first argument – the table over which it will iterate. In this case, that is supplied by the TOPN function on line 3, which simply provides a temporary table of the top three Products (well actually, potentially more than 3 in case of ties).

**<expression>** (Line 4): This is the expression that would be calculated for each row of <table> and in the end would be concatenated. We supply the *ProductName* here.

**<delimiter>** (Line 5): We supply comma as a delimiter here.

**<orderby_expression1>** (Line 6) and
**<order1>** (Line 7): If this argument is not provided then you may get results in no particular order. We would like to see *ProductName* sorted by [Total Sales] so that we show our top product first, then second ranked product and so on. Thus we supply [Total Sales] in Line 6 and specify DESC in Line 7.

## ISEMPTY()

 ISEMPTY(<table_expression>)

Wherever you were using logic like COUNTROWS(<table_expression>) = 0, you can now use a shortcut, ISEMPTY().

Example: We define a new measure

```
ProductNotSold =
ISEMPTY ( Sales )
```

| ProductKey | ProductName | ProductNotSold | Total Sales |
|---|---|---|---|
| 210 | HL Road Frame - Black, 58 | True | |
| 211 | HL Road Frame - Red, 58 | True | |
| 212 | Sport-100 Helmet, Red | True | |
| 213 | Sport-100 Helmet, Red | True | |
| 214 | Sport-100 Helmet, Red | False | $78,028 |
| 215 | Sport-100 Helmet, Black | True | |
| 216 | Sport-100 Helmet, Black | True | |
| 217 | Sport-100 Helmet, Black | False | $72,954 |
| 218 | Mountain Bike Socks, M | True | |

*Figure 579 ISEMPTY at work*

Our expectation is that ISEMPTY() is probably going to calculate faster than COUNTROWS()=0, since if you think about it, counting all the rows is lot more math than simply checking if a table is empty. You may only see a noticeable difference when working with really large datasets. Still though, even for readability reasons, ISEMPTY() should be preferred as a best practice.

# INTERSECT(), EXCEPT() and UNION()

INTERSECT(<LeftTable >, <RightTable>)

EXCEPT(<LeftTable >, <RightTable>)

UNION(<table_expression1>, <table_expression2> [,<table_expression>]...)

These functions come in handy when you are operating on lists and comparing and combining them in some manner. Here's how they work in general

**INTERSECT**: Returns the rows of left-side table which appear in right-side table.

**EXCEPT**: Returns the rows of left-side table which do not appear in right-side table.

**UNION**: Returns the union of the two tables whose columns match.

Here's a visual that may help:

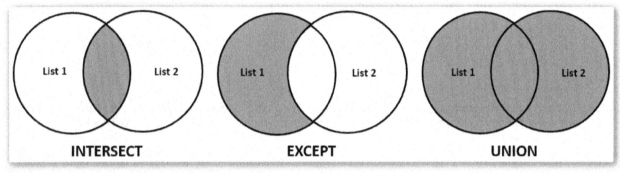

*Figure 580 INTERSECT, EXCEPT and UNION illustrated graphically*

Let's try these out with an example. Let's say we have

- List 1: List of Top 10 Products by Sales
- List 2: List of Top 10 Products by Margin

Here is how these lists look for the "Clothing" product category:

### List 1: Top 10 Products by Sales

| ProductName | Total Sales |
|---|---|
| Women's Mountain Shorts, L | $25,406 |
| Women's Mountain Shorts, M | $24,636 |
| Long-Sleeve Logo Jersey, L | $22,595 |
| Long-Sleeve Logo Jersey, M | $22,096 |
| Short-Sleeve Classic Jersey, XL | $22,082 |
| Short-Sleeve Classic Jersey, M | $21,974 |
| Short-Sleeve Classic Jersey, S | $21,920 |
| Long-Sleeve Logo Jersey, S | $21,446 |
| Women's Mountain Shorts, S | $21,277 |
| Long-Sleeve Logo Jersey, XL | $20,646 |

### List 2: Top 10 Products by Margin

| ProductName | Margin |
|---|---|
| Women's Mountain Shorts, L | $15,904 |
| Women's Mountain Shorts, M | $15,422 |
| Women's Mountain Shorts, S | $13,319 |
| Classic Vest, M | $7,910 |
| Classic Vest, L | $7,751 |
| Half-Finger Gloves, M | $7,650 |
| Half-Finger Gloves, S | $7,481 |
| Half-Finger Gloves, L | $6,792 |
| Classic Vest, S | $6,678 |
| Long-Sleeve Logo Jersey, L | $5,197 |

ProductCategory

☐ Select All
☐ Accessories
☐ Bikes
☑ Clothing
☐ Components

*Figure 581 Our Top 10 products by sales and by margin*

## INTERSECT()

Using INTERSECT, we want to determine the count of products that appear in List 1 *and* in List 2. Here's our measure

```
Count Products with TopSales AND TopMargin =
COUNTROWS (
    INTERSECT (
        TOPN ( 10, 'Product', [Total Sales] ),
        TOPN ( 10, 'Product', [Margin] )
    )
)
```

And here are the results:

*Figure 582 INTERSECT shows us the count of Products found in **both** List1 and List2. (We are using Power BI's "Card" Visualization to Display our measure here. We merely diagrammed the tables at the top so you can see which rows contribute to that count).*

## EXCEPT()

Using EXCEPT, we want to determine the count of products that appear in List 1 (Top 10 Sales) but *not* in List 2 (Top 10 Margin). Here's our measure

```
Count Products with TopSales and NOT TopMargin =
COUNTROWS (
    EXCEPT (
        TOPN ( 10, 'Product', [Total Sales] ),
        TOPN ( 10, 'Product', [Margin] )
    )
)
```

And here are the results:

*Figure 583 EXCEPT shows us the count of Products in List1 but **not** in List2. (We are using Power BI's "Card" Visualization to Display our measure here. We merely diagrammed the tables at the top so you can see which rows contribute to that count).*

# UNION()

Using UNION, we want to determine the count of products that appear in List 1 (Top 10 Sales) *or* in List 2 (Top 10 Margin). This one is a little tricky, since UNION() retains all duplicate rows. Therefore we write this one slightly differently.

Here's our measure, and this one definitely falls under "go ahead and treat this as a pattern."

```
Count Product with TopSales OR TopMargin =
VAR TopSalesOrMargin =
    UNION (
        TOPN ( 10, 'Product', [Total Sales] ),
        TOPN ( 10, 'Product', [Margin] )
    )
RETURN
    COUNTROWS ( SUMMARIZE ( TopSalesOrMargin, 'Product'[ProductKey] )
```

What just happened there?! Don't panic, we told you it was a pattern, no need to think too deeply ☺.

But OK, assuming you are still curious... firstly what is a VAR? VAR is used to declare a Variable. Yes, Variables are a new feature in DAX, we will talk about them in a moment. But for now, you can think of the measure as calculating in two steps.

**Step 1**: UNION our List 1 and List 2. However, UNION retains the duplicates, so we need to remove duplicates before we can count our rows (else your answer will always be 10 rows + 10 rows = 20). That's what Step 2 is for.

**Step 2**: SUMMARIZE then COUNTROWS. SUMMARIZE is a very versatile function, but one that we never teach in our two-day seminars. (Rob likes to say that this one is too hard for him, so why torture others?).

In truth it's not *that* bad, but it *is* rare that you would ever need it. SUMMARIZE returns a temporary table that, if we could see it, would strongly resemble a PivotTable – one with 'Product'[ProductKey] on Rows, and nothing on Columns or Values in this case. And we know that pivots remove dupes from Rows, collapsing duplicates into a single row of the pivot. So does SUMMARIZE.

So here, we are using SUMMARIZE merely to remove the duplicates (SQL folks can think of SUMMARIZE as "Group By" SQL clause). With duplicates removed, COUNTROWS gives us the desired result.

| ProductName | Total Sales | ProductName | Margin |
|---|---|---|---|
| Women's Mountain Shorts, L | $25,406 | Women's Mountain Shorts, L | $15,904 |
| Women's Mountain Shorts, M | $24,636 | Women's Mountain Shorts, M | $15,422 |
| Long-Sleeve Logo Jersey, L | $22,595 | Women's Mountain Shorts, S | $13,319 |
| Long-Sleeve Logo Jersey, M | $22,096 | Classic Vest, M | $7,910 |
| Short-Sleeve Classic Jersey, XL | $22,082 | Classic Vest, L | $7,751 |
| Short-Sleeve Classic Jersey, M | $21,974 | Half-Finger Gloves, M | $7,650 |
| Short-Sleeve Classic Jersey, S | $21,920 | Half-Finger Gloves, S | $7,481 |
| Long-Sleeve Logo Jersey, S | $21,446 | Half-Finger Gloves, L | $6,792 |
| Women's Mountain Shorts, S | $21,277 | Classic Vest, S | $6,678 |
| Long-Sleeve Logo Jersey, XL | $20,646 | Long-Sleeve Logo Jersey, L | $5,197 |

## 16

Count Product with TopSales OR TopMargin

*Figure 584 UNION and then SUMMARIZE gets us count of Products in List1 or in List2*

# More New Functions

These are just some of the new functions, for a complete list see http://ppvt.pro/newfxn. For updates on the new functionality released with Power BI Dekstop (expected on a monthly cycle) see http://ppvt.pro/pbiDesignerBlog.

# DAX Variables

## Variables Are like a Tape Recorder

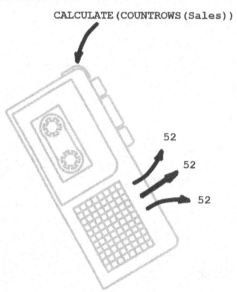

*Figure 585 DAX Variables let you "record" a value in one part of your formula, and "replay" that value multiple other places in your formula without re-calculating it every time.*

At a high level, Variables let us tell the DAX engine, "go evaluate an expression, remember the answer you get, and then use that answer elsewhere in the formula."

So it's sort of like a tape recorder (with apologies to those of you who are too young to have ever seen a tape recorder). Go "play" this chunk of a formula, "record" its value, and then "re-play" that value multiple times during the rest of the formula ☺

Oh, but it's been long enough now that we think it's time to repeat our warning...

 **Everything** in this chapter will ONLY work in Excel 2016 or newer, or in Power BI Desktop! **Nothing** in this chapter will work in Excel 2010 or Excel 2013!

## Variables Offer Three Benefits

Assuming you are running Excel 2016 or newer, or Power Pivot Desktop, there are three basic answers to the question, "why are Variables useful?"

 Three Benefits of Variables:
1. They make certain formulas "cleaner" - less tedious to write, and also easier to read and edit later on, by removing duplicate expressions from the formula.
2. They make certain formulas easier to write, with less conceptual worry about row context vs. filter context.
3. They make certain formulas perform faster, by not requiring the DAX engine to re-evaluate the same expression multiple times.

Of course, sometimes Variables can provide all of those benefits at the same time, but we think it's easier to cover each one separately, with its own example.

## Benefit One: Cleaner Formulas

Consider for a moment the following formula:

```
Transaction Count =
IF (
    CALCULATE ( COUNTROWS ( Sales ) ) > 0,
    CALCULATE ( COUNTROWS ( Sales ) ),
    -1
)
```

Pretty simple: we perform a calculation to see if it's greater than zero. If so, we return that same calculation as the output of our formula. Otherwise, we return -1 (or 0 or some other number – there's nothing special about -1 in this example).

Sadly this requires us to repeat that CALCULATE(COUNTROWS(…)) expression twice in our formula. Blech.

This is an age-old pattern that we've all seen, even back in traditional Excel formulas. It's quite similar to the IF(ISER-ROR(*some calc*), 0, *that same calc*) pattern actually. *That* pattern was made simpler with the IFERROR function, which allows us to write "*some calc*" only once.

But in our case we're not testing for an error, which means we can't use IFERROR to remove our duplicate expression.

Until Excel 2016 and Power BI Desktop, that is, because in *those* products, we can do this instead:

```
Transaction Count =
VAR RowCount =
    CALCULATE ( COUNTROWS ( Sales ) )
RETURN
    IF ( RowCount > 0, RowCount, -1 )
```

OK, that formula doesn't look a whole lot cleaner than the original. It's got these new keywords VAR and RETURN in there, and on net, it's actually *longer* than the original!

But bear with us… because sometimes, your repeated expression is *much* longer than the example we're using here. Let's stick with this example for the moment, because it illustrates the concepts quite nicely.

## The VAR Keyword

The first thing you will notice is that the VAR keyword does *not* appear in auto-complete:

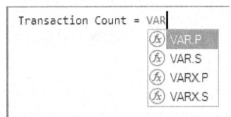

*Figure 586 Using Power BI Desktop, we see that VAR does not appear in autocomplete, which is admittedly a bit weird*

Don't worry, VAR *does* exist! Just type VAR, press the spacebar, and voila:

Transaction Count = VAR

*Figure 587 Note that VAR **does** appear in special blue font, indicating DAX knows that it's special*

Once the DAX engine sees the VAR keyword, it is expecting you to then immediately provide a <variable name> = <expression> block next, like we did above:

```
VAR RowCount =
    CALCULATE ( COUNTROWS ( Sales ) )
```

And let's see what the formula editor does with this:

Transaction Count = VAR RowCount = CALCULATE(COUNTROWS(Sales))

*Figure 588 RowCount is formatted in green, indicating that DAX knows that is a Variable we have created*

 So, in short, you put the VAR keyword at the front of a formula when you want to create a Variable, and then include a <variable name> = <expression> block. Yes, you can create multiple Variables within a single formula, in which case each <variable name> = <expression> block MUST be preceded by its own VAR keyword.

## The RETURN Keyword

Now that we have our VAR and our <variable name> = <expression> block, we tell the DAX engine "OK, enough with that Variable stuff, now we're going to do the normal old formula thing."

```
Transaction Count = VAR RowCount = CALCULATE(COUNTROWS(Sales)) RETURN
```

*Figure 589 The RETURN keyword also does **not** show up in autocomplete, but also like VAR, it **does** get recognized and formatted in blue*

Everything after RETURN, then behaves just like a normal formula. Well, except for the awesome fact that you can then reference your Variable by name, of course.

## Referencing a Variable

Using your Variable is then quite simple: just type its name!

After we reference the Variables in our completed formula, the Variable appears in green every time it shows up – both inside the VAR section, and inside the RETURN section:

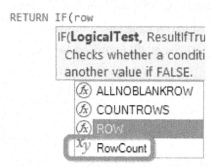

*Figure 590 Good news: Variable names do appear in autocomplete, and even get their own special icon!*

```
Transaction Count = VAR RowCount = CALCULATE(COUNTROWS(Sales)) RETURN IF(RowCount > 0, RowCount -1)
```

*Figure 591 Variable names always appear in green, both within the VAR section and within the RETURN section*

## Cleaner Formulas (Benefit One) Revisited

OK, with that groundwork laid down, we can consider another "with and without" example of formula simplification.

Another Example – Without Variables

```
AdjustedLeadTime =
SWITCH (
    [ProductCategory],
    "Bikes", CALCULATE (
        MAX ( 'Product'[DaysToManufacture] ),
        FILTER (
            'Product',
            'Product'[ProductCategory]
                = EARLIER ( 'Product'[ProductCategory] )
        )
    )
        + 3,
    "Clothing", CALCULATE (
        MAX ( 'Product'[DaysToManufacture] ),
        FILTER (
            'Product',
            'Product'[ProductCategory]
                = EARLIER ( 'Product'[ProductCategory] )
        )
    )
        + 2,
    "Accessories", CALCULATE (
        MAX ( 'Product'[DaysToManufacture] ),
        FILTER (
            'Product',
            'Product'[ProductCategory]
                = EARLIER ( 'Product'[ProductCategory] )
        )
    )
        + 1,
    "Components", CALCULATE (
```

```
        MAX ( 'Product'[DaysToManufacture] ),
        FILTER (
            'Product',
            'Product'[ProductCategory]
                = EARLIER ( 'Product'[ProductCategory] )
        )
    )
    + 4
)
```

And now the same formula, simplified using Variables...

```
AdjustedLeadTime =
VAR MaxCategoryDays =
    CALCULATE (
        MAX ( 'Product'[DaysToManufacture] ),
        FILTER (
            'Product',
            'Product'[ProductCategory]
                = EARLIER ( 'Product'[ProductCategory] )
        )
    )
RETURN
    SWITCH (
        [ProductCategory],
        "Bikes", MaxCategoryDays + 3,
        "Clothing", MaxCategoryDays + 2,
        "Accessories", MaxCategoryDays + 1,
        "Components", MaxCategoryDays + 4
    )
```

Which do *you* prefer? We strongly prefer the latter, especially in cases where we must "revisit" a formula later – merely reading and understanding it is much simpler with the Variable approach, but imagine having to *edit* said formula in four different places (which we often have to do without Variables).

## Benefit Two: Less "Mysterious" Formulas

### Example 1: Alternative to EARLIER?

Hey, remember that EARLIER function? Well, with Variables, you may decide to forgo the use of EARLIER and skip all of that mumbo-jumbo.

Here's the formula example that we used to explain EARLIER in a previous chapter:

```
CategorySalesWithEarlier =
CALCULATE (
    [Total Sales],
    FILTER (
        'Product',
        'Product'[ProductCategory] =
            EARLIER ( 'Product'[ProductCategory] )
    )
)
```

And here's the same thing, written using a Variable instead of EARLIER:

```
CategorySalesWithVariable =
VAR Category = 'Product'[ProductCategory]
RETURN
    CALCULATE (
        [Total Sales],
        FILTER ( 'Product',
          'Product'[ProductCategory] = Category )
    )
```

They both return the same results:

| ProductCategory | Transaction Count | AdjustedLeadTime | CategorySalesWithEarlier | CategorySalesWithVariable |
|---|---|---|---|---|
| Clothing | -1 | 2 | $339,772.61 | $339,772.61 |
| Clothing | 2190 | 2 | $339,772.61 | $339,772.61 |
| Accessories | 328 | 1 | $700,759.96 | $700,759.96 |
| Accessories | 249 | 1 | $700,759.96 | $700,759.96 |

*Figure 592 The version that employs EARLIER and the version that employs Variables yield the exact same results*

There are two ways to think about this:

1. "Sweet, that business with EARLIER confused me, I'm not ready to understand that yet, so yeah, I'll just use Variables for now and bypass all that heavy thinking."
2. "EARLIER isn't that bad really, so I can keep using it, but hey, *how* do Variables allow me to get the same result as EARLIER? I need to understand the machinery under the hood!"

As always, we are totally OK with you following a pattern. So type 1 people, go for it. Ignore the next three paragraphs.

Type 2 people, here's the answer: EARLIER is only required when you are evaluating a column's value from *within* a row iterator function like FILTER, and need to get the value from the "original row," also known as the value from the original row context. Outside of FILTER, getting that original value is simple – just reference the column.

Well that's the key here. Since the VAR block is evaluated once, outside of the FILTER function, the value for [Product-Category] respects the "this row" row context, and that value for the Category Variable is going to be "remembered," as a static value, for the rest of the calculation.

This doesn't mean that Variables can replace EARLIER in *all* circumstances, because in certain advanced situations, you might be juggling more than two row contexts (!), in which case no single value will suffice, but hey, *most* usage of EARLIER can be replaced with Variables if you so choose.

## Example 2: Measure References Inside FILTER (Within a Measure)

In the chapter on Row and Filter Context, we saw that *this* measure worked fine:

```
Transactions for Highest Price = CALCULATE(
    COUNTROWS(Sales),
    FILTER(
        Products,
        Products[ListPrice] = MAX ( Products[ListPrice] )
    )
)
```

But then if we defined a [Highest Price] measure and then used *that* inside our FILTER...

```
Highest Price = MAX ( Products[ListPrice] )
```

```
Transactions for Highest Price BROKEN = CALCULATE(
    COUNTROWS(Sales),
    FILTER(
        Products,
        Products[ListPrice] = [Highest Price]
    )
)
```

We got a "bogus" result in the pivot:

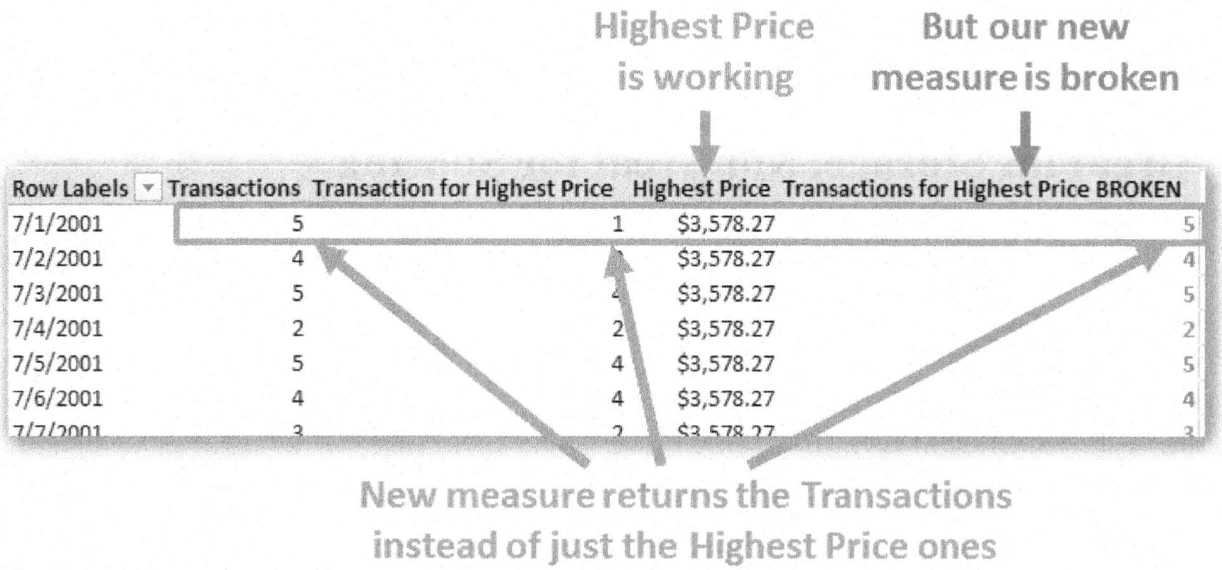

Highest Price
is working

But our new
measure is broken

| Row Labels ▼ | Transactions | Transaction for Highest Price | Highest Price | Transactions for Highest Price BROKEN |
|---|---|---|---|---|
| 7/1/2001 | 5 | 1 | $3,578.27 | 5 |
| 7/2/2001 | 4 |  | $3,578.27 | 4 |
| 7/3/2001 | 5 | 4 | $3,578.27 | 5 |
| 7/4/2001 | 2 | 2 | $3,578.27 | 2 |
| 7/5/2001 | 5 | 4 | $3,578.27 | 5 |
| 7/6/2001 | 4 | 4 | $3,578.27 | 4 |
| 7/7/2001 | 3 | 2 | $3,578.27 | 3 |

New measure returns the Transactions
instead of just the Highest Price ones

*Figure 593 The reasons for this are explained in that previous chapter, but boil down to the interaction between measure names, CALCULATE (the implied flavor), row context, and filter context.*

Turns out, we can re-write the measure like this:

```
Transactions for Highest Price FIXED =
VAR HighPrice = [Highest Price]
RETURN
    CALCULATE (
        COUNTROWS ( Sales ),
        FILTER ( Products, Products[ListPrice] = HighPrice )
    )
```

And this works just fine, as displayed here in Power BI Desktop:

| Date | Transactions for Highest Price FIXED |
|---|---|
| 7/1/2001 | 1 |
| 7/2/2001 | 2 |
| 7/3/2001 | 4 |
| 7/4/2001 | 2 |
| 7/5/2001 | 4 |
| 7/6/2001 | 4 |
| 7/7/2001 | 2 |
| 7/8/2001 | 2 |
| 7/9/2001 | 3 |
| 7/10/2001 | 2 |

*Figure 594 "FIXED" version of the measure (using Variables) returns the 1, 2, 4, 2... correct results*

Maybe this isn't all that much simpler, conceptually speaking, because VAR and RETURN are not exactly "introductory" concepts. But at least it does let you go back to the best practice of "I only write each formula once" – a rule you had to "break" when operating inside FILTER previously in such situations.

A small victory perhaps, but still a victory!

We are still getting used to Variables actually, and the simplifying power that they bring. A year from now we expect to be using them in ways we had not anticipated at time of writing.

# 28 - "YouTube for Data" – The Importance of a Server

## Files – Great for Storage, Not Great for Sharing

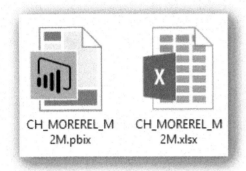

CH_MOREREL_M
2M.pbix

CH_MOREREL_M
2M.xlsx

*Figure 595 At the risk of being overly-obvious... everything we create in Power BI Desktop gets saved to a .PBIX file (left), or in the case of Power Pivot, to an .XLSX file (right)*

Everything we have done with Power Pivot so far, as well as with Power BI Desktop, has been saved to a file. And hey, files are great for storage, which is why they've been a feature of computing basically since the advent of magnetic storage (tapes, floppy disks, and hard drives).

But *storage* is typically not sufficient.

Maybe this *starts* out like a Model Railroad hobby - where you build something epic in your basement for *you*, and never share it with the world.

Pretty quickly though, in order to get "fair market value" out of your work, you will need to share it with others - your team, your manager, or maybe the entire organization. (We're not talking about your model train. You don't even have one of those. We're talking about your data models and reports here, please try to keep up ☺ )

Well, what is humanity's "go-to" method for sharing files? Yep, email. However, email has some serious flaws as a sharing mechanism. One might even get a bit harsh about it and say...

## Email Sucks as a Delivery Vehicle for Our Awesome Work!

*Figure 596 Email doesn't work that well as a sharing/publishing mechanism*

Email is a passable sharing/publishing mechanism on the surface, but there are definite drawbacks that become apparent over time:

- Files are often too big for email
- Others don't have the right version of Excel (or Power Pivot, or Power BI Desktop)
- Others want to use tablets and phones
- Email provides no security or protection for sensitive data and logic

- YOU, the author, are responsible for updating the files, distributing the latest, and reminding everyone to stop using the older versions
- Very quickly, there are too many versions of the file floating around to be trusted

## Network Distribution via File Shares? Not much better.

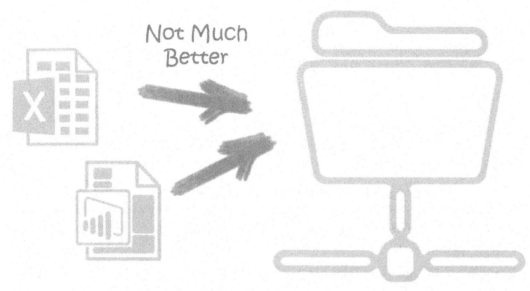

*Figure 597 Network shares are only slightly better than email*

Yeah yeah yeah. You've got a fancy network at your job, and you can save massive files out to the Z drive or whatever else you call it.

OK, that "fixes" the file size problem, sort of, but all of the other problems listed above are still in play. It's still chaotic, error-prone, and unfun.

So, when we say "email," we mean "anything that actually delivers the file to other people." Including network file servers.

("Sucks," by the way, may as well be an official software/techno term by now. We're pretty sure that, back in the day, the entire Excel for Windows engineering project started with someone saying, "you know what, Lotus 1-2-3 kinda sucks." History is made in such ways.)

## Parallels to Video Files, Circa 1998

Keep those drawbacks in mind, and let's look at another problem with similar characteristics. History has a powerful lesson to teach us.

### Parent, Grandparents, and Pictures of Cats

Back in the late 90s, the Internet was already a big deal. Our parents *and* grandparents had email addresses by this point in time, and they were *using* them. How do we remember? Because we were receiving dozens of forwarded email chains per day – jokes, top 10 lists, hoaxes, and images. Lots of entirely meaningless noise, primarily generated by family members who had lots of time on their hands.

These email chains were the precursor to Facebook, in other words.

By 1998, yes, we were already seeing multiple cute pictures of cats per day. Society had advanced to that point very quickly. (We suspect that in alien cultures it also unfolds that way: Step one, invent Internet. Step two, pictures of cats.)

But you know what was almost *never* being shared?

**Video. Video sharing was *not* a thing back then.**

If you wanted to share a video file with someone, it was VERY difficult. The files were too big for email, but even when you circumvented that obstacle, the person receiving the video had at BEST a 50% chance of being able to view it. For instance, if the video was produced on a Mac and the viewer only had a PC, they very often had to go track down and install additional software. Even when it was PC to PC, you often lacked the right video codec. So only the most dedicated nerds managed to share video files.

# YouTube Happens!

*Figure 598 YouTube changed video publishing from "share the file" to "upload and send link"*

YouTube changed all of that. No more sending large files, because YouTube compressed the files and also streamed them. No more worrying about the technology installed on the viewers' desktops either, because YouTube converted ALL videos to Adobe Flash, which everyone already had.

Video sharing EXPLODED.

 300 hours of video are uploaded to YouTube every minute. And every day people watch hundreds of millions of hours on YouTube and generate billions of views. (Source: http://ppvt.pro/ytStats)

People are watching on their desktops, their tablets, their phones, and on their Smart TVs and devices. By the way, half of YouTube views are on mobile devices!

## Importance of Web/Mobile

YouTube is just one example. If you look around, *many* of our interactions have moved away from "heavy" desktop applications, and onto web and mobile platforms.

Think of all the content you consume in a day. How much of it is shared with you via a link or a location, and how much of it actually arrives in the form of a file you can save to your desktop?

Sharing the file is just heavy, awkward, and inconvenient for everyone. Yes you could place your workbook files on a network share or online file share, but until your users can consume that information via a link, and without installing software, well, you lose.

 Research suggests that you can potentially double the success of BI adoption in your company by delivering reports to mobile devices. (Source: http://ppvt.pro/junderwood1)

# So We Need "YouTube for Data"

*Figure 599 We need this, for the same reasons that video needed YouTube, but actually we need it MORE than video did!*

YouTube opened the floodgates on video sharing by solving the file size problem and the software compatibility problem.

And we definitely have both of those problems in Power Pivot / Power BI (we even had them back in traditional Excel actually).

So, where's *our* version of YouTube?

How can we publish our work online, so users can consume it via web/mobile? Turns out, you have not one, but a few cloud/server sharing options. Here are the top three options as of Fall 2015:

- PowerBI.com (Cloud)
- SharePoint with SSAS Tabular (On-Premises)
- Excel Desktop connected SSAS Tabular (On-Premises)

Let's walk through PowerBI.com in detail, since it's the newest, and then briefly contrast the three options versus one another.

# PowerBI.com Quick Tour

We will first use PowerBI.com to demonstrate the 'YouTube for Data' paradigm. (And the usual disclaimer: since the interface is evolving rapidly, by the time you are reading this, we are certain at least some small things will have changed in appearance.)

## Step 1: Upload XLSX/PBIX File to PowerBI.com

If you are using Power BI Desktop, all you have to do is to click the "Publish" button to send it to PowerBI.com. You'll be prompted to sign-in to your PowerBI.com account, which you can create for free, if you do not already have one. (You can also upload your Power Pivot Excel workbooks very easily).

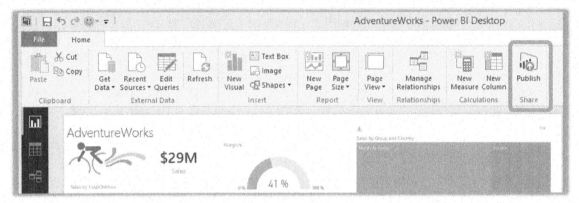

*Figure 600 Click Publish to upload a Power BI Desktop model to PowerBI.com*

Your dataset would be imported from the file and your reports would also be transferred to PowerBI.com. On PowerBI.com you also have the option to create new reports connected to the dataset and to schedule refresh for the dataset.

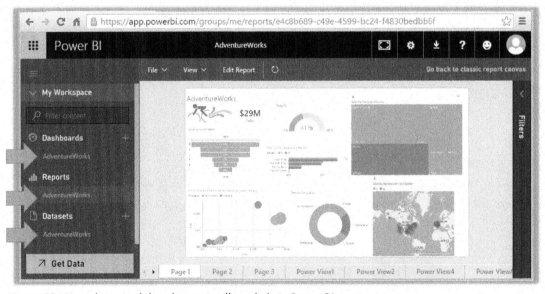

*Figure 601 Your data model and reports all made it to PowerBI.com*

There is another new element on PowerBI.com, the "**Dashboard**". It is initially empty, but you can pin elements from your report to the dashboard. You can then navigate to the dashboard and resize and arrange pinned items. You can also pin items from multiple reports to the same dashboard.

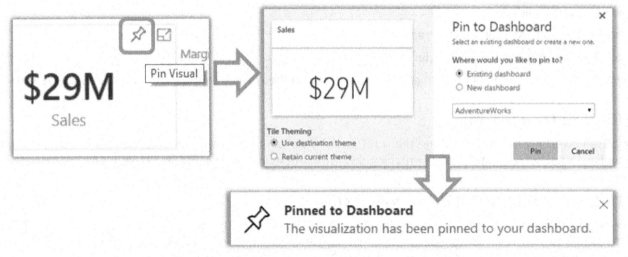

*Figure 602 Pin any element you like to your dashboard*

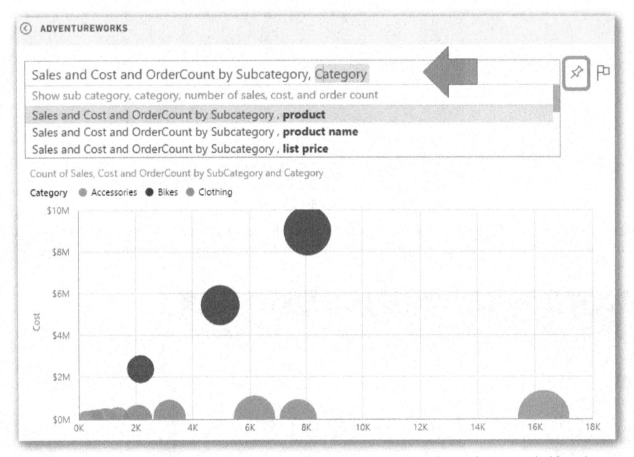

*Figure 603 You can also use natural language Q&A to ask your questions and pin the results to your dashboard*

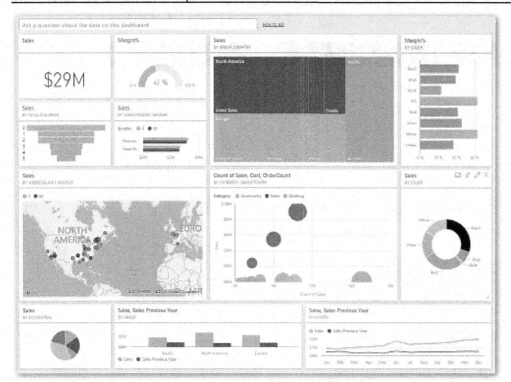

*Figure 604 Your dashboard would look a lot more interesting once you have pinned all the key visuals you need to monitor at a glance*

## Step 2: Sharing Your Dashboard

Next you can click 'Share' button and specify who you want to share the dashboard with.

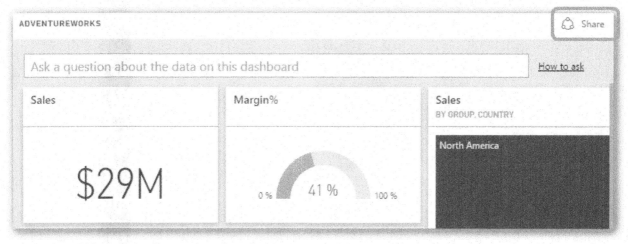

*Figure 605 Dashboards are better when shared*

*Figure 606 Recipients can open the dashboard from the link in the invitation email*

**That's it! The recipient can open the Dashboard in their desktop browser, or on their Windows, iOS (Apple) or Android mobile device** using the Power BI Mobile App (download from http://ppvt.pro/pbiDownload).

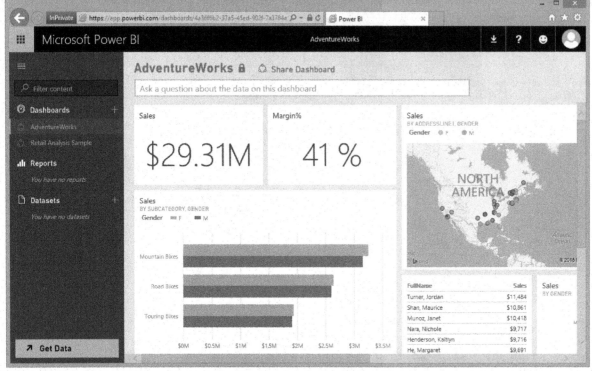

*Figure 607 View the dashboard on your desktop browser or...*

*Figure 608 On your Windows/iOS mobile device*

> Dashboard is the "unit of sharing" in PowerBI.com. There are no options (currently) to share a Report. However, when you share the Dashboard you are also sharing the underlying report. Recipient will be able to click the pinned elements to open the report (in their desktop browser at least). Also note that recipients can only view and not make any changes to the dashboard or report.

For a more detailed overview of PowerBI.com you can watch http://ppvt.pro/p3webinarRec

# Cloud/Server Option Comparison

Here is a quick comparison of the Server options currently available:

| | Interactive Consumption in Browser | Consumption on Mobile Devices | Securely Protect Data & Business Logic | Modern Dashboard Visuals | Automatic Scheduled Refresh | Connect from Desktop Excel and Create New Pivots | Installation and Setup Difficulty |
|---|---|---|---|---|---|---|---|
| PowerBI.com (Cloud) | Yes | Yes | Yes | Yes | Yes | TBD | Trivial to Medium |
| SharePoint plus SSAS Tabular (On-Premises) | Yes | No | Yes | No | Yes | Yes | Very High |
| Desktop Excel Plus SSAS Tabular (On-Premises) | No | No | Yes | No | Yes | Yes | Low to Medium |

*Figure 609 Subject to change as things evolve, but provides a good picture as of Fall 2015*

**Basically, if your company is "open" to the idea of the cloud,** PowerBI.com is by far your best bet. It provides the most functionality at the lowest price and hassle.

**If cloud is currently off-limits for your company,** that probably means you're going for the SharePoint + SSAS Tabular option, because most people want that web browser consumption experience.

**If you don't care about web browser access,** however, you can use desktop Excel as a "thin client" connected to SSAS Tabular. In this setup, basically *any* version of Excel is sufficient, no Power Pivot install required, no worries about 32- versus 64-bit, and no upgrades required. The important stuff – the data and the data model – are centrally located and protected on the SSAS Tabular server. The lightweight report workbooks themselves are files again, which re-opens some of those file-centric drawbacks we're trying to avoid, but keep in mind that those files are *much* smaller, and contain very little sensitive information relative to the data model on the server.

**If you have more questions about choosing a "YouTube for Data"** that's right for your organization, we at PowerPivot-Pro offer short roadmap planning sessions. We typically get you pointed confidently in the right direction with nothing more than a two-hour call. Drop us a note at http://www.PowerPivotPro.com/contact-us/ if you require this sort of assistance.

## Cloud/Server Sharing Option: Even More Valuable than YouTube

Guess what? Power Pivot / Power BI Workbooks benefit from cloud/server sharing even MORE than video! Here are some additional benefits from cloud/server sharing:

- Security
- Automatic data refresh
- Create multiple reports for various audience groups

Security and hands-free automatic data refresh are NOT things that typically matter for video. But oh boy, do they matter for reports, dashboards, and data models.

You can either leverage the data refresh options made available by your cloud/server platform, or use a tool like Power Update (see http://ppvt.pro/pwrupdate) to schedule automated refresh on your desktop. (We at PowerPivotPro had a hand in developing that utility in order to overcome limitations of server-driven refresh, but either way the important thing is that the server is where people "go" to see their dashboards and reports).

In our sharing by email scenario, here is a very common query that you would get

Q: Hey, can you send me the latest copy of the report?

Your answer can now be:

A: Just open the same URL that I sent you last time. The report is automatically refreshed daily (try to hide your satisfied smile when you say this).

# PS: Can We Ask You for a Special Favor?

Hopefully this book has given you the keys to start or sustain your own personal data revolution.

We would like to ask you for a favor: would you be kind enough to leave a review for this book on Amazon? Rather than cede control of our work to the big publishing houses, we remain staunchly independent, and rely on word of mouth and endorsement from real people rather than massive multinational marketing machines.

We like it this way, and think you do too – we get to write the way we like, rather than under the thumb of overzealous grammar editors.

So your review would be greatly appreciated!

Power On!
- Rob and Avi

# A1 - Power Pivot and SSAS Tabular: Two Tools for the Price of One (again!)

In this book we've made some bold claims about Power Pivot's impact on your career. We've used words like "programmer," "engineer," and "developer" to describe your changing role.

Excel Power Pivot is quite amazing. However at some point in your Power Pivot journey, you might discover a need to move to the big leagues. Maybe Power Pivot is no longer sufficient – your files are growing too big for desktops, or you've outgrown its "all or nothing" security access model. Well, meet Power Pivot's bigger sibling: SSAS Tabular.

Is it then time, to go enroll in an SSAS Tabular course? Nope. Since **SSAS Tabular is just Power Pivot's elder cousin and they share the same engine, all that you have learned so far applies directly to SSAS Tabular**. With SSAS Tabular, you can take your Power Pivot skills to even greater heights.

SSAS (SQL Server Analysis Services) has been Microsoft's flagship, industrial-strength BI platform for a long time: the "Apex Predator" of their BI platform. However the traditional product (now termed SSAS *Multidimensional*) was not easy to learn or use. SSAS Pros could charge a premium price for their skills.

But SSAS *Tabular* is the new game in town. Microsoft doesn't like to publicly say that SSAS Tabular supersedes and replaces SSAS Multidimensional… but trust us, that is precisely what is going on.

Even the longstanding "celebrities" of SSAS Multidimensional, such as Chris Webb, Marco Russo, and Alberto Ferrari, now use Tabular for most of their projects.

Neat huh? We all now speak the same language.

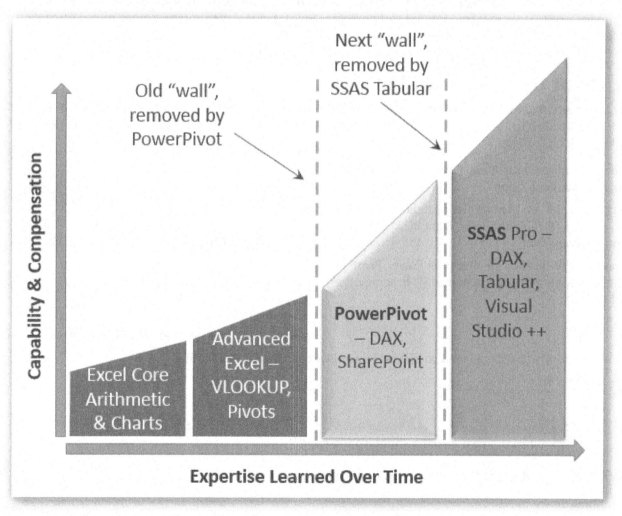

*Figure 610 Excel Users can scale new heights by learning Power Pivot and SSAS Tabular*

# SSAS Tabular Features

While the underlying engine in SSAS Tabular is the same as Power Pivot (it's the DAX engine), there are some key differentiating features

- **Robust and More Scalable**: Theoretically there is no limit on the number of rows your model can contain! We have worked on occasion with Tabular models with sizes in Terabytes; something that just isn't possible with Excel Power Pivot.

- **Advanced Features** like Partitions and Row Level Security. Partitions let you refresh only the most recent data, instead of the whole table. This can be really handy if you have a table with 100's of million rows. Row Level Security can check the identity of the User accessing the Data Model and grant access based on that. For example a North America Salesperson may only be able to see North America Sales data, even though the model contains Worldwide data.

- **Author Data Models in Visual Studio**: You can continue to author your Data Model in Excel Power Pivot and upload it to SSAS Tabular (we'll see this in action). But you also have the option to use Visual Studio for authoring Tabular Models. This opens up the advanced features (as above) and also has all the bells and whistles of Visual Studio. Like Integration with Source Control (to easily version control your Model), kind of stuff that developers care about.

- **Administrative/Scripting Capability**: SSAS falls under the SQL Server family, thus you have a lot of tools/options for Administrators. You can also script and automate tasks using the XMLA scripting language.

- **YouTube for Workbooks**: We covered this in the YouTube chapter. But just to remind you, SSAS Tabular allows hundreds of users to connect to Tabular Models from desktop Excel.

 One reason we love SSAS Tabular is that it's not only easy to use, it's also easy to install and administer. Get help from your DBA/IT team if you can. But setting up an SSAS Tabular server is within reach of Excel users. In fact you can be up and running in less than 30 minutes. See for yourself at http://ppvt.pro/pp2ssas (Compare this to SharePoint which is a beast to setup and administer)

# Power Pivot to SSAS Tabular

A good way to transition to SSAS Tabular is to continue to author your models in Excel Power Pivot and then "upload" them to SSAS Tabular. This will get you *most* of the benefits of SSAS Tabular while maintaining your familiar Excel-oriented development environment.

**Here is how to upload your Excel Power Pivot model to SSAS Tabular in two easy steps**.

**Step 1**: Open SQL Server Management Studio (SSMS) and connect to your SSAS Tabular Server. Right click and select "Restore from Power Pivot"

**Step 2**: Point to the location of the Excel Power Pivot file (Backup file) you want to upload (restore). Fill in some other details and click OK.

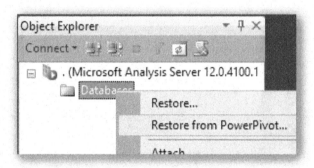

*Figure 611 Right click and select Restore from Power Pivot*

That's it, you're done! You have uploaded your Excel Power Pivot Model to SSAS Tabular.

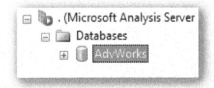

*Figure 612 Your Excel Power Pivot Model now available as SSAS Tabular Model*

Uh...okay, but how do we use it?

## Connect to SSAS Tabular from Excel

To connect to your Tabular Model from Excel, from the ribbon click Data > From Other Sources > From Analysis Services.

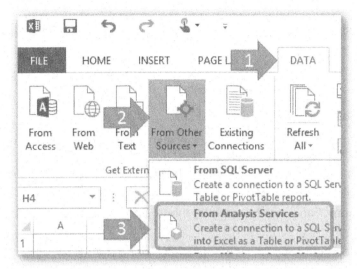

*Figure 613 Connecting to SSAS Tabular from Excel*

Specify the SSAS Tabular Server Name, select the Model you want to connect to then click Finish and OK.

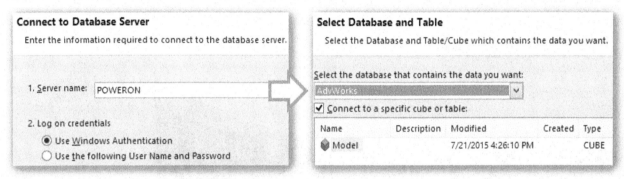

*Figure 614 Specify server name and select model*

That would give you a Pivot Table with a field list connected to the SSAS Tabular Model. Note that the field list has all the tables, columns, measures that existed in the Excel Power Pivot model we uploaded. (The measures are shown grouped at the top, in ∑Customers and ∑Sales).

This should be a familiar playground for any Excel user and building your first Pivot Table should be a snap.

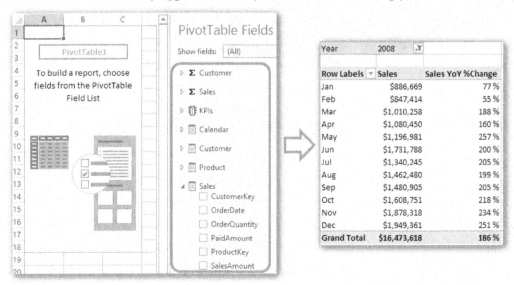

*Figure 615 Pivot Table connected to an SSAS Tabular Model*

If you were to save this file, its size would likely be a handful of Kilobytes (KBs). That is because this "Report" file does not store the complete Data Model. The Data Model is hosted on your SSAS Tabular server and could be a few Megabytes or several Terabytes. Your "report" files will always be small.

Almost all visualization tools support connecting to an SSAS Tabular Cube. PowerBI.com has a special Analysis Services Connector (download at http://ppvt.pro/pbiDownload) which would allow Power BI to connect to your SSAS Tabular Server.

You've seen how easy it is to upload an Excel Power Pivot model to SSAS Tabular Server. However, to go the next step in this journey you should consider using Visual Studio to author your Tabular Data Models.

# Going Further with SSAS Tabular: Visual Studio

To go further with SSAS, say to build large data models or to leverage some of the advanced features, you would need to switch to Visual Studio. This unnerved us to begin with, till we actually gave it a try. And to our delight, we found that it's quite similar to the Excel Power Pivot environment – so similar, in fact, that the heavyweight BI pros complain to Microsoft that "you only gave us the same quality tools as you put in Excel!" ☺

The easiest way to get started using Visual Studio is to "import" an Excel Power Pivot model into a new Visual Studio project.

We'll start by opening Visual Studio Ultimate – a real development tool. This is where SSAS Pros do their work, as well as web developers, mobile app developers, etc. – this is **the** programming tool from Microsoft:

*Figure 616 Visual Studio Ultimate: Even the name sounds impressive*

But rather than build something from scratch, let's try something simpler. There's a convenient option to Import from Power Pivot:

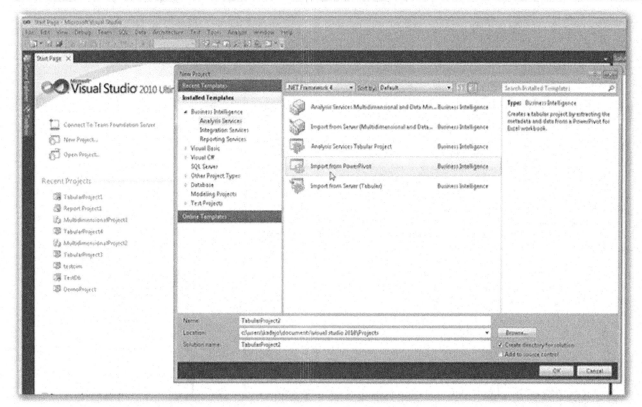

Figure 617 Import from Power Pivot

Guess what happens next? We browse for a Power Pivot workbook:

Figure 618 Just select a Power Pivot workbook

What we see next is a very, VERY familiar experience:

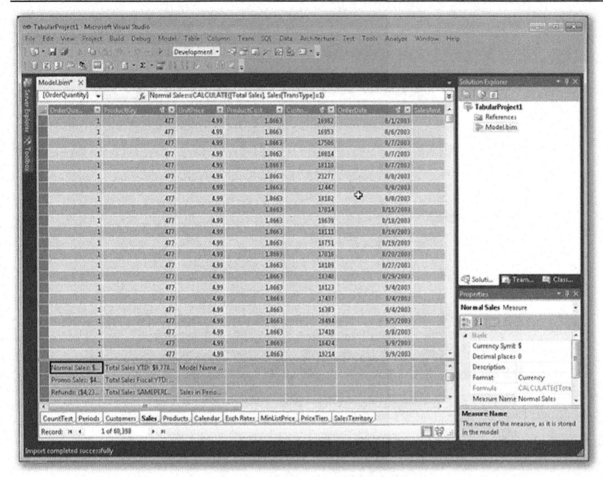

Figure 619 Our Power Pivot model used in this book, now loaded in Visual Studio!

Other than the blue tint versus green tint, and the treeview docked on the right, this is precisely what we see in the Power Pivot window! Tables, sheet tabs, etc.

Zooming in a bit, we continue the "identical to Power Pivot" theme:

| 1 | 477 | 4.99 | 1.8663 |
|---|---|---|---|
| Normal Sales: $... | Total Sales YTD: $9,770... | Model Name ... | |
| Promo Sales: $4... | Total Sales Fiscal YTD: ... | | |
| Refunds: ($4,23... | Total Sales SAMEPERI... | Sales in Perio... | |

| CountTest | Periods | Customers | **Sales** | Products | Calendar | Exch Rates | MinListP |

Figure 620 Measure grid and sheet tabs

Normal Sales:=CALCULATE([Total Sales], Sales[TransType]=1)

| | UnitPrice | | ProductCost | | Custo... | | |
|---|---|---|---|---|---|---|---|
| 477 | 4.99 | | 1.8663 | | 16982 | | |

Figure 621 DAX formula is exactly the same

We can even toggle into diagram view, which again looks identical:

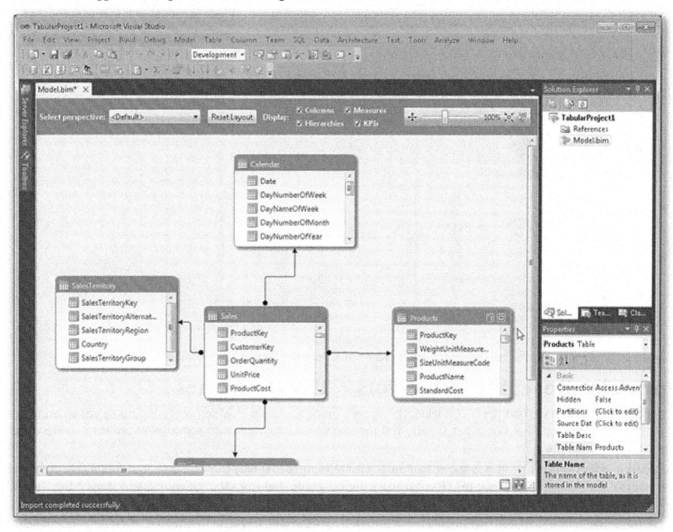

*Figure 622 Relationship view is also the same*

Thus you can easily import your existing Excel Power Pivot models and continue to develop them in Visual Studio. For more on SSAS, read some of our articles at http://ppvt.pro/pp2ssas and http://ppvt.pro/pp2tabular.

 **Do you have to make the transition to Visual Studio?** No, not at all. In fact, we didn't for a very long time. You've seen how you can upload your Excel Power Pivot workbooks to SharePoint, SSAS Tabular and PowerBI.com. Thus you can continue to use Excel Power Pivot but still leverage these platforms. However at some point, you may want to consider trying out Visual Studio to build large models or leverage some of the advanced features.

# Key Takeaways

- **Microsoft is betting heavily on "the Power Pivot way."** You don't "infect" your flagship product with something new unless that new thing is awesome. Power Pivot – that thing running on your desktop – is good enough for the heavyweight BI pros. Digest that thought.

- **There's an "upgrade path" for important Power Pivot models**. This is a great selling point for IT if they are nervous about Power Pivot. Unlike regular Excel workbooks, a Power Pivot workbook that becomes business critical CAN be "taken over" by IT, and made into something centralized and blessed, without having to rewrite it.

- **There's an "upgrade path" for Excel Pros**. With very little effort, an established Power Pivot pro can "change hats" and label herself a Business Intelligence Pro, a Tabular Modeler – even if she were "just" an Excel Pro a couple years ago. Again, not that she has to, because Power Pivot itself offers practically limitless power. She just can. Exciting huh?

# A2 - Cube Formulas – the End of GetPivotData()

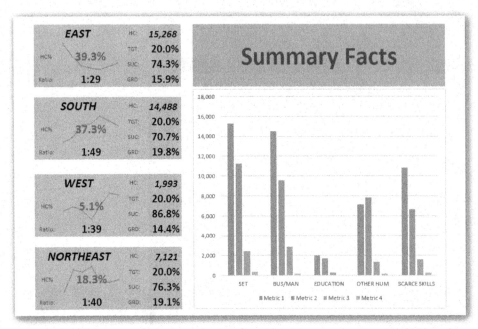

*Figure 623 This IS Excel. And this IS a live, interactive Power Pivot Report. But there are NO PivotTables ANYWHERE.*

## Formulas Reaching into Pivots = The Dark Ages

In the old days, before we had the DAX engine, there were many scenarios in which we found ourselves creating one or more pivots, "hiding" them on other sheets, and then *reaching into them with formulas* in order to create a final report on another sheet.

That part in italics was brutal. It was super tedious to create reports that way the first time, but *modifying* them was even worse. GETPIVOTDATA(), anyone? (The hardcore people graduated from that of course and started the INDEX(-MATCH()) game, but that merely "sucked less" and should not be considered a "good" solution).

But in those old days, there *were* essentially three different cases in which you were forced to do this:

1. When you needed the same pivot filtered a few different ways in order to produce a final report composed of ratios or percentages between those different subsets of the data.
2. When you had two Data tables, and therefore couldn't VLOOKUP them together into a single wide table, you produced two pivots and then built a report off of that.
3. When you simply needed a shape of report that a pivot could never give you.

Well, CALCULATE() means we never have to do #1 anymore – just build filters into the Measures themselves! And relationships mean we never have to do #2 anymore – see the chapters on Multiple Data Tables.

But #3... #3 is still a problem... until someone shows you *this* button...

## One Click That Will Change Your Life

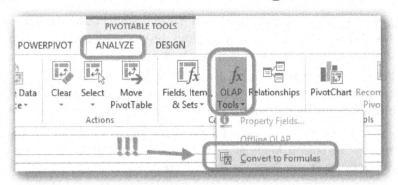

*Figure 624 Select a cell in ANY Power Pivot PivotTable, find this button on the ribbon, click it, and catch your breath*

**Seriously, go do that right now.** We'll wait right here.

<waiting>

Hey, you're back! Neat huh?

Did you try moving some cells around? How about inserting some blank spacer rows and columns?

To give you an idea, this was a pivot about 60 seconds before we took the screenshot:

| Location | Total Sales | Just Bike Sales | Total Margin | % Margin | Avg Sales Amt per Order |
|---|---|---|---|---|---|
| Grand Total | $9,770,900 | $9,162,325 | $4,049,695 | 41.4 % | $749 |
| Europe | $3,209,356 | $3,044,696 | $1,330,333 | 41.5 % | $855 |
| France | $922,179 | $870,222 | $382,037 | 41.4 % | $796 |
| Germany | $1,076,891 | $1,025,889 | $448,423 | 41.6 % | $909 |
| United Kingdom | $1,210,286 | $1,148,586 | $499,873 | 41.3 % | $859 |
| North America | $3,997,659 | $3,676,700 | $1,688,255 | 42.2 % | $621 |
| Canada | $673,628 | $581,425 | $290,533 | 43.1 % | $381 |
| Central | $233 | | $124 | 53.4 % | $47 |
| Northeast | $2,566 | $2,295 | $1,205 | 47.0 % | $513 |
| Northwest | $1,291,994 | $1,192,657 | $544,814 | 42.2 % | $643 |
| Southeast | $8,442 | $7,769 | $3,687 | 43.7 % | $844 |
| Southwest | $2,020,796 | $1,892,554 | $847,892 | 42.0 % | $767 |
| Australia | $2,563,884 | $2,440,928 | $1,031,106 | 40.2 % | $895 |

CalendarYear

| 2001 | 2002 | 2003 | **2004** |

*Figure 625 This used to be a pivot, before we clicked Convert to Formulas and made a few formatting tweaks*

# The Data Is Still "Live!"

And guess what? This isn't like Copy/Paste as Values. It's still 100% linked to your data model.

So for instance:

- Slicers that were connected to the pivot before conversion will STILL slice the numbers in these individual cells!
- When you refresh the underlying data model, these numbers will update!

**So these cube formulas are just as "live" as pivots** – it's just that you get MUCH finer-grained control over the layout of the report.

# You Can Also Write Them "From Scratch"

## For Starters, CUBEVALUE() Is All You Really Need

Converting a pivot is not the only way to use cube formulas. You can also write them manually, as long as you are working in a Power Pivot workbook.

For example, in any of the bike sales example workbooks, go to a cell on any sheet and enter this formula:

```
=CUBEVALUE("ThisWorkbookDataModel","[Measures].[Total Sales]",
"[Products].[Category].[All].[Bikes]")
```

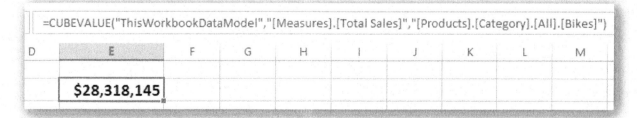

*Figure 626 You can type a CUBEVALUE formula directly into a cell, no need to convert a pivot*

That formula will fetch the [Total Sales] Measure's value, filtered to "Bikes." In fact, the DAX engine does not know the difference between a cube formula cell asking for a number versus a pivot asking for a number. (In this case, Products[Category]="Bikes" is sent in to the DAX engine as a coordinate, a filter context, just like what happens with pivots!)

Don't sweat the CUBEVALUE syntax in any depth, just follow the pattern above for now (or just convert pivots) and you will STILL be a hero.

 The first input to CUBEVALUE (and other cube functions) should be set to "PowerPivot Data" in Excel 2010, but "ThisWorkbookDataModel" in all subsequent versions.

## Adding a Slicer is easy...

If you want a cube formula cell to "listen" to a Slicer, that's easy too:

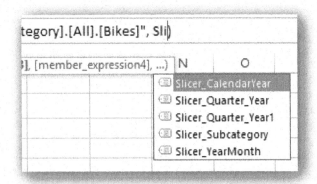

*Figure 627 Just add another argument to the CUBEVALUE and start typing "Slicer" – you will get an autocomplete list of all slicers in the workbook. Pick one and now that cell will "listen" to that Slicer!*

# Perspective – When to Use, Tradeoffs, Etc.

A few tips and principles:

1. Cube formula reports are "fixed axis" reports – meaning if you have a cube formula report that lists all the countries where you do business, and next month you start doing business in a new country, that new country will NOT appear in your report automatically. (Unlike in a pivot).
2. So if the shape and/or dimensions of your report need to change frequently, as the underlying data changes, cube formulas are not a good fit.
3. The places to use them, then, are for scorecards and key performance dashboards, as well as for single cells of "extra" information placed next to pivots and charts.
4. If you can make a pivot to do what you want, don't use cube formulas.
5. If you are tempted to write a formula that "grabs" a value out of a pivot, you should be using cube formulas instead (or CALCULATE or multi-data-table modeling, if it's one of those first two scenarios).

# More Information

We could probably write an entire book on cube formulas, but really, 90% of their value is easy to grasp, and already covered here.

If you do want to continue learning about them, here's a listing of articles on PowerPivotPro.com:

http://ppvt.pro/CubeFormulasCat2

# A3 - Some Common Error Messages

There are a handful of errors that you will see from time to time – error messages that sound scary but ultimately mean very little. We want to dedicate just a quick page or two and cover these, so that you know what to do when you see them.

## Addin is "Out of Sync"

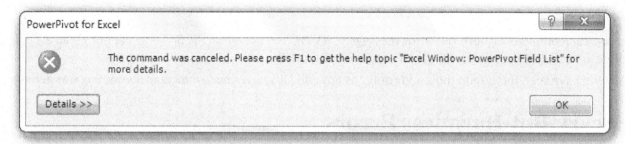

Figure 628 "The command was canceled"

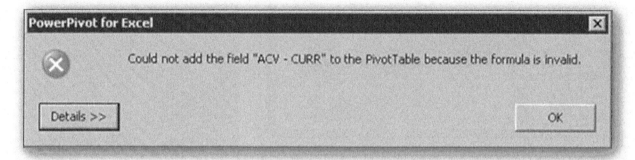

Figure 629 "Formula is invalid"

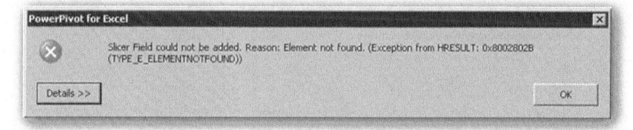

Figure 630 "Element not found"

All three of these indicate that the Power Pivot addin and Excel have gotten "out of sync" with each other. More specifically, Power Pivot knows about the field you are trying to add, but Excel does not think that field exists. This happens with fields you recently created – we have never seen this occur with a field that we have already used in a pivot.

The fix for this is essentially to reboot the Power Pivot addin.

You can do that by trying one of the three following techniques:

1.  Give up on the current pivot and create a new pivot. The new pivot will not have this problem.
2.  Turning off the Power Pivot addin (under COM Addins on the Developer tab of the ribbon, or under Excel Options > Addins > Manage COM Addins), and turn it back on.
3.  Saving and closing the workbook, closing Excel completely (all Excel windows closed!), then reopening the workbook.

Note that if you just added a table, column, or measure to your data model, and it's not showing up in your field list, the same fixes above will work.

# "Initialization of the Data Source Failed"

*Figure 631 We see this one all the time in 2010. It is 100% harmless.*

Simply put, you can completely ignore this error message. Click OK and everything is fine. We cannot recall a single instance where we clicked OK and something bad happened afterwards.

Quite literally, we have seen this popup thousands of times now, and it's never once indicated something was actually broken.

# Other Scary-But-Harmless Errors

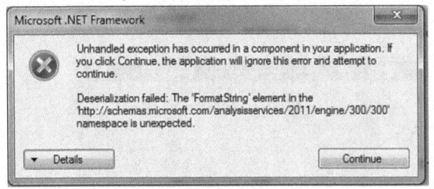

*Figure 632 These Unhandled Exceptions pop up from time to time, and very rarely indicate something is truly wrong. Just ignore them, and if something bad is happening afterward, restart Excel (or just the Power Pivot addin – see above).*

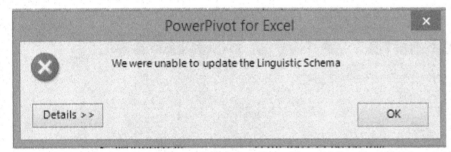

*Figure 633 Wow, Linguistic Schema failed to update. Oh noes! Totally, 100% ignorable. But it does give us a chuckle every time we see it. It's a virtual lock for the Error Message Hall of Fame.*

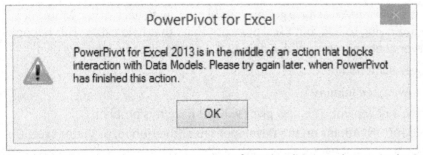

*Figure 634 If you see this one, you may be in formula editing mode over in the Power Pivot window. Just flip over there, hit the ESC key, and come back. If you are NOT editing a formula in the Power Pivot window, just close said Power Pivot window (this won't lose your work) and the error goes away.*

# Perspective

**Note that these problems will NEVER impact the consumers of your work.** They are merely an annoyance for us, the producers, and once a pivot is working, it stays working.

# A4 - People: The Most Powerful Feature of Power Pivot

Power Pivot is a pretty good piece of technology. It offers a lot of powerful new capabilities. But technology itself never changes the world – it's what *people* do with it that matters. The revolution, in other words, is not Power Pivot. The revolution is what *you*, the Excel Pro "army," are going to do with it (and are doing already).

In a similar vein, I (Rob) started the blog in late 2009. Without the readership, questions, and feedback of the blog audience, this book never would have happened. Many of the names below have been with me for a long time. Their support, enthusiasm, and adoption have been a huge help to me over the years. They have validated, repeatedly, my beliefs about the future of data and Excel's role in it. So here they are, some of the people on the very tip of the spear:

Refa Abay, Access Analytic (Jeff Robson), Rob Adams, Saul Mendez Aguirre, Chris Akina, Matthew Akins, Roger Alexander, Areef Ali, Tom Allan, Belinda L Allen, Matt Allington, Carl Allison, Husein 'ochenk' Alatas, Jeff Anderson, A.L. Apolloni, Alex Thomas Aranzamendi, David Araujo, Arilindo, Noam Arnold, Azhagappan Arunachalam, Jonathan Ashby, Mark Askey, Mark Ayo

Pablo Baez, Pamela O Baker, Lorenzo Baraldo, Rachel Barnette, Oskar H Diaz Barrenechea, Breanna Bartmann, Andrew Basey, Doug Beardmore, Hussein Belal, Bemvilac , Stephen Bennett, Robert Bentley, J L Berliet, Stanton Berlinsky, Roz Beste, Daphne Betts-Hemby, João Biagini, Stan Bialowas, Carsten Bieker, Doug Binkley, Ramon Drudis Biscarri, Antonio Blanco, Vernon P Blessing, Dan Bobrovsky, Thomas Boge, Anders Bogsnes, Gail Bolden, Mark Bond, Ivan Bondarenko, Erik Bonfrere, Paul Borela, Lucas Brisingamen, Dustin Broach, Quentin Brooke, Reena Brown, Shawn Brown, Stephanie Bruno, Haakon Thor Brunstad, Edward Bunt, Michael Bunyan, Doug Burke, Bweiss03

Jeff Cable, Charlton Calhoun, Angel Ortego Camacho, Dennis Campbell, Gerson Cano, Michael Carter, Guy-François Castella, Muness Castle, Catsnbettas, GLCauble, Natthorn Chaiyapruk, Chan Phooi Lai, Santiago Robert Chang Lay, Ken Chapman, Dr. Cody Charette, Petros Chatzipantazis (Spreadsheet1.com) , Krishna Cheruvu, Kenneth Cheung, Paul Chon, Qaisar Choudhary, Christophe, Huang Chung Chuan, Luann Clark, Barry Clarke, Thomas Coats, Nicholas Colebatch, Larry Compton, Steve Coons, Rob Corbin, Alex Cordero, Thomas P Costello Jr, Michael Couturier, Colleen Cravener, Colleen Cravener, Chris Criddle, Phil Cross, Anthony Crouchelli

Debra Dalgleish, Kellan Danielson, Meredith Darlington, Jay Dave, Heather Davis, O Depolito, Mary Myers DeVlugt, Bryan Dewberry, Tony Diepenbrock, Mike Dietterick, Joseph DiPisa, Sal Distefano, Jason Ditzel, Andrey Dmitriev, Mark Domeyer, Marcel Domingus, Paigemon Douraghi, Susan Draht, Bill Draper, Oz du Soleil, Stewart J Dunlop, Anand Dwivedi, Rachel Dyer, Steven Dyer

Mark Eames, John Egerter, Ted Eichinger, Dan English, Eric Entenman, James Enyart, Lori Eppright, Ernestas Ernis, Boje Ervenius, Gary Etherton, ExceleratorBI.com.au

Anton Fagerström, Luis Fajardo, Pedro Fardilha, Kelly Farmer, Søren Faurum, fazzbuilder, Peter H Feddema, Edward Feder, James F. Fedor, Imke Feldmann, Vicente Castello Ferrer, H. Fielding, Justin Fillip, Chris Finlan, Jeremy Firth, Randy Fitzgerald, Eric Flamm, Adam Flath, Jim Fleming, Lawrence Foat, Kåre Foged, James Follent, Kevin Follonier, Mike Foos, Norah Fox, Steve Fox, Brian Freeman, Urbano Freitas, Steve French, Yuri Friedman, Gordon Fuller, Scott Futryk

David Gainer, James Gammerman, Yesenia Garcia, Garth, Matthew Gaskins, Alan Gazaway, GDRIII, Graham Getty, Anthony Ghent, Forrest Gibson, Chris Gilbert, Adam Gilpatrick, Angela Girard, Tom Goishi, Jordan "Option Explicit" Goldmeier, Brett Goodman, Michael Goodwin, Martin Gorgas, Roger Govier, Donald Grassmann, Michael Greene, Jonathan Gregory, Kyle Grice, Alexander Grinberg, Mathew Grisham, S. Groeneveld, Matthew Grove

Christopher Haas, Rachel Haggard, David Haggarty, Dean Hale, Kyle Hale, Charlie Hall, Chris Hall, Elaine Hammer, Mohamed Ben Hamouda, John Hanson, Scott Hardin, Trevor Hardy, Sean Hare, Randy Harris, David Harshany, Ed Harvey, Kamal Hathi, Reid Havens, Mike Haynes, Dena Heathman, Sean Heffernan, Rüdiger Hein, Peter Heller, Philipp Heltewig, Roberta Henifin, John Henning, Gregory Hernandez, Staffan Hillberg, Staffan Hillberg, James Hinton, Brad Hobgood, David Hoey, Eric Hofrichter, Michael J Holleran II, Llewellyn Holtshausen, Carl Hooker, Jeffrey Hou, Nicolas Hubert, Melody Huckins, Gareth Hutchinson, John Hutchinson

Braulio Iglesia, Rod Ippisch

Stephen Jakubowski, Kristian Jansson, Amy Jarrow, Joseph Jasper, Bill Jelen, Stephen Jenkins, Jonny Johansen, John, Al Johnston, Jonathon, Melissa Jones, Tommy Jørgensen, Andy Josolyne, Amy Julian, Jumpingjacqs, Junk.Doo.Erz

Henri Kääriäinen, Ruth Kadel, Fred Kaffenberger, Fahim Kanji, Eric Kaplan, Greg Karl, William Karlin, Alison Katagiri, Michael Kelley, To Wai Keung, Scott Kevgas, Muhannad Khalaf, Alexander Khryakov, Don Knowles, Caitlin Knox, SRINIVAS

KOLLI, Don Kollmann, Eric C Kong, Sabareesh Kornipalli, Joel Kossol, Brad Kostreva, Manish Kotecha, Reuvain Krasner, Peter Kretzman, Johann Krugell, Olga Kryuchkova, Brian Kwartler

Jennifer Lachnite, Victor Andrés Araya Lagos, Philip Laliberte, Bas Land, Keith Lane, Stéphane Langer, Jonas Langeteig, Mike Lavalley, Matt Layfield, Alan Lazzarich, Michael S Lee, Arthur Lee, Rebekah Lensky, Joe Kwok Tai Leung , Jane Leung, David Lewinski, Geoff Lilley, En L, Charles Lincoln, Samantha Linden, Karen Lindenberg, Jonas Lindskog, Jeff Lingen, Timothy Lizotte, Amir Ljubovic, Chuck Lombardo, Joseph Looney, Mourad Louha, Inge Løvåsen, Kevin Lovell, David Lowzinski, Martin Lucas, John A. Luff, Mark Luhdorff, John Lythe

Jen Mackan, Andrew Mackay, Madison Power BI User Group, Akhil Mahajan, Michael Maher, Piotr Majcher, Rob Makepeace, Tomislav Mališ, Pawel Maminski, Mike Mann, Kristin Marceaux, Edward Marceski, Sharon Markatcheff, Cristin Marshall, Christian Masberg, Jeffrey Masse, Brian Mather, Tom Matthews, Steven Maxwell, Jim McAlister, Celeste McCabe, John McGough, Dan McGuane, Jeff McKinnis, Robin McLean, Wyatt McNabb, Renee Mcvety, Parth Mehta, Raul J. Benavente Mejías, Ken Melies, Shelly Meny, Craig Merry, Eddy Mertens, Mr. Metric, Colin Michael, Dennis Mickelsen, Microsoft Power BI Team, W Middelman, Mary Middleton, Kávási Mihály, Jonathan Miller, Josh Miller, David Mills, Li Min, Wayne Mircoff, Pinaki Mitra, Andreas Moosbrugger, Stephen A Morfey, Jeffrey S Morgan, Sean Morgan, Jeff Morris, Thomas Morris, Travis Morris, Lee Morton, Stephen Morton, Hans Mostafavi, Ted Murphy, Mike Murray, Seth Murray, www.MyExcelOnline.com

Hiroshi Nakanishi, Nanousers, Talat Nauman, Stephan Nelles, Tom Neo, Nevtek, Cristian Nicola, Mike J Nicoletti, Heather Nieman, Nmacabales , Bill Noonan, Jonas Nørgaard

Wendall F Oakes, Dave Ojeda, Brian O'Kelly, Omarosorno, David Onder, Cristopher Ong, Victor Ooi, Michael Ortenberg, Brad Osterloo, Kevin Overstreet, Remi Øvstebø, Jonathan Owen

Rafael Paim, Jose Paredes, Donald Parish, Jaehyun Park, Catherine Parkinson (@CatParky), Steve Parton, Brent Pearce, James Penko, Maureen Penzenik, Daniel Pereira Barbosa, Kirill Perian, Ylinen Pertti, Darrell Peterson, Michelle Pfann, Lap Phan, James Phillips, Rob Phillips, Chris M Pieper, Michael Piercefield, Lauri Pietarinen, Adam Pifer, Nicky Pike, John Pittman, Dan Popp, Martin Povey, Ppipl, Ketan Pradhan, Miguel Denis Prieto, David Primrose, Mary Ann Prunier, Psycho Bunny, Thomas F Puglia

Liu Qilong, Julie Quick, Frank Quillin

Lisa Radonich, Robinson Ramirez, Palakodeti Bangaru Rayudu, Maury Readinger, Nigel Reardon, Fran Reed, Sayth Renshaw, Micheal Reynolds, Tommy Reynolds, Tony Richards, Dale Rickard, Cecelia Rieb, Cecil Rivera, Juan Rivera, Bentley W Roberts, Monica Robinson, Hernan G. Rodriguez, Bill Rolison, Collin Roloff, Don Romano, Cliff Rosell, Jason Roth, Tony Rozwadowski, Michael J Rudzinski, Brian Russell, Ken W Russell, Rob Russell, Steven Rutt, Kevin Rutty

Egor Sadovnic, Grímur Sæmundsson, David Saez Cortell, Alexander Samogin, Sirajudeen Samsudeen, Alfonso Sanchez, Christy Sandberg, Bradley Sawler, Victor Scelba, Anthony J Schepis, Walter Schoevaars, Peter Schott, Don Schulze , Michael Schupp, Scott Schwartz, Tim Scott, Thomas Scullion, Mati Selg, Scott Senkeresty, Austin Senseman, David Seymour, Ron Shaeffer, Mike Shellito, Thomas Sherrouse, Kurt Shuler, Rich Siegmund, Brian Simmons, Mark S Sirianni, David Sisson, Dani Skrobar, Susan Slinkman, Lee Smith, Randy W Smith, Susan E Smith, John Snyder, Adam Soil, Jukka-Pekka Sokero, Dmitriy Solovev, Ghulam Soomro, Joseph Sorrenti, Scott St. Amant, Karen Stafford, Lou Stagner, Torbjörn Stamholt, Jeff Standen, Justin Stanley, Brent Starace, Lawrence Stein, Zackary Stephen, Andrew Stewart, Jon Stielstra, Henson D Sturgill, Antti Suanto, Ryan Sullivan, Bill Sundwall, Sam Suppe , Supraflyer, Peter Susen

Laurie Tack, Joe Takher-Smith, Sarah Talbot, James Tallman, Manolo Tamashiro, Tan Kwang Hui, Roberto Tapia, James Tarr, Dean Taunton, TenaciousData, Perry Thebeau, Mark Theirl, Supak Thienlikid, Thysvdw, Amy Ticsay, Andrew Toal, Vinnie Toaso, Andrew Todd, Hang Tran, Joe Treanor, Tviesturs, Don Tyrrell

Jen Underwood, Luis E Berdugo Urrutia, Tom Urtis

Vaasek, Mark Vaillancourt, Patrick Van De Belt, Wouter van der Schagt, Diderico van Eyl, Gary Van Meter, Brent Van Scoy, Klaas Vandenberghe, Roelof van Heerden, Roy Van Norstrand, Travis VanNoy, Eltjo Verweij, Vinoth , Tomi Vir, John Vizard, Sven Vosse

Tsui Wai Chun David, Ian Wainwright, Steve Wake, Ross Wallace, Anne Walsh, Mark Walter, CPA, Raphael Walter, Jeff Walters, Ross Waterston, Ronald Webb, Nathan Webster, Russ Webster, Darren Weinstock, Rob White, Rod Whiteley, Kevin Williams, Rick Williams, Bradford Wills, Rick Wilson, Ryan Wilson, Bradley Wing, Steven Wise, Bartholomew Wistuk, Sean Wong, Alan Wood, Daye Wu, Sam Wu

Kent Lau Chee Yong, Steve Young

Pete Zaker, Robert Zaufall, Nathan Zelany, Ido Zevulun

# Index

**ADAPTIVE**

We hope you loved the book!

# Now that you're hooked on Power BI, we'd love to show you more.

If you're eager to continue your BI journey, we offer a variety of customizable services for individuals and organizations.

- **Jumpstart**: Buckle up for our high speed, exceptional quality consulting service! See first tangible results in 5 business days!

- **Training**: Private training is available onsite and online for teams and individuals. Public classes are also available live, online monthly.

- **Consulting**: Discover new opportunities in your data. Lean, nimble and fast-paced project execution for organizations of any size.

www.p3adaptive.com

In 2013, Author Rob Collie founded P3 Adaptive to help organizations leverage their existing data with Power BI consulting and services.

Gold
# Microsoft Partner

■■ Microsoft

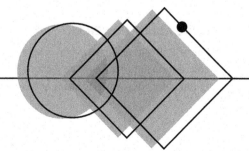